Correlations in Rosenzweig and Levinas

Correlations in
Rosenzweig and Levinas

Robert Gibbs

PRINCETON UNIVERSITY PRESS

PRINCETON, NEW JERSEY

Copyright © 1992 by Princeton University Press
Published by Princeton University Press, 41 William Street,
Princeton, New Jersey 08540
In the United Kingdom: Princeton University Press,
Chichester, West Sussex

Library of Congress Cataloging-in-Publication Data

Gibbs, Robert, 1958–
Correlations in Rosenzweig and Levinas / Robert Gibbs.
p.   cm.
Includes bibliographical references and index.
ISBN 0-691-07415-1
ISBN 0-691-02964-4 (pbk.)
1. Judaism and philosophy. 2. Judaism—20th century.
3. Rosenzweig, Franz, 1886–1929. 4. Levinas, Emmanuel—
Views on Judaism. 5. Philosophy, Jewish I. Title.
BM565.G44 1992
181'.06—dc20   92-7221

This book has been composed in Linotron Sabon

Princeton University Press books are printed on acid-free paper
and meet the guidelines for permanence and durability
of the Committee on Production Guidelines for Book Longevity
of the Council on Library Resources

First Princeton paperback printing, 1994

Printed in the United States of America

10 9 8 7 6 5 4 3 2

FOR ROBERT A. BAKER

may he be remembered for blessing

Contents

Acknowledgments

PORTIONS of this book appeared in earlier versions in other publications. I wish to thank those publications for their kind permission to reprint those materials here. Portions of Chapter 9 were first published as "Substitution: Marcel and Levinas," in *Philosophy and Theology,* Marquette University Quarterly, vol. 4 (Winter 1989): 171–85; portions of Chapter 1 as "Limits of Thought: Rosenzweig, Schelling, and Cohen," in *Zeitschrift für philosophische Forschung,* vol. 43 (October 1989): 618–40; and portions of Chapter 10 were first published in 1991 in University Press of America as " 'Greek' in the 'Hebrew' Writings of Emmanuel Levinas," in the edited volume, *Studies in Jewish Philosophy, Vol. II,* ed. by D. Novak and N. Samuelson.

I have received much support in the writing of this manuscript. From 1986 to 1988, the Mellon Humanities Faculty Development Fund at St. Louis University provided me the opportunity to meet with Emmanuel Levinas, attend the Rosenzweig Centenary conference in Kassel, West Germany, and conduct research on Part I of *The Star of Redemption.* In addition the Leo Baeck Institute and the DAAD supported my research of Rosenzweig's papers at the Leo Baeck Institute in New York during the summer of 1990. Finally, Princeton University also supported my research at the Leo Baeck Institute and travels to Paris to meet again with Levinas, as well as giving me a sabbatical leave in 1990 to conclude this book.

Beyond these more formal acknowledgments, there are also several people whom I wish to thank for their support and encouragement. First of all, Alan Udoff for proposing this interpretative study and then suggesting the name *Correlations.* My research commenced in St. Louis in a context of true collegiality with several remarkable philosophical minds. The reading circle we formed of James Bohman, Michael Barber, and J. Claude Evans was particularly nurturing and constructive. A second group, the Academy for Jewish Philosophy, has been both the recipient of the first airing of much of this work and the source of much helpful criticism. Norbert Samuelson, Peter Ochs, and Richard Cohen have been especially helpful to me. And here, in Princeton, my new colleagues, especially Jeff Stout and Cornel West, have not only encouraged me but have contributed to the development of this book considerably. In addition I wish to thank Edith Wyschogrod for leading the way in Levinas research in America and for helpful suggestions on this book. I also wish to recall Steven S. Schwarzschild, z"l, Professor of Philosophy at Washington University. He certainly is the person who would be most pleased to see a book that locates contemporary Jewish philosophy in a family whose progenitor is Hermann Cohen. Steven offered me true company and philosophical friendship in the years we both were in St. Louis. He remains the true first reader of this book.

Finally, I thank Deirdre and Ariel for sharing the computer, their table, their patience, and indeed their lives with me.

Abbreviations and Citations

ALL TRANSLATIONS in the text are my own. All citations follow the convention of citing the original-language text followed by a slash and a reference to an available English translation.

I cite Rosenzweig's works directly by volume. All such citations are to the recent collected works of Rosenzweig, entitled *Franz Rosenzweig: Der Mensch und sein Werk: Gesammelte Schriften*, published in four volumes (1974–1984) by Martinus Nijhoff, The Hague. These texts will be cited merely by volume and page. Please note that a citation of simply two page numbers is to *The Star of Redemption*.

(I, #, Date) Volume I includes letters and journal entries.

(/) Volume II contains the fourth edition of *Der Stern der Erlösung*, which was translated as *The Star of Redemption* by William W. Hallo (Boston: Beacon Press, 1971).

(III,) Volume III (*Zweistromland*) contains various essays and will be cited by volume and page (III, 148).

Levinas' works will be cited by the following abbreviations:

ADV *L'Au-delà du Verset*. Paris: Editions de Minuit, 1982.

AE *Autrement qu'être ou au-delà de l'Essence*. Dordrecht: Martinus Nijhoff, 1974. Trans. Alpohonso Lingis as *Otherwise than Being or Beyond Essence*. The Hague: Martinus Nijhoff, 1981.

CP *Collected Philosophical Papers*. Trans. Alpohonso Lingis. Phaenomenologica, vol. 100. Dordrecht: Martinus Nijhoff, 1987.

DL1 *Difficile Liberté*. Paris: Editions Albin Michel, 1963.

DL3 *Difficile Liberté*, 3d. edition. Paris: Le Livre de Poche, 1984 (minor corrections of 2d ed., Paris: Editions Albin Michel, 1976). Trans. Seán Hand as *Difficult Freedom: Essays on Judaism*. Baltimore: The Johns Hopkins University Press, 1990.

DVI *De Dieu qui Vient a L'Idée*. Paris: J. VRIN, 1982.

EE *De L'existence à l'existant*. 2d ed. Paris: J. VRIN, 1981. Trans. Alphonso Lingis as *Existents and Existants*. Dordrecht: Martinus Nijhoff, 1978.

EI *Ethique et L'infini*. Paris: Librairie Arthème Fayard, 1982. Trans. Richard Cohen as *Ethics and Infinity*. Pittsburgh: Duquesne University Press, 1985.

EN   *Entre Nous: Essais sur le penser-à-l-autre*. Paris: Bernard
            Grasset, 1991.
HAH   *Humanisme de l'Autre Homme*. Paris: Le Livre de Poche,
            1987. Reprinted and repaginated from Paris: Fata Mor-
            gana, 1972.
HDN   *A L'Heure des Nations*. Paris: Les Editions de Minuit, 1988.
HS   *Hors Sujet*. Paris: Fata Morgana, 1987.
L'Herne   *L'Herne: Emmanuel Levinas*, no. 60. Ed. Catherine Chalier
            and Miguel Abensour. Paris: Éditions de l'Herne, 1991.
LR   *The Levinas Reader*. Ed. by Seán Hand. London: Basil Black-
            well, 1989.
NP   *Noms Propres*. Paris: Le Livre de Poche, 1987; Paris: Fata
            Morgana, 1976.
QL   *Quatre Lectures Talmudique*. Paris: Les Editions de Minuit,
            1968. Trans. Annette Aronowicz in *Nine Talmudic Read-
            ings*. Bloomington: Indiana University Press, 1990.
SAS   *Du Sacré au Saint*. Paris: Les Editions de Minuit, 1977. Trans.
            Annette Aronowicz in *Nine Talmudic Readings*. Blooming-
            ton: Indiana University Press, 1990.
TI   *Totalité et Infini*. 4th ed. The Hague: Martinus Nijhoff, 1971
            (1st ed. 1961). Trans. Alphonso Lingis as *Totality and In-
            finity*. Pittsburgh: Duquesne University Press, 1969.
TO   *Le Temps et L'autre*. Paris: Quadrige, 1979. Trans. Richard
            Cohen as *Time and the Other*. Pittsburgh: Duquesne Uni-
            versity Press, 1987.

Correlations in Rosenzweig and Levinas

Philosophy and Its Others

EVER SINCE Hegel proclaimed himself to be the end of philosophy, philosophy has been resurrected in a strange, almost Hegelian, dialectical move. A thinker claims that something stands outside philosophy and so refuses the systematic logic that thinks everything. Philosophy sits rejected and chastened by this recourse to something other than itself. But this very effort to stand outside philosophy, independent of reason's empire, produces a new point of orientation for philosophy. The existing self, or everyday language, or the written text, or the will to power, or "the body," or . . . produce new philosophies: philosophy of the existing self, philosophy of writing, philosophy of the will. . . . At first glance Hegel seems to have won all too easily, for what looks more like the dialectic of sublation than philosophy recovering itself by moving through its others? But the philosophy that emerges after this recovery is not Hegel's, but is rather one which has become significantly other through the process—and so the notions we have of reason, of argument, of the purpose of philosophy, and indeed of the very orientation of philosophy are profoundly changed. Philosophy is replaced periodically with altered philosophies and thus cannot reign as the self-consciousness that assimilates everything else into its program, system, or project.

This process of altering philosophy, or of philosophy's conquest by its others, displays not the will to power of philosophy, but rather the perennial needs for a reexamination of reason and for reason itself to undergo alteration from its others, discovering in the process that reason is not clear to itself. The other teaches philosophy—philosophy resists, but ultimately is educated by the other and forgoes only its claim that philosophy is sovereign and complete, grounded and secure, a claim which even its others accepted in order to distance themselves. When the spokespeople for philosophy's others claim that they will not be philosophers, that their work is not philosophy, or in the academic context, that they cannot teach in Philosophy Departments, they are reacting to this claim which philosophy and its professors advance. But the thought and writing of philosophy's others redefine philosophy and become new philosophies, again vulnerable to still other others. Each other comes forward to claim its distinct critique of philosophy; each claims to have what has been missing all along, or at least since a wrong turn. Whether each other needs philosophy is more complex, but a certain striving for universal intelligibility, for persuasion in contrast to force, for justifying oneself to other others—these seem to emerge again and again as each other reorients philosophy as radically as it can.

This book explores an encounter with one of philosophy's others: the development of modern Jewish philosophy. Franz Rosenzweig and Emmanuel Levinas are its two most important philosophers in this century. Rosenzweig thought in the first quarter of the century, in the context of German late-idealism and early existentialism; Levinas lives in Paris, writing in French, the first expositor in France of Husserl, of Heidegger, and of their phenomenological method. These two take their stands as other against two different "philosophies"; they write in greatly disparate styles; they emerge from different Jewish milieus; their personal relations to Judaism and to Christianity are markedly different; and they live on opposite sides of the great chasm of modern Judaism: the Nazi destruction of European Jewry. Yet in their arguments with philosophy, they share an other. The Judaism they share is an ethics understood as concrete responsibility for others, correlate with the radical transcendence of God. This Judaism can again reorient philosophy.

Defining this Jewish other of philosophy, this radical ethics, is one of the several tasks of this book, and the book concludes with seven rubrics which serve as an agenda for this reorientation for philosophy. I will neither rehearse the centuries-long argument, nor recount the history of the theory of the argument that the geographic slogan "Athens or Jerusalem" names. The definition of the Jewish other in Rosenzweig and Levinas is permeated both by a tradition of Jewish discussions of ethics and of God's transcendence as well as by an interpretation of Jewish otherness given in the German philosophical tradition. Archaeology of the Jewish other that these two counterpoise against philosophy is a task for quite another, longer project. In place of archaeology a certain agenda emerges as delimiting that Jewish other, an agenda which varies for other thinkers and in other times. The rubrics of this agenda, however, retain a certain consistency, and the task here is to identify that agenda in Rosenzweig and Levinas.

A still more intricate task revolves around the title of this book: *Correlations*. For, while the term has various meanings, which I will sort in the first chapter, the meaning most important to this work refers to the relationship between philosophy and this one other, Judaism. The interaction between philosophy and Judaism is not one of two fixed terms in utter autonomy, but rather of two terms that become correlates of each other, each changing in itself through its relationship to the other. Philosophy does not simply assimilate Judaism, reducing and configuring it to fit within either its late-idealistic or phenomenological method, but neither does Judaism create a space which lies permanently outside philosophy.

Judaism can determine a new orientation for philosophy in the works of Levinas and Rosenzweig, as the importance of ethics and relations to the other are now gaining currency as a critical element of philosophy. Similarly, the very process of reorientation shows that Judaism does not permanently reside in itself, isolated and withdrawn from philosophy. It comes to meet philosophy, demanding a different perspective and offering new resources for a thus altered philosophy. These complex processes of correlation, alteration, obligation, and invitation define the central topic of this book. We will see not only how philosophy becomes Jewish, but also how philosophy and its other come into correlation and how the fall of one philosophical vision through criticism by its other creates a new philosophy.

I wish to begin here by introducing Rosenzweig and Levinas, indicating key features of their biographies and the importance of their works. Following that I will indicate the novelty and the strategy of this book, for my reading of each thinker is a departure from the standard view. The structure of this book will then appear in a brief outline.

Two Lives

In order to accentuate the differences between Rosenzweig and Levinas, some of which I mentioned earlier, I offer brief sketches that may help to measure the distance between the two men. Franz Rosenzweig was born in 1886, the only child of an assimilated German family. His intellectual path led from medicine, to history, and eventually to Jewish thought. His first major work, written under Friedrich Meinecke, was a biography called *Hegel and the State* in which he examined the development of Hegel's political philosophy through an intellectual biography. While under the sway of historicism, he had a harrowing conversation in 1913 with Eugen Rosenstock (later Rosenstock-Huessy). Rosenstock, himself a convert to Christianity from Judaism, persuaded Rosenzweig to convert. Rosenzweig chose to become Christian through a deeper appropriation of his own Judaism, but when he explored Judaism he discovered that it was sufficient and cancelled his plans to convert. Soon after, Rosenzweig went to Berlin to study with Hermann Cohen. Cohen was the leading Jewish thinker of his time, the pioneer of the Marburg School of neo-Kantianism. In his later years Cohen addressed Judaism directly in several works, works central not only to Rosenzweig's thought but to the themes of this book.

While Rosenzweig fought in World War I on the eastern front, he also managed to read and write copiously. He outlined and began his greatest work, *The Star of Redemption*, at the front and finished it at home. It is a monumental work and will occupy much of the discussion of this book.

While completing his return to Judaism and *The Star of Redemption*, Rosenzweig abandoned plans for an academic career. Instead, he founded the Frankfurt Free Jewish School, an adult education center. The Free School was part of Rosenzweig's efforts to rejuvenate the German-Jewish community by allowing traditional Jewish texts to speak to the well-educated Jewish intellectuals. Rosenzweig believed that the largely unfamiliar, traditional Jewish texts could still contribute to the lives of modern Jews. The Free School became a model for Jewish intellectual life in Europe and in America, and its students and teachers were the seminal group for twentieth-century Jewish thought: Rosenzweig himself, Buber, Scholem, Agnon, Erich Fromm, Leo Strauss, Ernst Simon, and Nahum Glatzer.

Soon after marrying in 1920, Rosenzweig was struck with amytrophic lateral sclerosis (Lou Gehrig's disease), and he deteriorated rapidly. The sclerosis left him able to communicate only by way of a special keyboard, but he lived and conducted a remarkable correspondence until 1929 (this in uncanny parallel to the contemporary physicist, Stephen Hawking). During that time he began a new German translation of Hebrew Scriptures with Martin Buber and translated a set of Judah Halevi's liturgical poems. He developed an innovative theory of translation, in which the goal was to remake the receptor language through the use of the original language. Rosenzweig's life centered around *The Star of Redemption*, but his tragic demise has spawned a certain kind of hagiographic treatment of both his life and his work.

Emmanuel Levinas was born in 1906 in Kovno, Lithuania. His family was "enlightened" and so pursued contemporary liberal culture, but was not assimilated as such. He grew up in the atmosphere of the intellectualist Lithuanian-Jewish community. The family survived the First World War, and in 1923 Levinas left the East for Strasbourg, France. He studied philosophy with Husserl and Heidegger in Freiberg. In 1929 he presented the first translation of Husserl into French, and soon after he wrote an important introduction to Husserl. He settled in Paris in 1930 (where he and his wife live today) and taught at the Normal School for the *Alliance Universelle Israélite*. The *Alliance* was a "modern" school network for Jewish communities throughout the Mediterranean; its Normal School was the training ground for the teachers who spread modern culture to what were often isolated and traditional Jewish communities.

Levinas volunteered for the army as a French citizen, was captured in 1940, and spent the Second World War doing hard labor in a POW camp in Germany. (Although the Jewish prisoners were segregated from the non-Jewish ones, they were not sent to the death camps because they were in the military.) Upon liberation Levinas returned to Paris and became principal of the Normal School. Like Rosenzweig he spent many years devoted to community education. In the late 1940s Levinas encountered Mordechai Shushani, a remarkable itinerant sage. It was Shushani who inspired Levinas to explore Talmudic and other Rabbinic texts, for Shushani was able to make their dense and dialogic style come alive in the contexts of contemporary philosophy and science.[1] Then, like Rosenzweig, Levinas innovated by adding classes in traditional Jewish texts (largely Talmud and medieval biblical commentaries) to the Normal School curriculum. In the context of the modernist vanguard *Alliance*, Levinas thus promoted a new reading of traditional sources.

Only in 1961, with the publication of his major work, *Totality and Infinity*, did Levinas receive a university position. First in Poitiers, and soon after in Paris at Nanterre, Levinas in his late fifties became a university professor. His influence today extends directly from students like Derrida, to his long-time friend Maurice Blanchot, to Lyotard, to the Solidarity movement, and to Latin American Liberation Theology. In 1974 Levinas published his second major work, *Otherwise than Being or Beyond Essence*. Levinas has also written several volumes of essays, including a series of works distinctly addressed to Jewish audiences.

Beyond the biographical distances, Levinas and Rosenzweig stand in relation to two distinct moments in twentieth-century philosophy: Levinas grapples constantly with phenomenological analyses pioneered by Husserl, while Rosenzweig took his point of departure from late idealism and the battle with historicism. Rosenzweig was trained in two different flavors of Neo-Kantian thought: the Marburg hyperrationalism of Hermann Cohen, and the humanistic thought of the Southwest German school. For him philosophy was the effort to know the essence of beings. The emergence of historicism, however, seemed to doom the philosophical attempts to provide foundations for knowledge. While Hegel had claimed to conceive all of history in a necessary dialectic culminating in his own thought, the later historicists went further. They accepted both the general claim that consciousness has a history, and its corollary that philosophy does not discover eternal truths, but is always historically conditioned. What the historicists rejected, on the other hand, was the existence of some overall purpose and plan to history's process. Neither the exploration of history nor the resources of consciousness seemed to Rosenzweig to offer definitive knowledge. The nihilistic crisis—represented by Nietzsche and the emergence of a philosophy of power and will—was the context from which Rosenzweig emerged with the combination of theology and philosophy he called "New Thinking." The concepts of Idealism, from Kant to Hegel and late Schelling, served as a vocabulary for Rosenzweig's thought. The attention to consciousness and subjectivity were exactly what he had to struggle through in order to emerge in a realm of free human interaction. The first half of this book links Rosenzweig's thought with these various strands. The various authors (Schelling, Cohen, Rosenstock-Huessy, Hegel, Weber, Troeltsch, and so on) are in a limited sense correlate to Rosenzweig; that is, they share themes, topics, and vocabulary on some points. I do not claim, however, that these correspondences display the mutual interrelationship that characterizes the correlation of Judaism and philosophy.

Levinas' philosophical context is dominated by Husserl's phenomenological analyses. Husserl's attempt to get 'to the things themselves' by phenomenological reduction, by examining the ways that phenomena appear in our consciousness, remains for Levinas the regulative goal of philosophy. The transformation of that method into an existentialism of situated, existing people, accomplished by Heidegger in *Being and Time,* signals for Levinas a crossing of a Rubicon. While Rosenzweig still had to move from the world of an ego's consciousness to the spatial world of living people, Levinas' thought began already with a life-world, with a set of concrete analyses of living people. Levinas' struggle thus is not to gain the spatiality of the world, but rather to discover how ethics occurs in that world. The Heideggerian turn to ontology poses for Levinas the challenge of how to construe the existential world. What Levinas finds is that both Heidegger's authenticity and Husserl's transcendental ego reduce the existential world by giving undue primacy to the self and its relationship to itself. The alterity of the other person is more fundamental than "the being of the being who asks about being."

Yet already some of the gap in Levinas' and Rosenzweig's contexts narrows, because Levinas' reading of both Husserl and Heidegger emphasizes exactly the themes that link phenomenology back to Idealism. In a brazen shorthand, Levinas reads Husserl as Fichte and Heidegger as Hegel. Levinas views Husserl's egology as, despite itself, too close to Fichte's philosophy of the 'I'; while Heidegger's resurrection of ontology is seen as parallel to the totalizing system in Hegel. Indeed, Heidegger surpasses Hegel, because his totality of ontology dispenses with the mechanistic dialectics of history and rests ultimately on the anonymity of Being itself. Levinas finds the ontological project to be one which must efface the other person, reducing the other's concrete and unique needs to a mere specification of being in general. Perhaps this idealistic reading of phenomenology emerges from the common concerns of Levinas and Rosenzweig.

In these personal and intellectual contexts each thinker fashioned distinctive works. Levinas' two major texts are written in a phenomenological style. *Totality and Infinity* makes use of Heideggerian analyses to argue against Heidegger. It is a grand text, interpreting intersubjectivity by contrasting ethics with a certain inward, assimilating thirst. It can easily be read as a rejection of Heidegger's *Being and Time.* Heidegger's preference for the ontological relation of a tool is replaced by a more basic joi de vivre of enjoying things. Authenticity is replaced by a being for the other, encountered face-to-face. And being beyond my death, in the discontinuity of the generations, in the life of my child, replaces Heidegger's being-towards-death. *Totality and Infinity* was widely recognized as one of the great phenomenological texts, and it has had serious impact in many circles where the phenomenological tradition is studied.

Levinas' second major work, *Otherwise than Being or Beyond Essence,* redevelops many of the analyses of *Totality and Infinity*, but with a narrower focus. Levinas explores the moment of encounter with an other, the moment of my responsibility. He shifts away from ontological language and moves to a richer and more paradoxical vocabulary of super-phenomenological terms. Levinas seeks to describe the rending of consciousness that occurs when the other approaches me, and he has become more aware of the problematic nature of describing that event in any language. Thus he gropes with concepts like 'enigma', 'obsession', 'substitution', and 'glory'. This text is clearly more mature than the first, but it also has had less widespread impact. Both works, however, are uncommonly dense and difficult, even for those familiar with the writings of Husserl, Heidegger, Merleau-Ponty, or Sartre.

Rosenzweig, on the other hand, wrote only one major text: *The Star of Redemption.* The work is composed of three parts, each of which is made up of three books and an introduction. The first part presents three elements (God, world, human [*Mensch*]); the second examines a sequence of relations between these elements (God's *creation* of the world, God's *revelation* to human beings, and humanity's *redemption* of the world); and the third explores two different communities (Judaism and Christianity) as instantiations of the goal of redemption and concludes with a theological exposition of truth. The three parts move from logic (I), to a performative theory of speech (II), to a theological social theory (III). Rosenzweig held that only the first part was genuine philosophy because the latter parts depended on empirical sensation. The relation of pure reason to reasoning that admits sensible data is a key issue in understanding the systematic structure of Rosenzweig's text.

The Star of Redemption is written in an idiolect of German, readily understood by only a small circle of relatives and friends of Rosenzweig's. In its time, the German-Jewish community recognized it as a work of genius, bought it loyally, and then consigned it to the bookcase, unread, because of its daunting style and size. *The Star of Redemption,* thus, has fared reasonably well but only as an icon. It has gone through four editions in German, is translated into French, English, and Hebrew, and is widely acknowledged in Jewish circles as a great book. Rosenzweig relented in 1925 and wrote an interpretative essay for the book, called "The

New Thinking"—the name Rosenzweig gave the sort of combination of philosophy and theology in *The Star of Redemption*. This essay was supposedly intended to provide the general Jewish intellectual community access to the book, but it too, like almost everything Rosenzweig wrote, is dense, idiosyncratic, and a long read. In my interpretations of the book, the essay serves as a continuing point of contact: I examine the text of *The Star of Redemption* itself, but "The New Thinking" is never out of view. I would claim that *The Star of Redemption* is the greatest work of Modern Jewish Thought, but it is also the hardest to read and so fails in its function as a published text.

The Star of Redemption's influence on later thinking is much more complex, because so few people could actually make sense of the book. Still, in the circles of Jewish intellectuals it has been influential for such thinkers as Gershom Scholem, Walter Benjamin, Emil Fackenheim, Leo Strauss, André Neher, and of course Levinas. The sequence of theological relations (Creation, Revelation, and Redemption) has become a standard rubric for Jewish theology, and the attempt to justify both Judaism and Christianity has inspired many people involved in interfaith dialogue. The rigorous philosophical appropriation of the text still lies ahead.

THE TASK

In this book I propose to revise the common receptions of Levinas and Rosenzweig. My major claim is twofold: that Levinas should be read as a Jewish thinker in the class of Rosenzweig and others, and that Rosenzweig should be read as a philosopher—specifically, a postmodern philosopher. I believe those who come to this book hoping to gain some insight into Levinas' thought will be rewarded doubly, because they will see that Rosenzweig also is a philosopher worthy of their interest. And those who expect to get some help with Rosenzweig's thought will also receive an extra measure, as Levinas will appear as a valuable companion.

The need to advance this claim emerges from the standard reception of the two thinkers. Levinas has been read as a philosopher, while the Jewish dimension of his thought has largely been ignored, or honored by a mention and then ignored. The significance of his long years at the Normal School, of his own Lithuanian heritage, and most of all of the learning with Shushani are not used to interpret his philosophical insights. And yet Levinas has a wide readership and is recognized as influential. Rosenzweig, on the other hand, has been relegated to the company of religious existentialists. In general, Jewish religious intellectuals make at least a nod in his direction, but few have tried, much less plumbed, *The Star of Redemption*. Beyond the ranks of rabbis, religion professors, and seminarians, Rosenzweig is almost unknown. The one exception is in Jewish-Christian dialogue, where he is often put into service. But as philosopher? Thus Levinas' influence is much more extensive and is as philosopher, not as Jewish Thinker. Levinas himself might desire it thus, because Rosenzweig's fate is not enviable. While I will pair Rosenzweig with philosophers, I will group Levinas not with Husserl and Heidegger, but with religious thinkers.

My task of rereading is made difficult by the very cause of the limitations of previous readings: the extreme obscurity and density of the works of both writers. *The Star of Redemption* is written in the private language of Rosenzweig's circle. He draws on various philosophical and theological vocabularies, denoting clusters of concepts by the use of a single word or phrase. (I must add that the English translation, while serviceable in parts, is not the product of a deep, sympathetic grasp of Rosenzweig's systematic concerns.) Rosenzweig's analyses thus are so cryptic that, unless one already knows the result, it is often virtually impossible to follow his line of reasoning. Due to this obscurity, much previous scholarship was left with little more than impressionistic and experiential readings. Levinas, on the other hand, writes in an extremely dense phenomenological style. His phenomenological analysis is blended with rhetorical excess in a French both heavily adorned and somehow broken. The lines of argument are repetitive and emphatic, yet one often wonders how the paradoxical results are achieved. Rosenzweig writes in rhythmic and sometimes witty periods; Levinas in long, rolling ones. Levinas has not been accessible, except to readers schooled in the phenomenological methods, and so remains largely unknown in American Jewish circles.

I wish to add that the flawed readings of Rosenzweig and Levinas are now being challenged in the secondary literature, little of which can be found in English. Still, I would like to cite here my major companions in this project, particularly the five volumes of essays on Rosenzweig that most reflect some of the challenges. There has been little written on Levinas' relationship to Rosenzweig, or even on his Jewish sources or writings. David Banon, Catherine Chalier, and Jean-Louis Schlegel contribute valuable essays to the recent volume *Les Cahiers de* La nuit surveillée: *Emmanuel Levinas*.[2] Several individuals, including Robert Bernasconi, Richard A. Cohen, and Edith Wyschogrod, have made significant connections between Levinas and Jewish thought. Finally, while this book was in press, Susan Handelman's new book appeared: *Fragments of Redemption: Jewish Thought and Literary Theory in Benjamin, Scholem, and Levinas*.[3] Her work complements the task of this book, placing Levinas in a Jewish context, albeit one largely of issues in literary theory. Moreover, she explores the relations of all three thinkers to Rosenzweig at some length, especially that of Levinas. There is conceptual and interpretative commonground in these two books, which, due to the timing of publication, I cannot explore in these pages.

With Rosenzweig the situation is more complex. In the last several years four important works have appeared. First, *Les Cahiers de* La nuit surveillée: *Franz Rosenzweig* drew together older pieces by and about Rosenzweig, but also included important essays by Stéphane Mosès and others.[4] Second, the proceedings of a centennial conference held in 1986 in Kassel, Germany, are available in two volumes.[5] Some of the innovations of my reading are closely related to essays in that work by Norbert M. Samuelson, Herman J. Heering, Bernhard Casper, Jeinz-Jürgen Görtz, Otto Pöggeler, Wendell S. Dietrich, and Alan Udoff. Third, Paul Mendes-Flohr has edited an excellent volume in which several of the same cast (Pöggeler, Casper, Mosès, and Mendes-Flohr himself) present essays which could enrich many of my interpretations.[6] Last, in 1982 Stéphane Mosès published *Système et Révélation,* a commentary on *The Star of Redemption.*[7] This is a substantial work which at times is in accord with my readings, at times in sharp disagreement. A complete treatment of Mosès, or indeed of any interpreter, is beyond the scope of this book. The burden of justifying my interpretations is borne, I hope, by the following text itself; moreover, I hope that this book will disperse these new approaches to both Rosenzweig and Levinas to a wider audience than that reached by the present scholarship.

But, I hasten to add, my claim is also problematic for each man: Levinas resists the title *Jewish Thinker,* and Rosenzweig refuses to be called a philosopher. The initial justification for my claim is the first topic in Chapter 1. I will provide a sketch of the family to which both men belong, a family of religious thinkers who pursue the sort of correlation I discussed in the opening pages—a reciprocal interaction of two independent modes of thought: philosophy and Judaism. That family sketch will offer a provisional view of how I will relocate both thinkers. I will also provide an introduction to Levinas' thought by enumerating the basic set of Rosenzweig's influences on him. Thereafter, I will largely confine myself to exploring each man in independence from the other, as the development of the double claim requires different forms of interpretation for each thinker. For Rosenzweig, the interpretation needed is one that shows how his method is still philosophical, even when he engages in theological matters. For Levinas, we need to see him in specifically religious contexts in order to appreciate how, even there, he does not cease to think in the correlational mode. Levinas will appear as a Jewish thinker adapting Rosenzweig only after Rosenzweig appears as a philosopher offering a theology which is neither fanatical, nor dogmatic, nor even apologetic.

The chapters on Rosenzweig follow the structure of *The Star of Redemption*. I focus on Rosenzweig's methods because, in terms of methods, he has been direly misunderstood. Once those methods are sufficiently clear, a diligent reader of *The Star of Redemption* will be capable of interpreting the specific analyses. The sequence of topics, however, also displays the systematic design of the work. I begin in Chapter 2 with Rosenzweig's logic (Part I of *The Star of Redemption*). He requires an innovation in logic so that individuality can be freed from an Hegelian dialectic which achieves a totality through the dyad individual/universal. Levinas will later appropriate the innovation in logic by contrasting totality with infinity, but Rosenzweig explores the limits of thought and discovers a way of holding opposites together without producing unity.

Chapters 3 and 4 then examine the heart of Rosenzweig's method: the turn to speech in Part II of *The Star of Redemption*. While pure reason with its logic undergirds the freedom of human and divine action, it cannot produce the reality of that freedom. Rosenzweig needs an a posteriori access to experience, but one that will not degenerate into private religious experience, which he calls fanaticism. He chooses the public realm of speech and later of social gesture. Theological concepts intrude here precisely because, according to Rosenzweig, human speech is never merely human. Speech opens up to a transcendence which breaks out of our humanly constructed world. The methodological breakthrough results from attendance to the performance of speech rather than to the cognitive function of language. Rosenzweig calls this 'grammatical thinking', but he is using a mixture of forms of analysis that today would include not only syntactics, but also semantics and pragmatics. In Chapter 3, I will locate this emphasis on performance in both historical and contemporary contexts in preparation for a presentation of Rosenzweig's own theory. I will develop that theory through an emphasis on mood (indicative, imperative, cohortative) as linked both to theological concepts and to differing forms of interrelation between speaker and addressee. By concentrating on the mood of utterances, Rosenzweig orients speech by the imperative—the speech of an 'I' to a 'you'. The corresponding theological concept is revelation, as Rosenzweig explores how the other is revealed to me through my hearing the other's commandment to love.

Chapter 4 will build upon that analysis of moods and address more general issues in philosophy of language. The first issue is the possibility of meaning. Rosenzweig claims that logic provides a kind of prelinguistics, which could be seen as a transcendental linguistics, constituting the conditions for semantics, syntactics, and pragmatics. The second issue is the origin of language, which Rosenzweig assigns to poetry. The question is how a written text, particularly the Bible, can serve as a script for the revelation that occurs in speaking. The act of reading a text in public allows the written words to become revelation again. An examination of Rosenzweig's midrashim (readings of biblical text) will demonstrate how the public nature of speaking displays the theological interruption in the human realm, because for Rosenzweig love itself is never merely human. Finally, the last issue is the question of theology: What place does the interrogative have in Rosenzweig's interpretation of speech by mood? The performance of asking certain questions seems to be an ineluctable challenge to the primacy of commandments for interpreting Jewish theology.

Chapters 5 and 6 display the pragmatist sense of verification in Rosenzweig's thought—just as the theological interpretation of relations performed in speech is proven by social praxis in Part III of *The Star of Redemption*. I offer a sociological reading of this part—a task Rosenzweig himself called for. The analyses of the theological concepts of creation, revelation, and redemption in the performance of speech cannot be confirmed until societies are formed that live out the social harmony announced in redemption. The enactment of redemption thus moves beyond speaking into social action, and so the task of the final part of *The Star of Redemption* is to present the forms of society that achieve redemption. In Chapter 5, I examine Rosenzweig's social theory in contrast to both nontheological and historical social theories. Rosenzweig has a remarkable sense of how social action brings eternity into time, but most significant is the problem of how to interpret the often contentious historical claims he makes. What Rosenzweig calls a philosophical sociology is characterized by a commitment to social reality that is not identical to a dependence on historical accuracy. Here contrasts with Meinecke, Wölfflin, Weber, and Troeltsch are most helpful.

Chapter 6 then provides the first results of my approach to reading Rosenzweig's text. Rosenzweig presents a social theory that is a duplex of politics and aesthetics. He interprets the State and Art as each struggling to overcome the incessant passing away of time; the State through force and resistance, Art by representing the loss and so overcoming it. Each social form is then transformed theologically without becoming the other: Judaism represents an overcoming of the state; Christianity of art. Most challenging is the recognition that the state and art do not merge, neither in their normal function nor in their theological form. That refusal of aestheticized politics itself depends not only on the social theory, but ultimately on the logic, with which my interpretation of *The Star of Redemption* began. The move from logic, to speech as performance, to a philosophical sociology is the central design of the work, and as such is not a random progression. Rather it displays Rosenzweig's keen and profound vision—that the task of Jewish thought (and, I would add, of contemporary philosophy) requires the connection of these different spheres of reflection. I am rehearsing that motion in this book in order to explore the significance of each sphere, but ultimately to offer an invitation to join the serial tasks.

The second part of this book examines how Levinas belongs in this family of Jewish thinkers; it proceeds by a set of recontextualizations rather than by a systematic presentation. Chapter 7 is a pivotal chapter, as I examine Levinas' Jewish writings in order to discover the correlation that moves from Jewish sources to philosophy. Levinas' own concept for that correlation is a translation into philosophical language. I will show not only that Levinas makes essential use of Jewish texts and ideas, but also that such use is not dogmatic or antiphilosophical. Rather, even as philosophy requires the reorientation from Judaism, Judaism on its own reaches out for a philosophical exposition of its insights.

Chapter 8 will return to the family portrait in order to examine the question of the other's uniqueness. The central question is the logic of uniqueness and its function in intensifying responsibility beyond the limits of thinking, which follows the logic of subordination of individuals to their species. I pair Levinas here with Hermann Cohen, because at first glance they are the furthest apart philosophically of the correlational thinkers. Cohen's effort to generate a unique, specific person through pure reason alerts us to the difficulties in using any philosophic method to justify the radical ethics of this group. Levinas' own struggle to reach beyond phenomenology to an experience that inverts the intentionality of Husserlian analyses appears, in comparison with Cohen's efforts, more clearly as struggle. In the process of examining these two thinkers' transgressing of their own philosophical methods, I will also discover lines of filiation in the family. Rosenzweig follows most closely upon Cohen, but both Buber and Levinas each choose only one side of Cohen's discussion of the ethical relation to an other.

From logic I move again to the performance of speaking. Chapter 9 is a commentary on parallel discussions in Gabriel Marcel and Levinas. The issue in these texts is the substitution for the other. Each thinker helps to show how the capacity to respond (*responsibility*) originates not in my spontaneity, but in the other. Autonomy appears as derivative from other-centered responsibility; the ability to choose to be ethical itself derives from the unchosen responsibility to the other. How ethics can arise from a responsibility I do not freely choose is perhaps the key philosophical question posed to the ethics I am exploring. It is also noteworthy that Marcel belongs to this family of correlations, even though he works in a Catholic theological tradition. Marcel helps illuminate the theological dimension of Levinas' work, while Levinas helps develop the asymmetry Marcel discovered in the performative nature of speaking. I justify my choice of commentary by further reflecting on themes introduced in Chapter 4 on a reader's responsibility.

Finally, I return in Chapter 10 to social theory, this time pairing Levinas with Marx. While Rosenzweig was linked with Weber and Troeltsch, this pairing of Levinas and Marx allows the discussion to focus on the economics of responsibility. Unlike the other partners for Levinas, Marx is neither clearly a religious thinker nor a proponent of Jewish correlation. The question of Marx's Jewishness will remain unexplored, but the set of concepts that constitute an overlapping of both thinkers has important Jewish resonance. The question is, How does one understand liberation as a public and economic action? I present parallel interpretations that are relevant to the development of contemporary Liberation Thought. For Levinas the key question is how the responsibility created in a face-to-face encounter with an other can be preserved in a social context with other others. Levinas' elliptical discussions of 'the third' portray a rationalizing of what was originally an excessive duty. Marx helps accentuate the economic dimension of Levinas' thought, while Levinas helps emphasize the relations to others that underlie Marx's earlier writings. The need for social theory again emerges, because the reality of the phenomenology of face-to-face speech opens out from itself onto the need for social change. My presentation of Levinas, beginning with the question of translation, then moving to the logic of uniqueness, through the performance of speech where responsibility begins, and ending in a discussion of social liberation, parallels the systematic design of Rosenzweig's *The Star of Redemption*. The set of pairings for Levinas follows the same sequence of spheres of reflection, displaying in another vein how Levinas may be seen as an adaptation of Rosenzweig.

This book concludes with a brief epilogue: a sequence of seven rubrics to serve as an agenda for Jewish philosophy. I draw together the family resemblances of the various thinkers under consideration here, beginning with the task of correlation. The other rubrics include the primacy of ethics; an essential sociality; messianic politics; a new and positive form of materiality; the suspension of the state; and, finally, the development of positive social institutions. These serve not only to draw together the interpretations of Rosenzweig and Levinas in this book, but also to set an agenda for future Jewish philosophy. Moreover, this agenda can become a program for philosophy in general, as philosophy and Judaism both will be brought into closer correlation.

CHAPTER 1

Correlations, Adaptation

THE RECIPROCAL relation between Judaism and philosophy in the works of Rosenzweig and Levinas requires some preliminary definition. To call it simply correlation is to gesture to a wide spectrum of possible relations. In this chapter I will identify the specific correlation between the two bodies of thought. Moreover, I will attempt to overcome the explicit and original resistance each thinker would have to my double claim. Levinas refuses the appelation "Jewish Thinker," and Rosenzweig claimed to have moved beyond philosophy. By sketching a family portrait of Hermann Cohen, Rosenzweig, and Levinas, I can offer the preliminary perspective of this book. And following that sketch, I will provide a brief account of the influence of Rosenzweig in Levinas' work, an account that will also introduce Levinas' own major ideas. Finally, I will offer the suggestion that we understand the relationship of Levinas and Rosenzweig neither as correlation in my specific sense, nor as translation, but as adaptation.

A FAMILY PORTRAIT

I wish to sketch a portrait to display the family resemblance of correlation—that Judaism and philosophy are correlative. The central figure for that concept of correlation is Hermann Cohen, the title of whose final work proclaims the connection between reason and Judaism: *Religion of Reason out of the Sources of Judaism*.[1] In this work Cohen claims that the method of correlation produces not only a relation between the 'I' and the 'you', but also and more importantly between a person and God. Before explaining Cohen's use of the term, however, I must separate this meaning of correlation from two other uses of the term.

The connection of philosophy and theology by the method of correlation might suggest Tillich's use of the term *correlation*. Tillich claims that theology provides the answers to philosophy's questions.[2] While he does recognize a mutual relationship between the two disciplines, and indeed is using a term descended from Cohen's, his use is far removed from that of these Jewish thinkers. Behind Tillich's use is some sense of the autonomy and reciprocity of the two disciplines, but both his limitations on philosophical inquiry and his claims of authority for the theological position are foreign to the family I am sketching. Rosenzweig and Levinas both explicitly reject the apologetic theology that Tillich proposes and similarly are, along with Cohen, far removed from any sort of church theology. Perhaps the greatest gap between Tillich and the family is that Tillich's theology eclipses ethics and its command behind a knowledge of the answers.

Furthermore, the correlation of the intentionality of the ego (*noesis*) and that of the phenomenal object (*noema*) in Husserl is not a member of this family either. Husserl distinguished the traditional search for a correlation between a thought and its object from a more radical correlation between phenomenologically reduced objects. He looked to the evidence in consciousness and bracketed the question of external reality. By bracketing realistic claims, he was able to discover the correlation in the realm of consciousness between noesis and noema. He determined that different kinds of intentionality (perception, memory, fantasy, etc.) have different kinds of correlate objects in consciousness.[3] This phenomenological correlation then serves as the foundation for any "realistic" or existing correlation. Levinas often insists that the relationship to an other breaks with this specifically Husserlian correlation—but that need not put him at odds with the correlation of Judaism and philosophy I am describing.

Rosenzweig claimed that Cohen broke through to existentialism only in his last work, *Religion of Reason*, precisely by adopting the method of correlation (III, 206). But Cohen made use of that method in a *technical* sense from the time of his *Logic of Pure Cognition* (1902),[4] and while the employment in the *Religion of Reason* is impressive, it is not unique. Chapters 4 and 8 will explore the various valences of Cohen's method and display the inadequacy of Rosenzweig's claim, but here I wish only to sketch the most central characteristics of his method. Cohen insists on the plurality of entities in order to allow for the possibility of ethics in general. He fights against monism and particularly pantheism in its many forms throughout his works because ethics, for Cohen, depends on the possibility that distinct agents can act undetermined by other agents. Cohen is also a rationalist of a particularly fierce variety. To admit a plurality of entities would be insufficient if there were not some rational mode of knowing each of them. Indeed, Cohen's critical epistemological perspective insists that we cannot know any thing in any way except through pure reason. The plurality of entities, therefore, must be produced through reason. This view of reason is not altogether popular today, but its value for Cohen is not compromised by his rejection of monism. Correlation is the rational cognition of plurality.

When Cohen then applies correlation in the theological sphere, we find him insisting both that God is separate from the world and that reason has a primacy over sensation. The radical transcendence of God, the utter lack of any mediation between God and human beings, is recognized through the use of human reason. Human reason, therefore, must be in correlation with divine reason. The bridge from God to the human must both leave each intact and also make revelation possible. Revelation emerges as a two-party relationship, in which both sides are changed but neither becomes submerged in the other. Knowledge of God, and in that sense God's existence for us, depends on our own rationality; conversely, our rationality and existence depend on the relationship we have to God as our creator.[5] This nonsymmetric correlation is the logical center of the family resemblance I am discussing.

The title of Cohen's work also displays a correlation between reason and Judaism. To draw out a concept of religion from the sources of Judaism need not compromise rationality, and, conversely, a religion of reason need not be non- or anti-Jewish. Judaism offers a historical body of thought, a unique resource for philosophy. But Judaism also has a natural inclination toward reason and so seeks the idealization that Cohen portrays in his book. By insisting on the universality of reason, Cohen rejects all empirical experience. Judaism's privilege is as source for reason's Religion, but this does not authorize the community to be exclusive. He develops this view of Judaism not from the outside, as philosopher, but from within, interpreting biblical and rabbinic texts. The very correlation with which I introduced this book—the mutual, asymmetric interaction of philosophy and Judaism—is found in Cohen's thought.

Rosenzweig, however, was suspicious of Cohen's claims to have achieved this correlation of reason and Judaism without recourse to existential experience, and he rejected the theory that reason could generate the plurality of separate and independent entities. But Rosenzweig augmented philosophy not with religious experience, which is the common view of his work, but with theological concepts. He portrayed both philosophy and theology as at dead ends: philosophy having lost its sense of purpose, theology its objectivity and historical validity. In the midst of the historicist crisis the two needed each other, and from such a need was born Rosenzweig's New Thinking.

Like Cohen, Rosenzweig insisted on the separation between God and human beings, and indeed Rosenzweig also protected the independence of the world as a third, separate entity. Rosenzweig designated these three as *elements* and assigned their constitution to philosophy. Their interaction, on the other hand, he discovered from theology in the sequence of concepts: Creation, Revelation, and Redemption. The absence of mediation was retained from Cohen, but the bridge of reason was abandoned in favor of a bridge of speech. Rosenzweig thus made the linguistic turn, focusing on the performance of speaking to correlate the three elements in their three relations.

Rosenzweig still retains, however, the correlation of theology and philosophy, through which both are changed. He is quick to claim that the New Thinking "is no theological thinking. At least not at all what one has had to understand as such heretofore. Neither in end nor in means" (III, 152). Rosenzweig rejects the approaches of both dogmatic and apologetic theology. Correlation is not merely a change produced in each term, but the mutuality of that change: "Theological problems are to be translated into human, and the human ones propelled into theological" (III, 153). Thus what for Cohen happens through reason, for Rosenzweig will transpire through spoken language; human questions and problems will require theological inquiry, and theological issues will gain their meaning in human terms. The two correlate elements (the human and the divine) require relationship with each other, but the terms do not collapse into one another.

However, Rosenzweig, like Cohen, also preserves a certain sort of philosophical universality in his correlation. While reason cannot serve any longer to bridge differences, speech is not a turn to religion or its experience. Cohen's religion is one of reason, but Rosenzweig, having criticized that reason, is left with no interest in the concept of religion. Theology, yes; religion, no.

> God did not create religion, rather the world. And when he reveals himself, the world still stands fast, indeed it becomes for the first time created. Revelation does not destroy the genuine paganism, the paganism of the creation, at all. It only lets the miracle of return and renewal happen. It is always present, and if past, then it is out of that past that stands at the beginning of human history—revelation to Adam. (III, 153)

Rosenzweig's use of theological concepts depends on the universally accessible, human experience of speech. Perhaps the most important reinterpretation in my book is intended to free Rosenzweig from the constraints of Jewish sectarianism. The theological concepts in a deep sense derive from Judaism, but their application is not exclusive and their validity does not derive from "Jewish religious experience." Revelation, and indeed creation and redemption, are accessible to all peoples of all cultures in all places, but they are not themselves the product of pure reason; rather, they emerge from speech. The shifts toward experience, theology, and speech are the bases of Rosenzweig's claim to be moving away from philosophy, but he still retains the desire for a thought which is not exclusive, but open universally.

But Rosenzweig can still appear as a kind of philosopher, for one of the least stable terms in the philosophical vocabulary requires examination: the term *philosophy* itself. My claim, quite simply, is that for the very reasons Rosenzweig disqualifies himself as a modern philosopher, he qualifies as a postmodern philosopher. The openness to theological matters and to Jewish sources eliminated him as a modern philosopher, because such a philosopher was, by definition, someone who could found all of his thought upon rational resources, someone who in principle would not have need for specific, historical, religious sources—someone, in short, who could not be a Jewish thinker. But in the postmodern use, philosophy includes particularities of tradition and of time and place, requiring only what Rosenzweig himself would require—that we abjure fanaticism and authoritarianism. Rosenzweig has become a philosopher because philosophy has been changed, if not by his work, then at least by the work of many who would be his proper companions. (And Rosenzweig's view that Cohen paved the way, that Cohen was the last great idealist who had broken through to experience only in his final work—that view depended on Rosenzweig's failure to see how Cohen had been correlating Jewish concepts with philosophy throughout his system. Cohen's purpose had eluded Rosenzweig, although many Protestant critics had always accused Cohen's thought of being tainted with Jewishness.)

The justification for the claim that Rosenzweig is a postmodern philosopher lies ahead. New Thinking is a break with modern philosophy, but in its desire to bind the arbitrary subjectivity of inner experience with the public interactions undertaken in speech and gesture, New Thinking backs away from both dogmatism and idiosyncratic, subjective experience. The welcoming of theology, therefore, is not a rejection of philosophy. Indeed, in the best sense of postmodern philosophy, Rosenzweig not only retains certain recognizably philosophical goals, he also preserves a positive role for modern philosophy itself (which he calls *Philosophy*). This positive evaluation of what modern philosophy can contribute may be a breakthrough for postmodern philosophy, one made possible by postmodern philosophy's acceptance of heterogeneous elements into its thought without assimilating them into a single model. The very abundance of Rosenzweig's system—that logic and a theory of speech, philosophical sociology with theological analyses of art and politics, and above all an ethics that orients intersubjective space without recourse to foundations—points to the plurality of methods and spheres of thought that characterizes postmodern philosophy.

In presenting such a view of Rosenzweig, I concur with Levinas, who more than anyone else has reopened *The Star of Redemption* for philosophical appropriation. Rosenzweig's turning to existing human beings and to spoken language does not signify to Levinas that Rosenzweig is beyond the realm of philosophy. Such reflection is exactly what constitutes philosophy for Levinas. Yet Levinas resists the title Jewish Thinker. He persists in segregating his philosophical work from his Jewish work. He even publishes them with different publishers. Both *Totality and In-*

finity and *Otherwise than Being* have extremely sparse explicit references to Jewish sources.[6] One might similarly notice that philosophers seldom appear in the Jewish writings—that, particularly in the Talmudic readings, Levinas focuses on current events and popular intellectuals, but avoids debate with philosophical forces. This segregation seems complete.

One must be only a bit more subtle to discover both the causes and the deeper philosophical method behind Levinas' thinking, for the former are superficial and the latter is once again in the family of the correlation. I believe that the intellectual atmosphere of Paris has more than a little to do with the segregation. Levinas wants his philosophic works to be received as such. The regnant postreligious consciousness, combined with a never completely absent anti-Semitic scent, makes the reception of boldly Jewish thought by the philosophical community difficult. Were everyone to think of religion as Cohen did, as ultimately neither exclusive nor sectarian, the problem would be reduced—and yet the Christian theological community might still be suspicious. Rosenzweig's own misappropriation as an existential Jew and his subsequent omission from intellectual discussion possibly serve as a warning to Levinas. Levinas was a doubled man for the central years of his life, developing his philosophy while serving as a leader and educator in the Jewish community. What he lived professionally is reflected in the refusal to be thought simply a Jewish educator. The canons of philosophical discourse seem to him to require that his work not appear limited by its relationship to Judaism. In this respect he seems closer to Cohen than to Rosenzweig.

Both Cohen and Levinas had wider readerships in their times than did Rosenzweig. Many secular and Christian intellectuals alike have drunk deeply from Levinas' well. Who knows if they would have been so accepting of a more overtly Jewish body of work. Rosenzweig may have made his thought inaccessible to the Jewish audience, yet one cannot but wonder if his philosophical impact has been lessened not merely by the religious dimension of his thought, but particularly by its Jewish identity in a period renowned for its virulent anti-Semitism.

Levinas' strategy of segregation is not, however, identical to his method of thinking. I will explore in Chapter 7 how Levinas' Jewish writings translate from Hebrew to Greek. At this point, however, I wish to mention only that his philosophical writings are yet a further translation from Jewish sources into philosophical terms. The Jewish writings present a distinctly philosophical reading of Jewish sources, one which demonstrates the inherently Jewish quality of this striving for philosophy. On the other side of the correlation, philosophy stands in greatest need of its other, of an ethics that breaks in upon the ontological pursuit of identity and autonomy. The yearning for transcendence, radical transcendence, for a relationship to an other that does not admit of assimilation, that yearning is philosophical to the core, but Levinas contrasts that desire for alterity with the dominant philosophical tradition which reigns complacently from Parmenides to Heidegger. Levinas claims that philosophy can be renovated, reoriented in pursuit of radical transcendence, in the service of ethics. While Rosenzweig felt compelled to step away from philosophy, Levinas finds that philosophy can become new, revising its canons of reason, proof, evidence, and so on. Thus Levinas attempts to make the correlate change in both philosphical and Jewish contexts.

However, the more theological context of correlation, that between the divine and the human, is strained in Levinas. Levinas retains only traces of the theological vocabulary of Cohen or Buber or Rosenzweig. God appears in his texts as a decisive absence, a trace, a force that can be felt behind the ethical encounter with other people, but never a presence. Yet despite this thinning of the theological vocabulary, Rosenzweig and Levinas remain quite close in their understanding of the exposition of theology—for it was Rosenzweig who claimed that theological problems had to be translated into human ones. Levinas carries that task out with a certain disguise, but it is a similar task nonetheless. Beyond negative theology, Jewish theological discussion often dissolves into the intensification of ethics. Levinas pursues that displacement with great power and offers to the philosophical world great insight into the correlate ethics of Jewish theology.

THE BASIC INFLUENCES

While I will show how Levinas' translation from Hebrew to Greek is consonant with Rosenzweig's New Thinking, I am unwilling to devote the book to the complex but somewhat superficial task of tracing the influence of Rosenzweig in Levinas' thought. Here, for a few pages, I will do what I have otherwise left to the reader: connect the dots. The kinds of connections possible are not merely between concepts, but also between the focuses and approaches of the two thinkers. A systematic reading of Rosenzweig's work will occupy the first half of this book. I will introduce Levinas here, on the other hand, by discussing several of his central themes. In the later chapters of this book I will explore Levinas' thought in conjunction with other thinkers (Cohen, Marcel, Marx), but I will not provide a systematic account of his thought. I will divide that introduction here into two parts: 1) the themes that Levinas explicitly acknowledges as Rosenzweig's, and 2) some themes that display an implicit correspondence.

Explicit Influences in Levinas

Levinas has written on Rosenzweig much less regularly than on Husserl, Heidegger, Descartes, or several other authors. The vocabulary Levinas employs is largely drawn from the phenomenological tradition and so does not sound like Rosenzweig's. Nonetheless, Levinas himself acknowledges in the preface to *Totality and Infinity*:

> We were struck by the opposition to the idea of totality in *The Star of Redemption* by Franz Rosenzweig, which is too often present in this book to be cited. But the presentation and the development of the notions employed are due completely to the phenomenological method. (TI xvi/28)

Levinas is most indebted to Rosenzweig for the critique of totality, a concept so basic to Levinas' project as to become the title of his book. What was Rosenzweig's "opposition to the idea of totality"?: his insistence on a radical separation of God, humanity, and the world. In place of totality, plurality succeeds. And that plurality is in principle nontotalizable, incapable of being regrouped and represented by the knower. The possibility of freedom, of ethics, of theological relations like creation or revelation all depend on the impossibility that one term could synthetically encompass everything. This radical breakup of the totality of being is a point of departure for the correlation outlined above.

Levinas wrote two essays on Rosenzweig in which he rehearses both Rosenzweig's biography and the main themes of *The Star of Redemption*.[7] Following these, Levinas only took up Rosenzweig again in two shorter pieces.[8] And with those writings we encompass the explicit discussions of Rosenzweig in Levinas' work. However, several key themes of his own work emerge in these essays and shorter pieces as he tries to revive interest in Rosenzweig's thought. First, Levinas claimed recently that the most important aspect of Rosenzweig's shattering of the 'all' is the discovery that a human has no genus, that each is unique.[9] I am unique and the other is unique, and even the third is unique. This topic is the focus of Chapter 8. The pluralism that replaces totality abandons the logic of subordinating members to their class. In Rosenzweig's logic, this is the 'Yes' of the unknowability of God or World or the Human to which the 'No' of will must still be added. That rational process of classification totalizes over the unique individual and presupposes that each has its being or its worth only by belonging to a more universal class. Even Heidegger's ontology subordinates the being of each person to the question of Being, which is given priority. Levinas finds in Rosenzweig the requirement that each person is an infinite end (and as such has unique worth) not subordinatable to some general assessment of human value.

Second, Levinas recognizes Rosenzweig's claim that love is experienced as a commandment and that such a claim follows a Jewish tradition of thought (HS 83). In Chapter 3, I will discuss Rosenzweig's assertion in terms of a kind of grammar. The paradoxical meaning is not obscure: In contrast to a sentimental notion of love as relaxation and comfort, we find the view that to love is to command, to trust so much as to impose a duty on the other. Or rather, as both Levinas and Rosenzweig will discuss, to find myself loved is to receive a command from the other, to be affirmed as the one capable of love and even required to love. Love is joyous, delightful, affirming, and so on precisely because it trusts me so far as to demand something of me. Love finds me adult and responsible—not comforted by release and escape.

Third, Levinas connects this claim by Rosenzweig with the further one that this responsibility to love is linked directly to the human responsibility for redemption (HS 85). Here again Levinas identifies a Jewish theme—not Heidegger's "only a God can save us," but rather that as adults, as loved and capable of loving, we human beings must redeem the world. No divine mediator can do the task for us. The love that commands me invests me with the capacity to make the world better. Without my effort, without human efforts, the world will remain unredeemed.

Fourth, Levinas notes that Rosenzweig deformalized time, discovering that past, present, and future are shaped by the events that happen in them (HS 85). Levinas explicitly compares this move to Heidegger and Bergson; it is the existentialist discovery that lived human time is structured around specific forms of experience and that temporality is not a uniform sequence of discrete 'now's. Both Rosenzweig and Levinas claim that temporality is fundamentally intersubjective, that our ethical relations to other people create the basic reality of time. Levinas himself has returned to the topic of time again and again throughout his career to pursue just this deformalization.

Fifth, Levinas gallantly defends Rosenzweig's claim that the Jewish people live outside of history, as an eternal people (DL3 273f./199f.). Rosenzweig discussed how the Jewish people roots itself in its own blood as a way of not binding itself to historical events. For Levinas this became the possibility of claiming a right to judge history and so to stand against the judgment of history. That judgment of history benefits the winners and assumes a totality in which the suffering of the losers is subordinated to the immanent results. In place of a totalizing judgment, Levinas proposes that a particular community can refuse the summation of the historical record. Such communities do not thus attain an absolute platform from which to retotalize over the others and so do not gain justification for self-righteous fanaticism. Rather, a community may witness, in its own suffering and in the suffering of other losers, that world history is not just. This sense that an ethical judgment can go against the winners is vouch-safed by a community exactly when it chooses to sever its destiny from the events of history. In the Western world that withdrawal is most of all a rejection of the political history of empires, and Levinas makes that suspension of world history a fulcrum for ethics. Thus the embrace of temporality is not the cancellation of the category of eternity, the reduction of reality to the immanent realm, but the function of eternity is characteristically ethical and as such is a fracturing of the totality which a historicist immanentism presupposes.

Finally, Levinas also explicitly praises Rosenzweig for resuscitating a concept of religion that is neither sectarian nor confessional (DL3 260/186). Levinas knows well Rosenzweig's own allergy to the term 'religion', but the range of concepts that Rosenzweig terms 'theological' can bear the term 'religion' if only we retain the correlational strictures, including the prohibition on totalizing over a particular religion (which would come down to some form of exclusion). What Levinas gains from Rosenzweig's labors is the possibility of exploring these 'theological'/'religious' relationships and concepts at the very deepest level of reflection—as the originary existential categories. This relocation of religion to that depth, coupled with its accessibility as nontotalizing, offers Levinas the specific philosophical task of his examination of ethics.

Recurring Concepts

To readers of Levinas, this list of Rosenzweig's explicit contributions must seem remarkable. In a small corner of Levinas' writings we find several guiding principles of what seems most distinctive in his thought. Beginning with the break with totality, and including the various points up to the current research on deformalized temporality, Levinas appears to be continuing Rosenzweig's projects—although he also seems to be a creative thinker in the exploration of several concepts that he fashioned for himself. The situation, however, is more complex, because the most-central concepts of Levinas' own genius are also related to Rosenzweig.

I will now introduce five concepts basic to Levinas' thought, and I will also indicate their antecedents in *The Star of Redemption*. These implicit links are only a glimpse of a scholastic task of large proportion but questionable worth—the glossing of Levinas' work with Rosenzweig's. At the same time I can lead you into Levinas' thought and so prepare the way for the second part of this book. I begin with a glimpse of the three-part structure of *Totality and Infinity*.

The most important place to start is with Levinas' key concept: the Face. Levinas' phenomenology climaxes in the moment when I am face to face with another person. In a face-to-face encounter, I find myself responsible for the other, bound to the other. The other's face commands me not to murder, not with words nor through the physiognomy of the other, but through the resistance of naked vulnerability. The relationship is asymmetrical, as I do not discover that the other is similarly responsible for, or answerable to, me; rather, I see the other as higher than me. The other comes to teach me, but not on any reciprocal condition—I must learn from the other whether or not the other wishes to learn from me. This experience of the other's height and of my responsibility draws out of me a response as I try to justify myself to the other. Speech begins in this apologetic mood. The deepest justification is not the use of reason to justify being ethical, but rather the ethically instigated need to reason in order to justify myself.

(In this book *I* is used in three ways: 1) as the authorial I who guides the motion through the chapters and also criticizes Rosenzweig and Levinas, 2) as a person who speaks, thinks, and, most importantly, becomes responsible, and 3) as the reification of the second I, in which case I is written in quotation marks [the 'I'] and is in opposition to the 'you' or the 'we'. The second use reflects the asymmetry of responsibility in the face-to-face encounter, because what I experience and what I find myself responsible for are not identical to what the other experiences and what I hold the other responsible for. The third use is in a complex tension with the second, a tension which will become clearer in the progress of the book.)

Although Rosenzweig also discusses faces in various contexts, including a mystical evocation of the face of God which concludes *The Star of Redemption*,[10] his description of two different kinds of 'listening' is particularly cogent. Rosenzweig distinguishes conversing from listening, and the goal described in the following passage is to cultivate this listening with one's ears. But the dialogue, with the interplay between the other's eyes and my words, is not unimportant for Rosenzweig:

> In dialogue one speaks who already hears, and not only if he speaks, indeed not for the most part as he speaks, rather just as much through his living listening [*Zuhören*], through the agreeing or doubting look of the eyes that speaks directly and raises the word to the lips. . . . There the one who speaks may not be the speaker of his own words, because where would he take his 'own' words except out of the speaking look of his hearer? (343/309)

Dialogue is the center of Rosenzweig's account of revelation. In the face-to-face encounter, the other's looking at me is the key to the dialogue. I speak, not in response to any spoken words, but in response to this look which speaks to me, which forces me to respond. The face signifies before spoken words, before language, and in *The Star of Redemption*

Rosenzweig explores the very drawing out the words of my response by the other's looking at me.

The me who is looked at does not come into existence at the moment I am seen. In order for me to learn from the other, to speak to the other, to be hospitable to the other, I must already be someone. Were I created in the moment when the other looks at me, I would have no resources, no inner freedom with which to become responsible. Levinas develops the concept of *ipseity*, of my corporeal uniqueness, drawing heavily on phenomenological sources. The individual person, before meeting an other, is a self-constituted, corporeal, specific self; not a member of the species, but in many key ways a self-created person. The intensity that allows me to fashion my own world is needed to create the infinite responsibility I have in relation to the other. Levinas examines this self which is recursive in order to understand the inversion of that self in the responsibility for the other.

As an introductory point, note that Rosenzweig devotes the whole of Part I of *The Star of Redemption* to the construction of independent elements. There in Book III, Rosenzweig discusses how a self has an authentic relationship to death, closed off from the world and from God. The very will and being that the self uses to enclose itself are the resources for its later relationships with God and others. I do not enter into those relationships of service and of learning from a position of dependence and insecurity, but rather from the highest moment of heroic self-sufficiency and independence. The life before encountering the face occupies the section of *Totality and Infinity* entitled "Interiority and Economy." While Levinas' analyses are original, the logic is directly appropriated from Rosenzweig. Moreover, when Levinas redevelops those analyses in *Otherwise than Being*, he constricts the analysis of that pre-ethical self from one of enjoyment to one of recursion and self-creation, as I will show in Chapter 9. That constriction leaves Levinas more firmly than ever indebted to Rosenzweig's analyses of the self.

After my meeting with the other, I am bound in responsibility. The socialization of that responsibility is complex, because I am bound not only to one other, but also to a third person—indeed, to all the others. In society I do not live out infinite responsibilities, and Levinas' point is not that I ought to. Rather, Levinas' question is, Why am I bound to society at all? If I were not bound infinitely to any individual, could I be bound to society? Would I ever enter a social contract? These issues will occupy the last chapter of this book, but here we need to look at what is one of the most striking responses in Levinas' *Totality and Infinity*: fecundity. Just as I am already a unique corporeal self before I meet the other, and just as that encounter is fully corporeal, indeed it depends on the very asymmetry of my spatiality (I am here, the other there), so, too, after approaching the face there is a distinctly corporeal social possibility, *fecundity*. My responsibility for my child is a paradigm for the responsibility I have for others, because I am responsible for all that my child does, while my child is not responsible for my actions. This model produces what Levinas will call 'religion' in *Totality and Infinity*. This highly contentious discussion (particularly because Levinas prefers a sexist vocabulary, where only paternity and filiation are relevant) clearly refers back to Rosenzweig's own contentious discussion of the Jewish people. There, too, corporeal descent is linked with the development of a nonpolitical form of sociality. Rosenzweig claimed that Judaism rested in the blood of the people, from generation to generation. This intergenerational point is striking in the context of Levinas; moreover, Levinas' phenomenological depiction of fecundity serves the parallel function of socialization of the one-to-another responsibility without compromising ethics by the negotiations of politics, which limit infinite responsibility.

I have indicated how each of the three major parts of *Totality and Infinity* is linked back to Rosenzweig's analyses in *The Star of Redemption*. But this introduction to Levinas' thought requires two significant additions from his later work, particularly *Otherwise than Being*. The two emerge as Levinas focuses more closely on the relationship of speech to responsibility. In order to clarify the moment of responsibility and the dynamics by which the other becomes my responsibility, Levinas narrows his analyses to the dynamics in the self and to the generation of language as response. The previous discussions of economics, where I am at home with myself, and of religion and politics, where the other and I merge into communities, now disappear from the analysis. But two significant additions come into focus: 1) the opposition between *le dire et le dit* (the saying and the said), and 2) the temporalization of the response—that one is committed, commanded, obliged, in a past that is not re-presentable; that, in Levinas' term, there is *diachrony*.

The opposition between *le dire et le dit* calls attention to the action of speech in opposition to the words that are spoken. Levinas must put all specific utterances, all linguistic types, under erasure—for the face of the other cannot be named, described, or even exposed in language. Levinas heeds and answers the critique of his attempt to employ language to name something outside it; he now refuses the totality that language creates and re-creates for thought. I would not say, however, that Levinas is forced to move away from the claims for language in *Totality and Infinity*, because even there he looked not at the cognitive function but at the ethical purpose in speaking. He insisted that the function of language was not to provide knowledge of the face, but was rather to offer an apology to the other. Still, by driving a clearer distinction between the practice and the words used, Levinas refocuses the question of how words can signify at all. Here the possibility that a word will have meaning for another person shows the prior exigency for speech to an other, the prior responsibility to answer for myself.

This distinction will dominate Chapters 3 and 4 on Rosenzweig's theology of speech as performance. Rosenzweig distinguishes two kinds of *Sprache* (language). There is a *sprechende Sprache*, (speaking language) and an *unausgesprochene Sprache* (unspoken language). The former corresponds to Levinas' *le dire*; it is the action or praxis of speaking, the speech that partakes of an intersubjective dynamics. Indeed Rosenzweig finds in speech the experience of revelation that I would call ethics. The unspoken language corresponds to Levinas' *le dit* and is the system of significations used for closing oneself up within oneself; language as a system of words offers knowledge, but here it is not put into action as a means of relating to others. The focus on the practical dynamics of two interlocutors, particularly in the act of revealing themselves to one another, is key for both thinkers.

Finally, there is this complicated temporality of diachrony. Levinas is afraid that were I able to choose my responsibility for others—or even derive it from reason, were it a product of an a priori reasoning—then I would misconstrue the passivity that lies at the heart of the experience. For Levinas there must be a moment that is not available to me in memory, a moment I cannot knit up in a narrative, and in that moment, to which I have no access in consciousness, I am chosen, elected, obliged. My narration is broken into by something that I cannot make part of the story. When Levinas calls this a past more distant than any past, and eventually a past that was never present, he echoes the whole logic of Part I of *The Star of Redemption*—a logic borrowed from Schelling. For Rosenzweig and Schelling too desired to secure the radical freedom for ethics against any rationally necessary process. Chapter 2 explores that logic, drawing lines back to Lurianic Kabbalah and forward to Levinas.

Our freedom is finite and depends on a situation that cannot be brought under our control. We have many ruses for gaining control, one of the greatest being the representation of the past in consciousness. To make us responsible requires that we not initiate or spontaneously begin the world, so there must be a past before the past we can remember. I sometimes misappropriate the geological term and call it a *deep past*. The theological name of this past is either creation or the eternity that precedes creation (here Rosenzweig and Levinas are not in simple agreement), but the very finitude of our freedom depends on some immovable obstacle to our spontaneity.

ADAPTATION

Before I conclude this overview of the relation between Rosenzweig and Levinas, I wish to offer some images for describing the particular affinity of Levinas for Rosenzweig. I might begin once again by calling this another equivocal correlation. No mutual relationship can exist between the two men; Rosenzweig died before Levinas read *The Star of Redemption*. Many of their ideas correspond, but that is not all that correlation means. If one is subtle, one might propose that whatever reception Rosenzweig will have in the next few years will depend on Levinas, so that Levinas can also affect Rosenzweig. But that is a relationship between the reception of a text and a living person, which is not truly a correlation. Of course, we could reduce Levinas also to his text and have a correlation between texts, but the ethical focus on the practices of writing and reading disappears if the texts relate directly to one another, independent of readers and their actions. Some sort of relationship does hold from Levinas to Rosenzweig, but it is not a correlation.

If the title I have chosen for this book is not so much deceitful as somewhat equivocal and ironic (as Levinas and Rosenzweig are not correlational in the central meaning I intend), then we would do well to look for other possible images of relations. The second choice is one of essence and accident, which might be put into service with the old rhetorical saw of a man and his clothes. Is there some essence of Jewish philosophy that dresses in different clothes when speaking German in the 1920s and French in the 1960s? This possibility haunts my book, but it fails for reasons that are too familiar to require lengthy discussion. Whatever essence or center Jewish philosophy might have, it could not claim to be completely detachable from all instantiations, nor are the different instantiations as distinct as different suits of clothes. A straightforward essence/accidence approach simply will not do.

A more subtle and interesting possibility is the idea of *translation*. Rosenzweig wrote translations and developed a remarkable theory of translation, while Levinas himself uses that term to depict his task of making Jewish concepts universal. Moreover, translation need not be a literal rendering of one term in one language into one term in the other. There is a certain play and control dictated by the limitations of the two languages. Levinas devotes a Talmudic reading to a text that explores how the Aramaic Targumim of Hebrew Scriptures are not simply literal (HDN 43ff.). Is Levinas' work a French phenomenological translation of Rosenzweig's German existentialism? I believe this is a closer image, but I suspect that Levinas' own creativity goes further than the freedom of a translator. He does not merely repeat, nor even selectively re-present,

Rosenzweig's ideas in a new language—although he certainly does do that in part. But if not translation, then what?

I propose we view their relationship as an *adaptation*. Rosenzweig's concepts require not merely new terminology and argumentation, but also a certain refashioning to bring different tones into focus and change the old thoughts to conform to the current circumstances. I believe that the Hebrew term *midrash* fits the relationship of Levinas and Rosenzweig in this way: Levinas creates a *drash*—makes an adaptation—of Rosenzweig. Would Levinas' work be possible without Rosenzweig? No— for Rosenzweig permeates Levinas' schema and even his key concepts. But Rosenzweig is nonetheless not merely presented in a new coat, nor is he simply dragged forward fifty years. The adaptation is recognizable both in relation to what it replaces and as an adaptation. I believe literary adaptations serve best to illustrate the relationship, whether of Brecht adapting Marlowe's *Edward II*, or Primo Levi Dante's *Inferno*, or even Buber's renditions of Hasidic tales. The search for an image of Levinas' relationship to Rosenzweig will never conclude, but the dependence and the creativity of adaptation seems a helpful image.

One might well ask, however, why Levinas adapted Rosenzweig with a parallel level of stylistic obscurity. For the adapter of a dense and cryptic thinker, there seem to be three choices: 1) to continue in the style of that thinker—as so much American deconstruction is really still written in a French idiom, 2) to render the original much more direct and clear, and 3) to replace one obscure style with another. Levinas seems to have chosen the third option at the expense of the second. One could object that the second runs the risk of popularizing and trivializing the original, as has been the case with the "existentialist" Rosenzweig who supposedly abandoned reason for religious experience. But not all straightforward prose has to cheapen its subject. While part of the justification for this book is the need for an expository style less impenetrable than that of the authors being discussed, I would also like to suggest that Levinas' choice of style was not simply obfuscatory nor malicious. The two thinkers are saying something remarkably similar, and they are loyal to these dense and obscure idioms because of their perception of what will garner respect from their audiences. Levinas' phenomenology, for example, is an intrinsic medium for his thought, because his French, intellectual audience demands that sort of methodology if it is to treat Levinas as a philosopher. And Rosenzweig developed a cryptic, dense style in order to respond to the demands of his circle of friends and to his sense of what the wider, German intellectual audience required.

Levinas or Rosenzweig might have misjudged their readers' needs, but because each was adapting a radical agenda by exceeding the normal bounds of a specific intellectual idiom, it is at least understandable why they retained those idioms, perhaps in an excessive and exorbitant form. Largely because I, as interpreter, perceive that my audience will not require such steadfast loyalty to either the phenomenological nor the neo-Kantian vocabulary, my interpretations will not focus on the stylistic nuances of Levinas' adaptation of Rosenzweig. Instead, I hold myself more free to examine both sides of the adaptation in a less-technical philosophical idiom. The resulting interpretations will produce both the common agenda for these thinkers and also the common pursuit of a correlation of Judaism and philosophy.

CHAPTER 2

The Logic of Limitation

THE PROPONENTS of the others that stand outside the grasp of philosophy are compelled to mark its limits. They reject the quest for total knowledge, and their resource is what cannot be known. We live in a time when the goal of encyclopedic knowledge, of a progressive discovery of all knowledge guided by a fully grounded method, seems obsolete. Due to regular announcements that we "do not know," philosophy appears to have reached its conclusion. We do not know what humanity is. We do not know God. We do not know what our world should be. We do not even know what philosophy is. If philosophers once had to learn to ask, "How can we know?" when philosophy was still proud, then in our time the question we are learning is "How can we not know?" But thus we lapse back into the very error of proud philosophy. Today's question truly should be "How can we know—that we do not know?" Our humility, our professions of ignorance, may after all be too confident—the confidence of skepticism. Philosophy's ignorance itself requires a critical turn.

The problem is all too familiar. Ever since Hegel announced his system, philosophy has been in a sort of joyous retreat. All stripes of thinkers have abandoned the identity of being and thinking. It has become commonplace to insist that there is something utterly incomprehensible about existence and reality. Philosophy now takes its cue from these incomprehensible realities and becomes philosophy of this or that other. Reason submits to the dominion of incontrovertible experience. This submission, however, has only rarely been an abandonment of philosophy. Reason and philosophy remain—benighted, humbled, but they remain. But this more modest, altered philosophy seems incapable of forgetting its past hopes of knowing all reality. The existentialists, most of all, seem perennially entangled with idealism; indeed, with Hegel. Modern philosophy does not simply disappear in the 'postmodern discourse'. Instead, the *modern* in 'postmodern' continues to play a vital role as the aspiration toward total knowledge against which the complaint (*post-*) is lodged. This need for recourse to idealism's speculative moves is an odd obverse for the sometimes arbitrary assumption of epistemological humility.

In this chapter I present Rosenzweig as heir to Hegelian speculation, even as he announces a turn from the totalizing systems of Hegel and philosophy. Despite his rejection of Idealism's attempt to grasp all reality in thought alone, Rosenzweig begins *The Star of Redemption* with one of the purest speculative constructions imaginable. His task is to revise logic to allow for the plurality of free individuals, individuals who would not be subsumed in the totalizing logic of particular/universal. A logic so recast would provide the contingency for both theological and ethical relations, as God could create the world freely and I could bear responsibility for your freedom. Rosenzweig's divergence from Hegel appears in his rejection of an unceasing movement of the dialectic of negation, as well as in a reconstruction of the coordination of opposites.

Rosenzweig's construction can also serve as representative for contemporary philosophy's entanglement with speculative idealism. His attention to the requirement for a modernist philosophical construction as a point of departure for a postmodern exploration provides insight into the issue of the relation of postmodern philosophy to its modern ancestor. Moreover, Rosenzweig's construction is the most rigorous critical reflection on knowing we do not know, or the logic of limitations. Thus he provides not only insight into our lingering involvement with speculative philosophy, but also a constructive exposition of the conditions for our epistemological humility, for knowing we do not know.

This chapter has three sections. The first is an introduction to Rosenzweig's break with modern philosophy—a break that occurred through a reflection on the incomprehensibility of death. Rosenzweig rejects Hegel's dialectic of the limit and the infinite, committing himself to protecting the unknowable from the tentacles of speculation. This negation of total knowledge is not the goal of Rosenzweig's thought, but serves only as the point of departure for the movement to the constructions of Part I of *The Star of Redemption*.

The second section is an exploration of the motivation for Rosenzweig's philosophical construction. To safeguard the incomprehensible from dialectical snares is to isolate what cannot be known. In a sort of shorthand we can say that we may know *what* exists, but that the *that* of its existence is incomprehensible, arising from radical freedom. A comparison with Schelling's *Weltalter* will help, as Schelling pioneered an existential dialectic that explored the not knowing the *that* of an existing being. He developed an introverted image of what exists in order to isolate the free actions of divine creation and of human moral action. Rosenzweig imitates Schelling, undergirding his empirical reflection on lived experience with an introverted construction.

The third section explores Rosenzweig's method of construction. Unlike Schelling, Rosenzweig insists on a pure, critical construction, so that what lies beyond the limits of thought will not in any way be dependent on what lies within those limits. Hermann Cohen's *Logic* provided valuable tools for Rosenzweig. Cohen insisted on an utterly pure, rational construction of the actual world of scientific knowledge—for him the only 'real world'. Rosenzweig borrows Cohen's mathematical reasoning to create an antithetical construction: Cohen claimed to construct an actual something from nothing; Rosenzweig uses the pure construction to found the hypothetical reality of what lies beyond the limits. In this way, while Cohen is still pursuing Kant's question of how we can know something, and Schelling is asking how can we not know something, Rosenzweig is pursuing the critical question of how we can know that we do not know something.

DEATH AND PHILOSOPHY

"From death, from the fear of death, all knowledge of the all commences" (3/3). This very first sentence of *The Star of Redemption*, with its arresting hesitation (" . . . the fear of . . . "), has more than rhetorical import for Rosenzweig. Philosophy has always been up to its neck in the fear of death, but has never admitted it. The philosopher, the one who fears and thinks, refuses to face his own death. But in order to deny his death—that "unthinkable annihilation" of himself which he can only fear—the philosopher insists that reality is identical with thought: what he cannot think (death) cannot be. In a grand evasion of his own fear, the philosopher denies the object of this fear: death is absolutely nothing. His own death becomes a mere separation of a body from his soul, which cannot die, like Socrates imagining the philosophical conversation continuing after death. But in order to accomplish this denial, the philosopher must undertake the totalizing philosophic project: knowing it all. If he can only think everything, can know it all, can complete the system, then in that moment of completion he will have proven that death is absolutely nothing (because it will have no place in the system).

Philosophy for Rosenzweig is this passionate desire to know it all. Modern philosophy has thought it all in self-reflective new ways. If the very project of knowing it all is real, then the project itself must be knowable. A system that merely *states* what everything in the world is would not be *knowing* it all. Nor would one that encompasses the origins and transcendent dimensions of everything be knowing it all. We now must ask how our knowing it all is possible, and so encompass our own efforts. Rosenzweig identifies Hegel as the culmination of the original, evasive, philosophical passion to know it all. Hegel brings the history of the project of knowing it all into the all (6/6). With that inclusion in the system, philosophy reaches its outer limit, its perfection. The 'I' that thinks, that can know it all, is the ultimate object, the last piece in the totality.

What justifies Rosenzweig's identification of Hegel as the end of philosophy is his interpretation of all philosophical speculation as ultimately bound to the goal of knowing it all—all philosophy proceeds under the equation of being and thinking. In that sense, what I would call modern philosophy may appear as the conclusion of a longer philosophical tradition, but it may also be that a rereading of the earlier stages will reveal that knowing it all was not the driving passion. In any case, Rosenzweig also must justify placing Hegel at the conclusion of what I call 'modern philosophy' and he calls simply 'philosophy'. If we attempt to elevate Kant's critical thought as the true goal of philosophy, we are left with Hegel's question: How is critical thought possible—what allows reason to critique itself? If we sever thinking from being and confine ourselves to reality (*Wirklichkeit*), we still desire to know that critical move itself. We still assert that the thinker, at least, truly is—or so runs the justification for asserting Hegelian priority even over a non-ontological mode of philosophical thinking. Even after Hegel, philosophy's pretension to arbitrate reality according to its rationality forces the admission that the project can only be completed along the lines of Hegel. Thus Hegel represents the dividing point: either one agrees that thinking is equivalent to being, including the being of the history of thinking, or one asserts that being is irrational.

To assert that reason cannot grasp the totality of some particular experience, or entity, or relationship, etc., is hardly uncommon today. Even philosophers accept what could be called the death of (modern) philosophy, the abandonment of the claim that all reality is thinkable. And yet, there are two false forms of humility possible here. One is a mere *unrealized* potential for knowing: we do not know how many moons Pluto has, but there is nothing inherently unknowable, nothing that cannot eventually be brought within the circle of the all. The second false form of humility allows only for an irrationality that dialectics ultimately recovers. This for Rosenzweig is the distinctive move of the Hegelian dialectics of limit and the infinite. Hegel expressly denies that there are limits to thought, by claiming that the very process of limitation displays the overcoming of that limit.[1] This is much the same as the 'bad infinity', which for Hegel is the impossible attempt to separate the infinite from the finite.[2] Thus, whenever we place a limit on thought and assert that beyond that limit lies the infinite, Hegel challenges that we have, through such thinking, already reappropriated that infinite and transcended the limit. Hegel's 'true infinity' is one that is present in the finite. This dialectical move is the main point of Rosenzweig's interpretation of philosophy in general and of Hegel in particular: The willful desire to know it all cannot tolerate anything beyond the limits of thought. Rosenzweig denies this reappropriation emphatically, claiming that he has to shatter Hegel's 'genuine infinity' in order to make the 'bad infinity' visible (284/254). The 'spurious irrational' (which can be captured in thought) is the child of Hegel's 'genuine infinity'—and thus the 'true irrational' (which does lie beyond the limits of thought) requires the destruction of the 'all', Hegel's infinite containing everything.

To dash that all into irrational pieces, Rosenzweig must insist on radical irrationality, unintelligibility—that we cannot know something. The dialectic does not arrive at its limit only to scale its walls. Rosenzweig finds the irrational 'x' at the very origin of the project to know it all. Death, or rather deaths, are the irrational 'somethings', and Rosenzweig begins his work on *The Star of Redemption* with haunting, terrifying images from the front. "Let a person crawl like a worm into the folds in the naked earth before the bullets of the blind, inexorable Death whizzing toward him"(3/3). Philosophy had reduced death to an absolute nothing, but Rosenzweig focuses on the something, the something*s*, which death is. "In the dark background of the world stand a thousand nothings as its inexhaustible presupposition—in place of the one nothing, which would be really nothing, there are a thousand nothings, which just because they are many, are something"(5/5). My death stands outside any system, as the unacknowledged spur to thought. Rosenzweig writes of the person, a totally determinate person, as an Ersatz, and identifies the uniqueness of each person by referring to the "first and last name" (10/10) of a person. Because death strikes each unique person, there are many deaths—the deaths of each first and last name. Several years before Heidegger, and several decades after Kierkegaard, Rosenzweig finds the individual's fear of death to be the ultimate refutation of philosophy and its claim that thought is identical to being.

My death is not an absolute nothing (as philosophy always wanted to pretend), but is a relative nothing, my nothing. Death is the exhaustion of the all. We arrive at a relative nothing, a residue of human reality that can never be known. This points the way to what I will call a 'negative anthropology' (Rosenzweig called it 'negative psychology'). No matter how much I know about myself, or about the human per se, I can never know this aspect of reality. Indeed, the door is now open to a reiterative process of negation. No matter what properties I choose, I cannot know all of a person because I can never know their death. Moreover, I can replicate this analysis with God and with the world, producing negative theology and negative cosmology. The cosmos is now set free from the rule of a totalizing logic and appears as an upsurge of three unencompassable entities; God is separated now from the world and from human subjectivity, free to retain a separate existence, a hidden nature, and a radically free will. Each element (God, world, human) can be determined as an unknown, a relative nothing of knowledge. One could aspire to that ignorance itself. In an incomplete critical move, we could demonstrate that we cannot know God (or the human, or the world). Negative theology for

Rosenzweig is the demonstration that each thing we know does not fit God. It takes a something of knowledge (the king, or the rock) and reduces it to a nothing of knowledge of God (not like the king, not like the rock, etc.). This move produces the relative nothing, the starting point of Rosenzweig's reflection. Rosenzweig displays that philosophy has now made this negative move in each of the three spheres. But *The Star of Redemption* as a whole becomes a motion away from this threefold ignorance.

Given pure thought's impotence in knowing these three realities, Rosenzweig must discover an impure or experiential access to reality. This is a generic problem for postmodern thought and usually involves some sort of nod toward empiricism. Rosenzweig's discovery, in Part II of *The Star of Redemption*, comes through a study of grammar. I pause here briefly to indicate the way that Rosenzweig transgresses the bounds of philosophy and its pure thought. This indication will aid in the evaluation of his lingering entanglement with pure thought in Part I; fuller discussions of the relation of pure thought and experience will come later, in Chapters 4 and 5.

To frame the problem, consider one's own unique person and one's death. Rosenzweig calls a philosopher who begins with her uniqueness and unique death a "viewpoint philosopher" (117/105). After Hegel (= philosophy), the subjectivity of the individual's life and passions have become the substance of 'philosophical' reflection. For Rosenzweig, Nietzsche best represents this sort of personal philosophy (21/18).[3] Had Rosenzweig given up on philosophy, he might have fashioned a sort of Jewish Nietzschean work. Instead, Rosenzweig fears Nietzsche and the viewpoint philosopher, fears that such thinking becomes mere fanaticism. If the Hegelian system and its logic and knowledge are exceeded by personal experience, then what can be used to justify one's view? How does personal experience become a resource for social life? Rosenzweig asks whether Nietzschean thought is still science (*Wissenschaft*) (117/105). He requires more than radical subjectivity. The thought of radical subjectivity disperses into myriads of individual philosophies—or worse, with the fragmentation of the self, into myriads of myriads, as my own subjectivity can then spawn its own myriad of thoughts. Rosenzweig's commitment to philosophy after the end of the traditional project of knowing it all requires the possibility of unity and objectivity.

How does one meet those requirements, having shattered the All of knowledge? Rosenzweig demands that philosophy retain the subjectivity of the existing person for its origin. That irrational fact cannot be compromised. But from that subjectivity he seeks a bridge to the "lucid clarity of infinite Objectivity" (117/106). The bridge for Rosenzweig comes from theology, which itself stands in need of philosophy. The method of thinking in this bridging provides for us the contrast with speculation, and we will overlook here the theological issues. Rosenzweig's method is one of reflection on the grammar of living speech. Philosophy, as idealism, seeks to comprehend everything through logic. In logic the unique person is rendered anonymous. Bound to the a priori, stipulating only what things may and may not be, but not what they are, logic reaches only mute essences, an individual in a genus and not the existing person. Indeed, the abstraction of logic from language is Idealism's way to overcome language and its grammatical categories (156/140). For Rosenzweig, to turn from logic to speech, language as spoken, is to turn to lived event (*Erlebnis*).

For Rosenzweig, speech provides the 'empirical' evidence that reason cannot provide for itself. The step beyond the limits of thought is a reflection on the grammar of speech as actually spoken. In this respect Rosenzweig is not unlike many other twentieth-century thinkers. For many the break with idealism is accomplished through reflection on speech, by trading in the formalism of logic for the speedier access to existence through spoken language.

THE STAR INSIDE OUT

That emergence into the sphere of speech and its grammar stands a long way off from the relative nothing of my death. According to Rosenzweig, a simple turn to the empirical evidence of speech will fail to yield grounded knowledge. In "The New Thinking," Rosenzweig refers to his method as absolute empiricism (III, 161). That *absolute* refers to the philosophical, logical, pure reflection that undergirds the recourse to lived experience. Part I of *The Star of Redemption* is the preparatory, philosophical construction of three irrational/unknowable, hypothetical somethings (God, world, human) from the three corresponding, relative nothings. That construction and even the need for it have always been recognized as a most difficult aspect of Rosenzweig's thought—doubly difficult as a result of the shorthand style of composition, which produces a dense text, and because the exercise in logic itself requires substantial familiarity with various philosophical systems.

Rosenzweig's greatest philosophical resource for principles of this reconstruction was Schelling.[4] Schelling, too, had faced the collapse of the Hegelian system and of the project to know it all. Indeed, Schelling is truly the first post-Hegelian philosopher, the first person to require an augmentation from experience in the wake of the vanity of Idealism—the first philosopher to claim the humility of ignorance. In his use of Schelling, Rosenzweig is again a typical existentialist. Kierkegaard, Heidegger, Jaspers, Marcel, and Tillich (to say nothing of other philosophers such as Feuerbach, Engels, Bakunin, and Habermas) all came to Schelling to hear the radical pronouncement of the death of philosophy.

Rosenzweig was closely involved with two books and two manuscripts when he conceived and wrote *The Star of Redemption*. The next chapter focuses on the two manuscripts; this chapter on the books. The first book was Schelling's *Weltalter (Ages of the World)*. Rosenzweig had a copy of the 1913 Reclam edition with him at the front and refers to it in correspondence of that time (I, #320, 11 Nov. 1916). And in a later letter Rosenzweig declares, "It is a great book to the last. Had it been completed, nobody except Jews would give two hoots for the *Star*" (I, #655, 18 Mar. 1921).

What did Rosenzweig find so compelling in the *Weltalter?* First and foremost, Schelling's rejection of Hegel's thought, and of idealism in general, on the matter of existence. For Schelling as for Rosenzweig, idealism meant the denial of the irrationality (and the freedom) at the heart of human existence. Schelling saw the idealistic project as an attempt to make a person his own Ground, the source of himself. For Schelling, as a Christian thinker, this is tantamount to deifying oneself and produces many disastrous results.[5] The core inadequacy of idealism was its reduction of freedom to necessity—both in the divine free act of creation and in subsequent, human, free actions. In order to dissolve freedom into necessity, idealism ignored the negative, contractive, dark aspect of reality.[6] By reducing all to light and affirmation, philosophy made everything thinkable and ignored the tensions of existence. In opposition, Schelling created a project that would protect freedom from a priori reason and its necessity. In its most basic sense, the fact of creation lies beyond the limits of knowledge. But all freedom must arise from a similar irrationality, a similar incomprehensible source. Even for the nontheological followers of Schelling, interest centers on that human freedom, freed from the chains of rational necessity (even be they dialectical) of the System.

Insofar as knowing is a priori and necessary, freedom must be made unknowable. Yet because freedom occurs in time, it can be known a posteriori. All knowledge of existence and of free action, therefore, is gained only through history, through a discourse that follows after the fact. What we cannot know a priori, then, is the transition, the discontinuity of temporal existence. Schelling grants to pure a priori reflection the ability to know what is, to know essences in their atemporality, but he proves that existence, the temporal order, cannot be similarly known. To explore our not knowing, Schelling must resort to history, and the *Weltalter* itself is a history. It is this history that Rosenzweig found particularly enticing.[7]

In order to isolate the incomprehensible free act, Schelling claims that what is prior to the free transition (the before) must be an introversion of what is made extroverted by the action (the after).[8] The before cannot determine that the action will occur; nonetheless, if there were no relation of the after to the before, we would not recognize the act. That there should be a free action is radically indeterminate, but what sort of action is possible is determined. Schelling holds that the only possible relation between the before and the after is introversion/extroversion. The most plausible explanation for this relation is that the alternatives are inadequate: an after completely dissimilar to the before is unrecognizable; a mere repetition of the before in the after would mean no free action; and, finally, if the after were a development that emerged from the before we would have slipped back into a necessary (unfree) process. The extroversion of one form provides radical discontinuity and the possibility of full re-cognition in a narrating of the event.

In the *Weltalter*, Schelling portrays this introverting/extroverting discontinuity between God before and after creation in order to make creation unknowable and hence free. Like most philosophers, Schelling is unwilling to abandon the unchangeableness of God's nature. But, he argues, if we reason from this to a God who is "eternally still, completely absorbed in itself, consumed by itself,"[9] then we are forced to make God undergo an essential change when creating. An Aristotelean thought thinking itself must be completely changed in order to create a world. Schelling comments that "no sort of thinking whatsoever can make this conceivable [*begreiflich*]."[10] (This comment is worthy of considerable reflection, as Schelling in most other ways is willing to tolerate the coincidence of contradictories in God's nature. Moreover, it is not merely that this sort of change is inconceivable, but the qualification "no sort of thinking whatsoever" would serve as a fine point of departure in exploring what different types of thinking Schelling considers possible.) We are left, at core, with a simple principle: In order to think of creation as a free act, we must posit a God who is alive, a God who is inwardly in eternal action. Then, as Schelling comments regularly, the internal can become outward without changing its nature—we can retain intelligibility of the *what* in the extroversion of free action.[11]

The history that Schelling must narrate is, therefore, not merely the history of the world or of world-historical events. Schelling is forced along this line of reasoning into theosophy. He must narrate the happenings within God prior to creation in order to be ignorant of why God created the world. Schelling's discussion of a prior contraction in God is the *tsim-tsum* of the Lurianic Kabbalists filtered through Boehme.[12] Following Boehme and other German mystics, Schelling reasons that prior to creation God has an inner life much like ours. Just as there is a succession of states in our life, so there is in God's internal life: "In divine life also as in all others, there is movement, progress."[13] The difference is that in God's life there is no threat of halting the circular cycles of always sublating lower states with higher ones. This cycling cannot be the temporal past, but is the eternal past in God. This past is a past that was never a present—an unpresentable past—thus not prior *in present time*. "The past time is no sublated time; the past can not truly be as a present, but must be as a past simultaneous with the present."[14] Schelling posits a series of eternities in place of one eternity, and it is into the past eternity that he places the development in God prior to creation. Here in Schelling is the deep past that later will become Levinas' diachrony. What is theosophy in Schelling will become ethics in Levinas, although Schelling's concern is also ultimately to secure the contingency of human moral freedom.

For all that, it would be hard to imagine something less to the taste of contemporary thought than theosophy. Whether Schelling expected assent to his various moves in constructing this deep past is open to question. Rosenzweig himself reluctantly found a need to reflect on Schelling's deep past. To provide a foundation for not knowing the free relations between God, world, and human, Rosenzweig was forced into this bizarre kind of historical reflection, constructing introverted elements prior to experience. While thinking through *The Star of Redemption*, he proposed a triad that describes the thought of Part I, for "in addition to *theo*logy and philo*sophy,* it now appears that the definitive third corner of sciences—I myself am still astonished by and reluctant at this thought—is theosophy"(III, 137). This third component of the triad he equates with "the eternal happening [*Geschehen*] in God." The theosophy (as Rosenzweig himself calls it) of Part I is, as in Schelling, the key to a narration of the present and the future. Moreover, Rosenzweig imitates Schelling by giving the names of three kinds of eternity to the three parts of *The Star of Redemption* ("The Elements or the Everbecoming Pre-World," "The Way or the All-time-renewed World," and "The Configuration or the Eternal Super-world"). These three eternities should not be seen as simply the extensions of the sequence of Part II—Creation, Revelation, Redemption. That sequence is inherently narratable, a sequence of terms that can be assembled and re-presented in a story that can appear in consciousness. The past of Part I and the future of Part III are not accessible to consciousness and never become present. Instead, they are simultaneous and do not move narratively from one to the next in time. The deep past, unlike the past of creation, always happens as past, at the very moment that is also present. The lived past, on the contrary, moves off and becomes further past as time goes by. Rosenzweig characterizes his Parts II and III as the completion to Schelling's *Weltalter*, as "the second book he [Schelling] tried to give" (III, 148).

The basic Lurianic theosophical move, the discontinuity over the introversion/extroversion, borrowed from Schelling guides Rosenzweig's construction in Part I of *The Star of Redemption*. In each of the three books of Part I, Rosenzweig constructs an element that is an introverted, hypothetical entity. The first is God. Rosenzweig follows Schelling, conceiving of this proto-God as an equation of nature and freedom.[15] Schelling constructs God's nature first, using the tension between God's love and God's being, dialectically knitting them into a contraction of God followed by an expansion—again following the principle that the negative must be considered and that internalization precedes externalization. This construction continues for two more steps in Schelling: the unity with the will makes for the proper internal creation in God; and then, finally, God turns out in the free act of creation. I will show below how Rosenzweig arrives at his equation of God's freedom with God's nature, which he symbolizes as 'A = A'. But what is significant is how both Rosenzweig and Schelling use the inversion of the constitutive elements to form the extroversion. Schelling writes:

> We are content to note, that the general course of events is the same as in nature, with the single difference, that arises because the negating power, which in nature is outward, in the spiritual essence is inward. One can say, therefore, that in nature the negating power is elevated and led inward; in the spiritual world it is drawn outward and lowered. . . . What is contraction in that, is expansion in this and vice versa.[16]

Rosenzweig writes:

> What flowed in as Yes, steps forth as No, and what as No, as Yes, just as one unpacks the contents of a suitcase in the opposite order one packed them in. As farcical as the metaphor seems to be, still we may use it seriously. (124/112–13)

Rosenzweig's major constructive impulse in *The Star of Redemption* is directly dependent on Schelling's *Weltalter*. The motivation, moreover, is the need for a turning inside out in order to preserve the intelligibility of what happens in freedom, while preserving the contingency and hence unintelligibility, the radical freedom, of whether the free act will be done. The free relations that occur in lived experience in spoken language require a logical foundation in order to yield rigorous knowledge. We move from Hegel's denial of the limits of thought, not to simple empiricism, but to a way of making the action of freedom unknowable, beyond the limit. Both Rosenzweig and Schelling insist on the indifference to existence of their introversions, and Rosenzweig also distinguishes between factuality (*Tatsächlichkeit*), which the elements have, and actuality (*Wirklichkeit*), which exceeds these constructions.

But there is a further application of the notion of limit here. The elements, constructed in their inward turning, are inaccessible to each other and so, of course, to human experience. We 'know' of them only as hypotheses, as factualities deprived of all reality. The missing externality of the elements rests on their inward turning, while their extroversion is the key to Rosenzweig's Part II, where each element turns inside out. Thus the elements secure the a posteriori experience, but as elements they can only be thought and never known.

A final observation of these dialectics of introversion/extroversion in *The Star of Redemption* considers the ultimate image of the work: the star of David composed of the overlapping triangles of Parts I and II, with a fire burning in the middle and light streaming out in rays. This image represents the eternal form of redemption, as the kingdom of God advances like rays of light to illuminate the whole cosmos. A bright star shines its light outward while its burns within, but the foundation in thought of this ultimate star must be an introversion. The very motion of light outward would be introverted with a motion of light inward, and the brilliant fire would be introverted into a stillness, an absence of all energy. This star turned inside out we now know as a black hole (although in Rosenzweig's time the theory had not yet been developed). If the star of redemption is the positive product, the result of exploration beyond pure thought, then in pure thought Rosenzweig must construct its opposite, the black hole.

And indeed there is a discussion of the hidden God in Part I of *The Star of Redemption* that closely approximates the black hole, although it is not noticed as such. When Rosenzweig discusses this interaction of freedom and nature, he discovers that their equality resembles a hyperbolic curve—that if God is all freedom, he has no nature, and vice versa. Rosenzweig's representation of the introverted God, 'A = A', equates freedom with nature. He argues that God's freedom seeks its nature, and hence he chooses to identify that side of God as 'A =', and not just as 'A', with the equal sign (=) representing freedom's desire. God's essence, on the other hand, seeks nothing; it rests in infinite silence of pure existence (*Dasein*). As the freedom nears essence, it comes into the jurisdiction of essence's inertia; each is then transformed through their proximity. Essence becomes necessity and fate; freedom becomes power and willfulness. The introverted God is the binding together of power and necessity. As freedom nears the stillness it loses its power, and when it finally reaches pure essence it is extinguished (33/31). Thus God's hidden nature, God's fate, is, as it were, a black hole, sucking infinite freedom into its stillness. Only after the extroversions in Part II will God become a constructive part of the star of redemption, a star which shines forth from its own inner blaze of light.

GETTING SOMETHING FROM NOTHING

What strikes any reader of Schelling's *Weltalter* is the questionable nature of the construction of the introverted God. If it is a foundation for understanding the incomprehensible act of freedom in creation, it is a twisted and obscure foundation. One cannot help suspecting that the whole construction is simply and irremediably arbitrary. Principles like "love is forever expanding" or "God must be the oldest of beings" are not nonsensical, but they are hardly indubitable.[17] What one suspects is that Schelling has imported into the introverted God just what he hoped to get out—or, rather, just what he had experienced in the created world. But that makes his theosophical reflection nothing short of an intellectual trick in which a game of mirrors makes empirically derived concepts look as if they provide a priori intelligibility for the empirical evidence that they presuppose. The project of defining a limit for our thinking has merely transgressed the limit, thereby expanding what we can know (or conjuring up some nonsense, if one has a severer judgment on Schelling).

Rosenzweig realizes that the introversion/extroversion scheme is the best means of preserving freedom in the interactions of the elements, but he requires a pure construction of those introverted elements. Rosenzweig claims that Schelling borrowed the chaos, the dark ground, from experience. Hegelian idealism had pretended that there was no darker side to reality, and Schelling made this repression visible, insisting that contraction, negation, etc., are always the first moment in love and generation.[18] Schelling brings this negative moment clearly to the fore, insisting at one point that love is forced to become hate and culminating in his hymn to pain and suffering as the way to holiness.[19]

On the basis of Schelling's exposé of this darkness, Rosenzweig criticizes all idealistic thought as dependent on chaos, the dark ground (153ff./138). Rosenzweig emphatically distances himself from Schelling (and the mystical tradition) with its godhead and the sort of theosophy based upon the darkness at the beginning of God. "It is no 'dark ground' nor anything else which can be named with Eckhart's, Böhme's or Schelling's words" (28/26). Rosenzweig requires a purer construction of the hypothetical, unknowable elements. He takes the introversion itself more seriously, struggling to think of what cannot be known without the presupposition of something given, something unintelligible, like evil. His existential dialectic thereby preserves the limits of thought.

Rosenzweig wrote *The Star of Redemption* with two books at his side: Schelling's *Weltalter* and Hermann Cohen's *Logic of Pure Cognition*. In a letter to his mother, written one week before starting to write *The Star of Redemption*, Rosenzweig said of the latter:

Cohen is insanely hard; I would never have believed that a philosophical book could still hold such difficulties for me. Moreover—whether understanding him is accordingly worthy, is not yet certain for me; I almost believe it is not. But now I have begun it and I am reading it through. (#553, 15 Aug. 1918)

Although Rosenzweig had studied with Cohen several years earlier in Berlin, only after Cohen's death did Rosenzweig finally read his teacher's system. Ironically, Cohen's *Logic* is written in relatively clear German prose, while Rosenzweig managed to create a text that is truly "insanely hard." The *Logic*, moreover, has decisive impact on the construction in Part I of *The Star of Redemption*. At the conclusion of the introduction, Rosenzweig extols Cohen for discovering how mathematics is an organon for thought, particularly through the Logic of Origins (23/21)—the point of departure for Cohen's *Logic*. Most of all, Rosenzweig appropriates the infinitesimal method, which Cohen had applied to generate something from nothing.[20] Indeed, even some of the most Schellingian passages describing the structure of *The Star of Redemption* are oddly qualified with terms of critical epistemology (*Erkenntniskritik*), leaving the unmistakable flavor of Cohen's Marburg neo-Kantian thought in one's mouth (96–97/88, 31/28, 45/42, 435/391).

To see how Cohen's pure cognition was valuable for Rosenzweig, a brief consideration of Cohen's overall project is required. Cohen argues emphatically for a radical idealism. Indeed, so strong is his claim for idealism that he can assert, "idealism is the true realism. Realism which is not based (*gegründet*) on the idealism of pure cognition is eclecticism."[21] By taking a critical epistemological turn, Cohen argues for the actuality of the objects of modern science. More critical still, he denies any given. Whereas Kant proved that the categories of the understanding are transcendental but must be applied to the manifold of sense intuition ("Concepts without intuition are empty"), Cohen argues that there is no given manifold or influx of sensible intuition. The pure forms of intuition—space and time—become categories for him. It is pure reason that generates (*erzeugt*) perception. Such a radical idealism asserts the stunning independence of knowledge from perception and refuses to accept the existential claims made for perceptible objects. "The stars are not given in Heaven, but we term 'given' the objects in the science of astronomy—in distinction even against the definitive opinion that the generation and treatment of thought is founded in sensibility."[22] Here, as in the *Logic*, Cohen draws upon an intellectual tradition running back to Book VII of Plato's *Republic* (529b), where the 'real' star is the one given in the mathematical science, and transcendent thought is not just looking up at the ceiling.[23]

The general structure of the argument in the *Logic* is a four-step construction from nothing to actuality. Cohen begins with the judgments of laws of thought in which he presents the basic structure of thought, which produces something out of nothing; in the second step he produces reality (*Realität*) out of nothing; in the third, reality becomes substance; and finally, in the fourth, the substances gain actuality (*Wirklichkeit*). Actuality is known purely, with no recourse to any given, to any sensible experience. This pure knowledge of actuality strikes most people as unreasonable. One must ask how the mathematical scientist knows the actual world. But the remarkable solution to the seemingly unconquerable problem of getting from the 'empty concepts' of reason to the objects of reality is found in the infinitesimal method. Calculus, with its generation of quantity from the infinitesimally small, accomplishes the production of something (the objects of reality, of science) from nothing.

Cohen claims that the infinitesimal method can generate quantity from quality.[24] Integration is a kind of rational reflection which generates a discrete variable (x) from an infinitesimal unit (dx). To integrate a curve over a continuous line, one adds up the area of very small rectangular bands between points on the curve and that line. Repeated additions, shrinking the width of the bands, produce closer approximations to the exact area between the curve and the line. Cohen's interpretation of integration notes that the possibility of determining the area by this approximation depends on a principle of continuity of the line—that we could not do the operation of shrinking the width of the bands repeatedly unless the line was strictly continuous. The width of the bands is represented by the symbol dx when we let the bands go as narrow as we want; dx, therefore, is the mathematical judgment of the line's continuity, but that judgment undergirds the approximation process and is not derivative from it. As the narrowest possible width, dx must be infinitesimally small, but then dx is both something (> 0) and nothing ($= 0$). As the judgment of continuity, dx can be as small as we wish and so ends up as nothing, but through integration it yields the real something (x), for the result of integration is a function dependent not on the infinitesimal dx, but on the real variable x. As a variable, the reality (*Realität*) of x is not the existence of some determinate thing, but only a variable in a function that defines a relation. In his ontology, Cohen's term for reality makes only the weaker claim of determinate definition (the stronger claim would be for objective actuality [*Wirklichkeit*]). The finite number that x represents is produced from the infinitely small number, and because the infinitesimal can never be given in sensation, Cohen demonstrates the purity of the thought of number.[25]

This level of reality in Cohen's ontology happens through the act of thinking numbers (not existing things), but it anticipates the higher level of actuality in a way directly linked to Kant's anticipations of experience.[26] What is real is still 'hypothetical', even for Cohen; nonetheless, to generate the finite from the infinitesimal without recourse to sensible intuition is a major accomplishment for pure cognition. The infinitesimal method's first triumph is the generation of something (x) from nothing (dx). In Cohen's *Logic,* that real x is further reflected through reiterative processes of infinitesimal judgments until it achieves actuality. This generation of actuality from pure reason does not concern us directly, but before interpreting Rosenzweig's appropriation of this first step, we need to survey Cohen's first class of judgments, because they establish the continuity and the possibility of the reasoning used in integration; that is, in the getting of something from nothing.

The judgment of origin is the first judgment in the *Logic.* Because nothing can be given, the origin will have to be nothing—but Cohen claims that it is a relative nothing, not an absolute nothing. The relative nothing is relative to something—It is the nothing of knowledge—and the concept of continuity discerns that this relative nothing borders on something.

> Being itself should receive its origin through the not-being. The not-being is not some correlate concept to being; rather the relative nothing designates only the springboard, with which the leap working towards continuity should be completed.[27]

The relative nothing is a mere means to originate something. Continuity as a law of thought is what allows us to integrate dx and produce x. Through the thought of continuity, reason overcomes the separation of being from nothing.

The judgment of identity is the second step in Cohen's construction. This is affirmation (A is A), but what is affirmed through identity is judgment itself.[28] Identity is neither equality nor comparison of something with itself; rather, it lies before all such relationships. Prior to a comparison of some determinate thing with itself there must be the stability of judging anything at all. Identity makes possible the judgment of a thing as comparable with itself or another. Identity precedes all representation.

The first set of judgments is completed in the judgment of contradiction. Such judgment secures the possibility of judgment by the act of negation. The exclusion of contradictions, of judgments that would contradict some judgment "A," is a condition for that judgment. The judgment of contradiction arises through the not of negation (*nicht der Vernichtung*), which Cohen carefully distinguishes from the nothing (*Nichts*) of the judgment of origins. While the relative nothing was an origin for thought and served as a means to something, the not of negation is a reflection upon judgment that solidifies the judgment of identity. Cohen claims that "negation is not, as one has assumed, a judgement about [*über*] a judgement; rather it is, if one would so like to say, a judgement prior to [*vor*] the judgement."[29] Only by excluding or denying certain forms of judgment can identity be preserved, and, hence, can judgment itself proceed. The three judgments provide a pure origin for thought; establish the possibility of judgments of identity; and then secure the factuality of such judgments by excluding what is not identical.

Despite Cohen's claims to construct all the way to actuality from nothing, Rosenzweig was attracted to this method, and especially to the first three forms of judgment. Here was the antidote to Schelling's romantic dependence on the dark side, for Cohen refused to borrow the chaos in his construction. There are echoes of Cohen's more radical idealism in Rosenzweig's critique of idealism's 'thing in itself', 'manifold of sensibility', and 'the given' (153/138). With the purity of Cohen's *Logic,* Rosenzweig could rid the introversion/extroversion construction of its arbitrary nature. Given the goal of an introverted element, the God who is constructed cannot have actuality (*Wirklichkeit*) (what we normally call God's existence), but only factuality (*Tatsächlichkeit*). Cohen's infinitesimal method produces just that sort of reality in its first moments.

Rosenzweig constructs what lies beyond the limits of knowledge with critical epistemology. The problem was as old as Socrates: I know that I don't know something. We then ask, What sort of thing must something be in order for it to be unknowable? What is the nature of the unknowable? This is the turn Schelling makes in exploring the contraction and dark ground, the abyss and the godhead. Critical epistemology always asked, What are the conditions of knowing something? Now we do not ask, What are the conditions of not knowing something?—rather, we ask, What are the conditions for knowing that we do not know something? This sort of reflection seems like a hall of mirrors. But if we are interested in constructing a hypothetical element that in its introverted nature cannot be known in actuality, then at least we are not creating a rabbit out of a hat. Because we construct something we cannot know, the strongest claim is that we hypothesize what that something would have to be if it did exist and we were unable to know it. Its existence will have to be provided from some source other than pure reason.

Rosenzweig begins with nothing—a relative nothing, the result of negative theology. He is clear that we are not presupposing the existence of God; we presuppose, rather, only our ignorance, our knowing nothing about God (27/25). We seek a pure knowledge of a factuality: a hypothetical without existence, because with reasoning alone we cannot find a real, acting God. We will not presuppose anything nor borrow any intuitions from sensation. Here is the place for modern philosophy's repudiation of presuppositions, with the notice that such philosophy is now working for the introverted entities, not for positive knowledge.

Following Cohen, Rosenzweig sets out two paths from this knowing nothing. The first is a path of affirmation (Cohen's judgment of origin, a 'Yes'); the second, of negation (Cohen's judgment of contradiction, a 'No'). Because of the continuity of something and nothing, there is a neighborhood—that is, something—around the nothing of knowledge. Along Rosenzweig's first path, God is the affirmation of that neighborhood (which at all times is not known by us). Because there is no boundary within the zone of that which we do not know, the affirmation of our ignorance of God is an infinite affirmation (29/26–27). God's nature must be this infinite essence of what we do not know. This is the 'something' we cannot know, the area beyond our capacity for knowledge.

The second path is one of saying 'No' to the nothing, the denial of our knowing. It breaks with our knowing without presupposing any 'something' that we *do* know, any 'Yes', but it does require an affirmation of the something we do *not* know. While the 'Yes' affirmed a district surrounding our ignorance, the 'No' is bound to our not knowing. The 'No' emerges from nothing as a refusal, a negation of our knowing. Like Cohen's third judgment, this is a judgment about judgment that allows for meaning. It is not an affirmation of something we know, but always a 'not otherwise'—a denial that what we do not know could become known; it is the freedom of denying, of negating (31/28–29). This is the freedom of the hidden God to deny any claim, any knowledge of God. God becomes an ever-evasive motion away from our attempts to know.

Finally, the two paths are bound together with the 'and', which could be tied to Cohen's second judgment of identity. In discussing the black hole in the last section, I spoke of how the two sides are bound together as represented by the equation 'A = A.' The two results undergo transformation through their equation. The 'thus' of the 'Yes', which in God's case is essence, becomes God's necessity and fate as the goal to which God's freedom approaches. That freedom is the 'not otherwise' of the 'No' of the second route, and it is changed in the neighborhood of God's essence into arbitrary will and power: God becomes a fated, arbitrary being. But this relationship of the two routes is not itself a third route. Rosenzweig halts the progress of the dialectic with this 'and', with this identity of the two routes. He prohibits us from making this third judgment liable to further negation, generating a fourth and so on. The two aspects of the hidden God, might and necessity, rest in that hidden God.

Rosenzweig makes use of geometric imagery for this construction, describing a boundary zone around the nothing generated through the infinitesimal method. When he refers to the two forms of proceeding as the 'Yes' and the 'No', he draws on both Schelling and Cohen; however, when he links these words with the neighbor and the escapee, respectively, he opts for Cohen and the infinitesimal. We are thinking in "the hypothesized boundary zone of the nothing" (28/26). That boundary zone (of neighborhood and path of escape) is in fact a Magic Circle of God's hidden factuality (ibid.). To determine what happens within that zone or circle is not to have advanced our knowledge about God, but to have explored the conditions for our knowing that we do not know God.

In an inversion of Cohen's conditions for knowing reality, Rosenzweig finds the two conditions for knowing we do not know: 1) the affirmation of an x that lies beyond our capacities to know, and 2) the denial of our capacities to know x. The two are related, and when bound together they define each of the three hypothetical elements, but they are not tautological. The epistemological transcendence is found in a positing of something ('thus'), a denial of our competence ('not otherwise'), and the combination of these two ('and').

These are very strong conditions. To be epistemologically humble in a rigorous manner requires that both conditions be met. To state that God (or human or world) is an irrational reality goes well beyond the claim that we do not yet know God (or . . .). It means that God (or . . .) would have to be something beyond our limits of reasoning, and that each attempt to know God (or . . .) would be refuted or denied. If only one of the two conditions is met (as Rosenzweig discusses with interpretations of China and India), then either reality collapses into an all that we cannot know, or we and our knowledge become nothing. Either the sphere of affirmation will envelop everything, and so we will not know everything, or the denial will advance unabated, so that we will know nothing.

Rosenzweig's goal in his construction of God remains both critical and introverted. He seeks conditions for knowing as a critical epistemologist, but they are conditions for knowing that we do not know God and so remain introverted. In order for us to know that we know nothing of God, God must be a binding together of essence (the neighborhood of our not knowing) and freedom (the denying that we know God). As arbitrary will, God's freedom prevents any knowledge of Him. What at first was incessant denial of all claims becomes the arbitrariness that refuses all attempts to discern what God wills. God's essence similarly becomes bound as fate and necessity. God must not simply reside in the neighborhood beyond the limits of our knowledge; God must also be unable to change to become something we do know. Rosenzweig interprets God's life as the exercise of that fated choice, that necessary arbitrariness. In order for us to know that we cannot know God, God would have to be arbitrarily choosing to negate our knowledge while a fated resident in the neighborhood beyond the limits of our knowledge (33–34/31).

This construction of God has its parallels in the constructions of the unknown world and the unknown human. In order to deepen the sense of the first construction, I will now pause and provide a parallel view of the third one: the human. The human who remains hidden and who is inaccessible to our knowledge is the being most familiar to us from Heidegger's existential analytic of Dasein. Rosenzweig discovered this introverted human, relating only to itself, an authentic being, several years before Heidegger wrote *Being and Time*. Moreover, the possibility of a pure construction of this human has important consequences for the later, relational human who responds to an other.

Such a construction is based on a different cause of unknowability: the human is transitory. The final blow to the all that philosophy tried to know was the deaths of specific people, and those deaths are now made the hallmark of the human. Human nature, which reason cannot know, is particularity, a particularity that is neither universal nor eternal, but the particularity of the individual, the single one (*Einzelner*). Rosenzweig distinguishes this from the particular subordinate to its class and emphasizes that the human essence is an individual essence, the ownmost essence of each, neither shared nor susceptible to rational deduction. This own being (*Eigensein*) is not part of a community or species essence. It is alone.

Human freedom, which composes the other part of this construction, is markedly different from divine freedom. Because all freedom is negation, freedom is in some sense always finite. Human freedom is further finite because it is marked by finite power. God has free power; humans have free will—they cannot always do what they want, but they can want whatever they will (71/66). Human will, like divine will, serves to make a person unknowable by negating (in will, if not in fact) any claim to know the human.

Thus the construction parallel to the construction of God: the human essence is finite, but unique and unpredictable and similarly undeducible, while human freedom provides a contrariness that refuses classification. Both parts, moreover, are also parallel in their relation to the nothing of knowledge of the human: The essence is a location of a neighborhood of ignorance around the idiosyncratic, unknown essence. The freedom is the negation of the ignorance that protects it from further attempts to pin it down. Rosenzweig represents these by the symbols 'B' and 'B ='.

The attraction toward the essence of this freedom brings together freedom and essence and produces the human self. The self emerges as human freedom becomes defiance and human essence becomes character. This self "wills nothing else except that which he is," and what the self is is a finite being—a being that has an end in death (73/68). To become a self, a human must learn to will to be itself, and by so doing, to cease to will according to the world and its categories. The self, in contrast to the person, does not belong to groups, communities, people, nations, and so on, but roots itself in its own being. Thus the task of becoming a self is a task of breaking with the world, not in physical withdrawal, but in focusing the will solely on one's own being—which is a finite being, a being with character. The symbol for this self is 'B = B'.

This self, moreover, in keeping with the point of the constructions, is a human who is hidden. He or she is enclosed in pure finitude. Rosenzweig writes of how one dies to the world, with the rational order of cognition and the social realm of society, in order to become a self that cannot be visible in the world. A human who has become a self still appears to be part of the world because willing to be oneself can itself never appear in the world. Moreover, the confrontation with death in the world, the death that is part of being worldly, is the most radical way of having one's will directed to one's own most being. Rosenzweig writes of how death, one's own death, becomes the ruling event (*Ereignis*) of the hero. The hero is the person who has become a self by resolutely confronting his or her own death. That hero, that human self, can no longer speak nor even scream to the world because as self it now lives its life in the most bitter inward seclusion. The heroic self, called to itself from the world, willing its own finite being, must keep silent. While Kierkegaard saw this as the demonic despair of shut-upedness, Heidegger would shortly describe it as the authentic mode of being in the world, of being human. For Rosenzweig, however, this heroic self is the human we cannot know, the pure construction of the human who is unknown and unknowable. When that self is extroverted in Part II of *The Star of Redemption* and is opened first to God and then to the world, that self will emerge beyond its heroic silence as a speaking and loving soul.

CONCLUSION: REASON AND DISCONTINUITY

Both the motivation for and the method of construction now stand before us as guides to the logic of limitation. Rosenzweig constructs introverted elements, elements without actuality, in order to set a foundation for the empirical resources he will lay hold of. In this he follows Schelling, exploring what we cannot know in order to preserve, within discourse, the irrationality of freedom and of creation. But Schelling was unwilling to conduct a pure philosophical construction, instead smuggling what was known from experience into his construction of the a priori introversion. Rosenzweig therefore avails himself of Cohen, using Cohen's infinitesimal method as a critical turn for determining the conditions of knowing that we do not know. Through Rosenzweig's construction, both the need for entanglement with speculative thought and the rigorous exploration of what philosophy's humiliation requires appear.

Nonetheless, there are several key issues that remain unresolved. The first is the question of the use (or abuse?) of Cohen. For Cohen, the infinitesimal method serves as the cornerstone for a positive (not introverted) construction, for the generation of what we do know. Reality soon leads to actuality in a nondialectical manner. Cohen might well ask why Rosenzweig is so convinced that thinking can produce reality (or as Rosenzweig calls it, factuality), but cannot produce actuality. Rosenzweig's response is the break with idealism and its equation of knowing and being. This question then forces Rosenzweig, and indeed all philosophy after the death of philosophy, back to the fundamental question: Is there an irrational actuality?

While Cohen would insist that we must ask what the conditions would be for knowing such an irrational actuality, be it death, or a hidden God, or a heroic, authentic self, Rosenzweig and his crowd claim that living experience (*Erlebnis*) requires that irrationality. However, the strength of the construction in Part I of *The Star of Redemption* is the rigor with which it stipulates the conditions for knowing that there is something irrational. The conditions themselves, of course, do not offer up such an entity. Ultimately, we go around the circle of experience and criticism of experience, because we then ask whether the very construction has not assimilated the irrational to the rational. On this score, at least, Rosenzweig seems most valiant and successful. The hypothetical constructions display the ability of reason to delimit itself, and through the denial, to enforce its own limitation.

This brings us back to Schelling. The need for an introversion/extroversion schema is at least as troublesome as the insistence on breaking the equation of thinking and being. Although reason must abandon its pretense to determine what happens (creation, free action), those very happenings remain mute or utterly ambiguous (devoid of any specific meaning) without a rational construction such as an inversion. We do not discover experience without preparation; rather, rationality can prepare us to understand experience in every respect *except* for the actuality of the happening. Existentialism never tires of Schelling, nor of idealism's reflections and speculations, because without these it would cease to think or reason. Schelling called all previous philosophy "negative philosophy," and his supplement from experience the "positive philosophy." Rosenzweig follows Schelling and anticipates much of postmodern thought by holding on to modern philosophy and its project as a negative pole. Philosophy continues to reason purely and to explore logic, even in the presence (or absence) of the irrational, the incomprehensible. Only the *discontinuity* of actuality, the radical freedom in time (contra Cohen and Hegel), allows for the irrational. It may be that to know that we do not know we must make use of philosophy's pure, rigorous logic, for only with such logic can we prevent philosophy from assimilating the discontinuity of actuality to the sphere of reason's dominion. Even if we now proceed to impure (postmodern) philosophy and accept the help of some sort of experience, we cannot dispense with the examination of the limits of pure reason, nor with the task of exhausting pure philosophy. The exercise in topology of Rosenzweig's construction displays that pure thought can achieve true critique, asserting a region beyond its limits while at the same time negating its own pretensions to reach beyond those limits. To ask pure reason to do more is preposterous; to allow it to do less is to lose all hope of speaking of existence.

CHAPTER 3

Speech as Performance (I):
The Grammar of Revelation

WHEN ROSENZWEIG reconstructs the philosophical task in Part I of *The Star of Redemption*, he intends a parallel reconstruction of theology in Part II. Theology also entered this century in crisis. On the one side we are threatened by the culmination of a tradition of religious thought that has elevated and isolated inward experience to the exclusion of all expression, all habit, and all communication; on the other side an equally threatening wall of water crests above us with its meager rationalism. And for better or worse, both waves are almost spent: the inwardness of religious experience (or 'existential' experience, its postreligious cousin) seems no longer to secure any thought or discourse but to be simply a withdrawal from all need to think or to speak or to write, while the dreams themselves of rationalism are almost gone. The turn toward language, the most recognizable turn of our century, emerges clearly enough in repudiation of both empty formalist reason and of utterly inward experience. Rosenzweig also joins this turn, but his turn to language in action, to spoken speech (and the read text), offers us a vision that transcends strictly philosophical views of language.

Rosenzweig claims that his New Thinking is a bridge between philosophy and theology. He identified philosophy with the activity of reason independent of experience and thus assigned it the constructions of what is unknown and unknowable discussed in the previous chapter. An examination of speech as performance will now provide access to the realm of experience in which the unknowable makes itself known to others. Rosenzweig claims that language in action not only opens the self to others, but that such opening or revealing of oneself requires a theological interpretation. Philosophical reason cannot construct communication; it requires a theological reality.

The acceptance of theology brings with it the fear that thought will become fanatical. Rosenzweig believes that he has avoided such fanaticism: "I have written the first Jewish Book which I know to be non-fanatical (namely Jewish and so non-fanatical, non-fanatical and so Jewish)" (I, #955, 18 Sept. 1924). Fanatical here bears a technical Kantian meaning as the appeal to some private consciousness of divine assistance—

what normally passes as 'religious experience'.[1] Kant expressly defines the *Schwärmer*, the fanatic, as one who identifies the specific aid that God's grace provides and who thus identifies some particular component of will as being God's.[2] Rosenzweig fears fanaticism because he is turning to some experience that goes beyond pure reasoning. That admission of experience risks the dissolution of all knowledge. Thought cannot avoid the move to the subjectivity of the personal philosopher's viewpoint, represented historically by Kierkegaard and Nietzsche, but will thought still be science (*Wissenschaft*)? (117/105). The lack of continuity with others, and eventually even with oneself, threatens to make this move to experience useless. In place of science, the temptation is fanaticism, that some arbitrary and fantastical claim will be true. "The concept of experience, in its inexhaustible youth, easily seduces even calm thought to fanatical excess" (123/111).

Speech as the revealing of oneself to another cannot be the vehicle of excessive inwardness. Moreover, the technical sense of the term 'fanatic' approaches our more usual sense when Rosenzweig discusses how the fanatic ignores his or her neighbor in pursuit of some privately revealed, ultimate goal (306/274). The requirement to meet and love the person in front of you is closely tied to the analysis of speech in Part II of *The Star of Redemption*. Speech disciplines the fanatic, while at the same time bringing thought from pure rationality into the world of existence.

Rosenzweig provides us not with a theory of religious experience,[3] but with something more challenging and more beneficial. For the theological dimension of his reflection on speech opens up the space of intersubjectivity and so deepens the freedom in that space as it accentuates our responsibility in the world of others. Speech as performance yields a grammar or a vocabulary for a nonfanatical theology and for philosophy of religion, but it also argues that a nontheological view of speech will not adequately describe intersubjective space. Rosenzweig sheds valuable light on the way that speech—language spoken to another—constitutes true social relationships .

In order to interpret the activities of opening ourselves to others, Rosenzweig has recourse to an analysis of general rules of speech, to a kind of grammar. He refers to his interpretation as grammatical thinking, but it is not clear that what he is doing is parallel to what a contemporary grammarian or a philosopher of syntactics would do. The grammar he presents will not be a positivistic one in which what any person says in any language will count as evidence. Grammar will be more like a guide to the different kinds of interaction and to the construction of experience. The kind of empiricism that Rosenzweig advocates will emerge in the discussions of the next four chapters, but we should understand his grammar as a broader and more imprecise field than current research in linguistics and philosophy of language provide.

The primary task of this chapter is to present the grammatical interpretation of speech which Rosenzweig gives in Part II of *The Star of Redemption*. The move to the performance of language puts Rosenzweig in two interesting contexts, each of which will help us approach his own interpretation. The analysis of performatives begun by Austin offers an important systematic parallel. Austin's distinction of constatives and performatives will set a conceptual stage for Rosenzweig's own emphasis on what we do with words. There is also a second, more important, context: Eugen Rosenstock-Huessy's *Applied Psychology*, a manuscript Rosenzweig read during the war. Rosenstock developed a grammatical theory of language and culture, and Rosenzweig used that grammatical theory as the major resource in developing his own interpretation of language. The chapter concludes with my presentation of the content of Rosenzweig's interpretation: the three moods of theology. Through a careful attention to the different kinds of performance enacted in differing moods of grammar, Rosenzweig develops a theological account of the relations between the elements constructed in Part I. In the next chapter I will continue the examination of Part II of *The Star of Redemption*. There I will examine the relations of grammar to logic, to reading and writing, and finally to the fourth mood of speech, the interrogative. The next chapter, then, will display the resources in Rosenzweig's interpretation of speech for overcoming the risks of fanaticism and of meaninglessness.

PERFORMING AND GRAMMAR

Rosenzweig needs not just a theory of language, not merely an account of what language is or even of how language correlates inner states to outer sounds. The linguistic turn can be a purely epistemic move, claiming only that all perception of truth happens in the medium of words. Wordiness itself does not focus Rosenzweig's interest. Rather speech, the speaking of language, the practice or performance, is Rosenzweig's concern. Rosenzweig claims that speech in action is a revelation of the hidden self, which is not to say that all use of language, all uttering of words, constitutes speech (see the next chapter). But true speech is "speech of the soul in which human inwardness reveals itself" (163/147). Even without examining the constructions of Part I of *The Star of Redemption*, one can easily recognize that words may be used to reveal oneself to another—to reveal precisely what may not be inferable from behavior, from past actions, from even an intimate knowledge of one's character. One can always surprise another with what one chooses to say—and, more importantly, I can always be surprised by what another says to me. This revealing of what is inscrutable and undetectable is the task of speech. This action, and not the structures of language, is what Rosenzweig analyzes in Part II, providing him with the bridge from logic to existence.

Austin's Performatives

Rosenzweig distinguishes sharply between unspoken language and speech. The gap between Part I and Part II of *The Star of Redemption* can be seen in the distance between the existential situation of a speaker and the reflection of a thinker. A speaker speaks to another person, a person who also has a mouth and can speak back. The concrete situation of speech helps determine what is happening when one speaks. Indeed, speech, as existential discourse, is between me and an other; it is not an impersonal discourse between third persons (him and her). As a practical act, speech enacts certain sorts of relations between me and that other. Beyond the making available of information or the communication of knowledge, the structure of responsibility itself is created in my response to another; in speaking together, we become a community. We do things with words.

In his time, Rosenzweig was one of only a few thinkers to study the practical side—the performative function—of language. Since then, however, writers as diverse as Austin and Derrida, Habermas and Grice, Searle, Chomsky, and so on, have developed different dimensions of the study of what we do with words. The technical and theoretical studies in the various fields of linguistics, semantics, syntactics, and pragmatics have much to contribute to Rosenzweig's somewhat simple and broad portrait of the performative nature of language. Rosenzweig's ways of interpreting speech cut across the fields that are now defined; at times his points are simply syntactic (looking at the meaning of grammatical structures), at others semantic (the performative meaning of specific pronouns), and at other times pragmatic (the situationally bound meaning of an utterance). The full exploration of the relationship of Rosenzweig and of Levinas with the current state of these fields is beyond the scope of this book, but a brief discussion of Austin's contribution may help provide a location for Rosenzweig's grammatical method. In addition, an early adaptation of Austin for theological discourse by Donald Evans, independent of Rosenzweig, shows interesting affinities. In general, Rosenzweig's work seems closest to the approach of speech-act theory, although his interest in performance is more intrinsically relational than Searle and his cohorts.[4]

Austin distinguishes between the use of language to perform an action (performative) and the use of language to state what is the case (constative).[5] He then analyzes different sorts of performatives: those in which one acts in the very speaking of the words ("I do"), and those in which one produces an action by speaking ("I got him to 'x' by saying 'y' "). He details the features or constitution of these sorts of utterances by exploring how each can fail. The whole range of performative forces, of ways of using words beyond merely declaring the state of affairs, emerges in his work. Of greatest interest, however, is that although Austin sequesters constatives at the outset (perhaps to give the philosophical scholars their much-desired bone), he later breaks down the very distinction that guides his analysis.[6] It turns out that there is performative force even in an assertion—that we are still doing something and so are prone to the same sorts of faults in action (as opposed merely to questions of truth) whenever we speak. For Rosenzweig the performative force of statements will appear as the difference between the indicative mood of speech and the unspeakable statements of logic. "All 'P' is 'X' " is not speech according to Rosenzweig, but "the box is big" is, precisely because when I say "the box is big" I am asserting the existence of the box and the world that contains it.

Donald D. Evans appropriated Austin's work early in his career by examining religious speech in terms of performative force.[7] Evans noted the need to analyze the concepts of revelation and prayer with a new logic for theological discourse, because in such speech the self is involved (implicated) in the utterance. With its sensitivity to performative forces, Austin's theory was a useful tool for such a study. To say "God created the world" is to say something also about myself, or rather to commit myself to certain attitudes and even to certain further actions. Evans provides a broader horizon than Austin by looking at the 'ordinary language' of believers, complete with their commitments enacted in speech. Still more interesting, he focused on the linguistic dimension of biblical theology—that God is asserted to create the world through speaking. While the interpretation of this last theme may require recourse solely to human speech, it serves to provide a theological horizon for the basic thrust of Austin's theory. Evans looks at our self-involvements in religious discourse, while Rosenzweig focuses not only on how our selves are involved, but on how our interactions themselves happen in speaking. But Evans raises the stakes by daring to look at a vocabulary that is both more intensively self-involved and more theological than that examined by other theorists. Rosenzweig will independently suggest a lexicon of greater intimacy, but Evans' work points in the direction of the religious dimension of performatives and shows how this sense of action and creation in speech is constitutive for any sort of biblical theology.

It is interesting to see how Evans has since moved away from analytic philosophy and this particular focus on language. His later phenomenological and psychological work expresses distrust of the merely public nature of religious speech and looks back to inner states and attitudes for the meaning of the language.[8] He argues that the private is not idiosyncratic, but that public proclamation need not reveal the private experience. Rosenzweig, in response, might invoke the self-revealing performance of imperatives in 'I-you' encounters as the key to moving from inward emotion to private interpersonal relationship and then, in addition, he might explore the importance of completing the 'I-you' in a public community that can say 'we'.

Grammatical Method: Rosenstock-Huessy

While there is an important possible conversation between Rosenzweig and contemporary philosophy of language, the second context for Rosenzweig's grammatical method is historically essential. Both psychologically and intellectually Rosenzweig's relation to Rosenstock-Huessy is an absolute key to the development of *The Star of Redemption*. Rosenzweig publicly acknowledges the debt in "The New Thinking," where he writes that his speech method was

> re-introduced by Hermann Cohen in his posthumous works [*Religion der Vernunft*]. This position of Cohen's was already known to me as I wrote, but I do not owe to him the decisive influence in the presentation of my book. Rather, to Eugen Rosenstock, whose now published "Angewandte Seelenkunde" was before me in its first draft, even a year and a half before I began to write. (III, 152)

We now have to broaden the context of influences on Rosenzweig in order to gain better understanding of what his method involves. For Part I we examined two books; for Part II we must explore two manuscripts. In Part I of *The Star of Redemption*, Cohen's *Logic* was a key to interpreting the pure constructions; in Part II, Cohen's *Religion*, available in the proofs Cohen had given to Rosenzweig, is the great contribution of Rosenzweig's mentor (I, #562, 30 Sept. 1918; #489, 5 Mar. 1918; #493, 9 Mar. 1918). Cohen does interpret speech in a significant way in the *Religion*, and Rosenzweig's interpretation of Cohen's manuscript will be the opening topic for the next chapter.

Rosenstock-Huessy—with whom Rosenzweig had an intellectually overcharged and psychologically overwhelming relationship—sent Rosenzweig a manuscript that was the key to developing the new method of grammatical thinking.[9] In the midst of a passionate correspondence, Rosenstock sent *Angewandte Seelenkunde (Applied Psychology)* to Rosenzweig in early 1917 (I, #380, 29 Mar. 1917; #361, 23 Feb. 1917). It is a manifesto for grammatical thinking, proposing grammar as the key to the life of the soul. Rosenstock advances a new method for approaching not only language, but, through language, also the social forms of art, legislation, and science. The central premise is that the soul must be capable of keeping silent, of hiding itself.[10] Speech is the breaching of that silence, and it is what structures the soul.

The problem that has been lurking throughout this section, however, is that neither Austin's philosophy nor later speech-act theory is a theory of grammar. Indeed, Austin rejects grammar as incapable of guiding his work, specifically switching from grammar (with mood, tense, person, and voice) to vocabulary.[11] The problem is that a given utterance can do different things; that there is no directly binding correspondence between the grammar of a sentence and its performative force. The argument for abandoning grammar inclines toward Austin and his followers in his favorite example—first person, indicative, present tense—because a whole range of performative forces are possible within that one, seemingly limited, grammatical type ("I 'x'" or "I 'y' that 'P' . . . "). The performative variations seem tied exclusively to semantics: ('wish' vs. 'command' vs. 'argue' vs. 'promise', etc.). But the issue is more complex precisely when we consider different moods—the imperative gives speech-act theory special problems—because so much of the performative force does seem coded to grammar. The sort of analysis that Austin et al. are interested in, particularly the separation of performatives from constatives (a somewhat tricky business in the long run), might not be served by grammar, but there is a great deal that grammar seems to offer.

A preliminary apology for grammar lies in the critique that Rosenstock-Huessy himself makes of 'School grammar'. His proposal for grammatical method itself requires a renovation of grammar in order to observe more carefully (and in some ways more imaginatively) what happens in speech. Indeed, Rosenstock-Huessy calls for an *Urgrammar*, a root grammar, or what we might call a *depth grammar*. He objects to the everyday use of language as mere tool, writes of traditional grammar as "impoverished," and criticizes the dependence on Greek school grammar: the school books preserve that grammar as a presupposition[12]; such grammar is a photograph of the surface.[13] Rosenstock-Huessy still examines empirical speech, but he analyzes different uses, much as he proposes a deeper interpretation of grammatical rules and principles.[14] But the value of this grammatical method, particularly under the suspicion of contemporary theory, must obviously lie in its application.

Rosenstock-Huessy takes up grammar in the longest section of *Angewandte Seelenkunde* by challenging the Greek tradition of making the first person (the 'I') the first form of the verb. Idealism made all experience center on the subject, the 'I', and made all knowledge originate in self-consciousness. The point of departure for Rosenstock's grammar is that the second person (the 'you') is originary: a child begins to become conscious of itself through the commands addressed to it[15]; and a person becomes a person by responding when addressed and thereby discovering the 'I' of the first person. The 'you' is the experience of being called; the 'I' of answering; the 'he, she, it' of what cannot give an answer, and therefore of what cannot be addressed. The soul thus becomes aware of itself first from outside, finding itself something other. The child discovers its 'I' as the ability to answer, to say 'yes' or 'no', to that call from the other.

We may move from person to mood and then find this grammatical interpretation of speech gaining greater depth. The imperative is linked with the second person; similarly, the first person is linked with the subjunctive, and the third person with the indicative. Rosenstock-Huessy begins with the first person, in which we express our own freedom. In song and prayer, we use the subjunctive in its various guises to express what the world might be.[16] The invocation of possibility, of conditions that are contrary to fact or are subject to doubt, of future possibilities within our agency—this space of our freedom is the range of the subjunctive mood.

The indicative, on the other hand, is the mood in which things are discussed in their being and existence. The question of being is a question to be addressed in the indicative; it is a question about the entity as a thing that cannot answer. The indicative is bound to the third person. Natural science and Heidegger's philosophy, yet to be written, to say nothing of the philosophy devoted to assertions (constatives), all treat this mood as if it were the only mood of speech.

Finally, the imperative is the mood directed to the nearest you (the neighbor). The imperative begins in love, which is transformative. Recall that self-consciousness and indeed speech begin in the second person who is commanded. The re-sponsibility of the second person, the ability to answer, is the re-sponse to an imperative. While the subjunctive needs a philosophy of freedom and self-consciousness, and the indicative one of objective laws and *Weltanschauung*, the imperative needs a philosophy of love and of the nearest you.

We next move to tense. The link will be from second person to the present; from third to the past; and from first to the future. The future is the world I would make; I may exercise my freedom and create my wish in the future. The indicative speaks of things, of objects that do not respond; knowledge of the world is representation, describing what was, fixing the quality to the object. The *re* in representation makes clear how the assertion of what *is* the case is always what *was* the being of the case (Aristotle's *to ti ēn einai*). The imperative in Rosenstock-Huessy's text, however, is not fully explained as the present. At issue, though, is the urgency and the presentness of the speaker in the speaking, in opposition to the re-presenting of the indicative and the deferring of the future in the optative. The grammar of the imperative will be much more important in Rosenzweig's discussion.

TABLE I
Rosenstock-Huessy's Grammar

Person	Mood	Tense	Quality
Second (You)	Imperative	Present	Addressed
First (I)	Subjunctive	Future	Responsible
Third (He, She, It)	Indicative	Past	Unanswerable

Rosenstock-Huessy continues his grammatical theory later in the essay with a discussion of number and of case. The issue of number is the transition from the individual soul to the community (*Gesellschaft*). He follows von Humboldt in arguing that the first person plural ('we') is not a sign of plurality (*Mehrheit*), but emerges from the dual.[17] At stake here is whether communities should be seen as collections of individual 'I's, that to say 'we' is to say 'I and I and I and I', or whether to say 'we' is to display a deeper bonding together of the community. Rosenstock-Huessy argues that the true 'we' includes not only 'I' but also 'you' and 'it', that 'we' is a fused unity of the singular grammatical persons. The common community is degenerate and is a mere collectivity; true unity, found through depth grammar, is one of God, world, and man. It is on just these points that Rosenzweig will clearly present a differing position. The unification of everything, both grammatically and theologically, is much more desirable for Rosenstock-Huessy than for Rosenzweig. However, before we leave off the discussion of Rosenstock-Huessy's grammar, we must note the opening up of the theological dimension, for while Rosenzweig presents the theology with great clarity and centrality, Rosenstock-Huessy has also broken the path from grammar to theology in his essay.

Here we turn to that odd title of the essay: *Angewandte Seelenkunde*. Why did Rosenstock-Huessy not call it *Praktische Psychologie?* The central oddity is not the presence of Germanic roots in place of Greek ones, but the substitution of *Seele* for *Psyche*. Since both mean soul, why emphasize *Seele?* Rosenstock-Huessy answers by claiming that psychology in his time is impoverished: it either reduces the soul to a physical principle (nerve center, etc.), or elevates it into a spiritual essence (*geistiges Wesen*; center of consciousness, etc.). In neither case is the soul seen in its religious dimension. Rosenstock-Huessy argues for a religious view of the soul, which means recognizing the soul's power of prophecy, that God could reveal Himself to that soul. (Rosenzweig forswears religion in favor of theology largely because the soul for him is faithful but not prophetic, thus not allowing the religious experience of prophecy as an inner revelation of God.)

When Rosenstock-Huessy discusses the emergence of speech, he focuses on the ability for the whole person, and not just the physical or spiritual parts, to speak. Only when "God calls, and I answer 'Here am I'" is the soul speaking as fully human.[18] Because the soul learns of itself first when addressed by an other, we must focus on understanding the soul as responsive. But Rosenstock-Huessy is quick to recognize that idols—the state, the 'I' of man, the world of things, etc.—can stand in for God as our addresser, and we can answer to such idols. Whomever we answer to is the absolute, the god in our world, but until we are converted to the true God, we cannot speak as human beings. Instead, we must either reduce ourselves merely to physical realities (third person) or elevate ourselves into idolatrous man-gods (first person).

Rosenstock-Huessy attacks everyday speech and the current state of psychology in order to reveal the uncommon reality, fully human speech, that answers to the one true God and not to some idol. The discovery of the second person, of the 'you' addressed by the other, is the discovery not only of the soul, but of revelation. It opens the life of the soul, for the first time, to the various persons and related moods, tenses, cases, etc. Previous discourse misused the words, failing to find the deepest and truest meaning of the different persons, tenses, moods, etc. Soul does not exclude body and spirit, but rather orients all three in a unification that is at the same time a unification with God and world. Thus the grammar itself is not identical with an empirical grammar of everyday speech, because words are often spoken in what we would normally call grammatically correct ways without actually performing the key functions that Rosenstock-Huessy assigns to them. The insights of his grammar, therefore, are drawn from a deeper and richer use of language, but are best articulated in his renovated grammar. The tension between the superficial use of grammatical forms and the fully human speech indicated by the grammatical thinking leads Rosenzweig to move beyond formal grammar to the grammatical analysis of specific types and even toward a pragmatic analysis of utterances.

Rosenstock-Huessy's essay had global impact on Part II of *The Star of Redemption*, as will be clear in a moment. The influence also includes interpretations of the life of the soul that go beyond the immediate concerns of this book, particularly the emphasis on shame and the discussion of suffering.[19] Rosenstock-Huessy's essay also proposes a theory of culture that is in many ways quite different from Rosenzweig's, and so I will not discuss it here. The relationship between the two men continued throughout Rosenzweig's life, and its further dimensions belong to a study of the personal genesis of *The Star of Redemption*. For this discussion, however, the grammatical method now lies before us in its barest form.

THE MOODS OF THEOLOGY

The three books of Part II of *The Star of Redemption* form a theological sequence: Creation, Revelation, and Redemption. Each term itself is a relationship of two of the elements from Part I: God created the world, God reveals Himself to people, and people ought to redeem the world (and God will redeem Himself).[20] The connection between these relationships and the construction of the introverted elements of Part I is the topic of the next chapter. But here I wish to present a reading of Rosenzweig's grammatical thinking. The theological sequence corresponds to three grammatical moods: indicative, imperative, and cohortative. Similarly, they correspond to the three tenses, past, present, and future, and also to different personal pronouns, the third person, the second and first person singular, and the first and second person plural.

TABLE II
Rosenzweig's Grammar

Theological Concept	Mood	Tense	Pronouns
Creation	Indicative	Past	He, She, It
Revelation	Imperative	Present	You, I
Redemption	Cohortative	Future	We, Ye—HE

The links to Rosenstock-Huessy are at once obvious, particularly with the tenses and the moods. Moreover, Rosenzweig also depends on a fundamental 'I-you' of being called by God as the orienting point of the whole sequence. Nonetheless, it is also clear that to make sense of Rosenzweig's grammar, we need to examine the theology linked to the grammatical nexus. At the outset, we see that the interpretation of plurals and of redemption markedly differ from those of Rosenstock-Huessy. In proceeding, we will see that the grammar of Rosenstock-Huessy's thinking will be enriched by examination of specific utterances and specific contexts.

Creation in the Indicative

The beginning of the sequence is the discussion of creation as found in the grammar of the third person, indicative, past tense. We move from logical formulas, which are not spoken, to indicative sentences (Austin's constatives), which follow a predicate logic but make existential claims. In the section called "Grammar of Logos (The Language of Cognition)," Rosenzweig provides a table of parts of speech (140–45/126–31). He begins with a 'Yes', one which will be unlimited, and finds that he needs an adjective that is a pure predicate and pure affirmation of value. Only the word 'good' will do. This choice is in obvious reminiscence of the biblical account of creation, but 'good' also takes up the ontological tradition. What is, first and foremost, is the goodness of existence.

Ontology moves in two counterpoised directions from this quality: 1) toward the objectivity of a substance/predicate ontology, and 2) toward the completedness (the grammatical sense of the perfect) of the act of existence. Rosenzweig develops each mode of ontological thought by creating a table of parts of speech. To reach the things of substance/predicate ontology, we move from quality to property (adjectives in general), and then to materiality (*Dinglichkeit*) (pronouns, especially indexicals, like 'this'). The destination is the objectivity of the substance (nouns), but the route continues through the indefinite articles to the definite articles, in each case moving to greater definition and independence. When we arrive at the substance ('this one') in which the predicates inhere, we know that substance as one of a genus. The grammar/ontology does not provide us with proper names, only with generic ones: the individual is known as a member of a class; and the grammar of the indicative grasps the world as objects with properties. To use the indicative mood is, therefore, to see the world as things with properties, located indexically—this one here—in space.

But there is a second side to this logic: the affirmation of reality, of existence. The contemporary shift from substance ontology to process ontology will not take us beyond this first of three grammatical logics in *The Star of Redemption*, this first mood. We need more than the substance ontology, because the coming into being of the beings (things) also appears in speaking in the indicative. Rosenzweig begins anew with the expressed (or implicit) 'is' (144/129). More than a copula, is invokes the act of existing and leads to other verbs. That verbality displays that the things with their properties are in motion; they are in time. The move to verbs is through the most adjectival form of a verb, the participle. The possibility of the act of existence begins with the infinitive of the verb. The infinitive emphasizes the process (*Vorgang*) itself and not the agency of some actor. As the temporal definition continues, the verb must become finite and is presented in the third person. Things are naturally spoken of in the third person, and the third person stands independent of whomever is speaking (while the first and second converse and are situationally defined). Finally, the verb achieves full determination as a finite verb in the past tense. Only when something is over, when the action is completed, is it fixed and thoroughly knowable. The first route, through substance ontology, has fixed the things in space; the second route, through process ontology, has fixed the coming into being in time.

TABLE III
The Tree of Parts of Speech

Good ⟨	adjectives	pronouns	indefinite article	definite article	noun
	copula	participles	infinitive	third person	past tense

For creation there remain two issues at this point: 1) What does Table III, complete with its ontological translation, have to do with creation? and 2) How does creation become known as such? The first issue requires an explanation of the subtitle of the section entitled "Grammar of Logos (The Language of Cognition)" in *The Star of Redemption*. What speech in the indicative does is know things. We are exploring what Austin called the constative, in which the use of language is limited to saying what is the case. But in order to know things in time we need to transform the processes of change into a sequence of completed states of rest. Rosenzweig claims that modern mathematics, particularly differential calculus, works in just that way (146/132). The use of language to describe what has happened (and so is the case) must always take the present and turn it into a sort of past tense (it even can do this with the future—science is predictive, etc.). The world is known in that basic mood of the indicative because it allows no play, the propositional content of the statement is in fact the case (not might have been or ought to be, etc.). The world is known in this doubled ontology of fixed time and space. But the world as presented in this indicative mood is not merely in the eye of the beholder. In fact, the function of this kind of speech is to claim the independence from the knower of the things as they have come to be. It is not that I wish or will something to exist, but that it (third person) is thus. The things now stand completed, their integrity instituted in the very definiteness of space and time of the doubled ontology. This is the existence of the world.

On the other hand, while the world now stands on its own—while the purpose of the indicative is to grant to the world its own integrity—the world has come into being. The language of pure reason and pure mathematical physics, in contrast, is atemporal and neither addresses specific time or space nor asserts the existence of the world. Empirical and scientific speech discover that the world is not the source of its own existence, even if it preserves itself through its own structure. The pastness of speech in the indicative evokes the creatureliness of the things, but it does not reveal their origin. The speech of constatives (as opposed to logical formulas) displays the independence of things from speech, while at the same gesturing to a deeper dependence of things upon a prior source.

This leads to the second issue. Rosenzweig is emphatic that without revelation the grammar of Table III, of the doubled ontology of the scientific worldview, cannot recognize the world as God's creation. The grammar of the indicative is a prediction of the contents of revelation, but it cannot be recognized as such until the event of revelation appears, allowing us to see that this ontological knowledge of the world was a prediction of something more. On its own terms the scientific worldview does not provide that awareness of revelation. Indeed, Rosenzweig devotes considerable time to showing how an attempt to produce all experience from the world as given in this ontological grammar runs aground precisely on both the independence of the things from the knower and on the inability of the things to bring themselves into existence. Fortunately, that critique of idealism is not helpful here, but the point is important: the world will be seen as God's creation only from the perspective of revelation.

Revelation in the Imperative

And so I turn to the second stage of grammar. Rosenzweig's interpretation of the imperative mood as revelation is a different kind of task. Here there is no table of parts of speech; instead, he provides tokens, even token dialogues, in order to interrupt the work of thought with the reality of spoken speech. Rosenzweig analyzes the semantics of personal pronouns here and also the pragmatics of specific dialogues. The parallel section in *The Star of Redemption* is "Grammar of Eros (The Language of Love)." Here we move to what is the first specific speech, and at the same time to what is clearly a performative. For the decisive utterance is the command from the lover: "Love me." The grammar of eros is an enhanced grammar of the imperative mood. Rosenzweig finds a profound asymmetry, one not based on gender, but rather based on the difference between being loved and loving.[21] The absolute separation of the divine from the human as established by Part I of *The Star of Redemption* is bridged now in the speech of revelation, the speech of a lover. Thus the fundamental function of speech, to reveal oneself to another, is according to Rosenzweig the task of the imperative, "Love me."

The root word of this dialogue is 'I'. While the 'good' of creation was the affirmation of existence, the 'I' is always a 'no', an objection. "I, however. . . ." I say 'I' only to voice my refusal to go along. 'I' is always said in a specific context; the 'I' and the 'you' are spoken in the context of myself and another. Speech now is found in specific words, not in the classes (the parts of speech) of the grammar of logic. We can abstract from the specific dialogue, but we will not understand 'I' as a member of the group of personal pronouns (194/173). 'I' is a here and 'you' is a there, creating a specific situation where space becomes nonsymmetric.

The performance orients space in a specific and nonobjectivisable way in relation to myself as speaker.

The dialogues Rosenzweig interprets are both local to the biblical text and at the same time representative of more general uses.[22] Rosenzweig starts with God's inner dialogue ("Let us make man in our image," Gen. 1.26), but excludes it because this is not truly dialogue in which the inner you here addressed could talk back. Indeed in "The New Thinking," Rosenzweig criticizes Platonic dialogue and the idea of thought as an inner dialogue. The inner dialogue is not yet speech, because speech is for someone else, a 'you' who has a mouth (III, 152). This 'I' said to an inner 'you' is not yet really 'I'.

But when the 'I' asks, "Where are you?" it reveals itself (Gen. 3.9). The 'I' believes that there is a 'you' outside it, and it seeks to see that 'you'. In the discussion in the garden, the man refuses to become a 'you' for God. His response is a retreat into the third person: "The woman gave . . . " (Gen. 3.12). He will not take responsibility, will not respond to the 'I' of God. This interpretation is both true enough, but also an interpretation; the man does speak of 'me', and even of 'you', but because he refuses to say 'I' to God, there is no dialogue. Here the praxis itself guides the grammatical interpretation, as the issue of revealing oneself helps construe the 'grammar'.

The next attempt for dialogue prepares for the full emergence of the grammar of love: God calls Abraham by name, as he calls so many other prophets, and the answer is "Here am I" (Gen. 22.1). Here the partner is singled out completely by name and responds as an 'I', as a soul. The significance of the proper name for the speaker and the hearer is key: For the speaker it finds a particular person, a unique other, spoken to in the vocative, not as a member of a class but as a 'you'.[23] For the hearer, to be called by name is to be fixed to myself, to be required to stand forward as an 'I'.

This prologue leads to the commandment at the core of all of Rosenzweig's grammar of performative speech: "Love me." (Or in biblical dress: "You shall love the Lord your God" (Deut. 6.5). Rosenzweig claims that this utterance is restricted: only the lover can speak it. If a third were to utter it, it would be preposterous, but the lover speaks it and Rosenzweig argues that the love of the lover can speak only thus. That God is commanding "Love *me*" when He commands love *the Lord your God* becomes clear only by considering the Song of Songs, a task Rosenzweig defers to the end of Book 2 of Part II, and one I defer to the next chapter.

Rosenzweig argues that only the command "Love me" is the speech of love. Why? Because the speech of love must itself love. As mentioned in Chapter 1, love for these Jewish thinkers is not primarily comforting or

compassionate, but rather commanding. It affirms and builds up the beloved by demanding love from him or her. We might suppose that "I love
you" is the characteristic speech of the lover, but while that declaration
proclaims a state of affairs, it does not enact love. I explain and even
affirm my love by proclaiming its reality to you, but that makes the present passion into the just-now past. As proclamation, the statement has a
performative function; not the function of love itself, but rather that of
cognition of completed things. Love for Rosenzweig is an action of the
present, an action not complete (such as the verbal forms of the indica-
tive/creation), but an action that happens right now—and the imperative
is the mood for expressing the 'right now'. The imperative grabs the next
moment and forces it to be present (while the indicative takes the present
moment and re-presents it into the past). Rosenzweig distinguishes commandment from law (*Gebot* vs. *Gesetz*), because a law builds for the
future, while a commandment is only for this moment. The grammatical
point, quite strikingly, goes emphatically beyond parts of speech and
moods because it requires the vocabulary of love; but at the same time
Rosenzweig is arguing that all imperatives derive their primary force
from this one command. Indeed, he states that all imperatives except the
command "Love me" can become law, because this one ceases to be itself
when it becomes law. Thus its function as pure command (imperative in
the fullest sense) is to measure all other imperatives. Just as all speech to
another requires 'I', so all imperatives emerge from this particular one.
Rosenzweig's promise to turn to specific words, utterances, and from
them to grammatical classes, has been fulfilled.

The grammar of eros, however, requires that the dialogue go forward—because we have not heard the beloved's response to the lover's
command. The soul of the beloved responds with shame. The temporality
of that interruptive present points out to the beloved that it was once
content within itself without being loved. The introverted self mistook
itself for a complete being. Once my complacent self-sufficiency is interrupted, I realize that my own heroism, my own self-sufficiency, was sin.
Only in response to love does one speak of this shame, this failure in the
past. Rosenzweig focuses on the utterance "I have sinned" as the response
to the command to love. But through important transformations, the beloved realizes that this past property actually defines the past self ("I was
a sinner"). As analysis of the performance, Rosenzweig is claiming that to
have sinned is to have been a sinner—which is not to say that all actions
make the actor simply into the agent of the act, but that the announcement of past failure, of the self-involved awareness of my shortcoming,
produces a new knowledge of myself.

This grammar continues, as "I was a sinner" becomes "I am a sinner."
Such a transformation is the overcoming of the initial shame in being

loved. This confession first of all takes the past person into the present person; the structure of the self-involvement includes the current speaking self. But that invocation of myself is only possible because I am now being loved. Only as the beloved can I acknowledge that sinfulness that is myself, because I annul it in acknowledging (confessing) it. The German word *Bekenntnis* has both the clearly performative force of confession and, at the same time, that interesting quasi-constative (and still also performative) meaning of acknowledge. For Rosenzweig this confession is itself the process of atonement (*Versöhnung*), which the soul undertakes in the presence of the lover's love. I can only come to terms with my own false self-reliance, my own illusion of completeness while lacking love, in the presence of my lover's demand to love. And as I speak my way through this process of accepting my past as mine, as myself, even including the self that has heard the command to love, I recognize that the past is not being held against me.[24] Indeed, the lover's love is more truly love, more unconditional, precisely because while I was still deluded, still proud and oblivious to my failure, even then the lover loved me. To confess myself as sinner is to know myself as loved, to be faithful.

> The confession of the still-present sinfulness, for which sake alone the past sins in general are confessed, is already no longer confession of sin—that is passed like the confessed sins themselves. It confesses not the lovelessness of the past, rather the soul speaks: I also now love, but still in this most present moment not as much as I—know myself loved. (201/181)

Rosenzweig's position is that the relation called revelation requires both a lover's opening oneself to a 'you' and a beloved's hearing that and responding with faith; which is the sureness that the momentary imperative is a continuing state of being loved which the beloved produces. Thus the soul answers the command finally with the utterance, "I am yours." The process of self-atonement before the lover allows the beloved to enact faith in speech. Faith, unlike love, is performed in the indicative, but that indicative is one located in the asymmetric space of an 'I' and a 'you'.

The dialogue continues with a new mode of cognition, as the lover then responds, "I have called you by name. You are mine." This utterance ties the present to the past and so operates for Rosenzweig as the decisive link between the grammar of love and the grammar of cognition. While the beloved has already discovered that its past requires connection to the present and is redressed in the presence of the lover's command to love, the lover also now sees that cognition itself takes place in the context of the interaction of an 'I' and a 'you'. The cognitive discourse of creation is fixed in time and place by the revelatory dialogue of an 'I' and a 'you'. The predicate logic of the confession, culminating in the assertion "I am yours," leads us to see that revelation as the lived experience in the urgent command reaches back to creation's indicative for meaning. Revelation displays how the predicate logic and process ontology lay a foundation of meaning for the lived experience of the speaking subject's love. But the focus of this display is the proper name, which lies beyond the parts of speech. With the proper name, a specific person in the here and now is singled out against the class, not included in the class. Authenticity for Rosenzweig is linked to the pragmatics of the proper name. Here the logic of cognition provides a grounding for the experience of love, because the cognition affords a fixed place and time through the predicate logic and the completed action of coming into being. The 'I', called to speak by its proper name, enables revelation to go beyond the impersonal discourse of creation. "The immediate determinacy of the proper name appears in place of the article. With the call of the proper name the word of revelation steps into real dialogue; the proper name makes the breech in the fixed wall of thinghood" (208/186). Hence the response, "I have called you by name. And you are mine" accomplishes this cognitive break-through—relating cognition to eros and experience to existence.

Rosenzweig's account of this dialogue takes one more step, in the prayer of the beloved. This is a prayer for the coming of the kingdom, which translates into a publication of the love, the desire that all the world should know and participate in this romance. But the prayer takes revelation beyond its own borders into redemption. Indeed, the move is out of the imperative and into the cohortative. The link to the cohortative is our concern here. Just as the imperative required a reference to the indicative, where knowledge created a secured system of meaning in which the love could become a lived experience, so love also requires a completion of the world, a path to verification in the objective order. Ultimately, speech will yield to action and to vision, which is the topic for the Chapters 5 and 6 of this book. But more immediately, speech in the imperative yields to a further use of language, speech that is redemptive, speech that creates the public community lacking in the isolated love dialogue.

Redemption in the Cohortative

Redemption for Rosenzweig is primarily the relation of human beings redeeming the world. The human action of love of the neighbor develops the inner capacities of created things for life and growth. In Book 3 of Part II of *The Star of Redemption*, the focus is still on speech and on how redemption can be studied in grammar. Rosenzweig calls the parallel section here "Grammar of Pathos (The Language of the Deed)." In contrast to 'good' and to 'I', here there is no root word. We are now in the realm of 'and', which does not become another 'Yes' and so does not generate a Hegelian dialectic. 'And' binds together the 'Yes' with the 'No'. In place of a root word, we now have a root sentence: "He is good." This sentence combines the two root words, but not without a significant transformation: God's 'I', which could command "love me," has become the third person 'He'. Unlike the speech of dialogue, which is specifically located, we are looking for a type that allows for universal and communal speech, because redemption is the formation of a universal community. Only God can say, "I am good," while everyone can say, "He is good." Rosenzweig's claims for this root sentence are huge:

> This is the root sentence of redemption, the roof over the house of speech; the sentence which is true in itself; the sentence that remains true regardless of how it is meant and from whichever mouth it comes. . . . All other speech forms must be bound to this sentence. And indeed, while the forms follow the root word of creation in a row of a material development like the individual sentences of a history, and while the root word of revelation disclosed a dialogue, here all of the speech forms bear and explicate the meaning of this sentence. (258/231)

Here the narrative and the dialogue are replaced by a choral song. This sentence becomes the refrain of a choral song, and its various forms will be interpreted in this third grammar. That song is antiphonal: a human voice sings its love of its neighbor, and the world answers with its coming to life. What the two voices sing together is the acknowledgment of God as good—as good creator and as good lover. The 'moral' effort of individual people is balanced by the transformation of the world, at its own pace and in its own way, and that balancing is represented by the 'and' of this sentence. When the beloved human turns to the neighbor in love, the beloved must affirm that its love is a response to its lover. My caring for my neighbor depends upon my lover's love. Hence the individual says, "He is good." When the world comes alive, moving beyond its existence as creation, it too does so because it was made for redemption, for life. It affirms that thus it was created, and thus the origin of its existence, which lies beyond or behind itself, is also good. Together the human and the world sing that God is a good redeemer.

But this mutual recognition that 'He is good' is not simply a proposition. The point of this joining function is not to make both sides come to the same recognition; quite beyond that, the singing of the individual to the world and of the world to the individual of one and the same text is itself the work of redemption. In the singing, the conformity is created, announced, and fulfilled. The work of redemption is the completion of the goal of creation and of the commandment to love. Rosenzweig's recourse to grammar is to show how certain acts of speaking can do that work. The sentence that is the root will now go through several forms before it spins out the grammar of the cohortative.

The coming together of a community is the task of singing. Rosenzweig holds that song begins as communal chant, and that the content of the song is only a function of the community formed by the singing (the script for these songs is the Psalter and its use in worship). Thus the song form of "He is good" is the form "Because [*denn*] he is good." We sing this song, we come to sing, because the origin of the existence of the world is the origin of our love. The key mood is the cohortative of the form "Let us sing" or "Let us thank" or "Let us praise." The cohortative has a self-reflective, performative force—I do not merely require that you do something (the imperative), I also place myself in the deed—but that self-reflective element is not the only key point. For Rosenzweig had shown that one imperative, the decisive "Love me," can be spoken only by one who also loves the beloved, by one who is already loving. The cohortative obliges me to join with the others. In using it I do not merely insist on a response to my love, but I join with my listeners. I overcome my isolation by forming a community. Here is a performative force that subtends all communal declarations ("we, the people, . . ."), because in saying "let us" we create the subject, the community. Before a 'we' can speak, we must first sing, we must first create our community.

Rosenzweig explains that this cohortative utterance precedes the proclamation "He is good." We gather ourselves in the cohortative in order to say "He is good," but to assemble the widest community we must sing of the goodness of both our lover and the existence of the world—only such praise and thanksgiving can draw all together. According to Rosenzweig, the dative case structures the unity of the cohortative singing of beloved and world; it represents the recipient of the gift, the person who is neither simply the subject of the action (the giver) nor the object acted upon (the gift). The community thus sings its thanks and praise "to God" as indirect object. The dative allows the recipient to retain its personality and its goal as destination of the action. The 'He' of "He is good" is then in the dative, in order to allow the community of humans and world to sing together.

We thus move to yet a third mode of knowing (*Erkenntnis*), namely acknowledgment (*Anerkennung*): In the context of creation there was the foundation, cognition on its own as knowledge of creatures; in the context of revelation there was confession as a knowing relation to the lover. Cognition and confession combine in acknowledgment, a knowing that binds the knower to the world in recognition of the lover. The community sings of God's goodness before it asks its own petitions. While the individual is fulfilled in praying, the prayer of the community for the coming of the kingdom is fulfilled before it is prayed—because the acknowledgment that God is good comes before the prayer. To make that acknowl-edgment is to redeem. But communal acknowledgment leads to individ-ual petition, which is the liturgical practice in both Jewish and many Christian communities. The kingdom comes, but it is not yet here—the individual is not fully in harmony with the world. That moment is still to come, it is not-yet.

For Rosenzweig, redemption is in the future tense. The use of the co-hortative, even in the present, anticipates a future. It does not predict like the indicative, which turns even future events into a kind of already past by re-presenting them in the future-perfect tense. Nor is the urgent imper-ative the key, precisely because its time is right now. The future of the cohortative is ours to make, and by asking us to do it, I provide us with an experience of the future today. Rosenzweig rejects the incrementalism of all notions of progress; the redemptive future could happen today. The future as future must be brought into the present. In Chapters 5 and 6, I will discuss how social action can accomplish that, but even when we are merely speaking we can bring the future into today as an anticipation—not as a prediction. The difference lies in the very action of the utterance: to convene the community, not to diagnose it.

If the tense of the cohortative utterance is future, the pronoun is unmis-takably first-person plural. Nonetheless, Rosenzweig, following Rosen-stock-Huessy and von Humboldt, argues that the 'we' is not a plural—at least not a mere collection of 'I' and 'I' and 'I'. The way to the 'we' is through the other person. Were the world redeemed, were the individual brought together with the whole world, then 'we' would be immediate and obvious, but because we can only anticipate that community, we must approach saying 'we' more cautiously. 'We', according to Ro-senzweig, cannot be understood on its own but requires for its meaning some further word as a limitation.

The move to community is through the neighbor, which Rosenzweig interprets by emphasizing the etymological sense of the nearest person. The dual serves as the number here, because just as the dual is unstable (which two?), so the relation to the neighbor always slides off into the next one after this one. To love your neighbor is not to become fixed on this one person to the exclusion of all others, but to recognize that this person could be anyone and that through this one I will come into contact with another one—who will then be my neighbor. The "we two" which is the dual is always transitional, leading to further "twos".

Rosenzweig interprets the command "To love your neighbour like yourself" as an emphasis on seeing the other as a 'you', as one who has been loved and so as one who can share with me. Playing on the etymol-ogy of neighbor/near one (*Nächste*), Rosenzweig claims that the nearest is such a 'you', but the neighbor is also a representative of other others, indeed of all others (267/240). The blindness of this love is precisely the willingness to treat whomever is nearest as the one to whom I must say, "Let us. . . ." To speak in the cohortative is to see the world already coming alive.

The wandering of the dual, from one neighbor to the next, when I discover again and again that both I and this other are ready to come together, that wandering generates a fuller 'we', a 'we' that can collect all of us and more. The 'we' is the sign of an all, of a universal community—and 'we' can only be narrowed. Its grammar is to claim all by inclusion. The 'I' and the 'you', however, are specific and require expansion. For Rosenzweig, the 'we' of choral singing is a multiphonal one in which each voice retains its integrity. "All voices here have become independent. Each sings the words according to its own melody of its soul, and still all the melodies fugue themselves in the same rhythm and combine into a harmony" (264/237). This vision of community that is both more than collectivity and still not totalizing monotony governs Rosenzweig's theory of speech. But before we relax, complacent that by speaking 'we' we now stand in a redeemed world, we must consider the counterpart of the 'we'.

Just as the 'I' could not be spoken except in love to a 'you', so the 'we' cannot be spoken alone. Because our world is unredeemed, 'we' is also joined. Rosenzweig's insight, however, breaks with the common view that language partitions the collectivities between 'us' and 'them'. In place of 'them', the objectifying plural of things (found in the indicative in the description of classes of finished objects), Rosenzweig discusses the 'ye', which we would normally call a second-person plural. For Rosenzweig the 'ye' is the dreadful word of judgment passed on the others who cannot be embraced in the 'we'. We say 'ye' to distinguish our community, but that requires the exclusion of 'ye' and hence a judgment, even a divine judgment, upon ye. The theological vision Rosenzweig develops here is particularly uncomfortable, but the performative possibilities for relations between communities is still valuable.

For what is clearer than that by speaking to a 'ye', we express our willingness to listen to ye—which perhaps in America is best served by 'y'all'? 'Y'all' is not objectifying. It presupposes that y'all will speak back, that dialogue is the nature of our interrelationship. The other group is not made up of individual 'you's bound together any more than we are simply a clump of 'I's, and the other community is one with whom we must speak. Rosenzweig limits that speech to the judgment, a pronouncement, that the others are God's enemies, but he does so only long enough to then turn that judgment against the 'we': if the 'we' cannot yet include everyone, then the 'we', too, is susceptible to judgment. Our saying 'we' can only be true in the future. As a performance asserting our current redeemed condition, it is still false. In the conclusion of his grammar, Rosenzweig indicates that the inability of the 'we' and the 'ye' to achieve a single community leaves the ultimate task of redemption to God (HE). These moves are among the most questionable theologically, but the ground they break is important.

The averse reaction to 'we's today, I would suggest, arises primarily from our failure to recognize several key points: 1) That the 'we' truly spoken allows multiple voices to come together, 2) That such a 'we' is formed through individuals, through the nearest as found in the dual, and that it never completely escapes the awareness of the 'we two', and 3) That 'we' is counterpoised both with 'they' and with 'y'all'. Were we only to have 'they' as its opposite, then to say 'we' is to objectify the excluded. But to say 'we' with a 'y'all' is to become aware that there are other groups, other communities fully constituted as a 'we', and it is to raise hope for true intercommunal communication.

Rosenzweig's sense that every 'we' is in fact a judgment of condemnation is discomforting, but it also signals the full power of speech. In that context he comments:

> The word that they sing is We. As song it would be a last, a full concluding chord. But it can be last as word as little as any other word can. The word is never last, it is never merely spoken. Rather, it is always also a speaking. That is the authentic secret of language, its own life: the word speaks. (264/237)

As much as words do, and they do a great deal, they also lead to further doings. When God resolves the disagreement between the 'we' and the 'y'all', God does not speak—God *does*. The performance of speech points beyond speech into a fuller account of action, which will be the topic of Chapter 5. The crisis for speech is the point at which communities come into interaction. But Rosenzweig's insight is that our discovery of ourselves in relation to others, our experience of time, even our knowledge of the world, all happen in speaking. The grammatical thinking, moreover, displays profound resources for interpreting the different relationships that happen in speaking to other people. As a guide for interpreting what happens in speaking, grammar is helpful. As a description, a grammar even of Rosenzweig's variety, with its pragmatic and semantic impulses, cannot pose as a rigorous demonstration. Not all speech, even in the imperative, reveals; nor does all speech in the cohortative redeem. That even grammatically correct utterances can fail to enact those relations is a key issue for the next chapter. Rosenzweig's claim, however, is that the theological relations do happen in performative speech and that we can analyze those performances with this grammar.

CHAPTER 4

Speech as Performance (II):
Logic, Reading, Questions

THE PRESENTATION of Rosenzweig's grammar of revelation does not itself resolve the serious problems in philosophy of language. My purpose
in presenting the grammar within the contexts only of performance and
of grammar was to provide a base of interpretation from which we now
can consider the key claims that Rosenzweig makes about this view of
language. In examining those claims, Rosenzweig's analysis will intersect
with several general questions about language, offering indications of
how he can contribute to contemporary conversation.

The first task in this chapter will be to see how it is possible for spoken
words to have meaning, for the performative relations between people do
not make words have meaning, nor does performance itself create meaning. It is logic, even one such as is found in Rosenzweig's constructions of
introverted elements in Part I of *The Star of Redemption*, that makes
speech capable of bearing meaning. Rosenzweig claims that the relation
of logic and speech is one of prophecy and fulfillment. The key text here
is Cohen's *Religion of Reason out of the Sources of Judaism*, which Rosenzweig read in manuscript form at the front. Cohen's deployment of the
concept of correlation offered Rosenzweig a glimpse of how reason and
speech could meet in a way parallel to the meeting of a human being and
God. These parallel correlations are transposed by Rosenzweig in order
to resolve epistemological problems besetting the empirical turn to spoken speech.

But if performance cannot create the possibility of meaning, it certainly
cannot create the words themselves. In addition to the prophecy for
speech that logic provides, speech also requires a second prophecy: the
language of the poets. We do not invent our words, but take them from
society. Rosenzweig explores the invention of language in his theory of
art, especially poetry. The second section of this chapter will explore this
aspect of Rosenzweig's aesthetics, contrasting Greek tragedy with modern drama. The proper context for Rosenzweig's interpretation of the
biblical text is poetry. When the move from poetic language to revealing
speech is refracted through the question of reading a text, the biblical text
appears as a revelatory text. The revelation that occurs in the public reading of the Bible finally leads to the justification of Rosenzweig's claim to

avoid fanaticism. Theology is not fanatical when it takes speech as its organon, because speech is precisely the insertion of the private experience into a public realm—it is the revealing of myself to others, not the withdrawal into some inaccessible space.

In the latter part of this chapter I will raise a critical question for Rosenzweig, namely that of questioning itself. The proper location of the interrogative is a problem both for grammar and for speech-act theory. In one key paragraph in *The Star of Redemption*, Rosenzweig discusses the open question. For us, questioning emerges as the central form of theological discourse. Not only the question, following disaster, as a cry against God, but also the incessant questions of biblical commentary, of midrashic explorations, and of halakhic inquiry. The tension between the imperative and the interrogative creates, I believe, the space for Jewish theological reflection.

PROPHETIC THINKING, FULFILLING SPEECH

One of the key joints in this book is the move from logic to speech, a move I first make in exploring Rosenzweig's thought. That connection, however, is not simply a displacement, that previously we studied logic and did pure philosophy, but now we abandon those studies and only examine speech. Rosenzweig called his method New Thinking not because he was proposing comparative linguistics in place of transcendental idealism, but because he held that logic and speech were closely linked. This jointure requires exploration in order to understand how a postmodern philosopher examines experience. The previous presentation of Rosenzweig's grammatical thinking in many ways offers the answer: through speech, through the various uses of language. But that grammar needs a relation to what thought can accomplish on its own, else it degenerates again to the arbitrary nihilism as a reductio of positivism. While speech appears from experience, from the opening of one to another, it still requires a prior grounding in logic. Just what sort of 'foundationalism' or 'transcendentalism' this is for Rosenzweig is the task of this section. Rosenzweig himself calls it 'absolute empiricism', and we might rest more comfortably remembering the rigorous avoidance of all existential claims, really of all cognitive claims, in the discussion of Part I.[1]

I will first consider the relation of prophecy and fulfillment in Rosenzweig's New Thinking. The correlation he proposes between theological concepts is also the one he proposes between the silent language of logic and the speaking language of revelation. Second, I will turn to Cohen's *Religion* to see what Cohen thought possible in the correlation of logic and speech in the context of the correlation of God and human beings, but also to discover what Rosenzweig held to be Cohen's existentialist turn. Rosenzweig saw Cohen unconsciously moving beyond logic into the study of speech in this last work—moving in a way that was almost identical to Rosenzweig's own method. Rosenzweig's claim about Cohen's work is false, but examining it will help considerably in grasping Rosenzweig's thought. Third, I will present the way that logic is made to undergird speech in *The Star of Redemption*. Rosenzweig's claims about the unspoken, logical proto-words ('yes', 'no', and 'and'), as well as about the logic of the sentence, will conclude this section's discussion.

New Thinking

Rosenzweig's basic insight in interpreting experience is that experience is temporally distended; that is, it takes time to have experience, time that is not uniform.[2] The problem is that a collapse into experience as pure immediacy is a collapse of all communicable knowledge, a lapse into mere arbitrary subjectivism. This rejection of all communication and of all knowledge, this fanaticism of the moment, has already appeared in this book as a danger to be feared. The distension of time, the stretching out from the past into the present as the separation of logic from experience, can now clarify the possibility for knowledge. Rosenzweig's central discussion of that distension occurs in the discussion of miracles, which serves as the introduction to Part II of *The Star of Redemption*.

Miracles fell out of favor with theologians at precisely the moment when personal, private, perspectival, and utterly arbitrary, subjective experience hit its zenith in philosophy. At first glance these two events seem unconnected, but Rosenzweig joins the two in the introduction to Part II of *The Star of Redemption*. The decisive issue in Rosenzweig's analysis is the contrast between two definitions of miracle: 1) the exception to the laws of nature, and 2) the fulfilled prophecy. Rosenzweig downplays the effect of the Enlightenment's critique of the exceptional miracle, claiming that the prohibition on exceptional events can be traced back through a series of enlightenments, of which the scientific, liberal one is not the most corrosive for belief in miracles. The enlightenment that did cause a crisis for belief in miracles was historical, for the historical enlightenment taught us that each age refashions history to serve its own purposes. This enlightenment threatened the second and genuine concept of the miracle, because a miracle requires that there first be a prophecy of some future event; the miracle itself only happens when an event that was previously prophesied occurs. A fulfilled prophecy, thus, is a miracle. The historical enlightenment prevented the verification of the prophecy (not of the miracle) by showing that every historian rewrites history to make the events that occurred look as if they were predicted by the past. The problem of the historical enlightenment is that we can no longer gain any independent access to past events. Without the securing of the prophecy, we suspect that there are no miracles.

The broader significance of this distension is not hard to see: current experience is not intrinsically meaningful. Human knowing is temporal, built from a past into a present. This is especially important for the concept of revelation: in order to reveal myself, or for someone to reveal herself to me, the event of revelation requires a past, a prior horizon into which the revealing occurs. Thus relational experience is temporal, simply put, because it is based on the prior establishment of the two terms. To experience myself might not require the same sort of past, but it would then be only the discrete moment of that present experience. A fuller sort of experience is narrative (but perhaps this is not so surprising today).

The problem is how to secure the past as past, how to prevent the past from continually shifting so as to be slave to the present and so to make the telling of the story (the performance) dominate and even fabricate the story being told. Theology lost its hold on miracles when it abandoned creation as a concept in favor of the self-authenticating present of revelation. If that Protestant theology then looked to the future, it was only for continuing progress, but it treated the past in a manner that was all too subject to the historicists' critique. The anchoring concept should have been creation, but for various reasons Protestant theology had little interest in creation. Rosenzweig's concept of creation, following much medieval Jewish thought, is not that of a historical phenomenon that happened 5700 years earlier. Instead, his concept is of an emergence from concealment, an emergence which has already taken place. A completed action suitable for narration—and not a question of the chronology of fossils.

In place of the self-authenticating revelation, Rosenzweig proposes the prophecy/fulfillment version of revelation. Creation contains a prophecy of revelation, which is then fulfilled in the commandments of revelation. Creation itself does not include that revelation—prophecy need not know that it is pointing ahead. Instead, the miracle experienced reveals that it is a fulfillment of something already known, but not known as prophecy. It is a semiotic issue: a prophecy is a sign, but one need not know that it signifies until what it signifies occurs. In retrospect, the signified displays that it was already signified by the sign. The linking of sign and signified, discovered retrospectively, is the miracle—and so provides us with the revelation.

In *The Star of Redemption*, Rosenzweig uses this structure of prophecy and fulfillment equivocally, doing heavy work in several ways, two of which are relevant. Within the interpretation of speech as performance in Part II, prophecy and fulfillment link creation and revelation. Creation as speech in the indicative does not in itself require any theological commitment: the created world is the world known by science. Only after we hear the command to love do we discern that the world is created by God, that the world is created in order to come to completion by coming alive in love. It is the independence of the scientific knowledge of the world that guarantees the important relation of creation to revelation. The table of parts of speech is a prophecy of the utterances in the dialogue, but we cannot see that until we have had the dialogue. But Rosenzweig also proposes this distension between Part I and Part II of *The Star of Redemption*. Part I, with its proto-cosmos, is a kind of prophecy of the experiential cosmos of Part II. And this is where the important discussion of New Thinking occurs (as introduction to Part II). Rosenzweig proposes that theology and philosophy should come together. Philosophy could provide a foundation by its pure constructions in Part I, and theology can provide the interpretation of the immediate experience (the concepts of Creation, Revelation, Redemption) in Part II. Here is the familial trait of a correlation. But as clear as the first kind of prophecy is about the distension in time between prophecy and fulfillment, the second one challenges that model, for the three eternities are coeternal: Part I is a past that was never present, just as Part III is a future that will never be present. The relationships between the three parts are not simply that Part I is the world of creation, that a narrative runs from I to II to III. The true narrative is only in Part II—and to be even more specific, in some ways only in the discussion of creation.[3]

Thus the way in which the philosophical construction serves to shore up the past prior to theological experience is a bizarre kind of temporality. The past of those constructions is a past that has no hint of presence—it is the deep past which is pure, without any taint of experience. It is a much purer past than the past represented, the past of the indicative voice (of a constative utterance). The present of the imperative, the present of 'love me', is the purest present, the decisive speech of theology. Only because Rosenzweig can claim to see a prophecy of that experience in the pure constructions of logic can he certify the miraculous nature of revelation.

But that leads us forcibly to the key issue here: logic, in the form of the infinitesimal mathematics, must itself be a prophecy of speech. "That language of logic is the prophecy of a real language of grammar" (121/109). This must mean that logic, like all prophecy, is a sign pointing to some future, independent event. Speech, on the other hand, is what is foretold, but it is unable to establish itself as revelation except through the conformity to the previous foretelling. Speech goes beyond logic, providing us the lived, temporal experience of people. But logic provides a kind of foundation for that speech, allowing us to recognize it as the miracle, as the form of freedom that it is. Logic does not necessarily produce communication or revelation, but it is a necessary condition—and, indeed, logic is suited for revelation. The gap between logic and speech, therefore, is the gap that secures both the basis and the contingency—the miracle—of our freedom to relate to others, the meaning of revealing ourselves.

Cohen's Correlation in His Religion

Rosenzweig claims that he develops this exploration of speech not only from Rosenstock-Huessy, as discussed in the last chapter, but also from Cohen, particularly the Cohen of *Religion*. Cohen precedes Rosenzweig in exploring the dialogic structure of God's revelation, focusing on atonement before God's love, which later became the center of Rosenzweig's analysis. Rosenzweig's interpretation of Cohen, though tendentious, is important for seeing the emergence of this link of logic and speech. Rosenzweig claimed that Cohen had transgressed the bounds of pure reason, traveled beyond the logic of generation, in developing the concept of correlation (III, 209). Cohen becomes for Rosenzweig a pioneer precisely by transgressing his own system. The idea of correlation, according to Rosenzweig's interpretation, is not purely rational but is in fact empirical and existential. Before we look at the specific interpretative claims about logic and speech in *The Star of Redemption*, I wish to see just what Rosenzweig may have developed from (even against the intention and thought of) Cohen.

As I discussed in Chapter 1, Cohen's correlation is the central concept informing the *Religion*. Alexander Altmann decisively and finally exploded Rosenzweig's interpretation of this concept as a crypto-existential move by tracing correlation through its various uses in Cohen's system, discovering a remarkable continuity and consistency in its function.[4] I am largely following his essay, but our interests are slightly different.

Logic requires the possibility of recognizing the correlation of two independent realities. To return to Cohen's *Logic*, we can see that correlation serves there both as the model for the process of generation and for interrelationship of twos. First and most important, the relation of dx and x is one of correlation, where the x is required as a goal if the dx is to have any meaning.[5] Cohen, however, does not claim that they are reciprocal, nor that there is a genuine plurality at this level. The next step is the correlation of time and space. In Cohen's system time emerges before space, but the inner form (time) must be thought with (*mitgedacht*) the outer one (space). Cohen's characteristic pure generation rests on the concept of correlation—that what is inner can generate its matched outer through pure reason. But the logic of correlation also has one more important step: the emergence of a genuine reciprocity through the category of the concept (*Begriff*). Cohen claims that any concept is not merely an answer, but is itself a question. Indeed, the emergence of a concept begins a "new kind of reciprocal determination, of reciprocal action, which is accomplished in the system of the concept: the reciprocity of question and answer."[6] Here we are as close as we will come to Tillich's use of the term. Cohen, however, is claiming that concepts engender new ways of thinking, spawning new questions. Because any conceptual answer is incomplete, systematic thought is always a task, never a totality. Moreover, conceptual thought becomes dynamic, generating further correlations.

In the *Ethics*, moreover, Cohen presents the 'I' and 'you' as a correlation. It seems odd that Altmann neglects these texts, because they point out much that Rosenzweig finds most 'existentialist' in the *Religion*—here in the very heart of the idealistic system. (My fuller analysis of these texts occurs in Chapter 8.) As Cohen seeks to develop self-consciousness, he discovers that the 'I' is correlate with the other. Indeed, his claim is that in self-consciousness the other comes first, and only through the other do I become aware of myself. Moreover, the key point of this correlation is that I and the other cannot collapse into each other.[7] To become aware of myself as I, I must first become aware of the other. Cohen rejects any attempt to spin the other out of myself, to begin with a Cartesian self-consciousness and generate the other from that. However, Cohen does not stop with an other, a 'he', but moves beyond that to the 'you'. Here again there is a correlation, as he sees the 'you' as a way of moving to community (not unlike Rosenzweig). The very separation of each party of the correlation is guaranteed by the rational structure in which they are produced. From Cohen's perspective, long before the *Religion*, rational correlation was a way of generating a plurality of persons.

Correlation, in Cohen's *Religion*, is a methodological reciprocity between our concepts of the human and the divine. We can neither understand what a human being is without understanding the same of God, nor vice versa. The basis of this correlation is the creation of the human being in reason. God has put the divine spirit in the human by investing the human with reason (both practical and theoretical). The human is thus created to rationally know and to love God; God creates the human in order to be known and loved. The more fully the human comes into relationship with God, the more fully human it becomes; the more fully the divine is brought into relationship with the human, the more fully articulated the divine becomes. Cohen is most of all concerned with the critical epistemological issues—what can be known (in both theoretical and practical modes) about the ideas of God and of the human. The uniqueness of God becomes the paradigm for grasping the uniqueness of the individual person. Cohen retains a profound idealism here, but he does banish all monism, keeping God and the human firmly separated. His constant rejection of pantheism keeps him from allowing any ontological mediation between the God who is and the world that becomes.

Cohen never waivers, therefore, on the pure method of generation. Correlation is not an overture to some given experience, some break with idealism. Yet, as unrelenting as Cohen is on his pure generation, there is a slight modulation on the question of language in Cohen's thought. Rosenzweig wishes to argue for the prophetic relation of logic and language, in some sense replacing reason with speech in the correlation of the human with the divine. It is as though human beings were created in speech (as opposed to in reason). We might, therefore, wish to look for the hints of some performative theory of speech in Cohen. An easy place to start is with the second-edition introduction to the *Logic*, because there Cohen refuses to examine language and insists on the primacy of logic. Logic, historically speaking for Cohen, is too dependent on grammar, particularly Greek grammar. The problem lies in the term *logos*, which means both speech and reason (*Vernunft*).[8] Both speech and reason can thus claim to have the contents of logic, but only reason can produce pure knowledge, can provide a foundation. Cohen repeatedly interprets issues in sentential logic as originating in a mathematical logic, and not in a spoken grammar, for the explicit purpose of freeing logic from any contingency or predetermining experience.[9] This founding of logic accomplished, the question could return: What is the status of speech and its grammar? Are they given in experience but founded on pure logic, or can they, too, be generated ultimately through the same pure rational method?

Just this doubt hovers over the discussions of the 'I' and 'you,' even in the *Ethics*. Consider this passage (italics mine):

> The other changes itself to I and you. You is not he. He would be the other. He stands in danger of becoming treated as it. You and I simply belong together. *I cannot say 'you', without relating myself to you;* without uniting the you in this relation to the I.[10]

The act of speaking the word 'you' is the issue. The 'I', 'you', 'he', and 'it' (no 'she' here) are obviously personal pronouns—hence are they borrowed from grammar, from the impure logic of speech. Or are they generated from pure reason? Perhaps we don't need to resolve Cohen's position, but we cannot help but see that the speaking of those specific words is what requires certain kinds of correlational ethics. Their meaning seems bound utterly with the speaking of them, as the performance itself requires a relation between the two people. This move is even more striking as we look at the key issue borrowed from Cohen's *Religion* in Rosenzweig's *The Star of Redemption*: confession.

Cohen argues that atonement is the ultimate goal of monotheistic religion. The Day of Atonement becomes the high point, the fulfillment of religious consciousness. Cohen harps on Rabbi Akiva's words, "Blessed are you, O Israel, for who cleanses you and before whom do you cleanse yourself? It is your father in Heaven."[11] Here is Rosenzweig's emphasis on confession as self-cleansing in the presence of God's love. But what is still more important for our purposes is the emphasis Cohen places on confession (*Bekenntnis*). The confession of sin is itself the punishment that the sinner takes upon himself.[12] Cohen insists that the purpose of punishment is to induce the sinner to will his or her own punishment (and thus to avoid violating autonomy)—and Cohen had made this point long before in the *Ethics*.[13] But Cohen also makes some interesting points about the act of confession. Confession must bring the new beginning of the repenting person into the public; it cannot be completed "in the silence and secrecy of the human heart."[14] Here is the need for a performance, a public act which must go beyond the mere inner thought or feeling, or even inner action. Confession is an extroversion (and Cohen goes on to generate the congregation as the proper community for this action).

For all that, the relation of logic and speech for Cohen is still slanted heavily away from Rosenzweig's own moves. The few times he does emphasize performative speech are not developed—indeed, it is hard to imagine Cohen not arguing that the effects produced in speech, the actions done by speaking to others, should themselves be determined by pure reason, constructed through generation in correlation. Rosenzweig certainly misunderstood what Cohen was doing in his *Religion*. On the other hand, Rosenzweig's own method of moving from pure logic to the grammar of speech is in some important ways suggested by that passage from the *Logic*. The reality of the extroversions, of the living relationships between correlates, could require augmentation from the other part of logic, speech. Pure logic can serve as a prophecy of speech precisely because it stands independent of all experience and so cannot be impugned as a rigged history. Not to say that logic itself has no history (a subject on which Cohen truly excels), but that the better we get at doing logic purely, the freer it becomes to serve as an independent foundation upon which speech will develop correlations. Cohen's attempt to use logic to accomplish all relations again seems least promising in the matter of accounting for the freedom, the contingency, of human interactions.

Urworte and Ursatz

But now it is time to examine just how Rosenzweig makes his prophetic link. The central task is to unearth a linguistics of pure logic—a logical prophecy of speech's own linguistics. The technical discussion of the logic that we met in the construction of the elements in the second chapter can wait no longer. This logic is both a mathematics constructed through the infinitesimal, and a prophecy of language, a formal logic of sentences (or propositions). As prophecy it signifies the revealing action of speech, which can only be fulfilled when people open themselves to others in speech. As mathematics, however, it stands prior to that performance of speech and is rigorously independent of Rosenzweig's grammatical thinking.

We may recall that the constructions were made of an affirmation of a nothing of knowledge, a negation of that nothing, and the binding of these two together, which Rosenzweig termed 'Yes', 'No', and 'And'. The 'Yes', particularly the first 'Yes' of God's essence, holds in it "the unlimited possibilities of reality. It is the proto-word (*Urwort*) of speech" (29/27). 'Yes' as a logical term does not speak, but opens up a realm of experiential possibility. It is not a sentence but it underlies words. "It is the silent escort of all sentence parts, the confirmation of the 'Sic', the 'amen' of each word. It gives each word in the sentence its right to existence" (ibid.). It is a confirmation of the potential for an individual word. The 'No', on the other hand, is a property of the sentence.

> The originary No is similarly actual in each word in the sentence, . . . While the Yes as 'Thus' con-firms the individual word, that is as its static enduring worth, independent from the place that it takes with the other words in the sentence; the No goes directly to this place of the word in the sentence. As 'not-other' it will be oriented in this single word's place, through its own particularity against the 'others'—not the static peculiarity, rather one dependent on the whole sentence, on the 'other' stable parts of the sentence. (34/32)

The 'Yes' and 'No' secure a possibility for a linguistics of words in sentences, a possibility for signification. They are empty, formal, and at the same time pure. 'Yes' secures the semantics, that individual words can have fixed meanings; 'No' secures the syntax, that the meaning of the words will depend on the interaction with the other words. 'Yes' and 'No' are not spoken words in this context, but are the pure prophecies of possible words. Rosenzweig does not think that words derive their meaning from the one or the other, but from both independently. He asserts that the smallest meaningful unit of speech is the sentence (that words on their own do not have meaning), but words do have a certain invariance of meaning in different sentences. Just as we needed both 'Yes' and 'No' to do the mathematics in the last chapter, we need them to secure both poles of meaning in the logic that is a prelinguistics here.

Moreover, Rosenzweig insists that at this point there are no sentences. 'Yes' and 'No' refer only to a prelanguage of algebraic symbols (equations); on their own they cannot make even a prelinguistic equation. 'And' is also needed, but while it serves to bring the two independent proto-words together it is not itself a proto-word. "No something emerges in it. It is not directly out of nothing, like Yes and No. Rather, it is the sign of the process which lets the finished form grow between what emerged in the Yes and No" (256/239). God's freedom became arbitrary choice; God's essence, fate. The 'And' serves to bind together the two independent (dare we say it, correlate) proto-words, without creating a synthesis. Rosenzweig harps on the co-originality of 'Yes' and 'No' because he refuses the Hegelian dialectic which forces the 'Yes' to bear a 'No' and the 'No' thus to become another 'Yes', bearing yet another 'No', etc. The necessary dialectic must be stopped at the beginning, with a separation (and correlation) of the two origins of logic and speech.

This prelinguistics is still more complex because in each book of Part I of *The Star of Redemption* Rosenzweig has another algebraic equation. The 'Yes's and the 'No's change form.[15] Rosenzweig explains with the third 'Yes' just what each 'Yes' contributes:

> In the first case [God, 'A'], the force was made actual that made the individual word have any meaning [*Sinn*] at all. In the second [world, '=A'] that force [was made actual] that secured the equality of its reference [*Bedeutung*]. Here [human, 'B'] the direction of the originary Yes appears in the force that founds the individual word not merely as one and always the same; rather as its specific meaning, but also in distinction from the specificity, which the individual use makes always new; rather as that specificity that the word has before all of its uses [e.g., character]. (70/65)

Thus the constitution of the possibility of the word's meaning has three steps: 1) the possibility of any meaning, 2) the sameness of reference, and 3) the specificity prior to specific usage. These are at the same time represented algebraically by 1) the universal formal affirmation ('A'), 2) the motion towards universal order (= 'A'), and 3) the specific formal affirmation ('B'). I will not continue decoding the letters, but this notion of pure formal prelinguistics displays the conditions for a word holding its meaning in different uses. Rosenzweig does not pile up three negative levels parallel to these positive ones, but we might well see that syntactical meaning will also juxtapose three steps: 1) the possibility of context, 2) the variation of context, and 3) the specificity of usage, with different words. In this sort of transcendental linguistics, we can see how Rosenzweig explored various aspects of philosophy of language which now would be more clearly distinguished. This securing of semantics, syntax, pragmatic constraint, and so on in a transcendental way has certain affinities to issues in Apel's and Habermas' work. Its somewhat suspicious emptiness is linked to what Rosenzweig himself requires: that this prelinguistics yield no insight into speech without the subsequent praxis of speaking. Rosenzweig's project involves seeing how the possibility of a sentence bearing specific meaning and reference depends on these modes of thought.

This linguistics of a prelanguage can now appear to serve the prophetic function for language. To make this claim, we need to move beyond what is clear enough: that Rosenzweig claims to determine these formal possibilities for speech without recourse to any experience. The purity of philosophical construction remains decisive. But we also need to establish two further claims: 1) that logic cannot construct all the way through speech, and 2) that speech does depend on this pure logic for a foundation.

The first claim is clarified in Rosenzweig's discussion of creation in which he distances himself from idealism, particularly from the sort in which reason generates everything (Cohen and Neoplatonism). Idealism refused to grant the temporal distension that marks the relation of creation and revelation. It wanted to derive revelation and even redemption on the grounds of the created world through the use of reason alone. Thus it dried up the freedom both in God's revelation and in human faith, to say nothing of the later freedoms found in redemption. But in order to force everything, to provide rational knowledge freed from the contingency of these two-party relationships, it could not trust speech.

> It lacked the simple trust in speech. Idealism was not disposed to take note and to answer this voice, which appears ungrounded, but all the more really sounds in people. It required grounds, accountability, calculability, everything that language could not offer, and invented Logic for itself, which offered all of these. It offered all of these, only not what language possessed: its self-evidence. (161/145)

Rosenzweig's complex critique of idealism culminates in the recognition that the criterion of pure rational knowledge forced the idealistic constructions of the world and of God to become ultimately derivative from the one who thinks and knows this cosmos, from the 'I'—the transcendental subject. Such an 'I' is not the 'I' of speech, because it must reduce God and world, in advance, to objects of its own cognition and will. But then there is no longer a relation (correlation?!) between two elements, and so logic remains logic, and in terms of Rosenzweig's system the idealist does not ever leave Part I. Idealism's flight from lived time, from the discontinuities of conversation, prevents it from grasping the deeper relations that emerge in speech.

The second claim is the key claim, particularly after the end of modern philosophy. Rosenzweig makes it most emphatically at the end of the introduction to Part II of *The Star of Redemption*. He writes of protowords as secret grounds that lie concealed under living speech (121/109). Elsewhere he speaks of them as grounding the being of the root words of speech (the table of grammar from Book 1, Part II). Rosenzweig's terms *Urwort* (proto-word) and *Stammwort* (root word) themselves provide an image of the relation, for the *ur* is the root, the *stamm* a stem. The proto-words are roots from which the spoken words of ontology—the stems—emerge (even though I have translated those spoken words with the almost English term *root-words*). The proto-words provide this rootedness, or, alternatively, "the solid ground under the feet" (122/109). And this image of a stem's relation to a root illuminates the moves in Part II in the discussions of 'I' and 'good', which are the first expression of the proto-words (*Urwort*) in speech. Their capacity to range across all speech, to affirm every existent thing ('good'), or to assert the radical specificity against everything else ('I') is grounded on the prior logic of 'Yes' and 'No'. Even the sentence ('He is good') depends on the logical work of 'And', joining the proto-words together. The analyses of speech as performance, with the various claims of universal deployment, syntactical implications, specific reference, etc., all are assured, and in fact prophesied, by the pure logic that Rosenzweig has constructed in Part I. The grammar of speech, with its performative qualities, is grounded on the possibilities that words will have stable meanings and that context (syntax) will have recognizable patterns. Even if we collapsed Rosenzweig's grammar back to Austin's semantic lists of different sorts of performatives, we would still need to examine what makes it possible for the word 'promise' to have the specific range of performative force it has. Because neither words nor the grammatical structure of speech are always and at every moment invented anew, the foundations for the use of language must underlie the specific speech of our time. The foundationalism here is not that of the idealist, leading organically to the construction of the house, but it also is not the avoidance of the conditions for meaning and reference which many who make the linguistic turn propose. The objective possibility for speech lies in a pure logic of silent symbols.

God Speaks with Human Language

If logic serves to ground spoken words but cannot produce them, where do the words come from? The possibility of revealing myself with sentences and words is not the same as the words I use to reveal myself. Rosenzweig discovers that there is not only one prelanguage, but two: logic and art.

> In the catalogue of language of the mute pre-world, it [mathematics] must share with art [*Kunst*], which is the language of the inexpressible. Similarly, from it the founding concepts, the essence, comes to expression. But art here is the subjective language, the "speech" to some extent of that mute world; Mathematics, as already noted in its necessary written-ness, is the objective language, the "meaning" of that silence. (139/125)

Mathematics is properly a written language, one of symbols and equations on a page, on a blackboard, on a VDT. No one "speaks" mathematics out loud, except in service to the written. But art, especially poetry, has already created an audible language, even a grammatically correct language, a language that is not yet speech. In this section we will trace that parallel prophecy, from a language used to maintain the isolation of people, to the speech in that language of the prophets, to the role of biblical texts in Rosenzweig's presentation of speech, to an explanation of how speech is theological without depending on any sort of religious experience.

Poetry and Prophecy

The first step is to repeat with this new prelanguage of art the claims made for the logical pre-language. The move to experience, to speech, requires a grounding of sorts in a prior language. Art serves as an unspeaking language, and it serves as a prophecy of the speech of revelation. Rosenzweig links the exploration of nonspeaking art to empiricism. The isolated experience of empiricism is not fully human because it lacks the distension in time. Without that distension, meaning and truth cannot be secured; instead, we are close to the arbitrary subjectivism of the fanatic. We must have learned a language before we speak and reveal ourselves; otherwise, revelation would be impossible.

> But because one has in reality the language in art before that time, while one's inner life is still inexpressible, then art is just the language of this still inexpressible, so it is evermore and thus language exists complete from creation, and so the miracle of speech of revelation becomes sign of divine creation and thus of genuine miracle. (212–13/190–91)

Rosenzweig treats art in three ways in *The Star of Redemption*. Only the first time is it the silent prelanguage of the inexpressible. Neither art nor any other gesture to the empirical in isolation will deliver us the knowledge or insight we are pursuing. This goes for linguistic usage as much as for measurements of the stars and planets. Only with that binding of prophecy and fulfillment, only with an established separation of past sign and present actuality, can we be freed from the doubts that our experience is arbitrary and our interpretation fantastical. What is quite amazing, moreover, is that Rosenzweig requires two prophecies—and while the one is altogether pure, the other (this one, art) is intrinsically subjective and empirical. Empiricism requires the distension in order to become secure—and the interpretation of speech requires that art has already created the language with which it will speak.

But what is that language? The language of the inexpressible (*unaussprechliche*). The words not of speech, but of the spoken (*Ausgesprochen*). But who utters such words, and what is it about which they cannot speak? The answer lies in ancient tragedy, in the introverted self constructed in Part I, Book 3, of *The Star of Redemption*. That construction produces the authentic self, a heroic person who wills himself, who wills to be his own finite being, who has an authentic resolution toward his own death. But he appears as the person who cannot reveal himself, who must stay burrowed into, buried within, himself. But how does someone display this lack of speech, this burrowing self? Not in a narrative, because the absence of self-revealing would not be missed in a narrative. Rather on the stage, in the drama. Rosenzweig comments: "Tragedy created just on this account the art form of drama: to be able to display the silence. In narrative poetry silence is the rule; the dramatic knows on the contrary only talk [*Reden*], and so thereby silence first becomes eloquent [*beredt*]" (83/77). Especially Aeschylus put the character on the stage to not reveal himself. In his plays there is much talking, and in the later attic plays even debating, but never the interrelationship of selves. The soliloquy, the role of the chorus, the absence of love scenes, all point to the absence of speech. The will of the self clashes with other wills, but wills only itself, and only to enclose (to burrow into) itself. But this means that ancient drama is an example of what we recognized the need for long ago: utterance that is not speech, in our technical sense of self-revelation.

The art before speech, the art that appears in Part I, is a self-enclosed, world-excluding, keeping-to-itself sort of art. Rosenzweig follows German thought and claims that ancient Greek art (and indeed culture as a whole) provides the needed example. He then extroverts that art in Part II, in his second discussion of art. In moves that I will not explore here, the separate, introverted dimensions of aesthetics become the bases for extroverted (relational or revelational) art. Our concern here is that the poets coin language—a language that could serve to constitute the theological relations, but which need not. Poetry may belong with thought, but it does not necessarily produce speech or revealing. Poetic language is humanity's. Poetic language is originally coined to withhold oneself, to isolate, and so to maintain one's own will and power. But its ultimate use (in revelation) will be to humiliate oneself and to be opened in speaking and listening. Like the pure logic, it stands on its own before the theological sequence of Part II gets started—and so can be a sign of revelation.

But how then does God reveal in this poetic language? God must speak in human words, so that we will be able to understand what God reveals. The exclusion of fanaticism requires that we insist on the public nature of revelation, which is why words are required. But even more strikingly, Rosenzweig rules out private conversation. God speaks to the people, but not with a heavenly voice. God speaks in the voice of the prophet:

> The prophet is not a mediator between God and man. He does not receive the revelation and then pass it on; rather, immediately the Voice of God sounds from out of him. God speaks as I immediately out of him. The genuine prophet

is not like a master of the great plagiarism who lets God talk and give to him the revelation which occurred in secret and then passes it on to the astonished bystanders. He does not let God talk at all, rather when he opens his mouth, God already speaks. (198/178)

It is with human words, from a human mouth, that God reveals God's self. God may speak out of any human mouth—we do not know who will speak the 'I', the 'I' that commands "Love me." Speech is revelation, when we abide by the uses of language discussed in Chapter 3. The performative relations that emerged in Rosenzweig's grammar are what constrain the appearance of this speaking of God; only the intensely ethical relations of commanding love and forming communities are grammatically required. We have excluded, in the meantime, the appeal to a private communication, and for some we may have taken the prophets down a notch. But we are now left with a series of problems that are all the more pressing: If anyone can be the vehicle of God's revelation, than how can we claim that it is from God? Why should it not be simply human? Why not just think of revelation as the self-disclosing of speech of two human beings? Why emphasize the theological dimension at all? Rosenzweig's answer lies in three sections of *The Star of Redemption*, one in each book of Part II, each called "The Word of God," and each an interpretation of a biblical text. By way of a digression on written texts, we can approach Rosenzweig's justification of a theological vocabulary to interpret speech as performance.

Writing and Reading

The digression is striking: I propose to shift to writing from speaking. While the transcendental prelinguistics of the last section drew us near to the projects of Habermas and Apel, the concern for the way in which writing is a performance can bring us into proximity with Derrida. Despite the obvious opposition in the appropriations of Austin's discussions of performatives between Derrida's interest in iteration and misquotation, and Habermas' focus on the conditions for communication, both are examining the contingency of communication. In Rosenzweig's terms, the question is how speech can be the act of opening oneself, but need not. Rosenzweig's examination of the two unspoken languages represents his struggle to account simultaneously for 1) the possibility of language's failure to become speech, and 2) the directedness (prophecy) in language toward revelatory speech. It would be ridiculous to claim that Habermas and Derrida are synthesized in Rosenzweig's *Star of Redemption*, but conversations can occur because Rosenzweig engages in a universal transcendental prelinguistics and also places a particular stress on the textuality of Holy Scripture.

Speech as performance seems utterly different from the written text. Speech is a lived event, but a book is a thing—and it can at most be given. Indeed, when Rosenzweig criticizes Islam, which is a continual foil to Judaism and Christianity in Part II,[16] he claims that Islam failed to understand the two-party aspect of revelation. Rosenzweig claims that revelation in Judaism and Christianity never becomes merely a book, but that

> the first word of revelation to Mohammad says: Read! The page of a book is shown to him. . . . The book is sent down from heaven. Can there be a more complete turning away from the representation that God Himself descended, giving Himself to people, giving Himself over to them? But He reigns in His highest heaven and sends to people—a Book. (186/166)

This marks a great distance. In genuine revelation God gives himself to people in loving them, in commanding them, in opening himself to them, who will yet have to receive, to be faithful. On the other hand, we have what many would call a traditional denigration of writing, of the text, and of Islam. But now we must climb back through Rosenzweig's own use of another book to see how writing, or perhaps better how reading, can serve revelation.

To put out a furthest point of reference, we should look ahead to Part III of *The Star of Redemption*, where the goal is to practice a new communal silence—not the silence of withdrawal and reserve, but the silence of illumination and community. The biblical text serves a key function in that redemptive silence. It is communal listening to the scriptural passage of the week that helps to form the community.

> Communal hearing, that would be nothing but hearing, the hearing where a group becomes 'all ears', arises not through a speaker, rather only through the retreat of a living speaking person behind the mere reader, and not only, but behind the reading person, rather back to the read word. (343/309)

Rosenzweig contrasts reading with political speech, in which interruptions are welcome, to emphasize that this listening to a text being read, a text that is shared, occurs without interruption and creates a solidarity. The text, moreover, is a pretext for a sermon. Such speech always recedes before the text. "Its essence is, therefore, not that it is a talk, but that it is exegesis; the reading of the written-word is the main thing" (344/310). The distinctive performance made possible by what is written is not in the act of writing but in the act of reading. Despite the bashing of the Muslims, Rosenzweig actually installs the written text—in its performance—at the center of theological community.

But we have already tipped our hand. The text, the book, is not revelation. But the text speaks when it is read. The reading of the text becomes a new speaking. And in addition to the recitation of the text, the reading also provides for preaching. But let Jewish form stand in for the Protestant one: reading is both recitation and midrash. Thus the Holy Scriptures are not the revelation, but reading and commenting upon them allows for revelation. (Barth's emphasis on the revelatory power of the Gospel preached in church is similar, while the overlap with Derrida is complex because Rosenzweig norms the iterability of the text with a performance that can reveal truly.) And so Rosenzweig, in those three sections in Part II mentioned earlier, engages in the second half of reading. He does not recite the texts, because the performance of *The Star of Redemption* is not to form a listening community. But he does create midrashim on three texts, and in so doing displays how the texts reveal that speech is theological.

Three Midrashim

The three texts Rosenzweig examines are Genesis 1.1–1.31, the Song of Songs, and Psalm 115. In each case Rosenzweig provides a 'grammatical analysis', displaying the conformity between the grammatical concepts of the three different moods (indicative, imperative, cohortative) and the grammatical performances in the texts. The last of the three texts focuses on how we sing of redemption despite its futural promise. It does not advance the discussion of the cohortative but displays it within the text. The other two midrashim, however, contain discussions that are more fruitful for our concerns.

Before presenting the first text, Rosenzweig discusses the place of belief and trust in speech. The elements of Part I, constructed with mathematical logic, were described and determined. But only with speech does belief truly enter. The route of Creation-Revelation-Redemption is believed. Rosenzweig admits that to believe this sequence is hard, because we live only in a specific moment and 'were not present at Creation', to say nothing of not having lived through all three. Yet speech is capable of joining together the lived experience of the miracle, of the conformity of prophecy and fulfillment that we have lived, with the whole route. And, says Rosenzweig, "to trust it [speech] is easy, because it is in us and around us, and nothing else like it comes to us from outside, just as it echoes from our inside to our outside" (167/151). Speech, if it can be made to connect these three moods, will do the job.

Speech opens up a theological dimension beyond trustworthiness because "the ways of God are different from the ways of people, but God's word and the human word are the same. What one hears in one's heart as one's own human speech is the word that comes out of the mouth of God" (167–68/151). This reaffirmation that God speaks in human words leads us to a deep trust—but it does not force us to see these words as

God's. Rosenzweig argues that the grammar he has expounded in Book 1 of *The Star of Redemption* is also the word God spoke and that we find written in Genesis. In the grammatical analysis (midrash) Rosenzweig singles out the parts of speech to show how the doubled ontologies deriving from the basic affirmation ('good') are the very structure of the biblical text. The person, tense, mood, and so on, all confirm the theology of speech in the indicative mood. Moreover, true dialogue does not appear in this text, but only intimates (prophesies) the true dialogue that occurs first in the revelation to Abraham, and then again to the prophets. The text serves to display the very theology that grammatical thinking constructed—except that in both cases there is no demonstration of God's authority. This speech lacks an author, and the biblical text can only assert God's speech, because God still does not speak with man. God remains unrevealed, even in creation.

And so we turn to the very heart of Rosenzweig's text. The second of three books in the second of three parts, which Rosenzweig himself named the *Herzbuch*, the text written in the throes of passionate love and the book in which lived experience breaks in and orients the whole work—most of all the theology of spoken speech. To approach the Song of Songs is a difficult matter. Rosenzweig begins with a prefatory discussion of simile. One might say that God's revelation is like a lover's love.

If speech is more than a comparison (*Vergleich*), and is now a simile or analogy (*Gleichnis*)—or in fact more, if human love is an analogue of divine love (or in fact more)—then the 'I' that we hear, which sounds opposite to our 'you', would also be discoverable in Scripture. Indeed, Rosenzweig has used Scripture throughout the dialogue of love as a script, as a source of the dialogue. Now he looks to the Song of Songs to confirm that the lover is divine. The Song of Songs requires a reading either as a human love lyric or as a mystic revelation of divine love, revealed in the purely sensual love lyric. Rosenzweig claims that only when we hear a text that reveals God's love directly, without the intervention of a simile, only when the command to love is heard as God's and not as 'like the human command to love', only then will the text reveal God's love.

Rosenzweig also recapitulates the history of interpretation, particularly the modern phases. For until the beginning of the nineteenth century, the text was always a revelation of God's love. The 'I' and 'you' were both between man and woman and between a soul and God. The text was at the same time transcendent and immanent—and neither stood as the 'real' of which the other was merely a simile. As presented in my grammatical analysis, a human loves because God loves her or him first (and not because God has a relationship somehow similar to that between lovers). But then the idea that God might love, love with the intensity and particularity of this sort of sensual lyric, became untenable. The text *could* not mean that, and so it became a merely human lyric. A person might love God, but God could not speak, could not demand love from an individual person with that lover's impatience. The next step was to take its lyricism away and to transform it from merely human to merely worldly. The desire and demand of an 'I' for a 'you' was replaced by an epic interaction of 'he' and 'she'. The text became a series of epic dramatic actions, and not only did God not love with that sensual desire, but human beings did not either.

Textual critical research, however, pulled itself back out of the mire. The clue to epicizing and fracturing the text was the different voices and persons, particularly the shepherd and the king. Folkloric research now revealed that peasants enact a royal wedding in order to magnify a peasant wedding. But that returns the lyrical and analogous to the Song of Songs, for the shepherd is made to feel himself a king in the midst of his peasant wedding—and that feeling like a king yields more. "And there a supersensuous reference surmounts a sensuous meaning: the shepherd who the groom is, is replaced by the king who he feels himself to be" (224/201). The analogy returns and becomes more than mere simile—the text announces that he becomes the king for the very moment of this love. Rosenzweig finds this return of analogy to be precisely the point:

> Love cannot be "purely human." Insofar as it speaks—and it must speak, because there is no other expression of love save speech—insofar as it speaks, it becomes already something superhuman; because the sensuousness of words is full to the brim with its divine supersense. Love is, like speech itself, sensuous-supersensuous. (224/201)

Love, like speech, serves as a binding between the human and the divine. My experience of being loved, my hearing of a command to love from another, cannot be merely human. I cannot hear that command from a heavenly voice, but the command to love comes from beyond the person who speaks. It is the radical nature of love, its intensity, urgency, and the weight behind it of infinite essence that corresponds to the introverted element we could construct through logic, the element that is God. Loved by another before I can love, the other is a medium of God's love for me. But the text before us, the Song of Songs, is unwilling to sever the sensuous, erotic, delicious, and delirious passion of human love from the divine. Rosenzweig does not claim that we will hear voices or see visions, that we will have some religious experience of the numinous. Rather, we will experience God's command to love through the voice and the words of a sensuous and probably sensual being. The Song of Songs, moreover, shows the performative reality of love: it is incessant, full of 'I', demanding, wistful, always in the present, lacking a plan or a sense of history, and most of all it is direct speech—it is the revealing of the lovers to one another, the revealing of their love. To read the text is to perform a script not of epic drama, but of lyric revelation. Here to speak is to love, to reveal oneself as loving—not by proclamation, but by commandment. But such revelation—such love, such speech—is already to experience the transcendent demand, the infinite command.

Rosenzweig can thus perform a midrashic reading and draw the confirmation of his grammatical analyses from the text of Holy Scripture. The human-superhuman dimensions of this experience of speech require interpretations—but the distension, the diachronic lapse between both art and logic and this experience of speech provide the solidity to recognize that this transcendence is the revelation of God. A mere romantic (and Rosenzweig is obviously a romantic, though not a mere one) would be content to invoke some higher power—call it love, or Being, or spirit. But such an invocation would have no ground. To limit the range, indeed to focus and ground the interpretation of the human-superhuman dimension in love, requires that long before speaking and loving occur, some prior signification has been established, even if that prior sign cannot be read altogether for what it is. If Rosenzweig's theology instructs us, if it leads us to see the divine side of love and speech, then it accomplishes this precisely by all of the creaks and groans of the systematic architecture.

The performance of *The Star of Redemption* itself is awkward and retrospective. I doubt that Rosenzweig believed that the neopagan, the person who held solely to the authenticity of the hero, the language that is still silent, would accept the account of revelation offered there. Nor is it likely that the post-Christian, secularized philosopher, or person-in-the-street agnostic would be persuaded that whatever love life he or she might have was the experience of divine revelation. Whatever else *The Star of Redemption* is, it is not a persuasive tract. But the New Thinking Rosenzweig does perform is not merely a rehash of romanticism and late idealism. The unpredictability and utter contingency of this most personal experience, of love, is preserved without abandoning thought to the rampant fantasies and vagaries of fanatical thinking. Rosenzweig struggles to hold the objectivity of interpretation and the inner experiential reality together. At the same time, he confirms that binding with midrashic readings of Scripture.

THE QUESTION OF THEOLOGY

Rosenzweig concludes his midrash on the Song of Songs with the issue of the publication (*Veröffentlichung*) of the miracle of love. This desire to publicize is itself expressed in the scream (*Schrei*), for the lovers' dialogue goes beyond itself, yearning for an opening up of the world for their love.

This is on the one hand a transition from revelation to redemption, but it is also an important stopping point. In the grammatical analysis of revelation, Rosenzweig also ended with this scream, which he viewed as an open question. In this concluding section of Chapter 4, our question for Rosenzweig becomes the topic.

Our question, beyond the architectural inversion and extroversion, beyond the romantic hymns of love in love, our question comes from across the abyss of the Holocaust. Where is God? And why was God silent, absent, impotent, anything but loving, in the atrocities of this century? These questions might best be lodged with the next chapter, when Rosenzweig's historical vision is at issue, but perhaps if we travel with him, then we must wonder what kind of theological speech performances are these questions. Our theology today seems to consist in large measure of questions. Indeed, we might go one step further: we wish to interrogate God on God's role and absence in these events. Can we ask God a question? Rosenzweig has ruled out the private conversation with heavenly voices, leaving us talking with human words and human speakers, even if speaking to God. Whom do we ask?

This section begins with an attempt to reconstruct the grammar through an exploration of the missing mood of Rosenzweig's grammar: the interrogative. The questions that Rosenzweig does explore, both the seeking of a 'you' and the scream, will provide us with some analyses from which to develop this new mood. But then we must broaden the questioning and reclaim the interrogative as the mood for Jewish theological inquiry. Questioning can be removed from the indicative representation of what is the case and be placed in tension with the command to be given an answer. The question emerges as a relation much more tenuous and dependent on the other than the imperative. I conclude with a hint of the possibility that speech, and through it theology, could be coordinated around the polarity between the interrogative and the imperative, between questioning and commandment.

The first problem, but not the most complex, is that the interrogative is not a mood, at least not according to Rosenzweig nor to Rosenstock-Huessy—and in this they follow grammatical tradition. Insofar as grammar is our guide to speech as performance, there appears to be no distinctive performative relation to an other that is represented by the question. Yet if the imperative both reveals my self and demands from another, while the cohortative includes me and convokes a 'we', then can we not see how the interrogative invites the other's speech? It is true that the interrogative has many uses (as does the imperative), but it is not clear that we may not find a basic performative relation for use in interpreting the theological issues. The questioner seems to stand in a certain kind of ignorance, one that speaks of some desire to know, and at the same time, some failure of self-sufficiency. I ask of another, revealing my ignorance and my insufficiency to discover for myself.

We might even go further and try to distinguish the difference between being asked and being commanded. The latter can produce faith, as the other reveals herself to me in the command. What do I do when another asks me a question? What is the reception of the invitation? Being asked, like being commanded, does seem to put me in the other's service—but the need to answer the former is different from the capacity to be already answerable, which the command requires. Before the command I discover my guilt and my ability to respond and to answer for my own past. In answering a question, I discover either my ability or my incapacity to satisfy the questioner in the present. A dialogue of question and answer, or more likely of question and question, opens up the present, whereas the command's urgency overwhelms it. The temporality of interrogation is more complicated than I wish to explore here, but already some of the features of this mood come into view.

The grammarians' resistance to the interrogative may well go back to the Greek grammars. And despite the sketch above, it is clear that interrogatives have varying performative forces. The questions that are most relevant are not the informational ones, the question that is really a kind of crypto-indicative, where both the questioner and the questioned are irrelevant. The presence of pronouns, especially of the 'you', characterizes the questions that have clearest implications for theology. And the question after the 'you' is one of the two questions that Rosenzweig does interpret.

When the 'I' first breaks out of itself, it asks, "Where are you?" Rosenzweig links this to God's asking for Adam in the garden (Gen. 3.9), but he pushes this further (195/175). This is a revealing of the 'I', because it now believes in the existence of a 'you'; it just doesn't know where to find it. This is not a representational problem (such as, What is the essence of a 'you'?), but is a problem for spatial experience—Where are you, so I can talk with you? Even in seeking another, the self reveals itself, and the question displays the yearning of the self for another. A question is an opening up toward the relationship and is already speech, even before the 'you' speaks.

But the second question is the harder one, because Rosenzweig describes the scream as an open question (206/185). The scream is a cry for redemption, an open question to the redeemer—Why does God tarry? The unfulfilled wish for redemption stands as a question of the lovers' dialogue. The dialogue is thus bracketed by a question before and a question after, for redemption goes beyond love/revelation. But at this one critical moment when revelation breaks out of itself and threatens the dialogue, here for one and only one time in all of the grammatical analyses does Rosenzweig resort to the grammar of Hebrew Scriptures. "The speech-usage of the proto-speech of revelation expressed itself very deeply such an 'oh, that you' through the form of a question: 'Who would give, that you. . . .' " (206/185) The *mi yiten* is a remarkable form. In Hebrew Scriptures this question expresses a wish, a wish that the person asked for were actually present. It asks for an absent actor—most often God. It is the grammatical speciality of Job (appearing eleven times, and asking for God to be near, to speak, to write, and so on). The phrase that Rosenzweig draws on in the discussion of publication at the end of his midrash on the Song of Songs begins with this same phrase. It is a questioning of faith, of God. It is marked by a form of despair, but it does not abandon the hope for the dialogue. In place of the question that seeks an interlocutor in a certain kind of innocence, this is the question of the betrayed, of the survivor. And it is the question, literally, Who will give? The 'who' here is the question of contemporary theology. Who will God act in or through or with? Who is God become? Who speaks God's words? We wonder whether we now address God more as a 'you', or as this fundamental question 'who?'

The Hebrew grammar obtrudes itself here perhaps because it is so compact, so much the form that enacts or performs this relationship to God. But Rosenzweig is forced here to make an empirical grammatical move to a specific language. Indeed, some of the problems of grammar have been swept under the rug—the absence of gendered 'you's in German, the evanescence of the optative from Greek into Latin, to say nothing of the absence of a present tense in Hebrew with the false isomorphism of perfect and imperfect into past and future. Rosenzweig has failed as a comparative linguist, but we may wonder at how to make this grammatical thinking work with spoken speech. Rosenzweig himself admits that he is interested not in languages but in speech (III, 86). Here, at this crucial moment, he breaks into empirical grammar and in a genuine sense orients his whole theory of grammar.

We may benefit from Rosenzweig's two questions. They are ours. That scream is so eerie, most of all to our ears and eyes, because the scream is the very category that writers of the Holocaust invoke. Edmond Jabès, the master of the question, writes, "The light of Israel is a scream to the infinite".[17] For Jabès, the scream is the speech left us after the destruction, but like Rosenzweig he sees this as the speech of Israel. Rosenzweig could write that Jews are always survivors (450/404), and his identification of the scream may help to displace our assumptions that everything written before the atrocities of this century cannot address us after. We interrogate God most when God seems absent. We are not awaiting an answer, and we are still speaking to others. We are imploring both ourselves and others to hurry redemption, to save our common humanity from itself. And yet we ask it of God, much as we name the first lover/commander God, because that redemption transcends the merely human, even though it appears only in the human.

But the theology of the question includes more than this sublime and painful question. We must also return to the typical Jewish questions, the questions abundant in rabbinic texts: "From what time in the evening may the *Shema* be recited?" "What is the reason for this?" "From what verse does this come?" "But is it not?" "What is the difference?" These are the questions that have found especially in Jabès' work a contemporary resonance.

Are these questions the searching after a partner? Are they the scream that implores and hurries the messiah? If grammatical form is to serve as a theological organon, then the questions of Talmud and Mishnah must be an orienting point, just as the scream of the open question.

By orienting not only the imperative, but also the indicative and the subjunctive (Rosenzweig's cohortative), by the question, we would open theological discourse to a truly nonsystematic alternative. Our questions are directed to specific interlocutors; moreover, even the questions directed at God would appear as questions for ourselves, for humanity. And in a significant twist, to develop the grammar of such questions we would need to turn not only to the analysis of the interrogative of current philosophy of language, but even more to the textbook on questions—to Talmud and Midrash. Our questions are not their questions, but we have much to learn about the way one questions God by questioning the text; how one questions oneself by asking a question of another; and how another's questions of me are my questions for myself.

Rosenzweig succeeds in displacing the indicative with the imperative. He shows us how speech is first of all a social interaction and, therefore, that speech originates in a space oriented by the other's command for me. His analyses of moods allows us to interpret that space by considering the different fields of interaction. The installation of the imperative as the primary mood of interaction, however, requires adjustment with the interrogative. Just as we must preserve the aspect of the command that is not merely cognitive, so the question deserves more respect, preventing the reduction of the performances of questioning and being questioned to simply an exchange of information. The performance of the exchange itself must be our focus. But between the question and the command there is a complex interchange, one which Rosenzweig notices but does not develop. The possibility for discovering theological insight in a postmodern world seems to lie here, in the intersection of two moods of human speech.

CHAPTER 5

Eternity and Society (I):
Sociology and History

WHILE THE MOVE from logic to speech clearly broached the walls of pure reason with the admission of experience, the full relation of reason and empiricism in Rosenzweig's *Star of Redemption* requires a further step: a move into a futural verification of theology. Such a verification is not a testing of a hypothesis, but is rather a transformation of reality. The sphere for that transformation is society, because redemption will occur in the social world; the science for verification, therefore, is sociology. In Part III of *The Star of Redemption*, Rosenzweig produces a social theory of prescription, a theory that displays the sort of social practices which illumine the task of redemption.

This chapter will examine how Rosenzweig's social theory emerges from the need for eternity and then will clarify the relation of Rosenzweig's sociology to historical studies. The next chapter will then present the basic structure of his social theory: politics and art are the two ways of making eternity enter into worldly time. Rosenzweig is not unique in looking to sociology for an interpretation of religion and theology; in interpretations following upon Durkheim and Weber, religion now often appears as a social function, emerging from specific social contexts and serving various functions, including the formation of character and the bestowal of meaning. But sociology does not usually require the concept of eternity for its work. Like several members of the Frankfurt School, Rosenzweig requires a social theory that does not merely describe historical social practices and institutions; rather, he looks for a normative process to occur in social practice—for social practice to perform redemption. The tension between what happens in some societies and what ought to happen, between the immanence of current social practices and the transcendence of what should occur, that tension is complex and hard to isolate.

The Star of Redemption has been received as a kind of encyclopedia, but I am unaware that anyone has thought that Rosenzweig was actually proposing a general social theory. I will explore the methodology of the third part of *The Star of Redemption*, offering a reading that does not see Rosenzweig's task as ultimately a description of the two churches (Judaism and Christianity), as an attempt to do some sort of liturgical theology. The two communities (which Rosenzweig won't even call religions) are distinctive societies. They define two forms of bringing eternity and society together, but they also illuminate a fuller theory of what society is and, more importantly, what it is for. Rosenzweig argues that the purpose of society is communally to overcome death and time, to bring eternity into the world. This overcoming of temporality occurs both externally, through the organization and power of the state, and inwardly, through the artistic development of the individual's hope in the face of tragedy. While social forms in general achieve these overcomings, Judaism and Christianity are ideal types for this bringing of eternity into our lives. The partner to the linguistic turn in Part II is the sociological turn in Part III.

The third part of *The Star of Redemption* has a unique function in the system: it is the verification (*Bewährung*) of the theology of Part II. This is not Popper's verification, but is Rosenzweig's term for the making of the whole truth appear in the present moment of experience (437/393). Just as Part I provided a structure and so a meaning to the moment of speaking and hearing, so Part III will make the whole theological sequence true by binding up the present experience with the social practices that redeem the world. This task of verifying recognizes that redemption is a social category, the forming of a truly universal community, one in which each person will sing in his or her own voice but together will constitute a grand harmony; the vivifying of the world, turning all social institutions into ways of loving. This vision of redemption requires complex social practices, and thus the method for studying redemption is social theory.

For readers who are Rosenzweig scholars, I expect that the reorientation I am proposing here is both within reach but at the same time disruptive of a reading that sees Rosenzweig as a kind of dogmatic liturgical theorist. But for readers who are interested in social theory and perhaps not interested in theology and even less in liturgy, I suspect that the theological nature of Rosenzweig's claims will be startling. His theory of society is unabashedly theological—and this is clearest in the very conjunction of eternity and society. He takes his place with the early-twentieth-century sociological interpreters of religion, but maintains a theological viewpoint. On the other hand, this shift to sociology displaces both dogmatic and apologetic theology by a theological project that is more universally accessible even as it is more rooted in communal life. My aim is to displace the 'church theologian' Rosenzweig while at the same time attempting to raise the stakes for social theory.

This chapter begins with reflection on the need for society—particularly the need for social action and social change. I will address methodological questions first. Rosenzweig's view of the social construction of temporality is creative. The theme of eternity and social change suggests that Rosenzweig will approach society historically. Rosenzweig's use of history is contestable, as many of the interpretations of specific communities are simply inaccurate. In this chapter I will examine again the relation of philosophy and empiricism, focusing on the question of the place of history in the study of sociology. First, I will locate Rosenzweig's view of history in the historical school of Meinecke, who developed the history of ideas. Next, I will distinguish what Rosenzweig calls 'philosophical sociology' from 'historical sociology' as represented by Weber. And finally, I will confront the challenge brought by secular culture and discuss Rosenzweig's interpretation of contemporary Christianity, drawing on late Schelling and in proximity to Troeltsch. While Rosenzweig claims that sociology will allow him to avoid both dogmatic and apologetic theology, I will show how we must disengage his historical claims in order to make sense of his social theory.

SOCIAL TIME

The last chapter showed Rosenzweig embracing speech for theological reflection in order to move beyond the purely inward experience of the individual. The use of speech centers around the dialogue of an 'I' and a 'you', a dialogue which at root is a lover's exchange. The awareness of being loved happens in the intimacy of this loving dialogue, but even as the individual reaches awareness of his or her creatureliness through this private dialogue, an awareness of being loved and created for love which is unavailable in isolation, so too the lovers fulfill their awareness of the task of redemption only in communities. The lovers require a social grouping, even if only a neighbor, a few friends, a child. The move from the discussion of revelation, with its lovers' dialogue, to redemption, where we address a neighbor cohortatively to convoke a community, is a broadening of the circle of love, required by the very structure of love. Love is not fulfilled on the honeymoon.

But the emergence of families and of circles of friends is a slow route to the redemption of the world. In our world we often are thrown back on love and small circles in order to find real connections with others. But still we discern that society itself, the world, needs redemption. The discovery of these micro communities leaves us worrying that the macro problems will go unaddressed. My friends, my family, and the outreaching efforts to individuals, one at a time, seem too slow. Our own lives are socially realized, and we cannot avoid implication in the injustice of the world. Even our withdrawal into small circles still depends on the greater world for its material, and even its personal, needs. We desire to take hold of society as society, to institute social changes that will redress social injustice, discrimination, and unfounded hatred. The process of convoking a 'we' through one-to-one speech must yield some social action. The efforts to change or to redeem society as such is the subject of the third part of *The Star of Redemption*. Such social action will have to be accomplished at a communal level, not merely at the level of individual action.

So we might understand what social action is, Rosenzweig provides us with a complex social theory, an account of why societies exist and how they work. The process of hurrying redemption, referred to in traditional Jewish mysticism as "hurrying the kingdom," is displayed by the communities of prayer, for prayer now becomes the request for insight into what our society should become. Rosenzweig examines the social structures and practices of the Jewish and Christian communities both to discover ways for a community to discern the direction of social changes and to see how communities take part in the work of redeeming the world.

From this starting point of the tempo of redemption and the need to hurry it up, I move to the once familiar issues of temporality and eternity. Rosenzweig continues the basic metaphysical opposition of these terms, but at the same time he begins the deformalization of time. The discovery of the social forming of time, that temporality is structured socially, is central to Rosenzweig's argument. But before we can see society at work, we first need to become clearer about what time and eternity are.

We may begin with the Heraclitan flux. In itself time is simply a river that flows; the disappearance of the now, sliding off into the past. Were there no social structures, the law of time would be that everything must die. This inexorable truth is not eluded by the social structures and practices we are exploring—the individual person, animal, rock, or whatever is not preserved, and there is no other world in which things can live on after death. But society builds itself to endure; everything passes, but a community as such can perdure. Overcoming the death of temporality is not achieved by denying death, but by forming a society where others continue to live after my death.

Eternity, on the other hand, is not simple atemporality. Eternity for Rosenzweig is not the reality that is out of time; rather, it is the intensive possibility of completeness in each moment of time. "Eternity is this: that everything is at each point and in each moment" (378/341). Rosenzweig negotiates the opposition of time and eternity by refusing the ecstatic alternative: there is no way of escaping time—one must live in time, aware of one's own passing away and that time itself is always passing. He also rejects the move that renders the world always the same, for that produces only the static denial of loss which was philosophy's totalizing strategy. And he similarly refuses the ever advancing time of eternal progress, which fails to see that eternity is a possibility for each moment and instead defers eternity to a distant future—a future which can never come into any moment. But if one cannot escape time to enter eternity, one has the alternate possibility of bringing eternity into time. One then strives to make eternity happen in time, to make some moment of time fill up with the intensive unity of everything.

This over-full moment of time, this eternity in time, Rosenzweig links to (of all things!) the notion of an eternal recurrence. But while Nietzsche used this mystic doctrine for paradoxical purposes, for Rosenzweig the idea is much less paradoxical. The overcoming of the flux requires a new birth simultaneous with a passing away. Each end must be a new beginning. The recurrence comes in because, if one moment disappears and another replaces it, we have that infinite sequence of fully temporal moments, but one which defers eternity until we can unite the whole sequence. Rosenzweig requires a coming back of the same at the very moment of its passing away, for that would realize the intensive possibility of eternity. Time must be restructured from an endless sequence, not to the constant persistence of one thing, but rather to the continuous passing and return of the same. The hour for Rosenzweig serves as this structure of temporality, because as it ceases, the next one starts, and each hour is the same as each other one (322/290). Similarly, the week, the month, the year, all have the remarkable quality of being countable precisely because each unit is equal. The clock strikes the hour, announcing the passing of the last hour and the beginning of this one.

These units of time serve as an introductory image of how eternity is made to enter time. We notice at once that human time is not lived as the flux, that society does reckon time, that periodization is all but universal. But for Rosenzweig that indicates that our socially structured temporality is both at one remove from the naked flux and, more significantly, one step closer to the task of making eternity enter time—that society struggles in its temporality to make redemption happen now by realizing the possibility that everything can be at this very moment.

Rosenzweig's intensive eternity appears most clearly in contrast with eternal progress. Once we see that both ecstasis from time and the reduction of time to stasis are impossible, eternal progress is a popular alternative. For Rosenzweig the key issue is the possibility that eternity will break in at any time and not only after some traversal of a historical period. The Messiah is coming today, as the famous story from the Talmud goes (Sanhedrin 98a). In his notebooks from the front, Rosenzweig insists that Jewish and Christian revelation, in opposition to Plato as representative of pagan thought, focuses on apocalyptic possibilities (III, 68–72). Time is not merely an image of eternity, but eternity can happen in time, not by taking some time, but by interrupting it. This interruption is not unlike the striking of the hour by the clock, which interrupts the flow of time to designate that the passing of time is simultaneous with the recurrence of the hour.

The opposing view of eternal progress appears in *The Star of Redemption* as the Islamic concept of redemption, which Rosenzweig links to the modern concepts of eternal progress (253/227). He rejects the use of the adjective because 'eternal' progress is really only 'unending'. It represents the notion that Cohen had championed that history can be construed as a continuing progress, at no time during which is eternity (or redemption) realized. This steady improvement toward an unrealizable ideal makes no allowance for the hurrying that concerns us. The very futurity of the redemption of the world is lost when we construct it as a continuous function of the present—it becomes a representable, narratable future and not one for which we must join in action. "Without such an anticipation the moment is not eternal, rather it is an ever enduring further dragging along on the long highway of time" (254/227). In place of eternity we have the ever-becoming, the perduration that characterized the elements in Part I of *The Star of Redemption*. The very reduction of eternity to continuity and perduration in time is an evasion of the introversion/extroversion schema. Eternal progress collapses into eternal stasis because the eternal extension cannot allow the future its true futurity. The point of the introversion/extroversion schema is to recognize the discontinuity of freedom, and that interruptive moment of freedom is what makes even today, this very moment, a moment in which redemption can happen. "Today, if you heed his voice" (Ps. 95.7), that Talmudic story quotes. If we respond, eternity happens today.

Rosenzweig analyzes the human struggle to make of time more than an ever-flowing river. The preliminary solution appears by considering how human societies live time—that time is not experienced by people in its astronomical or geological dimensions. Yet unlike Heidegger and Bergson, Rosenzweig does not think that regularity in time is derivative or unfortunate. The temporality that allows us to count time, to reflect it and not merely to float in the river or even to swim in the current, that innovation is culture. Playing on a favorite etymology, Rosenzweig links culture with cult and finds that temporality appears in primitive agrarian cults by turning time into cycles, into ever-repeated units of time (325/292). Rosenzweig holds that the birth of culture is linked to the advent of calendars, of books of hours, of regularly appointed rites. More, this acculturation itself is an attempt to bring eternity into time. Any social theory will require the very coordinates of time and eternity, which we heretofore held in suspicion.

But these cultic cycles hold even more, for Rosenzweig uses their public or social nature to advance another claim. The coming of eternity into time, the hurrying of redemption, at first seems at best a magical effect of the cult. Theurgy and magic are hardly intimate with Rosenzweig's concept of redemption. Redemption is the forming of a universal community, the emergence of a true community that can say 'we'. The public nature of the cult, the publication of the times, the democratization of time, is itself the formation of that community. Just as singing together is redemptive, so is public time. In an almost shocking reversal of Heidegger and Bergson's evaluation of the emergence of public time, Rosenzweig recognizes in it the hurrying of redemption. If the priests or magi have private control of the cult, then they retard the coming redemption, but if the year, the hour, the week, the month, the times for matins (*Shachrit*) and vespers (*Ma'ariv*) are common knowledge, then the community forms already in this structuring of time.

Human culture emerges with its structuring of time, creating the shared communal experience of temporality. The key to the units of time is the interruption of the flow, the interruption that brings eternity into time. The reckoning of time is a positive result of sociality, the axis on which to locate the structures and related practices that hurry redemption. Socialized people experience time in a structured form. We live in a publicly formed temporality, which is neither the infinite, uniform dimension of scientific time, nor the ever-flowing river. Moreover, because that public nature of time extends throughout human culture, Rosenzweig's theory is not limited to Judaism and Christianity, but is a theory of society or culture in general. The hour and the week cannot be merely Jewish. (The next section will address the significance of those two particular communities for Rosenzweig's social theory, but we see at the outset that Rosenzweig concerns himself with more universal characteristics of society.)

While I am unable to escape my own death sentence, we as a community may achieve life socially. The egocentric concern over my own destiny after my death is replaced by the social view of how our society might live by bringing life into the world. The experience of love, which was enacted in speech, revealed that through an other I can overcome death. That revelation becomes true by making the world true to it. But even more decisive, this redemptive community does its work in the future. The obvious incompleteness of all present communities, the persistence of structures of death, of oppression and degradation, prevents, or ought to prevent, us from assuming that the world, or even some portion of it, stands already redeemed. Rosenzweig rejects modern constructions of progress, not only for metaphysical reasons, but most of all, because of the collapse of European civilization in the First World War. The war, coupled with the decadence of the beginning of the century, purged him of all confidence that history is unerringly moving in a positive direction. Redemption is not complete, and, significantly, we cannot count on history to move in the right direction.

Thus whatever truth our theological views and pragmatic analyses have will ultimately rest in a future verification. The truth of the concept of redemption is not yet available, but by hurrying the kingdom we can hope to verify the claims we might make. Rosenzweig advances a messianic concept of truth: the truth becomes true at that moment of the ultimate interruption. This vision calls for a redemption of the world as the verification of the experience of revelation. Until that moment—which can be today—our concepts and the exhortation to redeem the world are not yet true, as *true* becomes a verb. The result is a new emphasis on practice, particularly social practice, as the means of verifying those views. Clearly this is not the verification that is so closely bound with epistemological theories of falsification, because the failure of communities to form in this redemptive way does not disprove Rosenzweig's theology. Accepting that the world is not yet redeemed, Rosenzweig concedes that his position is falsifiable by reference to current social practices and conditions. But in that moment he also ducks away from this positivist reproach, for he calls us to change the world and not merely to reflect it accurately. We cannot see our own experience of revelation as bringing eternity into a moment until we make the world true. Until then, the truth of our experience remains unverified.

The key to the interpretation of cultic practice, of social practices and institutions, is the practice of the participants. Indeed, Rosenzweig moves in the third part of *The Star of Redemption* away from the analysis of speech as performance and toward a theory of mute practices—to a theory of gesture: not what people say, but what they are doing while they speak, what people do together in society, is the new focus. Moreover, the bracketing of speech becomes absolute as Rosenzweig looks to the creation of social silence—that a community performs certain actions and speaks certain words in order ultimately to transcend language and reach pure gesture. The illumination of the goal for which people pray is itself a vision, not a word. Almost reversing himself, Rosenzweig now claims that silence is higher than speech. The resolution of the tension between this silence and the silence of Part I is complex, but the basic insight is that the earlier silence is one of withholding oneself from all others, while the silence achieved in Part III is to be the consummation of relation with others. The latter silence is only available through the speech, the revelation, of Part II, but revelation is not the end of the route. Thus the move out from inward experience is not completed in communal speech or even singing, but in a still broader community in which gesture replaces speech. Social theory will have to focus on the actions people perform in society and no longer on the script of speeches.

PLACE-HOLDERS AND HISTORICAL CLAIMS

Before we can take even one step further, however, we must confront the most obvious objections, from which we can discern some important methodological values in Rosenzweig's social theory. The objections come to us from the refutations of history, which maintain that Rosenzweig has advanced historically false claims about existing religious communities. The two most flagrant claims are 1) that Judaism exists outside of history, and 2) that Christianity is spreading and must continue to spread over the whole world. We all are too familiar with the philosophical claim in historical dress: that with the Holocaust and the founding of the State of Israel, Judaism has reentered history. Similarly, most theologians would no longer be complacent about the church militant conquering the pagan world for the one, true way. And what the theologians thus reflect are the 'historical facts'—that Christianity is no longer conquering the world and has no good prospects for such a conquest. These obvious "mistakes" in Rosenzweig's system seem to doom his verification from the start.

But the failure of Rosenzweig's system is more pervasive, because throughout *The Star of Redemption* Rosenzweig has not taken history half seriously enough. His accounts of Greece, China, and India in Part I seem barely historical, while his constant use of Islam in Part II reflects an embarrassing prejudice. In short, it seems that every time Rosenzweig tries to make any claim on the basis of historical facts, he is at best half-right; his empirical claims are false. For many social theorists that pretty well ends this chapter; indeed, it causes one to doubt the worth of this book as a whole.

The question we thus have broached is the place of empirical evidence in this sort of Jewish thought, and Rosenzweig's answer seems miserable. But I have made the rejection too easy and, indeed, the 'historical' claims too simple. We must examine what Rosenzweig thought his method was, particularly in relation to history. I am afraid that I will once again do what a philosopher likes to do when confronted by historians challenging the historical accuracy of some position: turn the tables and raise philosophical questions for the historians considering historiography. Rosenzweig completed a dissertation on Hegel with Friedrich Meinecke, one of the great historians of his day. What was historical for Meinecke and for Rosenzweig is not necessarily what counts as history for some contemporary observers. The prominence of ideas in creating history is a methodological move that both men make, a move as subject to critique by materialist interpretations of history then as it would be now. Until we recognize the justification for such an idealist reading of the historical record, we cannot begin to understand what Rosenzweig was trying to do.

Ideas of History

The first step is to recognize Rosenzweig's own view of historical thought.[1] Rosenzweig's training as a historian was of a particularly intellectualist kind. His own dissertation, *Hegel and the State,* written before the war but published directly after it, was a kind of intellectual biography, tracing the development of Hegel's political thought by looking for a biographical development of the key concepts.[2] The origin of that work was a short chapter (five pages in the English edition) of Meinecke's main work, *Cosmopolitanism and the National State.*[3] I can spare you the complexities of Meinecke's account of German political history in the eighteenth and nineteenth centuries, but two key qualities of his account are noteworthy. First and most important, the history of forging a nation is viewed largely through the written works of philosophers and occasionally those of statesmen. The result is that intellectual history is the axis on which political and social events are plotted. This is not a regal history of kings and wars, but it is also not an economic history of prices, technologies of production, and distribution of wealth. The details of interest are subtle shadings of ideological concepts, and to them is given the burden of conducting history. The justification of history as 'history of ideas' is not argued in detail, but Meinecke holds that the conflicts between universal and national forces take place in the ideas and personalities of men.

> The examination of political ideas can never be separated from great personalities, from creative thinkers. We must attempt to grasp these ideas at their high source and not on the broad plain of so-called public opinion, in the insignificant political dailies.[4]

While the heritage of Hegelian idealism, and indeed of the nineteenth century in general, resounds in this turn to the great thinkers, we might well pause and question the counterclaim that history is not led by creative people. Meinecke's historiography is not devoid of examinations of the specific conflicts that shaped the creative leaders' ideas of nation, of culture, of the state, etc. But the assumption that ideas are always formed after the fact, as ideology, and that their sole function is to entrench and expand already established oppressive power relations is obviously too grand an assumption. For better and worse, modern people act in relation to ideas, even those ideas closely related to political ideology. Ideas move people, and history must discover the genesis of new ideas in tandem with the effective history those ideas produce. The role of consciousness need not be absolute for us to accord ideas an important role in the development of modern history.

Second, despite the questionable commitments in the basic thesis (that the highest form of cosmopolitanism is found in the nation state), Meinecke advances a strongly historicist view of history. There is no fundamental orientation or evaluation of the flow of ideas, and ultimately the power of certain ideas is held up as a measure of their worth. Indeed, a central idea was the importance of power in forming the nation state: that the disregard for power in national politics produces poor history and poor politics. Rosenzweig found this historicism disturbing, and while he accepted the importance of seeing intellectual developments within historical contexts, he longed for a proper orientation for judging history.

Rosenzweig's studies in history, moreover, were not limited to Meinecke. Indeed, it was ironic that he himself saw that the cure for his commitments to Meinecke was the study of art history with Wölfflin (III, 114; see also I, #797, Aug. 1922, and I, #902, 27 Jan. 1924). Wölfflin was a leading art historian, Burckhardt's successor in Basle. His own specialty was the transition from the classical to the baroque, and his analysis was broad and conceptual. Rosenzweig heard Wölfflin's lectures in Berlin in 1910 and was greatly taken with them (I, #182, 28 Oct. 1910). Wölfflin showed Rosenzweig that history was not ultimately that of politics and the nation state, but that artistic style could organize the material of history according to other principles. Two fundamental commitments of the German historical tradition exemplified by Meinecke were disrupted by the Basle historian: history need not be divided by nations, each with its own unique development, nor must history focus on political power and a certain kind of 'realism'. Rosenzweig's emphasis on aesthetics in *The Star of Redemption* comes from this respect for Wölfflin. While Meinecke's political vision is transcended by negation in Book 1 of Part III, Wölfflin's history of aesthetics is transcended by appropriation in Book 2. History thus appears not as the world history of political power, but as the grand, conceptual art history that cuts across political (and historicist) perspectives.

Wölfflin, however, did not cure Rosenzweig's case of the historicists disease. Rosenzweig's search for some truth that would not be subject to the relativity of historicism culminated in a request to Rosenstock-Huessy that led to his response in the form of *Angewandte Seelenkunde* (I, #330). Thus the historicist crisis for Rosenzweig led to the solution, the turn to speech. But the result is that historical eras and cultures then are located on axes of that grammatical thinking. The study of past communities cannot verify that grammatical thinking, because the speakers themselves create a new community. History at best might exemplify the concepts of grammar, but historicism has ruled history out as a proof (this was the crisis discussed in Chapter 4). The social theory Rosenzweig proposes will analyze societies for what they should become and will not take the historical record as its point of departure.

Perhaps one methodological quote will display the basic orientation of Rosenzweig to history.

> My form of thought is the *simile*. I hunt in material for *symptoms*. For example, Islam for me is not important as an essential *piece* of church history, rather because it makes church history transparent. History itself is for me elucidation of the concept. From church history I read off what love, faith and hope are. (III, 114)

Here is not only an unabashed preference for ideas, but truly a turning upside-down of Meinecke's history of ideas. The ideas, and not their history, is the goal, and it is not that we need to follow the ideas to understand history, but that history might help us out in understanding the ideas. Moreover, we can see here a willingness to reduce historical reference to place holding. Islam will never be much more than that in Rosenzweig's work. On the other hand, this passage does not make clear whether reason could hope to generate the ideas to be understood from itself. Rosenzweig's move to experience, in fact, precludes such an a priori move. The grammatical analysis of the performance of speaking arises from existential human speech—but how does that relate to history?

Perhaps we can see just what relationship occurs between history and grammatical thinking by considering again the importance of temporality in the analysis of speech in Part II of *The Star of Redemption*. The truth of experience relies upon the distension between past, present, and future, which is expressed in speech by different moods as well as tenses. Creation occurs in the indicative, in the doubled ontology that describes what has come to be. Moreover, speech itself relies upon a deep past, the past that was never present, as provided in Part I by mathematical language and poetic creativity. Neither of these pasts [1) the creation of what has come to be, and 2) the deep past of unspoken language] is provided by historians. Instead, in a remarkable inversion, Rosenzweig links the narration of historians to these pasts:

> What is then called [historical] narration? The one who tells, does not want to say how it "authentically" was [*"eigentlich" gewesen*], rather how it actually is come to be [*wirklich zugegangen ist*]. (III, 148)

This "correction" of Ranke's famous dictum is followed by a discussion of how historians in general are not exercised by determining 'the facts', but rather by the elucidation of the processes of realization of ideas and names and concepts in their own reality. Historical narrativity relies on the narrativity of creation, which provides a transcendental condition, if you will, for the very task of history. The importance of certain ideas remains, but the ideas are provided from either speech and its grammar or from pure philosophical thought. The very task of the historian is conformed to the task of narration from the discussion of the indicative and the doubled ontology of the creation of the world. But the task of redemption becomes excluded from history, because redemption is not narrated but is instead a matter for communal cohortation.

Neither Dogmatics nor Apologetics

The Star of Redemption switches from history to some sort of social theory in analyzing the task of redemption. Societies are to be known as representing ideal types or sorts, not as historically documented, fixed realities. This places Rosenzweig in a fascinating parallel with Max Weber, fascinating in part because Rosenzweig was largely ignorant of Weber's work. Rosenzweig had not read much Weber at the time he wrote The Star of Redemption, hence Weber is not part of the context for Rosenzweig's work. Rosenzweig did, however, write a remarkable appraisal of Weber in a letter from August 1921:

> I am reading Max Weber's Ancient Judaism, which I really would have read during the war. It is too bad that I didn't do it. I could have worked it up well with The Star. It is the same historically as what I announced philosophically. The sobriety of the observation in both cases leads to the same result and has set right what the idealizing spiritualization recorded. . . . It is another proof that nothing at all depends on whether one "believes" in the "loving God," rather only if one opens one's five senses and sees the facts—in the danger that thus the loving God will come in through them. (I, #670, 15 Aug. 1921)

Rosenzweig sees his project as being the same as Weber's—with the same result: that the faults of an idealizing spiritualization are now corrected. Thus Rosenzweig's turn to experience may not be historical, but neither is it based on the tradition of idealization. The paradigm of idealizing interpretation occurs in a discussion of bad Christian theology. There the theologians interpret Judaism not in relation to a people with social reality, but as the mere idea of people; Zion is similarly interpreted as the mere idea of the center of the world, and Christ as the mere idea of humanity (461/415). However conceptually centered Rosenzweig's approach to sociology is, it will always require that Judaism and Christianity be interpreted as societies, and not as metaphors for ideas.

The August 15 letter requires a three-step discussion: First I wish to explain why Rosenzweig might think that Weber was so close to him. Once that parallel is established, we can proceed to step two and see what Rosenzweig's claim for philosophy, in place of history, offers. And third, in interpreting the last lines of the letter, we might discover Rosenzweig's rejection of apologetic thinking in favor of sociology.

Unfortunately, this is not the place to explore the importance of Weber's work in its own terms. What can emerge here are similarities with Rosenzweig both in content and in method. *Ancient Judaism* is Weber's book which so closely resembled Rosenzweig's.[5] Weber was no expert in the field of biblical studies, but he contributed something of lasting quality in his sociological analyses of both the biblical society and of the formation of the Bible as document. One of the most striking similarities in content is the accounts of prophecy. Weber, too, focuses on the voice of God speaking out of the mouth of the prophet. Indeed, what Rosenzweig states quickly in one paragraph occupies Weber for several pages and becomes the focus for a chapter of his work.

The most important parallel between the two works is the reflection on the Jews as a pariah people. Weber's term is truly unfortunate, and at times he substitutes 'guest people', but the issue is identical with Rosenzweig's discussion of severing the connection of the people to the land, which I will take up in the next chapter. Weber focuses on the pacifism of the prophets and on the retrospective reading of the patriarchs as pacifist, while Rosenzweig will see the renunciation of military force as distinctive for the definition of the community; Weber discusses limitations on table fellowship in establishing an in-group/out-group definition, while Rosenzweig will emphasize the internal dynamics of table fellowship; and so on. The fundamental sociological construction of the community with strong ties in both bloodlines and table fellowship—and without political autonomy—is extremely similar in both thinkers.

The form of analysis is also shared, and here it is not merely the discussion of Judaism, but also the focus on the social practices of Judaism, that draws our attention. The texts are seen to reflect social practices, and the task of the interpreter is to discover what those institutions and practices were. Rosenzweig explicitly rejects the interpretation of Dogmatic Theology, claiming that, though it may postulate a social viewpoint, it ignores the question of how the society of the church is actualized. Trying to discover how Christianity forms a community, Rosenzweig attacks dogmatics:

We are not helped here with the dogmatic answer "Christ" any more than we might have been pleased in the last book [on Judaism] with the answer "The Torah," which a Jewish Dogmatics might well have given to the question of community-building in Judaism. Rather we want to know directly how then the community grounded on the dogmatic grounds achieves reality for itself. (378/341)

Dogmatics, as opposed to the New Thinking, presupposes both its authority and the efficacy of dogma. Rosenzweig usually discusses Christian Dogmatics as the model for Jewish Dogmatics (as he does in this quote), and he questions whether the theological project can be undertaken with the authority of a presumed social institution, the church (see III, 488). The important issue is how to form a community like the church; that is, to find what social practices can constitute such a community. But dogmatics presupposes the community's existence and speaks from the church rather than about the practices that form it. As a consequence, dogmatics assumes that dogma themselves explain or justify the church. In the Jewish context, the dogmatic possibility is that the Jewish community is based on the revelation to the 600,000 Jews at Sinai. Rosenzweig's concern, on the other hand, is to discover what practices members of a community must engage in to constitute a community and allow the revelation at Sinai to become theirs. The practices must justify the dogma, just as they constitute the community—and so the study of the social practices is not derived from the dogma and stands independent of dogmatic theology.

We now turn to the difference Rosenzweig discerns, between himself and Weber: Rosenzweig did his sociology *philosophically*, while Weber did his *historically*. Quite remarkably, Weber did not claim to discover new facts, but rather new interpretations of how things came to be— much like Rosenzweig's basic definition of the value of history.[6] But while Weber might have been pursuing the proper historian's task and, in addition, following the right focus in seeing history sociologically, he still was indebted to the inadequate theological concepts that governed his approach to history. Today we might reproach Weber for not being historically accurate. For instance, exclusion of outsiders is not a central aspect of Jewish society in late antiquity. One might argue that better historical research, consultation of other documents, of archeological data, etc., were needed. But Rosenzweig, for his part, might measure the error rather in terms of the bad theology that governed both the sources for Weber's work and his conceptual scheme. A theological vision that did not make the status of guest people dependent on an exclusivist claim is required before we can even see that the Jews were not firmly walled off

from the ancient world. That reorientation of vision requires an enrich-
ment of philosophy beyond totalizing philosophical concepts—it requires
a breakthrough in thought such as that achieved by Cohen, or Rosenzweig, or Levinas, to a plurality that cannot be totalized. With a logic
of totality, a guest people will necessarily appear exclusivist. Weber failed
not because he was not a good enough historian, but because the philosophical background of his history was not good enough.[7]

Rosenzweig, on the other hand, may not be a good enough historian,
but at least his social theory will emerge with sufficient philosophical resources to allow us to interpret the various evidence from ancient Judaism. Rosenzweig in particular broke with totality in such a decisive way
that he can require a plurality of communities with distinctive social practices, and he can see that plurality as necessary for the theological task of
redemption. The philosophical logic makes possible a breakthrough in
theology, and this allows for a sociology that in principle requires a plurality of communities.

The *philosophical* sociology (in contrast to Weber's historical sociology) is not to be confused with a merely philosophical/rational vision.
Rosenzweig must navigate carefully between the idealizing that ignores
society and the historicism that dissolves not only theology but also any
kind of genuine knowledge. His sociology exists between the outer
bounds of a pure Hegelian, idealizing view which neglects the actual practices of ideal types of communities, and the historian's commitment to the
uniqueness of each moment in which a specific practice is performed in a
specific community, a commitment which dissolves all sociological
knowledge in a solvent of skepticism. The social practices of Rosenzweig's sociology, quite beyond reason's domain, verify theological concepts (Creation, Revelation, Redemption), themselves provided from
speech and not from pure reason. However, Rosenzweig calls his sociology *philosophical* precisely to distinguish it from any dogmatic theological vision.

Moreover, Rosenzweig excludes theological apologetics for a different
but enlightening reason. Apologetics takes a stand based on the individual's position. We are beyond the mere play of ideas. When apologetics
succeeds, it avoids fanaticism because it discovers the common humanity
that lies in the deepest recesses of the self. Apologetics arises in an attempt
to defend oneself, but it is permanently skewed and must always speak
from my perspective and not *about* my perspective (III, 679).[8] As apolo-
gist I cannot verify (in Rosenzweig's sense of the term) my experience,
because my defense of myself requires that I dissolve the particularity of
my social world in order to discover that inner essence which is universal.
Having found a germ of universality within, I have abandoned the externality of my social practices and so can no longer speak as Jew or as

Christian, but only as nonsocialized human being (III, 686). Verification, however, requires that we bind the inner experience of speaking with the social practices that are neither totalizing universals nor dogmatically exclusive. Just as Rosenzweig dares to claim that his is the first nonfanatical Jewish thought, so he also claims that his thought is the first about Judaism (and Christianity) that goes beyond apologetics (III, 156). Indeed, in order to achieve that sociological interpretation of lived Judaism (not mere ideas, nor merely the inner conviction of the believer), Rosenzweig admits of his descriptions of the two communities that "the two will not be completely fair" ("*die beiden nicht ganz gerecht wird*") (III, 156). This compromise is required to achieve systematic thought that can act as a bridge between the inner conviction and the external and visible structures—because life itself is lived both inwardly and outwardly, and the 'and' joining the two is the very key to understanding our life. (This bridging of inner and outer is, as Arthur Cohen notes, a shorthand for the goal of *The Star of Redemption*, as the performative theory of speech is the bridge from the introverted elements of Part I to the objective social reality of Part III.)[9] The move to sociology is thus neither dogmatic (and idealizing) nor apologetic (and subjectivizing).

Rosenzweig's concluding sentence in the passage of this letter about Weber—

It is another proof, that nothing at all depends on whether one "believes" in the "loving God," rather only if one opens one's five senses and sees the facts—in the danger that thus the loving God will come in through them.

—claims that Weber, in a nonapologetic study, had discovered the very social practices that verify the theology Rosenzweig expounds. The verification is not dependent, therefore, on some private experience of grace, nor on the authority of an ecclesiastic body, but is found in the social practices and institutions of this community. Weber might not recognize just what these social practices are doing vis-à-vis Rosenzweig's account of theology, but still he is displaying the sociological and hence objective proof of Rosenzweig's thought.

It is just that kind of sociological verification that pushes Rosenzweig's analyses beyond the bounds of dogmatic and apologetic theology—because the social practices are not restricted to the Jewish community. The ideal types, including the guest people, are instantiated in part by many communities, and Rosenzweig's social theory is therefore not merely a depiction of two specific theological communities, but of social practices that are realized in various societies and at various historical moments. Just as in the last chapter I argued that Rosenzweig's turn to experience was in no sense fanatical and arbitrary, but was a turn to the universal possession of the human race, so in this chapter I argue that the sociological turn is not a retreat to a doubled dogmatic theology of the Jewish and Christian churches, but is also a turn to a general theory in which those two communities are important examples. Not only must we loosen the historical judgments, but we must also loosen the localized claims if we are to see how a sociology is happening here.

Judaism and Christianity only can claim to realize socially what is universally possible for the human race. Indeed, the other historical communities (Islam, Greece, China, and India) are not excluded from the concepts of Part II of *The Star of Redemption* (and not even, I would argue, from the concepts of Part III). Rosenzweig's struggle to create a Jewish system that is neither dogmatic nor apologetic produces a remarkable affirmation of the Greeks, with their misconception of the world as only plastic cosmos, the human as only tragic and heroic, and the gods as only mythic:

> The mythical Olympus, the plastic cosmos, the tragic hero are not thus done away with, are not 'has-beens', they are not essences in the strong sense of the word. When they prayed, the actual Greeks were of course not heard by Zeus or Apollo, rather naturally by God, and they also did not live in the cosmos, but rather in the created world, whose sun, our sun, also shone on Homer; and he was no attic tragic-hero, but a poor man like us. But even though these three configurations never actually were, they are still the presupposition of all of our truth. . . . The spiritual forms that were isolated and thus became visible only here in world history, only in Spengler's "Apollonian Culture", they are in all life as its secret, invisible presupposition, whether life is younger or older, whether it was itself an historical form or remained historically invisible life. (III, 146)

The social reality of ancient Greece represents an instantiation of the pagan experience of reality, the reality of the life without relationship between God, world, and humanity. That society, although misunderstanding itself, still offers a kind of true vision—the truth of introversion. The function of Part I of *The Star of Redemption* is not to document the historical expression of this truth, but to see in that historical form the manifestation of the perennial philosophy that refuses revelation—the human condition of isolation and introversion. As instantiation of that introverted way of life, Greece is still part of our lives.

But more important, the Greek historical person was also capable of prayer to our God. He was as capable of relations, of revealing himself to another, of joining in forming a chorus as anyone else has been. Not only philosophy is perennial—theology is, too. The questions and constructions of reason are valid for any age, and the theological concepts also are available to any age. The emphasis on the nonfanatic dimension of new thinking, that speech is available wherever people have lived, in any time, that those concepts do not depend on some historical privilege, transgresses history and historicism. What then of Part III?

> Only because and insofar as these both [Judaism and Christianity] renew the "revelation to Adam," only that far is New Thinking Jewish or Christian thinking. However, only and insofar as and because Paganism in its historical forms forgot or disavowed this revelation to Adam, who was as little pagan as he was Jew or Christian, only thus is this Paganism hardened for itself into an historical form, only thus is it thoroughly not perennial: precisely in its independence and having become form is it completely untrue. (III, 154)

The criterion to distinguish one historical community from another is not access to revelation, but avowal and consciousness of it. Rosenzweig repeats that fervent prayer went up to God, and so bound God and the praying person in relation; God did not wait for Sinai or Golgatha to hear prayers. But social forms (accessible in empirical, historical studies) can display and enhance these relations, or they can disavow them and reject them.

Rosenzweig's presentations of Judaism and of Christianity emerge as an effort to work out the question of how to make the eternal come into time (III, 156). He presents the external forms and practices of the two communities, always guided by the systematic problem. Those historical communities will not necessarily conform at any time and will necessarily not conform at all times to the sociological portrait Rosenzweig draws ("not be completely fair"). If the sociology is not ultimately an empirical portrait, but is rather a contrast of two ideal communities, each striving to bring eternity into time, then perhaps we need not labor under the task of qualifying, justifying, and criticizing Rosenzweig's portraits of Judaism and Christianity by reference to what Jews or Christians actually do. Instead, we might just as well turn our gaze to the claims that are made for these portraits: that they show us how societies make eternity come into time. In short, I will divert our reading of *The Star of Redemption* from questions of historical accuracy to the function that sociology is intended to serve: to the systematic promise that animated Rosenzweig.

Secularization and the Last Church

One last global historical critique. Rosenzweig hardly explores the full range of social forms that have appeared, but one that seems so distinctly prominent in historical reality and yet absent from his account is the secular modern society. When Rosenzweig partitions the world into the Jews and the Christians, he seems to have forgotten that the society of secular institutions and practices is dominant. Rosenzweig addresses this objection with reflections on Goethe and Nietzsche. In both cases the individual represents the supposedly desocialized individuality which is the hallmark of our society. Indeed, it is not hard to see that Rosenzweig's interpretation of modern culture as a third stage of Christianity is more than adequate to the task of interpreting secular society. Moreover, this last stage can provide insight into the challenges of postmodernity.

But we need to begin by examining, if only briefly, Rosenzweig's three stages of Christianity. These stages are liberally adapted form Schelling's comments in his later lectures on revelation. Schelling ended the lectures by reflecting on the history of the church and dividing it into three stages: the Petrine, the Pauline, and the Johannine.[10] He divides these stages into a past, a present, and a future church, each under the initially historical leadership of the named apostles, but then becoming the Catholic, Protestant, and finally (yet to come) Universal church. Schelling refuses to champion Protestantism against Catholicism absolutely, but insists that it is a transition and that it too must be overcome.[11] The triadic nature is reminiscent of so many other triads in Schelling, particularly in its temporalized interpretation. The Johannine epoch (the one of greatest interest for us) is remarkably underdetermined—messianic in an almost empty way. But one passage is particularly interesting.

> My standpoint in general is that of Christianity in the totality of its historical developments. My goal is that first truly universal church (if church is still the right word here), that is built only in spirit, and can endure only in the perfected understanding of Christianity, only in its actual fusion with universal science and knowledge. As long as Christ is in secret, not only for the individual members of the church, but rather for the church itself, so long as a church secures its full task within, as in a locked shrine to which no one has the key even to display it from afar, just that long has Protestantism not borne its true fruit.[12]

What Schelling envisions is the disappearance of the church as such—that it will cease to be a sacred space and will become one with the world, particularly the world of science, philosophy, knowledge, etc. This new conversion of the world is not to be done with the sword (that happens in the Petrine age), but through a meeting of thought and culture. But what the new 'church' will look like is quite beyond Schelling.

Rosenzweig's appropriation is quite distinct. He all but ignores New Testament authority and exegesis, but he focuses on the different processes of conversion. Rosenzweig's basic insight is that Christianity always means the process of becoming Christian. The Christian is a converted pagan (again the perenniality of the Greek social forms). In Peter's church pagans were converted forcibly in their bodies; in Paul's, inwardly through the soul; and in John's the task will be to transform the outward world, the social world, which is still pagan. Peter's conversion by its use of force only produced a physical conversion—although one of whole communities, nations, etc. But now the structures, the practices, the very life must be converted.

While Schelling sees these three churches as a model for temporality, Rosenzweig sees them as historical events, and for him the Johannine church has already begun. Its first church father is *Johann* Wolfgang von Goethe. Goethe died in 1832, nine years before Schelling's lectures on revelation, but Schelling foresaw the last church only in messianic time. Why Goethe? Because, as Rosenzweig says, Goethe claims to be both a pagan and "the only Christian" (315/283). The significance of his claim to be a unique Christian is the development of the modern self-consciousness of individuality, of personality, of vocation. But he sees himself also as pagan because he must convert his own life. Rosenzweig sees this self-creativity, of which Goethe is a founding father, as the emergence of the Johannine church. Authenticity is critical; it is the beginning of the last church.

This third church does not build new churches, and it does not convert new peoples. It has no distinct forms of its own, but takes over what has been produced in the two earlier churches and unites them by bringing them to life. Rosenzweig's fundamental association of redemption with universality and life recurs here. Key moments in the life of this new church are the recognition of the Eastern Orthodox church and the emancipation of the Jews. The French Revolution and the spread of the ideals of liberty, equality, and fraternity are necessary preconditions of redemption. These events, which are not ultimately churchy, but which instead open up into modern/'secular' politics, are part of the Johannine church.

This opening out into the public realm is discussed more fully in Rosenzweig's treatment of Christianity in Book 2 of Part III. There we have both a general accommodation of political and national holidays into the church calendar (signaling the acceptance of 'secular' events into the eternalization of the the community's lived time) (410/368) and also a remarkable discussion of how dance needs to flow out of the church (415/373). The medieval festival and its modern adaptation are the zenith of the discussion of Christian sociology—a zenith reached precisely by this need to flow from the church into the streets:

> The space of the church streams out into the outside that surrounds it. Its time organizes the stream of time that flows past it, but it must itself first produce its world from the outside world. It does not simply carry it outwards, as it brought out its laws of its space and of its time, rather because it goes outwards to all peoples, its receives its own law from the outside first—from working under the law of the world. It does not have its end in its walls. (415/373)

Like Schelling's *Verschmelzung* or *fusion*, Rosenzweig's outward motion is not simply imperial, but requires that sort of fusing of horizons.

The church, in its last stage, must take up the profane world. Its 'conquest' will thus not be an imposition, but a breathing through the world as it is. The redemption of the world is not ultimately revolution or conquest, but the breathing of new life into the structures of the world as we find it. But this means that Rosenzweig would reject any notion that the goal is to lead the world into the established church. Not the fortifying of the church against the world in order to become a bastion of orthopraxis in a secular world, but the more intricate task of learning from the world in order to transform the world (and not so much in order to preserve the church). The Johannine epoch is one in which the church empties itself into the world with respect for and intimacy with the world's laws. Apparently secular celebrations, like popular festivals and state holidays, in which time is structured and all can participate, are the innovations of this last church.

Rosenzweig admires Goethe because Goethe knew that the ultimate task was to convert his own life, to respect the structures, the history, the social reality of his own life, and through that to imitate Christ. He thus begins the work of the Johannine church. But what is lacking in Goethe is the completion of the task, because he only discovers his own life, his own time—he lacks the public, world-enlivening reality of redemption. Goethe, by being the great individual, fails to live with a community. Rosenzweig explains that failure in terms unusual but now familiar: Goethe lacks eternity (320/288). The public time, the communal celebration of conversion, the public participation in hurrying the kingdom is lacking. Temporality can be experienced in the paradigm of authentic individuality: eternity requires a community.

For our purposes, however, Goethe is not the question. Rather, in our world church attendance has dropped and Christianity appears to be diminished. Christianity is not 'conquering' or even converting the world, yet Rosenzweig's analysis of the Johannine church allows for a profound acceptance of this post-Christian age. Rosenzweig quite remarkably pairs Goethe with the first Antichrist, Nietzsche; each makes his own biography essential to his individual tasks. But Rosenzweig can accept each as part of an age that is still Christian. It does not look all that churchy, and Rosenzweig knows it, but the culture of our world has itself become Christian. The dissemination of the ideals of the French Revolution, the discovery of tolerance for other religions, the very dominance of the Christian calendar, all show that the world may be less Pauline and Petrine, but that it is still Christian in this post-Christian age.

But if such secularization of Christianity is part of Christianity, then Rosenzweig's historical claim about the spread of Christianity, indeed his whole presentation of Christian liturgy, is not a Church Dogmatics. The social forms and practices that he presents, especially for Christianity, must be reinterpreted as a perspective on modern and even postmodern society. The neo-orthodox's loss is our gain, as Rosenzweig at least is trying to describe contemporary society not in opposition to the church, but rather through the same practices in their most self-conscious reality (through the church). In an essay written in 1918, "Science and Life," Rosenzweig calls for a renewal of theology (the science of the title) as the key to renewal of the life of the Jewish community (III, 483). Immediately, he addresses the challenge that theology is chained to our ancestor's time, or that it is chained to piety—that theology is outmoded for modernity. He looks to Christianity and raises the question in its world in order to gain some insight into what might be possible for Judaism. Yet he answers that a free, pure, scientific theology can indeed arise (and not in bondage to religious sentiment). Moreover, he offers the hope that such theology might serve the community of the next century more than it serves the contemporary one. The theology he proposes is the one we find in *The Star of Redemption*, but the point to notice is that Rosenzweig is not ignoring the 'threat' of secularism, nor is he writing theology in a pietistic mood. Moreover, the post-Christian world is still Christian and still requires theological concepts in order to continue its life.

At the end of this chapter, let me suggest a last parallel: the work of Ernst Troeltsch. Rosenzweig did not read much Troeltsch; he did not like the earlier work on Augustine, and almost certainly did not explore his major work, *The Social Teachings of the Christian Churches*.[13] The parallel with Weber is particularly interesting, because Troeltsch and Weber were close colleagues, developing sociology of religion together. Rosenzweig was influenced by neither, but is in close proximity to each: Weber on Judaism, Troeltsch on Christianity. That he approved of Weber and was hostile to Troeltsch may have to do with the theological commitment of Troeltsch, particularly in an exchange with Cohen.[14] In any case, Troeltsch explored both the social teaching and the social practices of the Christian churches. His approach was not as focused on the specific practices of the communities as was Rosenzweig's, but still many of their conclusions are remarkably similar.

Perhaps the most basic and important point of agreement between Troeltsch and Rosenzweig is that Christianity must draw upon the society around it. Troeltsch turns to the need for an objective compromise with the world as the best hope for Christianity. Like Rosenzweig's call to take on the laws of the world in order to redeem it, Troeltsch's defense of church in opposition to sect elevates the positive relationship to the world.[15] Troeltsch's own account of the modern church links not only the orthodox churches but also the secular socialists to the constellation of Christianity. Moreover, he looks at the the social phenomena of idealism and romanticism as derivatives of medieval mysticism, emphasizing the individualistic shortcomings of such views. While Troeltsch does not emphasize aesthetics as Rosenzweig will, his sense of the sociological verification of the theological claims is remarkably close to Rosenzweig's.

Rosenzweig's discussion of the Johannine church, therefore, is not only conceptually adequate to meet the challenge of postmodernity and secularism, it is also in close proximity to one of the most important Christian theological turns of this century. While we would not want to ignore the distance between the orthodox Christian confessions and the secular world that now surrounds them, we should also not ignore the distinctive theological filiation of modern secularism. If Christianity for Rosenzweig is not to be interpreted as a dogmatically constituted church, but is rather a particular instantiation of a set of social practices and institutions, then we may find that that sociological Christianity is not limited to state churches.

The generalizing moves of Rosenzweig's social theory now stand defended against the easy criticisms of its falsification by history. What we have gained by generalizing is precisely the opportunity to see the value of this theory to interpret social practices. As a theologian, Rosenzweig tries to avoid both dogmatics and apologetics. The result is a theological sociology, wherein society appears as concrete practices and institutions normed by the goal of redemption. Society and social theory will receive their ultimate truth only in the future. We may have lost the so-called existential thrust of Rosenzweig's theory, but in its place stands a social theory that is yet to be verified by further social action.

We may now recover the social concepts behind the concrete analyses. The goal is to find out what motivates Rosenzweig's interpretations—what determines them, given that they are not adequate historically. The empirical move in Rosenzweig is not a historian's; rather, empiricism is saddled with the task of making the conceptual claims become true. Society is where those claims will have to be enacted; history itself cannot verify the claims, but only displays some of the possibilities for the claims, sketching a range of possibility in which they could be true. But this is an empiricism of the future—that we can make society conform to these concepts, and so redeem the world. At the same time, the theological dimension of this sociology is not an excuse to adopt a dogmatic, idealizing interpretation of society. Redemption happens in society *as society,* and not merely in the play of ideas allegorically drawn from society. Redemption's futurity means that the social realization is a task and not a given past event. But this reading offers Rosenzweig to intellectual circles that may not harbor interest in theological communities, much less in church dogmatics. The possibility of applying Rosenzweig's social theory to social reality is broadened, as the task set for redemption is available for any community.

CHAPTER 6

Eternity and Society (II): Politics vs. Aesthetics

WHILE SEVERAL of the methodological issues in Rosenzweig's social theory are now resolved, the specific claims that he makes about society in general, and about Jewish and Christian societies in particular, await exposition. The guiding light for that exposition is the first topic of my discussion of sociology: the importance of eternity. Social theory will be split into two different ways of making eternity take place in time. Both in a nontheological context, where the social realm disregards the theological concepts of Creation, Revelation, and Redemption, and in the specific theological communities of Judaism and Christianity, society's practices and structures are separable into the practices that force time to hold eternity and those that structure the flowing of time from within it. Social theory becomes political theory in the first case and aesthetics in the second. What I will do in this chapter is explore these two dimensions of social theory, first in the pagan context—the underlying sociality of our various societies. Second, I will show Rosenzweig's interpretation of the theological transformations of those two dimensions in Judaism and Christianity, respectively. And finally, I will conclude with some reflections on the perpetual animosity between these two communities and its implication for social theory in general.

FORM AND FORCE (GESTALT AND GEWALT)

Late in *The Star of Redemption*, indeed in the final pages, Rosenzweig announces that pagan society (the substrate of all society) has two idols. "Those eternal gods of Paganism, in which it survives until the end of time, the state and art, the former the idol of the materialists, the latter of the personalists" (468/421). Rosenzweig claims that the State fights against time by forbidding its flow and that Art drifts with time. Thus the two are poised against each other, as their two transformations will be as well. Politics strives for the eternity of 'forevermore', and so abandons or ignores time; art accepts the laws of perishing, but abandons eternity—particularly in its communal dimension. Rosenzweig does not present these two general dimensions in the way that I will in this section, isolating them from transformations in the two communities of Judaism and

Christianity. In *The Star of Redemption*, the State and Art are discussed most extensively in contrast with Judaism and Christianity. It is not an altogether difficult task, however, to pull together views of each of these two dimensions of society. The result is a generic portrait of society. I will begin with the more general philosophy of society, to show how society is constituted by its relation to the passing of time.

We begin with the state. "For the peoples, the world is pure temporality. But the state is the necessarily ever renewed attempt of the people to achieve eternity in time"(369/332). Rosenzweig speaks of how we seek to dam the stream of time, to make it stop flowing:

> Out of the pure running off of time, to which the peoples are in themselves surrendered, the state must seek to make a circuit. The enduring change of their life must be recast into preservation and renewal in order to bring it into a circuit that would in itself have the possibility of being eternal. Life establishes an apparently unredeemable quarrel between preservation and renewal. It wants only to change. The law of change forbids that anything that continues should change itself and that anything that is in change should preserve itself. Life knows neither mere rest nor mere motion. And since time cannot be denied, motion wins. You cannot step in the same river twice. History appears to pass away into this unrestrained change and alteration. Then the state comes and suspends its law over the alteration. Now for the first time there is something that endures. (369/332–33)

The state attempts to dam the flow of time, to make the river stop. Its attempt requires power, power in two forms: external and internal. The state defends itself against aggressors, against other states, and it must also exercise power over its own people. The former is the attempt to deny its own mortality, that this people will disappear from history; the latter is the coercion that attempts to force this society to retain its inner nature against the movements that would produce a change in kind. But in each case Rosenzweig finds that the task is to arrest time, to create a permanent, atemporal society, and that such a task requires force. The goal of the state is self-preservation; its essence is force. Force directed against the outside binds a people to a land:

> A people forces its roots into the night of the same dead and thus life-giving earth and takes from its permanence guarantee of its own permanence. It firmly fastens its will for eternity to the soil and for its dominion to its territory. (332/299)

To be attached to the earth, and in fact to this particular piece of earth, is one route to resisting the bitter law that everything passes. We hope that by such connection to something that does not pass we too will achieve that atemporal permanence. But Rosenzweig spells out the irony:

in order to secure ourselves, we must be willing to risk our lives for our land. The military is the institution of force that protects our land. We must fight against all other peoples who would take or even share our land. The whole nexus of boundaries, defenses, and the military arises through this connection to this piece of real estate, deriving its force from our social desire for eternity, or at least our dread of communal death. But the results are disappointing—because we then drench our land with our life, with our blood. The blood-soaked earth endures, and the peoples pass away. "So the earth betrays the people who had entrusted its permanence to it. The land itself indeed endures, but the people disappear from it" (333/300). National wars ultimately are only battles, because all empires fall. No people has survived intact on its native soil; some last longer than others, but even the most stable (unchanging) nations have passed away and other peoples now live on their soil.

Rosenzweig notes that the struggle for political permanence has changed in the modern world. In the ancient world, the historical moment of paganism, a people fought knowing full well that it could lose—the life and death of a nation was a natural fact. The idea of an eternal people, that a people as such had to be eternal, emerges in world history through Augustine's criticism of Cicero. Rosenzweig recognizes that if our people is mortal, then there is a bittersweet love of country in repressed acknowledgment of that mortality (366/330, 338/304). With the explicit conviction that this people cannot die, modern nationalism appears after the emergence of the nation-state from under the church. War moves to the very center of the purpose of the state. "The ancient states had public cults, offerings, festivals and so on as the midpoint of their political existence. But war that was waged against the enemy at the border and certainly shielded those pagan altars was not itself the offering, not itself the cultic action, not itself the altar" (367/330). War is not foreign to the ancient state, but it serves both national security and also the public cult.

Rosenzweig views the modern state as a descendant of Christianity and sees in the modern, total war not a rejection of medieval Christianity, but rather a development of the idea of holy war (perhaps in a different costume). National security has replaced the cult as the center of the modern state, and the quest for self-preservation preempts all other purposes. The thirst for eternity, for permanence, has been made transparent and governs the state. Whether Rosenzweig views Machiavelli or Bismarck as the master of modern, nationalistic state politics, the sociological point is that, more than the ancients, we now require a state precisely to achieve our imitation of eternity: the military power to be secure against invaders.

Force, however, governs the domestic side of politics as well. A people also roots itself in its own laws and customs. Its very identity is thus its social customs and the codified regulations of society. The continuity of society depends on the tradition of these practices from the past ("the power of habit") and their ability to fix the practices for tomorrow. In its internal life, a society strives for endurance through this repetition and renewal for the future. The laws govern time through our own culture; that is, we live in time and preserve our society with law (336/303).

In order to maintain society against the changes of life, it is necessary periodically to re-found the law and its right (*Recht*). Force (*Gewalt*) is the renewal of the right—or the order of practices codified into law (370/ 333). But practices must appear to be old, to be traditional. Thus the state requires force in order to adapt the social practices and institutions to the changes of time. The state stands in between the inherited customs and the innovative practices; it uses force both to change the old and also to slow the emergence of the new. It is both conservative and progressive— but it thus is bound to the temporal/historical changes of the people. It tries to hold back the flow of time, and so dresses up the renewal of institutions in more laws, laws which pretend to be old, but which at the same time try to prevent the future from taking its own shape. The present moment of force reconstructs the past and controls the future. And yet that present is not truly eternal, but is the attempt to prevent its own disappearance. For every society follows the law of time: that it must pass away. The state innovates or renovates society in order to keep it alive, but it does so under the illusion that it is only repeating the past.

One hears in the distance a reiteration of Hegel's thoughts about the police and the military. Rosenzweig sees war and revolution as the two continuing threats to the state, the two perennial denials of its eternity. The state may never dispense with physical violence. It battles the natural degeneration of the society as well as the external threats—in each case using force against the natural effects of time. It must both wage war, risking its life against outsiders, and battle against the stagnation and degeneration of its own culture. It forces the moment to become eternal, claiming that our way of life is based on ancient ways of our founding fathers and that our country will never disappear from world history. This very society, this very nation at this moment, is the way it has always been and will always be. But "the moment remains completely a moment: it passes. However, so long as it has not passed, it is in itself a little eternity" (371/334). New customs can become institutions dressed up to look traditional and can be the push to a different future converted to a continuation of today—and so the state makes even change appear under the guise of stasis, of order. Rosenzweig recognizes the hour, the cultic accounting of time, in these little eternities of nationhood. The creation of temporality or lived time depends on this double use of force. World history is the product of states; eternity, however, begins to appear in time by the action of the state. Politics does not achieve true eternity, but it points the way and even takes us much of the way. Its deficiencies are already appearing, but only contrast with different social forms will illuminate how correct its goal was despite the failure of its means.

The other dimension of sociology, art or culture (*Kunst*), requires a more inferential reading of Rosenzweig. Because Judaism appears in *The Star of Redemption* as an overturning of the state the state is defined quite explicitly; but because Christianity appears as a higher kind of art, Rosenzweig does not isolate the sociological reality of art as clearly. Which is not to say that art has not been discussed thematically. Indeed, aside from the inversions and mechanisms of the logic of 'Yes', 'No', and 'And', no topic has been more nearly ubiquitous. Art concludes each of the books of Part I, with grounding concepts of art as introverted. It extroverts in each book in Part II, with the concepts of artist, work of art, and audience. Finally, it emerges as social, as participatory, in Part III in the portrait of Christianity.

Like the state, art struggles with time; above all, with the passing away of everything. The social forms of culture, of art, arise as an attempt to structure the flow of time into a social temporality, into some sort of eternity in time. The contrast of art and politics centers around their different approach: for the state the use of force is defining, for art it is structure itself. In German the contrast is between *Gewalt* (force) and *Gestalt* (structure or form). But while the state tries to deny time its due, to make something exist that will not pass away, art celebrates and commemorates that very passing away. Art represents suffering not to deny it but to structure or to form it and to structure the inherent loss experienced in time. Following Cohen in some crucial ways, Rosenzweig opts for an interpretation of art as the human production of passions. The suffering of passing away is reproduced in art and overcome in the representation. Rosenzweig states that art is tragic in content (the passing away), but comic in form: "Art as production [*Darstellung*] is that which is tragic and comic in one" (419/376). Art must structure the passing away of time, and so it does not let us forget the suffering of death and loss. But unlike a mere consciousness of loss, such as grief, art also offers us an overcoming of that loss. We recall the suffering of our youth and so overcome it; we renew ourselves with the remembrance of past suffering, and art forges this circle of recollection.

The great temptation and power of art is its purity. "High art" is a disinterested reflection offering nothing to the world. It is the idealistic flight from the real world. Idealism that pretends to be 'too good' for reality "is usually only a flight from the all too common reality into a dream land" (394/355). The escape from the common world of society is selfishness. The purity of expression, the contempt and disavowal of the real world, is the reservoir for overcoming loss. The suffering due to time becomes a pure experience, removed from the world and offering another world as a consolation for the transience of this one. But because of this power to withdraw and so reflect, art is capable of overcoming the loss.

Rosenzweig's account of the personal experience of art occurs in Part II. There he distinguishes the idealist's desire for pure art from the possibility to apply art to change the world. He discusses how the mistrust in language was accompanied by a new trust in art—not in beauty, but in beautiful art (163/146). The aestheticization of thought was a trust in what humanity could make for itself, but for Rosenzweig this trust was a move back to the pagan alternative: a language of already spoken words, the poets' creation prior to revelation of one to an other. Rosenzweig did not refuse that moment, but he criticized it by reference to the possibility of an artist revealing him- or herself to an audience through a work. The question of the audience becomes the question of redemption and socialization of art in Part III.

But the more basic experience of art, the structuring of loss in that tragicomic moment, precedes the full application in the community. Thus in Part II we find the three basic divisions of art and a corresponding set of three central qualities. It is through these divisions and qualities that art accomplishes its fundamental task of structuring loss. In the next section, I will explore how these divisions become applied to produce a socialization of their function, which remains only individual in the more limited social forms (Paganism, Idealism, etc.).

The divisions are plastic, musical, and poetic arts. The plastic arts structure space; the musical time; the poetic a complete world. In their unapplied forms the plastic arts are painting and sculpture, which in their ability to capture a moment do not simply pull the objects out of time, but rather make the fragility of the moment, the soon-to-be-gone quality of it, stand out. Their dominant quality is epic. For Rosenzweig the epic quality is the fullness of detail, the unity of the content of the work.

The musical arts structure time itself, producing its very flow. Their dominant quality is lyric, by which Rosenzweig means the inner distinctiveness of the individual, as that individuality passes away and is integrated into a whole. Rosenzweig admits that epicism and lyricism are in each piece of art, but that they have a more proper place in their respective divisions. The epic requires taking in everything in one moment; the lyric requires the perception of the disappearance of the individual. Thus epicism is found in a synoptic view of a painting, while lyricism is found in the duration of the melody.

The final division is the poetic, which resides in both space and time through the representation of thoughts. In poetic arts the words bring together both the wealth of detail and the individuality at its moment of loss in the third quality: the dramatic. Like so much else in Rosenzweig's thought we find the third element as the combination, the 'And', of the previous two. In the case of poetry, the element is thought, much as time and space were the elements of music and plastic arts. The result, quite remarkably, is the authentically living art (273/245), because a human appears in the poetic arts, in the dramatic quality. Without thought or words, only a dumb figure or a blind song appear. Now a living person takes the stage—with words. Poetic arts are shared by the Greeks and the Hebrews—while the Hebrews suspect plastic arts and the Greeks suspected music. "Poetry provides structure like conversation [rede], because it gives more than both: it provides representational thought, in which both are alive as one" (273/245).

Again, Rosenzweig insists that all art has all three qualities—epic, lyric, and dramatic—but he claims that each division of the arts has a special intimacy with one of the forms, and that the dramatic quality requires the other two. Rosenzweig develops these three qualities further but that is not relevant here. Our concern is how we structure the flow of time through art. Space, time, and thought are the media in which we create a recollection of loss. The world we create for ourselves must at first transcend and depart from the world we live in with its unstoppable flux. But art may also return to refashion the world, to celebrate in comedy the tragedy of loss.

The task of the next section will be to display how art can become world changing. The idealistic retreat into a world, a space, a time removed from the flux will be turned around and overcome by applied art forms in each of the three divisions. The Christian transformation of those applied art forms will lead beyond that application to an insight into the ultimate eternalizing of social reality under the guidance of art. But art must first take us away before it may bring us back to redeem the world. The specific social uses of art are hardly unique to one time or culture. Christianity's specific claim will only be relative to the general social practices related to redemption. But one more aside may help us see the view of society that Rosenzweig presents.

If we pause and consider the logic of 'Yes' and 'No', we may find that society in general, as opposed to that under the theological social forms yet to be presented, represents a clear 'Yes' and 'No'. The state struggles to say 'Yes' to the world, to affirm its community in the face of the passing away brought by time. Its will is resolute, and it sacrifices its own 'essence' in order to survive. Here is will without essence, 'for itself' without 'in itself', 'Yes' without 'No'. On the other hand, Art represents a 'No' to the world, to the task of redemption. Art offers a way to reside within oneself. The aesthete has accepted time's threat, but rests content with her own transcendence of that loss in the structured experiences she can control. She has no interest in expanding her 'salvation' to others. Here is essence without will, 'in itself' without 'for itself', 'No' without 'Yes'.

Obviously, the next step is to turn state and art inside out. From the state will emerge a profound 'No' to world history, to world development—which will at the same time be the deepest 'Yes' to its own self. And from art will emerge a deep 'Yes' to the world, an attempt to bring to it a transformed art—and this transformed art would discover that the individual was not at rest but was only on the way. I know that at some point this begins to feel mechanical, and so it is, but at least Rosenzweig himself did not play out the architectonic of 'Yes' and 'No' at this point. What is interesting, however, is that these inversions do not take the Hegelian point of view, in which the two opposites (or rather contradictories) simply go over into each other and thus generate a third term. State and art retain their own integrity, even as they are overcome by the theological social forms. And while each turns inside out, neither becomes what the other was. Thus the messianic politics that dispenses with force is at no time akin to the idealistic art. It is because of this lack of reciprocal dependence that I have lingered in this section to present something Rosenzweig himself did not: the account of politics and of art independent of their theological social forms. Only on the basis of these fundamental social forms can the theological forms accomplish the redemption that they do—and that has much to do with the way that even the nontheological social forms strive for eternity. We do not wait for Judaism or Christianity to enter the picture before we can see how society aims for eternity. And quite strikingly, it aims in two opposite manners, through two distinct sets of social practices and institutions: objectively, through the use of force in the state; and, in the realm of personality and inwardness, through the structuring of experience in art.

Gestures of Eternity

At last we may explore the claims made for the two theological communities—the standard task in interpreting Part III of *The Star of Redemption*. Again, I repeat the decisive methodological conclusion made above, that the task is in no sense dogmatic. If Judaism and Christianity distinguish themselves, it must be by the social forms that are not uniquely possible for them, nor even uniquely practiced by them, but only by the emphasis and self-consciousness of those forms in these two contexts. All societies may form around a common table or in a public space. I will draw out the very accessibility of the theological social forms in order to accentuate the sociological nature of Rosenzweig's analysis. The question of authority itself, particularly in relation to revealed tradition, is overlooked in Rosenzweig's treatment. This produces a certain one-sidedness in his account as well as a deep resistance to diachronic considerations in the development of social forms. On the other hand, Rosenzweig's analysis offers a sort of social phenomenology of practices and institutions which develops his basic thesis about society and eternity.

We may now follow Rosenzweig through his discussion of Judaism precisely as the *Aufhebung* (sublimation) of the state and politics. In an interesting reminiscence of the Hegelian distinction between good and bad infinites, Judaism appears once again as a bad infinite; Judaism does not work with the state in transcending it, but instead utterly rejects it. Christianity, on the other hand, transcends art by retaining it and reforming it in a better mode. Rosenzweig presents Judaism first as the rejection of the state with its use of force. He then proceeds to discuss the social practices that create the community from within.

The most important rejection in rejecting the state is that of the people's connection to land. By abandoning the land, the community loses its need for an army, for war, in short for all external forms of violence. What replaces this patriotism? At first approximation, the land is rendered holy and, as such, unpossessable. Rosenzweig is not only observing the exile and dispersion as a historical fact; rather, he emphasizes that even when the people took possession of the land, it held that the land was God's. (Here the proximity to Weber's interpretation is apparent.) The autocthonous connection to a land is uprooted at the outset (the sojourn in Egypt, the exodus, the wandering in the desert—all formative moments in the self-consciousness of the community), and this unrootedness is developed in the Babylonian exile and becomes permanent in the dispersion after the fall of the Second Temple.

But surely Jews always desired the land, desired to return. Rosenzweig holds that, because they never owned the land, their desire was an insatiable desire, a desire for a holy land, which no possession of real estate, no habitation of specific hills and valleys, could ever satisfy. Whether the community lives on the soil of the Rhineland or the banks of the Hudson, or even in the hills of Galilee, it is never at home. Rosenzweig was no Zionist,[1] but his point is that while a Jew in exile longs for land, the land he longs for is not a piece of soil. By making land into the holy land, the community dispossessed itself and separated its desire from the struggle for geopolitical power.

But there is a second way for the people to survive, a way that is primary for Rosenzweig: through its own blood. The people roots itself in its body, in its generations, and not in the lifeless soil. Rosenzweig speaks as though no other people has ever done this, that all others have been rooted only to soil, but one must wonder whether this form of preservation is not in some measure universal (Judaism hardly has a monopoly on reproduction). Perhaps this blood community is stronger in Judaism precisely because it has sacrificed its link to land, but the evocation of a blood community is both historically questionable (Jews welcomed and even solicited converts in antiquity) and philosophically troubling (a potentially catastrophic racism lurks here). So here, as elsewhere in the accounts of Jewish and Christian sociology, our questions remain even as we seek sociological insight. It is not clear that the abandonment of ancestral soil must be matched with a potentially racist idea of blood. In any case, the first move is the characteristic move to a society that has stripped politics of its force: the willingness to wander and not possess a specific piece of land through the sanctification and eternalization of the land desired. Holy land, which cannot be owned, replaces geophysical land, which must be fought for.

This logic repeats in the discussion of laws. From the changing web of law, changed and preserved by the state's use of force, the community may freeze its law and make that law eternal. The set of customs and practices are made into a holy law, which can no more change nor coerce than the holy land could be possessed or fought for. These laws are binding for all time—there is no human legislature, no process of revolution and change, no conservation against the change. The people, thus, do not know normal life. Their customs from the past and their regulations for the future are made to stand still, continuously. Their life is anachronistic, or perhaps better, futuristic, or simply atemporal. Rosenzweig is drawing a fine line here, because the state must pretend to serve the same function. Innovations in Jewish law must appear as though given in the eternal law (338/304), but a state must renew its old law (370/334). The histories of law will thus look different: Jewish changes will be a continued unfolding of an original revelation, but all will have already been revealed at Sinai. Thus the temporal motion is a continuous dragging of the present to the past. Normal history would show a continuous progress and renewal; the origin would be preserved, but the future would promise new hope and new law. The temporal motion is a dragging along of what can be saved from the past into the demands of future. (Rosenzweig criticizes Islamic law for making the law appear at once in Mohammad's proclamations, in contrast to the deductions in the present of Talmud and canon law [241/216]). Eternalizing the law does not eradicate the history of law any more than legislation and revolution achieve eternity for the state. The gap is socially constructed by the refusal to submit the practices of the community to the flow of history. The correlate, which Rosenzweig notes, is that the people float in history more completely because their own law and land are now eternal and not subject to history's threats.

Rosenzweig also finds a third dimension of communal life, in addition to land and law, that Judaism eternalizes: language. I omitted language in discussing the state in the last section because language is not as central to the coercion by the state. The most one would say is that it is the medium of force. But the contrast here is again in the elevation of one's language to a holy language. For languages change, grow, and even die, and as such are correlate with the life of a people. Here is exile again, because in order to make Hebrew a holy language the Jews had to live in another language. The languages in which they lived changed, lived, and died. The holy language was reserved only for liturgy and study. The sanctification of their language "diverts the ultimacy of feeling away from the everyday; it prevents the eternal people from ever living completely at one with time" (335/302). Rosenzweig finds this diversion to be a disruption of freedom and unreservedness, because the language one speaks is 'only' an everyday language. While others lived and prayed the same language and so could invest the everyday with the meanings of the holy—and at the same time lost their liturgy when their life changed—the Jews never could trust the foreign language in which they found themselves. Hebrew cannot die because it is not bound to history; it is not used for everyday speech.[2]

These three eternalizations and resulting alienations show how Jewish society negates the historical struggles of political nations by sublimation (*Aufhebung*). But the inner constitution of the community, its own structuring of time, is still lacking. To eternalize one's relation to land, law, and language may succeed in pulling one out of time, but how does one still live with time? The core for Rosenzweig's presentation is the formation of a community that can be silent together. The alienation from living language is only complete in the moment of silence. Rosenzweig emphasizes the mistrust of the power of language balanced against an inner trust in the power of silence (335/302). As I discussed above, the goal of society is a new silence, a communal experience that is distinguished, by its communal character, from the silence before speech. Transcending from politics, that silence is created through communal hearing, eating, and bowing.

Rosenzweig distinguishes three stages of redemption in the portrait of the Jewish community, as expressed in his marginal titles added for the second edition of *The Star of Redemption*: sociology of the mass, sociology of the community, and, finally, sociology of the whole. These three stages are correlated to the three constitutive actions for community: hearing, eating, and greeting one another. In each stage Rosenzweig shows how the social practice offers an alternative to the force of the state in constituting community. These activities are hardly unique to Judaism. Our first step is to see the basic social form, which will already display the alternative to force and the state. Only after we see how force is transcended, how redemptive community is created, should we observe the specifically Jewish instantiation of the social form. The specificity of that community will lie in its self-consciousness and to some extent in its more absolute or pure expression. But these activities are common to societies around the world.

First, hearing. The community must learn to hear in a way different from listening in dialogue. I discussed this in the first chapter, but here the emphasis is on the nondialogue in which there is no need to say anything in response. The political speech stands in contrast to the speaking that produces pure hearing, in that a political speech draws out the crowd into applause, into cheers and boos. The politician incites the audience to become partisan and vocal. In opposition, Rosenzweig offers the reading of a text. The more fixed what is said, the less the audience focuses on the speaker and on responding. The reading of a publicly held scripture is the speech that best produces hearing in the crowd, because it asks the crowd to hear together, to find itself as addressed community, but it does not incite the crowd to answer. In the fourth chapter I discussed the way that the biblical text is read and then interpreted, making the written word come alive. Here we see that reading the text works as an inversion of political speech. The politician's purpose is to amass support for the particular platform, the specific innovations or conservative plans of his or her party and cause. Political speech is harangue and slogan. But true community emerges from the silence of listening to the reading of the text.

One need only think of Plato's *Ion* to see that pagans gathered to hear texts read. Literate societies often institutionalize public readings for which a community of hearers is formed without the coercion and the rhetorical ploys of political address. Even oral societies depend on public recitations of fixed texts. These public performances might also create a calendar of festivals. The cult is different from the assembly in this way, and the resulting community is not polarized nor positioned for the innovative progress of law.

What does characterize the Jewish community in Rosenzweig's account is that the cycle of reading is a celebration of the week, as the readings are done on the Sabbath. The liturgy of the Sabbath makes explicit the sequence Creation, Revelation, Redemption. The reading of the portion from the Torah, however, is the core of Rosenzweig's interpretation, and he describes how the blessings before and after link the individual, the text, and the community in the pattern we have been discussing. The yearly cycle of readings brings eternity into time, but the focus is on how the community learns to keep silent before the text.

The second social form is eating in common. This companionship transforms the society of hearers. Here is a group of people who feed themselves. Eating is a renewal of the life of the body, a renewal that brings life and requires material reality. But eating together brings life to the community, for there is a fundamental equality in our bodily existence which we avow in eating together. Even though we do not cheer for the reader of the text, we do not become equal to that leader until we eat together. Eating in common produces not only equality but also the awareness of our own freedom, experienced in satisfying our hunger. We may obey the reading, but we cannot do so freely until we have eaten.

Companionship, breaking bread together, thus creates the free and equal community. Rosenzweig discounts what is said at table, even were it common hearing again, in order to focus on the social requirement that each be fed. The contrast here is with the domestic politics of command and law. While hearing was contrasted with the struggle to acquire power, with the formation of parties and the motivation of crowds into action, eating together is contrasted with the exercise of executive power in the constituted state. However the state derives its authority, once established it exercises it without the necessity of equal regard. It now has amassed sufficient authority to govern, and so it must: taxing according to its laws, punishing criminals, regulating commerce, etc. Eating together subverts authority and prevents its exercise. We all must be fed, and we all experience our freedom in eating together, sharing in the mutual joy of each other's satisfaction.

Eating together is commemorated in festivals—communal feasts—in many cultures. Again, many other societies establish a calendar of feasts, which differ from sacrificial offerings precisely because they are not the exclusive privilege of the priests. Rosenzweig entitles this stage "the sociology of the community," because we live our common satisfaction eating together. He emphasizes the self-consciousness of Judaism by looking at the three pilgrimage festivals: Passover, the Feast of Weeks, and the Feast of Tabernacles. Again they follow the theological sequence (Creation, Revelation, Redemption), but the key festival is Passover, with its liturgically explicit seder.

In the process of the Passover seder, two social performances enact the equality of the community. First, the emphasis on inclusion is not only stated in the ritual, but more importantly, is performed through the gesture of the youngest child asking the four questions. Rosenzweig interprets that gesture as follows:

> This is really the signal of the genuine free sociability in opposition to all instruction, which always involves mastery, in which companionship is never constituted, that here the relation to the one who is nearest to the periphery of the circle 'gives the law' for the level of the conversation. It must include even him. No one who is physically present may remain spiritually excluded. The freedom of companionship is always the freedom of all who belong to it. Thus the meal becomes a sign of the call of the people to freedom. (352–53/318)

The physical community is united by the food in such a way that freedom is enacted. No question is too stupid or too ignorant. The least person must be included, not merely as vessel to be filled, but with epistemic priority. The liturgy thus makes conscious the fundamental sharing of freedom that happens in the common eating.

Rosenzweig continues his discussion of the Passover seder, revealing how the authority of the leader disintegrates through the process of the feast. When the meal is complete and the participants are still drinking, the authority of the liturgy, of the convener and leader, dissolves. Sated with food and happy with wine, the group gains independence and through companionship displaces authority. Here not only is the model of teacher and student inverted, so that equality means the student's question is primary, but also the authority (in Rosenzweig's discussion and Jewish tradition, patriarchal authority vested in the father of the house, literally Master of the house [*Baal ha-Bayit*]) is dissolved into equality. The common meal so commemorated and made self-conscious creates a community of equals, free in spirit because they are united in their material needs. And this is the *Aufhebung* of political authority exercised by the state.

The final action is greeting one another. From a crowd, to a community, to the whole. The problem is clear: the meal creates only a community of those who sit together. Insofar as such a community eats in silence, it is not the silence of redemption, because those who are not at table are not silent. Rosenzweig recognizes that a club excludes the uninvited, those who are not called by the communal hearing. But the guests through table fellowship became a community, and afterward they know each other and so greet one another when they meet again. Greetings have the prior condition of familiarity, even if only an introduction before a handshake. Rosenzweig now turns his attention to the gestures of greeting, for the silence of the greeting is the silence that completes the community.

The immediate problem is that a true redemptive greeting is impossible because there is no universal companionship. Rosenzweig elevates the greeting to that which constitutes the community of those who know each other, but no community of everyone knowing each other exists. There is no easy solution to the problem, because the silence of greeting is the perfected silence, the silence not of being closed to one another, but of everyone being open and known to each other. "Only if everything keeps silent would silence be perfected and the community universal [*die Gemeinschaft all-gemein*]" (357/322). The greeting of recognition within the community must be the point of departure.

The contrast between politics and religion is most explicit here, for the gestures of community and recognition in the political society are military salutes and flag waving. Here the authority, the necessity of force, reaches it social peak—because the army is drawn together into a community and the people become unified in saluting the flag or the president or the monarch. The obeisance to a ruler or an image of the state is based on the faith that the nation will live forever and in some way has always existed. Here we see the state expressing the social reaching for eternity in time.

The gesture that enacts a true eternal community is not a raising of one's arm in obedience to a ruler, or to a state. On the contrary, the gesture of eternal community is bowing. Lowering one's body in obedience to . . . to God. In place of the willed eternity of the state, one greets the eternal Lord. One transcends the sociological forms of the state—with its war as a means to eternity—by bowing before a God who transcends the temporality of states and history. The political salutes are bound to fate, to the historical fate of the state, and so exclude both the universality of redemption and also the eternity of it.

But how can we distinguish these gestures? Rosenzweig emphasizes how the bowing is prepared for by the meal and the recitation of the text—that the power structure has already been leveled through companionship. This gesture is not to a king, to a general, nor even to an elected official, but is only to God. The authority and power is displaced from the realm of visible and temporal locations. In addition, the God to whom the bowing occurs is not the local deity, but is the God of the whole world. Hence one step in overcoming the particularity of the community is thus completed.

But the social phenomena extend to our gestures of greeting one another, both as individuals and as communities. The theological dimension emerges in terms of this displacement of authority from the human centers to the divine. Here a move to Judaism seems more quickly needed. The bowing that Rosenzweig focuses on is the prostration on the Day of Atonement (Yom Kippur). While his interpretation is of great interest in many respects, only the question of what the bowing accomplishes for the community is relevant here.

This bowing is linked to the scream for forgiveness as a silent enacting of that scream. Here the petition for forgiveness, the question and petition for universal redemption, takes place through the communal bowing. The congregation feels this nearness to God, through the recitation of the text that describes the high priest's service in the Holy of Holies in the Temple, and at the mention of the unpronounceable name the congregation now bows, as the community used to bow in the Temple courtyard. Rosenzweig emphasizes the bowing itself—the congregational common action and the interpretation given it liturgically. The bowing is interpreted in terms of a key prayer in the liturgy (the *Alenu*), in which the congregation prays for that time

when every knee will bow before God, and when every idol shall have disappeared from the earth, when the world will become established in the Kingdom of God and all children of flesh shall call on Your name, all evil ones of the earth will turn themselves to You and all will accept the yoke of Your Kingdom. (359–60/324)

Rosenzweig reorganizes the prayer, however, and the result is in some way a dilution of the point he wishes to make. Consider the standard version:

We therefore hope in You, O Lord our God, that we may speedily behold the glory of Your might, when idols will have disappeared from the earth and idolatry will be utterly destroyed, when the world will be established in the Kingdom of God, and all children of flesh will call on Your Name, and all evil ones of the earth will turn themselves to You. *Let all the inhabitants of the world perceive and know* that unto You every knee must bow, *every tongue must swear allegiance. Before You, O Lord our God, let them bow and worship: and unto Your glorious name let them give honour; let them all accept the yoke of Your Kingdom, and You reign over them speedily and for ever and ever.*[3]

The liturgical examination of this extremely old prayer, a prayer which begins by extolling the unique relation of the Jews with God and ends with this strongest universalism, would be worthy of a whole chapter. Rosenzweig's own reconciliation of the limitations of this one community and its representation of the whole world both depart and return to this prayer. Indeed, the very correlation of Jewish thought with philosophy could be interpreted through this prayer. But for now I would like to say that Rosenzweig's jumbled quoting actually obscures the significance of the bowing. In the first stanza (with its emphasis on uniqueness), the prayer says: "We bend the knee and bow before you and give thanks to you, king of king of kings, the holy one blessed be He, who stretched for the heavens and laid the foundations of the earth."[4] While God is recognized as a God of the whole world, the 'we' is the particular community that recognizes God as such. This bowing is then linked to the hoped-for bowing by the whole world in the second stanza. And in that second stanza the contrast between idolatry, political oaths, and obeisance is made clear—only God should be so served with bowing and swearing.

Rosenzweig fills out the discussion of this particular bowing with his moment of both greatest individualism and greatest chauvinism. This requires from an interpreter two responses: a further stretching to see how individualism is bound with universalism, and a more explicit recasting of Rosenzweig's thought, for his claim here may not be sympathetically viewed. The great effort occurs because Rosenzweig sees the individual bowing in his death shroud, pleading both as an individual and at the same time for humanity. The greatest individuality of the single person standing before God, near to God, represents all humanity. The depth and isolation of myself, recognizing the great oppositions that lie within me, allow me to stand in for all humanity. I pray for everyone and everything, accepting responsibility for the faults of all. This individuality—rather, this uniqueness—sharpened by the gestures and the liturgical speech, makes me capable of bearing the world. Such a paradoxical uniqueness will be the topic for Chapters 8 and 9.

Our critical distance, however, comes because Rosenzweig holds that such a bowing individual recognizes that he (she) is already redeemed. For Rosenzweig this bowing bears the certainty of eternity in this life. This certainty of redemption, the conviction of already being eternal, is a falsification of our lives. Here dogmatism obtrudes irreducibly—dogmatism both in its theological sense and in its more common sense of reproach. We may recast the claim that a Jew is already eternal and certain of eternity, in several ways. This is not a marginal claim in Rosenzweig's *Star of Redemption,* and the following reinterpretations clearly break with the plain sense of the text.

Levinas proposes that the claim that the Jew is already eternal stands for a willingness to stand in judgment of history—and not to submit to history's judgment.[5] The eternity becomes a completed suspension of history's dominion—but this, too, seems an ideal that Judaism never has fully attained. Or, we might emphasize the confession that Rosenzweig places at this climax: "He, this God of love, He alone is God" (364/327). We could argue that the act of making this recognition is itself a taste of eternity in this world: to so enact God's love and God's uniqueness is to make eternity come into time. Or we might instead emphasize the foretaste of eternity in this bowing, looking at the experience phenomenologically. To be eternal then could mean being certain that the world is promised for redemption. Such reinterpretations are still a genuine distance from Rosenzweig's numerous repetitions of the claim that Judaism is already at the end, already completed in itself. That claim is refuted from within *The Star of Redemption,* because Judaism still has need for a calendar. This community, like all others, still lives in time. Even if the individual, or even the individual community, can stand for all humanity, it stands only as promise and not as the completion of that humanity. The calendar cycles display that Judaism too knows that the world lies unredeemed, that the universal bowing has not yet occurred. Judaism may represent the certainty of the promise, but that is not the same as existing as already eternal.

But let us return from this profound problem in Rosenzweig's interpretation of Judaism to our concern for sociology. Greeting is a form of communal gesture that requires familiarity with or recognition of the other. Bowing is the strongest example of such gestures because in it one offers one's self, one's pride and strength, in obeisance to the other. Bowing can be political and serve the state, as offering one's own body, especially one's arms, for the state's use of force in the military. Bowing also allows, however, for an *Aufhebung* of that force in serving a universal God, a God who is neither visible nor requires force. Such bowing to God undercuts the authority of the state and the concern for historical domination. Indeed, precisely as the conclusion of hearing and companionship, such a bowing by a community reinforces the supersession of political social forms. Each person appears ready for death in the deepest physical equality. Thus bowing before God fulfills the community that is oriented beyond force.

Before turning to Christianity and its transformation of art, I would once again repeat that such social practices are not uniquely Jewish, or even Western or monotheist. Certainly other societies can also displace political allegiance, power, and force with the freedom, equality, and unforced universalism of these practices. Judaism, for Rosenzweig, has accomplished a life that instantiates these practices more completely, and in so doing it has suspended the demands of world history and of its bearers (the state) and its engines (military and police force). The Jewish people survive in the midst of history, with a kind of history, but without the clamor for world historical presence. In the cycles of recitation, of festivals, and of bowing in the face of death, we find an alternative society to the more common one constituted by a political dimension. Christianity also has no monopoly on its social practices, but it has achieved a different but equally important way of bringing eternity into time through society. It accepts time and history much more, like the art it appropriates, but Christianity forces history into an eternal schema.

As preparation for the specific social changes that Christianity represents in the arts, we should pause and consider Rosenzweig's fundamental claim for these changes: that such a society is the eternal way. While Judaism represented the eternal life, a life whose cycles close it off from history and politics, Christianity is to be a way through the world and its time. But how, then, eternal and not merely temporal? Rosenzweig finds the answer in the Christian concept of epoch.

The world knows epochs only in the past. An epoch is the stability of the past moment—of the Roman Empire, for instance. The durability of the past, in opposition to its ever flowing off as mere time, gives us access to it. If Christianity is to be an eternal way and neither avoid history nor dissolve into time, its eternity must be secured by making the present of its way into an epoch itself. Rosenzweig sees the Augustinian schema, in which the temporal world is a path between two eternities (before Creation and after Redemption), as the way of producing a present epoch. Whether Rosenzweig discusses the historical epochs—before Christ

(B.C.), between Christ's resurrection and the second coming (A.D.), and after the Last Judgment (?)—or the more metaphysical epochs—two eternities surrounding the temporal order—the present has been secured as an epoch.

The Christian present is on the way from Christ's coming to his coming again, but no point on this historical way is any closer to origin or conclusion (376/338–39). Thus historical progress is not itself what provides the transition from one epoch to another. The advance along the way always keeps one in the same nearness to God. Here is Ranke at the expense of Hegel and of all incrementalism. This makes the way of the Christian eternal—one never arrives because one lives in this epoch. One always is on the way. Rosenzweig speaks of how every point is midpoint and so in every moment, in every present, a Christian sees the origin in Christ and the conclusion in redemption as near and present. Christianity makes every moment, whether past, present, or future, into a living present. The nature of that present is a preparation for the redemptive community. Christianity is the process of forming a universal society. Its practices do not constitute the community (as the Jewish ones did), but rather prepare for that community. Christianity will be a set of social practices that lead one to the redemptive sort of community, but do not actually produce that community.

Because Christianity represents the alternative to epochizing history, of living in and through history, Christianity comes to represent for Rosenzweig the *Aufhebung* of the social forms of art. Art, too, took up a location in the flow of time and 'worked with it'. The configuring of the process of loss, which characterizes art in general, needs a transformation, however. The aesthetic flight from the all-too-common world must be replaced by an artistic creation of a common world. The sense of epochs, of periods in history, shows the dimension of Christianity that is corporate, social, 'objectified spirit'. We begin the movement from the individual's idealized experience to a social reality. There are two coordinate motions here: from the pure to the applied, and from the spectator to the participant. The move to application is the move to structure the world in the world, to bring change in the social reality through art. The move from the spectator to the participant is the move that makes redemption, in Rosenzweig's technical sense, possible—that art is something that we all do, not that somebody does for us. Clearly these two motions are linked, and they culminate in the festival, in dancing in the streets.

The first of the applied arts is architecture. It is the application of the plastic arts, for it takes the artistic creation of space and fixes it in the world. Rosenzweig contrasts the paintings and sculpture shown in museums or in galleries with buildings themselves. The plastic artist has created ideal spaces, revealed through the artwork itself. The frame of the painting, the pedestal for the sculpture, these are expressions of the collision of the ideal space of the art with the real space of the viewer. Each piece fights off its context and so establishes itself as isolated individual.

Art becomes more than mere art, more than pure art, as it inserts itself into the space of this world. Rosenzweig compares the space of pure art to the space of the mathematician: there is no intrinsic orientation, no here that is not at the same time a there, no above or below, etc. But architecture fixes points on the crust of the globe with plumb line and sextant, and structures the space of the world through artistic power. The architect builds the building in which the sculpture and painting will be displayed—he gives them their home. The decorative arts emerge not as mere ornament, but—just the opposite—as "awake to their true life"; that is, they now give form to the space in which people work, live, meet, and pray. Rosenzweig does not denigrate decoration, nor does he attack pure art—it is just that the capacity of pure art, the ability to structure space, is only fully alive or fully awake when it works in human space. Architecture is the first of the applied arts because it gives orientation to the world in which we live and so bears the responsibility for making space conducive to community.

So far, we have architecture in its various guises, but no Christianity. The distinct contribution of Christianity is the church—as building. Yet its distinction is not churchy, but is altogether an expression of the function of a building; for the church as building is for Rosenzweig distinguished by its exemplary generation (*Erzeugung*) of the feeling of unification before that unification itself occurs (397/357). The church is one room, with its own distinctive floorplan. Its unity generates the awareness in all who enter it that this is a place in which a community forms. Because Rosenzweig is interested in developing a contrast with pure art, he focuses on the contrast with a great painting or sculpture—for in the church those art forms come home, whether the glass at Saint Chapelle or Michelangelo's *Moses*. But the contrast with politics is also interesting, because the assembly rooms seem to serve a parallel function. The difference is obvious, however; the assembly honors division of left and right, or parties, and the speech in it creates power and authority of one over others. The speech in the church is the lectionary that, following the previous analysis, creates community and silence.

The church, thus, is a preparation for the reading, and it provides a preparatory aesthetic. The feeling of unification into community prepares those who enter to hear in the way discussed before. While a formed people may enter any room and be ready to hear, a sampler of the world, an unformed group, requires this previous unification. The church is one space in which consensus and silence most exist. Thus the primary move from pure to applied art is signaled by the structuring of the space we live in, and its ultimate purpose is displayed in creating a space in which we can all feel we belong together—even before we have become a community.

The second art Christianity transforms is music. What is transformed is even more ideal, more removed from the world. Music creates an ideal time, a time removed from the real time of our world. But while plastic arts allow one to forget the real space of the world, the lyricism of music allows one to forget both the real time of the world and even the music itself. It allows for a withdrawal into the created emotions, detaching both from the real time and from the structuring of ideal time. Epicism retains awareness of the art working on the audience, but lyricism cancels out the artwork to allow pure inwardness.

The solution is the use of music in the church and, in this case, in commemorating the church calendar. Bach's cantatas, for instance, represent the specific location in time of church music. That calendar itself arises in relation to revelation—for revelation fixes a before and after and so orients the music of the church. Fleeing historicism, Rosenzweig's search for orientation in history found revelation to be the key; and, through music in the church, music becomes music in the world and, as such, fundamentally oriented.

Rosenzweig equivocates at this point about participation. On the one hand, his theory clearly requires communal singing. Such singing is the realization of community that was only granted its possibility by the architect. On the other hand, Rosenzweig wishes to allow for listening to the sung mass (perhaps for systematic reasons, or perhaps for empirical ones). The result is that he needs to argue that listening to music is not like listening to a reading, and that such listening to music only prepares one for community and does not constitute a community. Again, art is left to prepare one for the community that is to come. The distance from the concert hall becomes more subtle, and Rosenzweig is left only with the calendar and its orientation of time through the year.

But we could insist that a community is constituted by the singing and that the calendar is a result of the difference between a concert and participation. The calendar celebrates the theological concepts that make such communal singing possible (which seems the point of the second part of The Star of Redemption). Then some other texts in Rosenzweig's sociology themselves 'sing'—particularly the progress Rosenzweig finds from the architecture (preparation for community) to the reading of the lectionary (call to community) to the communal singing (formation of community). Here the relation between singing and eating might be worthy of some reflection. Rosenzweig's analysis of music is that it prepares for the sacrament of the Lord's Supper as the Christian reappropriation of the

Passover seder. Singing is interpreted as a prelude to the community that eats together.

One key problem is that, while redemptive community is ultimately one of silence, choral singing seems to announce that community while forcing words out of everyone's mouth. Rosenzweig's characteristically brilliant solution is that one learns to silence the authentic, unique speech: my specific words fall silent as we sing together; I learn to find a silence, a residing in the words of the group (the comparison with Quakers would be most interesting here). The fixed liturgy itself raises words and sentences up to a level of holiness (not unlike the Jewish relation to land, etc.) and pulls them out of history. At the same time a fixed liturgy is chanted or sung. The words lose their role as expression, as personal communication, and become "elevated to a common valid height of feeling" (403/363). Rosenzweig goes so far as to say that only when the melody of the prayer is chanted unreflectively, only when one hums along and need not think about the words, only then has a silent community been obtained. Through song and its structuring of time, its generation of emotions, the words of communication are elevated and dissolved into the chant of communal silence.

The third and final sociological analysis in Book 2 is that of the festival or pageant (*carnivale*). Here poetry and the poetic arts achieve their transformation by becoming participatory in a bold way. We move from books, to dramaturgy and drama performed, and conclude with a dance that streams forth from the church and allows each person to join in. My discussion here was anticipated in the last chapter, in the discussion of the Johannine church, but in terms of sociology of the arts we can still bring more light to the matter.

Drama differs from other poetic arts because it repeats the same application and confrontation of the ideal world with the real world. The aesthete thinks that a play actually takes place in the text and not on the stage. But the purpose of staging a play is to make poetic arts confront reality. "The hybrid effect of theatre comes from the struggle, in which the ideal world of the work must necessarily prove itself there in the reality of an assembled audience" (413/371). The performance here of body and soul, of the characters speaking words and acting in their world, confronts the spectators' world. But drama is only one step, because it is still burdened with words and has not yet achieved silence.

The next step is to dance, for the motion from speech to gesture is completed in art by dance. One's own body is the medium, and the gesture communicates in the fullest sense. Not gesture as saying something, nor gesture as drawing forth an action from the other, "but the gesture, which is totally free, become totally creative and no longer for this or that, nor towards this one or that one. The gesture completes the human totally for being, to his or her human-ity and thereby to humanity itself"

(413/372). As gesture replaces speech, the body discovers not only its place in space, but its creation of a world. When this movement is placed within the theological framework, then the world created is actually the world of creation re-created. That is, the world is redeemed through the fulfillment of human community, constituted through gesture.

The preparation for the gesture of community, for the bowing, is dance, for in dance the dramatic element of art is brought back into the real world. Dance is the participatory art form per se—Rosenzweig claims that it has or should have no spectators, but is the cooperative activity by which a people knows itself. Not ballet, but parades and carnivals, festivals and public celebrations. This public art completes Rosenzweig's aesthetics precisely because here art achieves its greatest application, as the festival world transforms the real world, with no remainder. Here is the creation of a common emotion, through the participation of each person in his or her self. In a characteristically epigrammatic comment, Rosenzweig takes this public gesture of dance one step further and reduces it to the glance (*Blick*). I have already commented upon Levinas' appropriation of this for ethics. One need only consider the appropriation by Benjamin for aesthetics. The glance as gesture has purgative power greater than action or speech. It structures the world to bring us to the redemptive community.

Just as architecture became Christian in the church as preparation for reading the lectionary, and music became preparation for the Lord's Supper, so dance comes home to the church as preparation for the sacrament of baptism. Baptism is the culmination of dance, and it leads to the procession from the church. For Rosenzweig baptism is the essence of Christianity, as the Christian is on the way, just started, and going forth into the world. But clearly any initiating rite, especially one that dwells on gesture, is parallel to this sacrament. While Rosenzweig claimed that only the Hasidic Jew knew liturgical dance, in many churches liturgical dance is now at home. Moreover, public dancing is in no sense the unique possession of Christianity. Last, it seems a short step from this Johannine church and its post-Christian Christianity to the festival's place in the experience and ideology of the student revolts in Paris in 1968. I would not claim that Rosenzweig is a prophet, but rather that his aesthetics has room for much more than church art and its traditions, and indeed offers a context for much that we would find novel in our culture.

ETERNAL ENMITY

The last section of this chapter offers no grand synthesis of the sociological examination provided. On the contrary, Rosenzweig insists at some length on the permanence of the tension between not only the state and art, not only the sociology that focuses on politics and that which dwells

on aesthetics, but even more on a tension between the theological transformations of force and structures. We might collect the six sections of
sociology in *The Star of Redemption* and discuss how redemptive communities form through these inversions of political structures and artistic
practices, but Rosenzweig sees the two communities and the sociological
alternatives that constitute them as in permanent tension. The prolonged
justification of both Jewish and Christian communities is exceptional in
Jewish or Christian theological discussion. The solution itself is troubling
precisely because it restores a certain imperial church and a de-histori-
cized Judaism. That was the problem of the previous chapter.

Following the struggle to maintain a sociological angle of inquiry
through the various sociological discussions of the two communities,
cannot we say more about "the enmity for all time" between the two
communities (462/415)? We might begin by considering how the refusal
of politics, the rejection of the judgment of world history, does not land
us immediately in an aestheticist's position. For the society that rejects
politics in the social practices of hearing, eating, and bowing ends up as
one of the great iconoclastic societies. Pure art, representational art, art as
escape from the world, is quite despised by the very same group that
struggles with its rejection of politics.

The transcendence of politics retains the political desire to refuse time
its dominion. Politics tries to force eternity from time; but the society that
rejects the political solution still aims to live as society—pure aesthetic
flight is not an option because that would abandon the social interactions
of this world. To transcend politics requires a motion through the political, retaining the social dimension and the insight into authority and
power in order to transcend the use of force.

Similarly, the transcendence of art does not produce the political order.
The structuring of time and the acceptance of loss that characterize art
are retained in the cultivation of inward states conducive to forming communities. Force is not advocated; rather, creativity is. Thus art and politics, both in their own place and as retained through theological societies,
do not combine. To say that there is enmity between Judaism and Christianity is to recognize that the failures of the state to establish eternal dominion through force, and of art to structure our loss communally cannot
be solved by a simple combination of the two into some aestheticized
politics. But even if that miserable combination of force and idealistic
escape from reality is obviously objectionable, what is more subtle is that
even the transformations—messianic politics and redemptive aesthetics—
do not belong together. These two groupings of social forms resolve the
social struggle for eternity in opposed ways. For while the one chooses the
temporal cycling of the calendar as a way to withdraw from world history, the other uses the cycling to permeate world history with the emotions conducive to redemptive community. Transcended art is propaedeu-

tic in the best sense, leading the world to become a true community. The transcended politics, on the other hand, withdraws from the world. The two will fit together, but not on the social plane, not in this world, and not in this world's time.

The balance of the tensions between messianic politics and redemptive aesthetics, moreover, points to differing capacities for social criticism. Judaism, as the *Aufhebung* of politics, involves a criticism opposed to the place of force in society. It measures social practices against an ideal of no force, of utter peace. Politics is criticized by a pacificism, but may not simply escape into aesthetics. On the other hand, the *Aufhebung* of art, Christianity, must adopt the "laws of the world" and aim for some sort of fusion of horizons, some basic preservation of the society that it changes. It measures social practices against an ideal of universal participation, but not in terms of a basic renunciation of the world or any aspect of it. All of the world can be redeemed through an enlivening, redemptive art. Thus the rejection of force may often look 'utopian', while the sublimation of the arts may look too acquiescent to the unredeemed world. The 'Christian' form of social criticism will have a clear ideal but will preserve the world as it is; the 'Jewish' will be more radical in its rejection. The two forms of social criticism, like the two sets of social practices, balance each other but cannot simply unite.

Ultimately the tension could be seen as the different temporality of the communities: the Jewish drags the present generation back to the past, finding the current moment as a means to live the past. The 'today' of revelation is in fact that day at Sinai, the day at the Red Sea, the day of each covenant. Christianity, on the other hand, struggles to make every day a today—to bring all of time into the present. It unifies past, present, and future into the present epoch. The two social forms could be linked together as the Christian preparation for the Jewish completion. Christianity draws different moments in the river of time into the present, and Judaism leads that gathering in the present back to the past. The separation of that 'making past' and 'making present' itself repeats the basic distension in time that is the structure of revelation, the structure of signification. The theological sociology of Part III of *The Star of Redemption*, therefore, repeats and so verifies the basic insight into the theological temporality discovered in Part II. One society achieves eternity by making present, another by making the present into the past—and the two repeat as sign and referent, as promise and fulfillment, the same theological structure. Were the two to collapse, were society to somehow become all a present making or all a past making, society would no longer be capable of verifying the temporal nature of our truth.

The ultimate question of this discussion—How can society have anything to do with eternity?—is now more intelligible. Eternity enters as a goal and brings with it a theological dimension for social theory, but it does not serve as the foundation of the social theory. A kind of social phenomenology, one ladened with systematic constraints, lays out the terrain. The theological dimension cannot found this sociology, nor can it become simply a sociological theology. Rather, the account of society must stand as verification of the theology of speech. Throughout *The Star of Redemption*, however, Rosenzweig offers a new perspective on temporality. His introduction of eternity does not invalidate all of history and lived temporality. He argues that our struggle to make time eternal actually creates our culture and the humanly created temporality of our lives. Time on its own is not what we experience, either internally or externally. But the philosopher's flight from time is inadequate for our lives. The fear of death, the awareness that everything must pass, is a basic horizon for all human existence. But rather than flee that horizon for some atemporality, Rosenzweig looks at how we structure that flowing and passing with the help of eternity itself. We create eternity within time, and so structure our temporality, making our culture. The fullest forms of such creativity lie in a politics without force and a participatory art. These two social configurations create the greatest eternalization available in society. *The Star of Redemption* requires a social vision self-consciously theological and universally available to guide our performance of the task of redemption.

CHAPTER 7

Correlations, Translation

IN THIS CHAPTER I turn to the works of Levinas. The sequence of topics in the following chapters parallels the sequence in the first part of the book: from the question of correlation to the logic of separation; to the performance of speech; and finally to social theory. Rosenzweig has presented these topics systematically in *The Star of Redemption,* allowing me the direct approach of interpreting his book. For Levinas these topics require a quite different approach, because he has struggled to avoid appearing as a Jewish theologian, even one as philosophical as Rosenzweig. The manner of proceeding will be an exploration of Levinas in tandem with various partners, in an effort to illuminate the prevalence of Rosenzweig's logic and of Jewish philosophy in general within Levinas' adaptations. The carefully constructed system of Rosenzweig will remain as a background for these pairings, as we move over similar terrain with a different guide, but I will not elaborate the precise nature of the adaptation and appropriation by Levinas. Instead, I hope to relocate Levinas' thought in a freer manner, challenging the familiar interpretation of Levinas which ignores the relation to religion in general and Judaism in specific.

The first step, however, is to notice how the most 'Jewish' of his works are still philosophical. Indeed, he discovers in Jewish sources not only resources for philosophical reflection, but also an inherently Jewish desire for philosophy. In short, in this chapter I will explore the correlation, in the specific sense of this book, of philosophy and Judaism in the midst of Levinas nonphilosophical writings. That correlation places Levinas' work in an altered context—one of much greater intimacy with Judaism—that is most dramatically represented by a series of colloquiums at which Levinas has spoken for the last thirty years.

On 24 May 1957, a small group of Jewish intellectuals met at Versailles for the first Colloquium of French-speaking Jewish Intellectuals, sponsored by the World Jewish Congress. They had no specific mandate at the outset, but by the time the proceedings of the first three colloquiums were published in 1963, André Neher could write of the need for those who lead the battle on every field (Jewish Intellectuals) finally to take to the one field they ignore—Judaism. In a series of yearly colloquiums, this group meets to discuss topical and foundational issues in Jewish thought. What became clear within three meetings was that there was an extreme need for education based on traditional Jewish sources. In a pattern that stretched through the 1960s, a biblical lesson and a Talmudic lesson, each dealing with the topic for that year, were placed side-by-side. There was consensus on the need for this, and, indeed, the first volume of proceedings is dedicated in part to the two respective commentators, André Neher and Emmanuel Levinas, who are called "the soul and foundation" of the colloquiums.

Levinas did not present such a commentary at the first colloquium, nor even at the second. At the second he presented a paper on Franz Rosenzweig, which was one of the two papers I discussed at length in Chapter 1. Levinas embraced Rosenzweig's claim that the Jew exists outside of history. He, like Vladimir Jankélévitch, Jean Wahl, Robert Misrahi, Émile Touati, and others, participated mainly as a philosopher. But the debate over Rosenzweig's claim that the Jews existed outside of history by abandoning politics led to the topic for the next colloquium: Jewish morality and politics. There in 1960, Levinas presented his first Talmudic commentary, on Messianism and History based on Sanhedrin 99a. At the conclusion of that third colloquium there was a clamor among the intellectuals for Talmudic commentaries in order to bring traditional wisdom to bear on contemporary discussions. Following that discussion, Levinas presented only Talmudic commentaries to this group, for the most part one per year at each colloquium. Over the years, these commentaries were gathered together in four separate books. When we include *Difficile Liberté*, which contains the first two commentaries with a large set of essays from the 1950s and 60s, we have, in those five books, Levinas' Jewish Thought.[1]

Levinas' Jewish Thought. At first glance, an inopportune name. In the Introduction I indicated that all of Levinas' thought is Jewish in the specific sense of this book. These five books are hardly unphilosophical, but they are not the general philosophy of the major works (and several other collections). These writings do not claim to be philosophy and are intended for a general, usually Jewish, audience. But when we consider in what way they might be termed Jewish, we discover some confusion. They are not Jewish as a matter of dogmatism, nor even in the style of apologetic theology. Levinas' interpretation of Talmud, for instance, is not pietistic nor even rooted in a confessional stance. To avoid the embarrassment of the term 'Jewish Thought', I now adopt one of Levinas' own terms: these Talmudic commentaries and the essays in *Difficile Liberté* constitute Levinas' 'Hebrew' writings—written, to be sure, in French (the first three only recently translated into English). On the other hand are a series of books and articles, key among them *Totality and Infinity, Otherwise than Being*, and *On God who Comes to the Idea*, that Levinas calls his 'Greek' thought. Also written in French.

In order to explore the relation of 'Greek' and 'Hebrew' in Levinas' thought, I must first clarify how he sees their distinction. The distinction is one of modes of thought; it is not a historical claim. Levinas at times makes the distinction between 'Greek' wisdom and 'Hebrew' wisdom, but most often between 'Greek' language and 'Hebrew' language—which, of course, does not literally mean language, since all is written in French. But 'Greek' represents the style of that language, which is universal, conceptual, antimetaphorical, and philosophical. 'Greek' is the language of the university; it is the common language of the West. Levinas' 'Greek' writings, therefore, are written for university/universal discourse. They are philosophy proper. These are the works of philosophy for which Levinas has gained deserved fame. In them Levinas characterizes that Western tradition critically in various guises: as the pursuit of totality, as the attempt to reduce the other to the same, as the rule of ontology—in each case as an-ethical, if not anti-ethical. He takes his stand in those philosophical works against the 'Greek' tradition, but he speaks to it in its own words. The way that 'Hebrew' thoughts appear in these philosophical works is a topic worthy of much study.

Levinas characterizes 'Hebrew' language much less fully. It is, most of all, the language of the Bible—and here, too, language means a way of thought. Levinas often refers to it simply as 'Biblical Thought'. 'Hebrew' is not the grammarians' Biblical Hebrew; rather, it is the Sages' mode of thought. The texts of Midrash and Talmud are written in it, and students argue in it when reading those texts. 'Hebrew' is essentially social, spoken in conversations over texts, and its manner of conceiving is concrete, practical, and above all, always ethical. Levinas' own 'Hebrew' writings are spoken in Jewish contexts; indeed, most of all at these colloquiums of the French-speaking Jewish Intellectuals.

The task for a whole volume would be to trace the role of 'Hebrew' as teacher in Levinas' 'Greek' works. In an almost perverse way, I propose here to look at the reverse motion of correlation: how does 'Greek' appear in Levinas' 'Hebrew' writings. The eventual result will be to notice that Levinas' discussion of Judaism requires Judaism to seek out philosophy, to seek out a 'Greek' translation of its thought. And what is almost more scandalous is that Levinas does not claim to borrow or translate from the philosophical tradition into Jewish thought. In this chapter, however, Jewish philosophy will justify its own attempt to approach Western concepts and principles. The difficulties of making such a move require a careful analysis of Levinas' treatment of 'Greek' in his writings and commentaries written for a Jewish audience. Such an analysis will proceed in four steps.

I begin by presenting Levinas' three images of 'Greek' in these commentaries. Though always distinct from 'Hebrew', 'Greek' itself is evaluated in varying degrees of criticism, as Levinas develops an increasingly positive evaluation of 'Greek'. Second, I will briefly discuss translation as Levinas' general concept of the relation of 'Greek' and 'Hebrew'. Here is the correlation producing new resources for philosophy from Jewish sources. Of greatest importance will be the way in which the key 'Greek' concepts are direct conceptual translations of traditional Jewish thought. Third, I will explore Levinas' hermeneutics for reading 'Hebrew' texts. He makes a strong claim that biblical texts can be approached Jewishly only through Midrash and Talmud. Moreover, he designs his own style of reading in such a way as to avoid both a historical-philological reading and a pietistic, Halakhic reading of Rabbinic texts. What is most striking is the almost exclusive interest in Aggadah rather than in Halakhah. This leads to an emphasis on a philosophical, universal mode of thought within the Talmud.

It turns out that 'Greece' is not only a topic for discussion in the 'Hebrew' writings, but that, even more, it is the way of reading. Thus the final issue is, To what extent is the 'Greek' in the 'Hebrew' an imposition on the text? The avoidance of several key dimensions of Talmudic commentary reflects an external limitation on Levinas' 'Jewish' thought. And yet, there is one last response from Levinas, for he also displays how the call for 'Greek' is intrinsic within the 'Hebrew', that Jewish thought solicits philosophical reflection. This leads to two final questions: 1) Is philosophy beholden to Jewish thought for experiences and concepts? Is 'Greek' incapable of its own independent access to this radical ethics? and 2) Is the identification of Jewish thought as the 'Greek' in the 'Hebrew' adequate for Jewish thought? If there is some aspect of Jewish thought that cannot be translated into philosophy, is translation an ideal or only a necessary evil?

FROM POLITICS TO RHETORIC

Although there is a consistent perspective on 'Greek' in the Talmudic lectures, there is also a subtle transformation in Levinas' acceptance of 'Greek' thought. In the context of his philosophical work of the late 1950s and 1960s, his deeply critical view of 'Greek' is obvious. But his appropriation of 'Greek' thought and his limited defense of it in the later commentaries is somewhat puzzling. I will present three images of 'Greek' in Levinas' commentaries, more or less chronologically. First, 'Greek' is the rule of the universal, the power of a political state. Second, it is the love of knowledge, the desire to know in an an-ethical way, the 'Western Odyssey' of consciousness, the return of all knowing to self-knowledge. Third, 'Greek' is the language of rhetoric, at which point 'Greek' wisdom is re-evaluated.

Levinas' elevation of ethics to 'First Philosophy' produces a rejection of the judgment of history, replacing it with the ethical judgment upon history. Coordinate with that is a critique of state political power. Although

Levinas justifies politics in several of his writings, such justification is precisely through the ethical. His critique of the West, of the 'Greek', is first of all a critique of its elevation of politics, or power, to ultimacy.

In his first Talmudic commentaries, on Sanhedrin 98b–99a, the discussions of when the Messiah will come and Who it will be, Levinas identifies 'Greek' as the politics of the universal. The universal subordinates individuals and their various moral codes under one, anonymous rule:

> What in effect is this drive towards the universality of a political order? It consists of confronting different beliefs—a multiplicity of coherent discourses—and discovering one coherent discourse that encompasses all, and which precisely is the universal order. . . . But that precisely is the destiny of Western philosophy and its logic that recognizes itself as a political condition, so that the full expression of the truth coincides with the constitution of a Universal State (through wars and revolutions). (#4, DL3 135/94)[2]

The coincidence of truth and politics is most important here. Levinas in a grand manner rejects 'Greek' immanentism. 'Greek' only knows a universal that reduces or ignores the individual and which must occur in history. Ultimately, it reduces all questions of individual mores to a universal. Levinas criticizes 'Greek' logic as forming its universals at the expense of the individual. For Levinas, the ethical obligates me in the face of an other; my objection against the universal is not ultimately for my sake as the unique individual, but is for the sake of the other person, whose individuality is lost.

'Greek' here as elsewhere is contrasted with 'Hebrew', which is indeed a second politics and a second universal. In contrast to the 'Greek' politics of world empire and conquest, Levinas in bold rhetorical flourishes describes a second relationship to immanent politics:

> Assume for a moment that the political life does not seem like a dialectical adjustment of humanity, of one with another, but seems like an infernal cycle of violence and foolishness [deraison] . . . assume that you have lost the meaning of politics and the consciousness of its grandeur—that the nonsense or the non-value of world politics is your first certainty, that you are a people outside other peoples (and that appropriately is what "a people who sojourn apart" or "people who are not counted amongst the peoples" means), assume that you are a people capable of a diaspora—capable of keeping itself outside, alone and abandoned, and you have a vision altogether different of universality. It no longer needs to be subordinated to confrontation. (#4, DL3 136/94)

Here, perhaps, we see a license afforded Levinas by his audience, for amongst Jews he is free to express the despair at politics that follows not only the Holocaust, but indeed the millenia of abandonment—and of survival. But such despair is not the rejection of universalism, but only of the universal that violates the individual. In its place is a universalism that for Levinas is Messianism proper, that is bound to my unique responsibility for an other unique person. 'Hebrew' universalism is intrinsically bound to particularism. In the uncounted Colloquium with the Algerian Jews, Levinas discusses a particularist universalism, explaining it as "the very mystery of the moral phenomenon: the moral act that I alone myself can do, that I must do in the strongest sense of myself to make a sacrifice—that is morality itself" (#Z, 239). Obligation is universal; any other whom I meet I am bound to, but I and no one else, I as unique and irreplaceable, I have these duties. The 'Hebrew' universality never allows the Jews to dissolve into the others, to lose the obligations they cannot disavow. The particularism, thus, is not opposed to the universal scope of responsibility, but it does preserve my duty as mine, refusing to dissolve it into a duty of the universal community. Such universalism cannot be achieved by war in any of its guises. It requires I serve everyone, and in that sense I accommodate each person by invitation and solicitude, not by subordination to a principle. Of course, this is not realized in our world now, but it is just the demand for historical confirmation which 'Hebrew' thought rejects. "Above all, this means that Israel does not measure its morality by the political—but only by its universality, which is the messianic itself" (#4, DL3 137). 'Hebrew' politics must not measure itself against historical progress, but vice versa (#10, SAS 45/114).

The second image of 'Greek' is closely related to the first. If 'Greek' represents a politics of totalitarian states and a universalism that destroys individuals, then at its core 'Greek' is a mode of knowing, a fundamental relation to the other of assimilation. The 'Greek' conquest of others threatens the other, not the self. The universal becomes a way of the self, of the 'I', to subordinate all to itself. Levinas has often contrasted Odysseus to Abraham: the one who journeys into the unknown in order to return to himself vs. the one whose travels lead to a new and unfamiliar place. As philosopher (in the 'Greek' writings), Levinas develops a profound attack on the Western tradition as reducing all knowledge of others to knowledge of oneself, to the reflexivity of the knower knowing his act of knowing. This fundamentally narcissistic circle of consciousness is the foundation of our Western philosophy (#11, SAS 67/127).

Levinas' most prolonged attack on 'Greek' and philosophy in the 'Hebrew' works is an essay on temptation, or rather, on the temptation of temptation, a commentary on Shabbat 88a–b, focusing on the "we will do and we will hearken" of Exodus 24.7. This accepting and pledging prior to knowing what is to be done has both troubled and defined Jewish Thinkers for centuries. One's natural reaction is that such obedience is foolish and, worse, immoral. But Levinas wishes to dislodge the opposition that governs the reaction: either one knows or one doesn't, but if you don't then to proceed to pledge obedience is immoral and naive; either one is naive (fanatical), or one knows what one is agreeing to do. Levinas contrasts this opposition, which he calls 'Greek', with a 'Hebrew' opposition. The 'Hebrew' alternatives are an adult option for the good, which is prior to the freedom to choose between good and evil, and an option of evasion, of deferring responsibility for the sake of self-control. That even this latter alternative derives from the option for the good is the topic of Chapter 9. Here our concern is with the analysis of both the 'Greek' opposition and with its deeply evasive character.

What is so challenging in this commentary by Levinas is that he announces that philosophy represents both this commonsense opposition and, further, the attempt to know what you are agreeing to do. Philosophy becomes the temptation of temptation. To be open to what is asked and then resist, that is temptation, but to know what would be tempting and not even be tempted is the temptation of temptation. 'Greek' here means the retreat from the imperative of obligation (which one would do or not) to a seemingly disinterested distance where the question is one of knowing what would be required. That moment of knowledge tempts us and is what makes temptation tempting.

For the 'Greek', knowledge precedes action. One must know the action prior to doing it in order to choose the good freely. And already the privileges are given to me both to know and to act.

> It is necessary to experience [*éprouver*] everything for oneself, but to experience still without experiencing, in advance, without binding oneself in the world. For to experience is simply already to be engaged, to choose, to live, to restrict oneself. To know is to experience without experiencing, before living. We wish to know before we act. But we want only to know completely, with our appropriate evidence. Nothing undertaken without knowing it all, nothing known without having gone to see oneself, which may be the misadventures of exploration. A dangerous life but, rest assured, one in the world of truths. Seen thus, the temptation of temptation is, as we said, philosophy itself. Noble temptation, already barely tempting and much more courageous. Courage in security, a firm place in our old Europe. (#6, QL 75–76/34)

Philosophy advocates a detachment in which one can feel slightly tempted and then overcome the temptation. Its cowardice depends on a leisure, and indeed on a privilege, of security. Because knowing always reinstalls the self after it has tasted the various other choices, it not only preserves the self, but makes the self feel as though it had been brave, had explored the possibilities. But so long as the self chooses on its own, in freedom, it is always only choosing its own freedom, its activity as chooser. Even its flirtation with temptation is an exercise of itself choosing its own exercise. But by scouting out the options, by exploring temptations, the self conserves its own freedom. Levinas accuses Christianity of often submitting to this process and of accepting the fundamental opposition of naiveté or philosophy.

The 'Hebrew' alternative is found in the acceptance of the Torah prior to knowing it. On the one hand, there is a choice for good without the temptation and without naiveté. To accept the Torah is not irrational, but is rather a kind of reasoning prior to 'Greek' reason. There is a truth here that is not based on hypotheses, on ideas, on an attempt to know (#6, QL 104/48)—a truth prior to the separation of knowing/doing. On the other hand, the exultation and evasion of the command produces the alternative of self-governing which is the 'Greek' opposition. The very freedom of knowing, of discursive reason, of philosophy, is founded on an unchosen freedom, a finite freedom. Here the concept of election, of being chosen, is the alternative to a 'Greek' domination of the other by the knowing self. Prior to the commandments to do good and to avoid evil is the commandment of commandments, the commandment of obedience—which is the foundation of all freedom, even that of knowing.

Thus, in the first two images, 'Greek' represents the lesser member of an opposition with 'Hebrew'. The 'Greek' is both the realm of politics and the realm of self-founding knowing, and as such Levinas criticizes it profoundly. In each case, 'Greek' thought is thought that is deaf to ethics, enslaved to the self through either politics or speculation. In the third image, 'Greek' gains a more ambiguous characterization, as Levinas seems to qualify his radical dismissal of the tradition. He now distinguishes between 'Greek' language and 'Greek' wisdom, and he identifies the Talmudic critique of Greece with the language.

The first clear statement to this effect is in the commentary on Menahot 99b–100a (#17, ADV 43–44). The argument concerns whether anyone should have time to study Greek wisdom, since the book of the Torah shall be always in one's mouth (Josh. 1.8). The Sages are quite opposed to any time for Greeks, but Levinas wishes to save 'Greek' thought. He makes a distinction between Greek science and arts, with the clarity of their reason, and Greek rhetoric. Emphasizing the Hellenistic culture and its courtly and diplomatic use of Greek, Levinas contends that Sages oppose sophistry, not philosophy. The apology for 'Greek'—and here I mean also Levinas' own 'Greek' writings, his proper philosophical works—continues explaining the vulnerability of true wisdom to prostitution and pollution. Here 'Greek' becomes dual: on the one hand, it is the sneaky, deceptive, manipulative art of rhetoric; on the other, it is the wisdom of philosophy, the pathos of its drama, the glory of architecture, and so on.

The rehabilitation of 'Greek' continues in a commentary on Yoma 10a called "Who Plays Last?" (#20, ADV 78). The first and striking move is that here the universal politics of the first image of 'Greek' is ascribed to Rome. It is not hard to see what motivates that textually, and even philosophically, because Rome is the descendant of Greece and made empire into a total world. But at the same time, this universal politics, so reviled twenty years earlier, is now praised as a positive moment. It still is not moral, but it serves to domesticate humanity from its animalistic struggle for power (#20, ADV 84). Aside from the Messiah, Rome with its bad, 'Greek' universalism is given the last play.

If Rome now plays the role of bad universal, then 'Greek' now becomes the pursuit of the *kalon*, of beauty and nobility. Greece represents the sublimation and transformation of the will to power, from crude head-bashing to the artistic, spiritual, delicate oppression of the aristocracy. As such it is a positive move, but it then appears as less universal than Rome. Indeed, in Levinas' reflections on the necessity of separation between the elite and the many, he echoes Nietzsche's interpretation of power and distance. Levinas grants that nobility only to criticize its immorality in the strongest terms (#20, ADV 79–80).

I will conclude this rehabilitation, such as it is, with reference to a remarkable commentary on Megillah 9a–b (#23, HDN 43ff.). Here the distinction between 'Greek' wisdom and language is made by reference to Baba Kama 83a (#23, HDN 64). Whether the Sages mean the first two images of 'Greek' wisdom (philosophy and bad universals) or the rhetoric of the sophists is not the point, because Levinas goes on to praise the language excessively. Again, there is a warrant in the text, because the Mishnah grants special privileges to translations into Greek. Levinas praises it for its beauty—a beauty one could link to the rhetorical power, as the Talmud puns. But Levinas goes on to praise Greek's order, clarity, lack of prejudice, and methodical power, and he terms it the language of demystification, demythifying, depoetisizing. It is the prose of commentary and hermeneutics because it demetamorphosizes metaphors.

Surely we cannot fail to note that Levinas has transformed his critique. What began as an attack on the Western tradition of politics and of philosophy, now under the same banner, has become a salute of the tradition as powerful and beautiful. This is no contradiction, for what was criticized then is still submitted to criticism. (Levinas does not abandon that first image. In a recent interview he calls the universal politics 'Greek' in order to criticize it.)[3] What does emerge, however, is a second factor: the 'Greek' language. This new, positive evaluation of the language is a necessary step to providing a consistent self-understanding for Levinas' two bodies of writing. I cannot but think that Levinas had to rediscover a positive 'Greek' to justify writing so much in 'Greek'. The critique remains, but there now is room, even in the 'Hebrew' writings, for Japheth.

Translation into 'Greek'

Despite the sometimes severely critical and hostile images of 'Greek', Levinas maintained his role as a philosopher, as a 'Greek' writer. Nonetheless, in his mature work (starting with *Totality and Infinity*), Levinas indicates the possibility that there is a profound agreement between the 'Greek' and the 'Hebrew'—indeed, that his own 'Greek' writings are translations from the 'Hebrew'.

The concept of translation here is, of course, not linguistic, but 'linguistic'; that is, from one mode of thought to another. In a later commentary, Levinas indicates that to move from 'Hebrew' to a universal discourse is exactly that translation 'into Greek' (#21, ADV 94). Universal, as indicated above, is the province of 'Greek', but only insofar as it is taken in a practical and nontechnical sense. What he means by "speaking in Greek" is "the mode of expressing ideas according to our university practices of presentation and interpretation" (HDN 203). Indeed, the motivation for such university language is rhetorical or even apologetic. Levinas in 1970 explained that he used 'Greek' terms to convince objectors that he was doing philosophy while commenting on Talmudic texts (#11, SAS 58/122). Apologetic discourse itself would require a further discussion, as for Levinas all discourse is an apology, an address to justify oneself to the other. Moreover, Levinas distinguishes two ways of reading Talmud: an uncritical way, and a way that is translation—an attempt to justify itself to a different mode of thought wherein justification depends on self manifestation.[4]

This appearance in a 'Greek' court is thus, most of all, an attempt to speak to the 'Greeks'—to the world that does not attend the colloquiums. In several writings, and in some historical reflection, it becomes clear that Levinas holds that the 'Greek' would not on its own think the key 'Hebrew' thoughts. On the concluding page of one of his 'Hebrew' books, Levinas declares that "we have the large task of announcing in Greek the principles of which Greece is ignorant" (ADV 233–34/LR 287). In contrasting 'Greek' and 'Hebrew' in the 1960s, Levinas at one point emphasizes that 'Greek' does not have a concept of responsibility for the other, that the Aeschylean mercy of the *Eumenides* is not the responsibility for each other found in the Talmud (#8, QL 182f./87f.). 'Hebrew' provides nourishment for the philosopher (QL 12/4). Clearly, there is a way of assimilating 'Hebrew' thought into 'Greek' in this image; of biting, chewing, and then digesting the 'Hebrew' concepts by the voracious knower of 'Greek'—which is paradoxical because Levinas claims that the inadequacy of 'Greek' is precisely that it knows not by doing responsibility for the other, but by assimilating the other into the same.

The clearest examples of Levinas' translation are the coupled terms *Kedousha/ethique* and *Hochma/sagesse*. The first (holiness/ethics) represents the translation of the various uses of the biblical and Jewish concept of holiness into a philosophical concept of ethics. Holiness, which seems to relate the human and the divine, is translated as a relation between human beings. Levinas claims that Kedousha should be translated into 'Greek' (French) as *sainteté* (holiness), in opposition to *le sacré* (the sacred), in order to distance it from the mythic and magical, spiritually empowered, etc. The desacralization of the world is what allows that full translation of the relations to God to become realized in our relations with other people.

Similarly, the second couple (wisdom/wisdom) represents a transformation of the 'Greek' (French) concept: while the philosopher-sage of the 'Greek' is one who knows him or herself, and from that the world, the 'Hebrew' wise one is one who fears God first of all, one whose wisdom begins in receiving the commandments. Responsibility is made central in such wisdom, while self-relation is thus reoriented in bringing the 'Hebrew' into the 'Greek'.

In the case of the two most central concepts—the face (*le visage*) of *Totality and Infinity*, and substitution of *Otherwise than Being*—Levinas clearly develops the ideas in 'Hebrew' writings, while also developing Jewish ideas. Because these are the central concepts of his 'Greek' work, I will pause here to show his translation at work.

Levinas' phenomenology climaxes in the moment I am face to face with another person. The face is the experience that lies at the root of ethics for Levinas (see Chapter 1). In encountering an other, I am prohibited from murdering him by his face. My obligation to be for the other rests in his human face, not as a cluster of nose and eyes, etc., but as an announcement of my responsibility for him, my duties. The separation between the other and myself is an inassimilable difference proclaimed in the other's face. I cannot make him mine, nor reduce him to my cognition of him. This concept emerges in the Hebrew word *lifné*, which means literally "to the face," or "before." The significance of standing in front of someone (before the other's face) has a particular resonance in Hebrew and in the Bible. It is the set of related meanings of the preposition (before) and the noun (face) that Levinas 'translates' in the concept of the face.

Levinas developed the idea of the face in several philosophical ('Greek') essays from the mid 1950s that lead up to *Totality and Infinity*. But the route to this distinctive idea begins in *Time and the Other* (1948). He makes reference to a face-to-face (*face-à-face*) encounter, but he explicitly links it to the widow and the orphan in order to bring out the responsibility, drawing again on 'Hebrew' writings (TO 73/83). Levinas first develops the face properly in a 'Greek' work in 1951, the essay "Ontology: is it fundamental?" (EN 13). He departs from a Heideggerian perspective by arguing that the relation to another person is not ontological but is, in Levinas' own sense of the term, *religion*. The invocation of a religion without sacrality, a religion of relations to others, of sociality, is a familiar theme in Levinas' writings. The face appears in this context as the similarly familiar meaning of the command not to murder. The key to this discussion is the opposition to 'Greek' ontology.

An almost contemporary discussion appears in a 'Hebrew' text, "Ethics and Spirit," in *Difficult Freedom*. This is the first essay in this first and most important of Levinas' 'Hebrew' texts. There he again explores the supremacy of ethics over cognition. Moreover, Levinas in this essay juxtaposes 'Greek' and 'Hebrew' and makes a strong critique of the former as deaf to the latter. Much of the discussion of the face is shared between these two essays; in addition, religion here appears by its proper name: Judaism. (Not that this is a religion only for Jews, but that it is the determining perspective of Judaism; that spirituality always moves from myself to the other person, before others, in responsibility for the other who has a face.)

Similarly, 'substitution' has a 'Hebrew' origin, originating in the responsibility that each person pledges for every other. This topic appears frequently both in the Bible and in Rabbinic texts. In Levinas' writings it occurs first in the commentary on Shabbat 88a–b in 1964: I am substitute for the other, even hostage for the other (#6, QL 108/50). This is the concept of election, of being chosen, prior to choosing. Levinas redevelops the concept in a later essay called "Substitution" (1968), which then became the core of his second major 'Greek' work, *Otherwise than Being*. I will not explore Levinas' interpretation of that responsibility for each other here, because Chapter 9 will offer a commentary of the text. But we should notice that this concept is one that also must move from the 'Hebrew' writings to the 'Greek'.

There are several other examples of such translations; for instance, Levinas' insistence that God is not-present in our relations to God and so should be addressed in the third person. This opposes Buber's and Marcel's address to God as Absolute Thou. That address is also linked to the motion in addressing another person, wherein I discover that the one whom I address as you (the formal *vous* for Levinas) actually appears as a third person. Levinas calls this appearance of the thirdness of the other person before whose face I stand *illeity*. But the emergence of that thirdness from the face-to-face relation reflects a translation of the opening words of a Hebrew blessing. One says, "Blessed are you, O Lord our God,

Ruler of the universe . . ." and there is a similar discovery that what seems a second person (are you) must be addressed as a third (Ruler) (EI 102/ 106). Moreover, in the 'Hebrew' writings, Levinas has occasionally displayed this very act of translating, most clearly in an essay on "The Name of God According to Certain Talmudic Texts" (ADV 143–58). After developing his basic "theology" from Talmudic sources, he appends a section entitled *"La Philosophie,"* in which he tries to show that the same concepts can be developed independent of the authority of Scripture and its exegesis (ADV 155). Thus, even in a 'Hebrew' writing, we find Levinas engaging in translation.

PHILOSOPHICAL HERMENEUTICS

In order to see the 'Greek' in Levinas' 'Hebrew' writings, we must also consider how Levinas reads 'Hebrew' texts. Indeed, 'Greek' has an even more central place in the manner of reading than as a subject of commentary. To recognize the centrality of 'Greek' requires first, however, an understanding of what reading 'Hebrew' is.

Levinas often refers to 'Hebrew' as "Biblical thought," but he also points out that the Bible is not read on its own. In the Jewish tradition, access to 'Hebrew' is gained through the writings of the Sages, through Midrash and Talmud. Indeed, 'Hebrew' is not the Bible per se, but the Bible through the Sages, and thus 'Hebrew' means the work of the Sages in interpreting the Bible. This point seems uncontroversial, and Levinas has made it from the first colloquium until the latest. He says in the commentary on Megillah 9a–b that "biblical wisdom is inseparable from Midrash, the fruit of centuries of spiritual life constituting a chain of the tradition where thought at once transmits and renews itself" (#23, HDN 62). He interprets the Halakhic concept that holy texts "render the hands impure" as a prohibition of direct reading of biblical texts. Only someone who is brazen treats the biblical texts as tame enough to be read without the medium of the traditional interpretations (#22, HDN 33). Moreover, 'Hebrew' texts direct our interpretation to the multiplicity of meanings in the biblical text. Talmudic references to the Bible are not proof-texts; rather, the Sages draw upon the contexts and the difficulties in the biblical text (#5, p. 478). The 'Hebrew' texts go beyond the letter of the biblical text, soliciting the multiple meanings of it (#6, QL 86/39).

The texts of the Sages have their own characteristics. Levinas loves to tell how the words of the rabbis are like burning cinders. Why not flaming ones? Because one must blow on them in order to produce their light. 'Hebrew' texts are difficult, in that the reading requires strenuous effort. This is due, according to Levinas, primarily to the absence of rhetoric in the Talmud and Midrash. He describes the style or manner of Talmudic texts as

> a manner of such height which makes due with—or uses—a certain nudity of words, a certain brevity of phrases, as if it were still gesture, and which fulfils itself in allusions. It mistrusts rhetoric raising the prestige of sorcerers at the core of all language, already weaving the plot of a text. A manner that remains thus absolutely sobered because of its indifference even to style, which is to say, to writing. A sobriety which goes beyond that of proper modern exegetes. (SAS 7–8/91)

The Talmudic text alludes to and even recreates its setting as conversation in a school. It records the oscillating of different sides and refuses to resolve the dialectic into a synthesis. "It is a dialogue where there is no Socrates facing a young man. Shmuel is not Socrates, neither is Rav. Both have the clarity, the modesty and the irony of Socrates" (#3, p. 289). Moreover, because the argument continues from schoolroom into the text, the text, rejoins the schoolroom. Talmud is meant to be read in a society (#5, QL 54/24). This ongoing argument, served by the text as intermediary, requires a text that avoids the ruses and conclusions of rhetoric. Here we see the most rigorous contrast of 'Hebrew' and 'Greek', because the former is the unrhetorical form par excellence, just as 'Greek' exceeds in its rhetorical power. Levinas' argument over rhetoric is a sort of miniature version of the larger-scale issues. He claims that this unrhetorical quality is defining of all 'Hebrew' thought, both biblical and Talmudic (ADV 166/LR 197), but that it is clearest in the Talmud, for the text preserves the argument in all of its disjointed qualities, pursuing the personalities and the arguments while refusing to become a text that would sweep over the reader.

Levinas' own writing is not Talmudic in that sense, but is, rather, exceptionally rhetorical. His 'Greek' writings have an exhortative and even prophetic quality rarely met in philosophy. But his 'Hebrew' writings also have a bold and extreme rhetoric. His interpretations manage to transform the indifference to style and to plot in the 'Hebrew' texts into a continuous, consecutive, and interconnected flow of ideas. Unlike others whose texts sabotage the reader's expectations of prose—Derrida for example—Levinas does not create a text that requires 'Hebrew' reading, but produces a text in his commentaries that has become prose, rather the bold prose of rhetoric! Levinas is well aware of this and, indeed, has set as his task, even in these 'Hebrew' writings, the translation into modern language—and as such into something much more indebted to the language of the university ('Greek'). In the preface to the first volume of the commentaries, he explains that he will not only interpret the text according to its own conventions, but that he will also try to translate the meaning suggested by what is given in the text into modern language, which is to say into problems which preoccupy a person educated by spiritual sources other than those of Judaism and whose confluence constitutes our civilization. (QL 15/5)

Annette Aronowicz, in her introduction to the English translation of the first two French volumes, examines the translation that Levinas performs. Clearly, the 'Hebrew' of the Talmudic text in itself, even translated into French, requires some further translation in order to connect to other readers. The question, however, remains, whether Levinas' translations into 'Greek' are proper to the 'Hebrew' texts.

This paradoxical presence of 'Greek' within 'Hebrew' writings becomes clearer still when we explore Levinas' own attempt to situate his 'Hebrew' writings within a spectrum of ways of reading 'Hebrew' texts. Levinas claims that his reading is neither philological and hence 'scientific', nor pious and thus Halakhic, but is broadly philosophical. Recall my introductory comments: Levinas began to deliver these commentaries in the context of colloquiums of Jewish intellectuals. That group included genuine Talmudists as well as philosophers, and of course many other types of less- and more-educated Jewish intellectuals. Levinas was only one philosopher among many. He fashioned a role wherein he, as philosopher, presented Talmudic texts to an audience that, to a large extent, knew nothing of traditional Jewish texts. Moreover, the group was not 'confessional'; indeed, some of the members were avowed atheists. Levinas praises the two alternative approaches to the texts (pious and philological) for what each can contribute. Indeed, he emphasizes that the readings of Talmud by the orthodox community have preserved Judaism through the centuries (SAS 8/91). And Levinas is forever apologizing to the Talmudic Sages present for his interpretations, which do not follow their piety. He states that his 'philosophical' reading will explain much that "goes without saying." As for philology and scientific criticism, Levinas has respect, but he suspects that such criticism could prevent the text from addressing us today. Both the traditional wisdom and the findings of historical studies are valuable, and Levinas often draws on each.

Levinas' ultimate choice is to disengage the theological language, particularly of the orthodox (#5, QL 33/14). Indeed, at one point he blatantly criticizes theosophy in which the Sages sometimes indulged and announces that it is the very negation of philosophy (#6, QL 71/32). In place of the other approaches, Levinas chooses a philosophical approach to the 'Hebrew' texts. He is going to allow the texts to speak independently of faith or piety. In this sense, he refuses to be called a Jewish Thinker, even in his 'Hebrew' writings, if that means that his thought is logically derivative from some personal, credal posture. The commentaries are "addressed to reason" and can be so because they speak of attitudes prior to philosophy, attitudes and experiences that ask for philosophical treatment (#5, QL 33–34/15).

Levinas insists that the prephilosophical experiences that lie at the core of the Talmud are not religious, but moral. Philosophical commentary begins with ethical experience and moves from there to theology. Levinas admits that the inverse move is "more edifying and more pious," but it is no longer philosophy (#6, QL 71/32). Moreover, the philosophical approach is justified because the Sages themselves recapture a rational meaning from biblical texts (QL 18/7). Similarly, he claims that the ethical meaning is the ultimate meaning in 'Hebrew' texts (SAS 10/93). Thus, Levinas will conduct his 'Hebrew' writings as a philosopher, making the ethical, nondogmatic, nonapologetic, and certainly nonfanatical experiences the touchstone of his reading.

This he carries over into one of the striking eccentricities of his commentaries: their preponderance of Aggadah and absence of Halakhah. Surely an orthodox commentator would not choose to focus his interpretation on the texts that Levinas does, for the serious, pragmatic issues of ethics occur in the subtle and casuistic reasoning of Halakhah. Levinas' own account of the difference between Halakhah and Aggadah supplements his frequent protestations of ignorance and incompetence in Halakhah, which, according to him, is a teaching of conduct; Aggadah is a teaching of "the philosophical meaning—religious and moral—of that conduct" (#16, SAS 155/182, 177/194). Levinas goes so far as to say that Aggadah is the presentation of philosophical views in the Talmud, or the properly religious thought of Israel. Given a philosophical approach, Levinas' choice of Aggadic portions is reasonable. Still, there is a question of whether a philosophical reading of the Halakhic portions is not also possible. Indeed, Levinas' own teacher, the mysterious Shushani, addressed this very challenge to Levinas.[5]

I will draw this discussion of hermeneutics to a close with Shushani, because Levinas claims repeatedly to have learned his manner of reading 'Hebrew' texts from this remarkable teacher (and neither from his Lithuanian education, nor from his other Parisian, Jewish counterparts). Levinas' account of Shushani's influence is so extreme that one might well ascribe to him the source of Levinas' goal of translation, and even of the lived experience of the face. One further teaching of Shushani is key to Levinas' hermeneutics of 'Hebrew' texts: whenever the text speaks of 'Israel', we are to read it as all of humanity. Shushani teaches that there is no legitimate taint of racism or exclusivity in the Talmudic texts; that, to the contrary, their claims are universalistic (#4, DL3 121/83). Levinas almost always cites Shushani when making this claim. Levinas also cites a more paradoxical aphorism of Shushani: "The Bible is particular to Israel; the Talmud is its clear thought on a universal plane" (#3, p. 288).

'HEBREW'S' DEMAND FOR 'GREEK'

We have come quite a cycle. Levinas' 'Hebrew' writings are not commentary on the Bible, the true representative of 'Hebrew', because the only legitimate reading of the Bible is through the Talmud. Moreover, the Talmud breaks with the particularism of the Bible and universalizes through reason. Thus the only legitimate reading of 'Hebrew', of biblical thought, is one which seeks a universalized reading. The best reading of 'Hebrew', therefore, is philosophical—is in 'Greek'! If 'Greek' requires nourishment from the 'Hebrew' texts, have we now only made progress to the converse, that 'Hebrew' requires a fulfillment in 'Greek'? It appears so, with profound philosophical consequences. But before exploring the consequences, we should explore Levinas' repeated claim that 'Hebrew' has a need to seek a 'Greek' expression.

In 1975, for a colloquium on "Facing the War," Levinas commented on Baba Kama 60a–b. It is a passage that discusses damages due to fire, but it leads from Halakhah into Aggadah and concludes with a story about R. Ammi and R. Assi pestering R. Isaac with a question. Each sage demands Halakhah or Aggadah exclusively, thus preventing R. Isaac from answering the other. Eventually he quiets them with a tale, an Aggadic story, followed by a Halakhah. For Levinas, this text displays the power to derive Aggadah from Halakhah and to return then to reformulate the Halakhah. In his introduction he makes the distinction referred to above, but continues further:

> In fact, it is a Halakhah, which is to say, a lesson that teaches *conduct* to be maintained, that states a law. But the Halakhah in the text itself, and *without provocation by an interpreter*, transforms itself into Aggadah, into a homiletic text, which as you may know, is the mode under which, in Talmudic thought, philosophical views, which is to say, the properly religious thought of Israel, is presented. (I do not regret having brought philosophy and religion together in my preceding sentence. For me, philosophy derives [*dérive*] from religion. It is called for by religion adrift [*en dérive*], and in all likelihood religion is always adrift.) And this Aggadic interpretation of Halakhah relating to the fire concludes with a new Halakhic teaching; the text thus goes from Halakhah to Aggadah and from Aggadah to Halakhah. (#16, SAS 155–56/182)

This cycle of Halakhah and Aggadah is itself representative of a cycle of religion and philosophy (a correlation) within the 'Hebrew'. Levinas is claiming that 'Hebrew' thought itself calls for the 'Greek', for philosophical reasoning. In the 'Hebrew' there is also a movement back into Halakhah, into practical matters. We must note, though, that Levinas himself does not make this movement back after his movement through philosophy.

However, there is not only this basic cycling or call for philosophy in the 'Hebrew', for Levinas also makes clear that there is a fundamental need for the 'Greek' language. After his first Talmudic lecture, Levinas claimed that there was more content in the 'Hebrew' than in a translation into 'Greek' (#3, p. 358). 'Greek' works with abstract concepts, with concepts striving toward univocal meaning, clear and distinct definition. 'Hebrew', on the other hand, works with polysemy, with the shattering of the term, producing a society of readings and commentaries. For all that, Levinas admits in a discussion following his commentary on the question of the Septuagint that, despite the pragmatic quality of 'Hebrew', despite its special fecundity, "in the final analysis, one speaks of all of this in conceptual language" (#23, p. 368). It simply is impossible to remain in 'Hebrew', at least for Levinas. Just as his commentaries create prose, create a written text from the shards of arguments of the school, so he translates the concrete examples of the Talmudic text into more general concepts, in an appeal to reason.

That one must speak in conceptual language is the key to recognizing that 'Hebrew' itself calls for 'Greek'. Levinas regularly makes the point that the Sages themselves are pursuing universality. Moreover, although in a different 'language', the Sages' thought is "radical enough to also satisfy the requirements of philosophy" (#3, DL3 101/68). Thus Levinas does not need to borrow 'Greek' to justify his 'Greek' interpretation of the 'Hebrew' texts; rather, the 'Hebrew' text itself contains this movement into 'Greek'. This need for 'Greek' expressed within the 'Hebrew' is most emphatic in Levinas' interpretation of that passage on the Septuagint. The biblical text stating that Japheth resides in the tents of Shem (Gen. 9.27) becomes a justification for translating Scripture (Shem) into Greek (Japheth). Levinas calls this opening of 'Hebrew' to a language without prejudices "a necessary test" (#23, HDN 62), a spiritual test, which reveals the merit of the tradition in its willingness to translate.

Levinas, despite his apologies and humility, has both a 'Greek' and a 'Hebrew' justification for his reading of Talmud. For the 'Greek' he merely notes that there are resources in the 'Hebrew' texts that have been ignored in the 'Greek' tradition, and which he can translate into 'Greek' terms. For the 'Hebrew', he notes that the very movement from Bible to Talmud, from written law to oral law, and more specifically within Talmud from Halakhah to Aggadah, is the movement from particularity and pragmatics to conceptual, even universalist, thought. These two justifications, of course, are coordinate rather than forced precisely because 'Hebrew' on its own looks to 'Greek' expression. For our purposes, it is critical to note that Levinas offers a deeply Jewish justification for the task of correlating the Jewish and the philosophic concepts. Here is an other of philosophy reaching out toward philosophy in order to provide it with what it cannot get from itself (or at least what is has not previously provided for itself).

There are two remaining questions to consider in this theme of translation. While in his philosophical writings, Levinas makes little effort to mitigate his critique of 'Greek', employing the images with which this paper began and so justifying the move to the other; in the 'Hebrew' writings, we do not find much discussion of why 'Greek' must look to 'Hebrew'. If the experiences (the face, substitution, etc.) that form the core of the 'Greek' reflection are prephilosophical, the very same ones which are available in the 'Hebrew', then we might well not need the 'Hebrew'. If we could draw more upon, for example, Plato's 'Good beyond Being', or even Kant's 'primacy of Practical Reason', we might find resources in the 'Greek' tradition. It is just this issue that seems to confuse Levinas, for at times he must defend the universality of such prephilosophic experiences and even points in the direction of an ethical manner of 'Greek' thought. At other times, for instance in discussing Aeschylus and responsibility for others, Levinas claims that Judaism has something unique to offer.

Such confusion leads to the more profound problem with Levinas' embrace of translation as the image of what I call correlation. If translation were able to be completed, if the uniqueness could be translated entirely and hence lose its uniqueness, then 'Greek' would triumph in logical form over 'Hebrew' with its particularist universality. The question of a remainder in translation, an untranslatable core, has serious implications. Whatever can be translated into 'Greek' could be viewed as what is not truly 'Hebrew'. André Neher can argue against Levinas' reading of Judaism that it is a philosopher's reading and so must discover, to no one's surprise, a philosophical Judaism (#1, p. 50). Jewish thinkers are exercised by the tension between universalism and particularity in Judaism, but has Levinas preserved in method what he established in content? Has the translation project itself not "sold out" to the 'Greek'? The very first question in the debate following Levinas' commentary on the Septuagint passages cited the other Rabbinic texts comparing that translation to the Golden Calf!

Early on, Levinas contends that 'Hebrew' says more or otherwise than can be said in the 'Greek'. In the first of his commentaries, he claims that the meaning of the Talmudic argument is not simply transposable into a philosophical language (#3, DL3 101/68). In its context, he seems to say that philosophers will not be happy with the Talmud. Talmud will not seem conceptual, not 'Greek', enough (#3, DL3 96/64). But the question is more subtle, and it is not until the commentary on the passage about the Septuagint that Levinas comes back to this untranslatable quality. If at first he feared that he could not persuade 'Greek's of the 'Hebrew' wisdom, he now begins to question whether 'Greek' will not shortchange 'Hebrew'. For this was the Sages' concern with translations. Levinas often proclaims that the Septuagint is incomplete (#21, ADV 94); the "authentic spirituality" of the 'Hebrew' text cannot be adequately rendered by the 'Greek'. The Gemara lists fifteen corrections in the translation into 'Greek', corrections made so as to prevent confusions that a 'literal' 'Hebrew' reading in 'Greek' might have produced. In those cases the 'Hebrew' cannot be rendered into 'Greek', but must be changed in translation. The original 'Hebrew' signifies in a way that becomes unacceptable in 'Greek' and so remains untranslated, indeed untranslatable.

The questions whether 'Hebrew' is fully translatable into 'Greek' and whether 'Greek' needs nourishment from 'Hebrew' are fundamental issues for Jewish philosophy today and, by extension, for other others of philosophy. We stand in need of apology not only to Jews for being philosophers, but to philosophers for being Jews. Levinas' most famous and perhaps greatest critic, Jacques Derrida, taunts him by ending his challenging article from 1963 (long before the translation image became Levinas' standard) with Joyce's mocking motto on Lynch's cap in Circe's Circle: "Jewgreek is greekjew. Extremes meet."[6] For us these questions challenge our understanding of both philosophy and Judaism, and that challenge delimits the topic for the correlation with which I title this book. If philosophy must be the conquest of the other by the same, the dominance of knowing before doing, the preservation of our own freedom at all costs, then it seems Judaism must have only limited interaction with it, for Philosophy threatens only to assimilate what it can take and to never become changed itself. Similarly, if Judaism is not primarily a search for universality through particularity and through texts, but is perhaps more exclusivistic, more racial (or ethnic), more historical in the scientific sense of the term, then it too, for its own sake, must shun the philosophers, for it should then make a camp outside the ditch that marks off the settlement of philosophical thought.

But the results of Levinas' own exploration of 'Hebrew' texts, in concord with other Jewish philosophers, show that philosophy can become other and that Judaism seeks universality through its own particularity. For philosophy the result of the examination of these writings is the articulation of a changed logic: a universality that is not totalizing and an obedience that is neither knowing nor naive. The activity of philosophizing can be oriented by the ethical responsibility for the other. For Judaism, in a parallel but not mirrored way, these writings point out the possibility for a translation of Rabbinic texts and thinking into modern language—a possibility which Levinas holds is a necessary test for that thought. While in the nineteenth century the appropriation of Judaism by philosophy produced claims about the essence of Judaism, today, perhaps for the first time, philosophy can receive the insight of its other without reducing that other to a philosophical framework. The possibility for a nonassimilating reorientation of philosophy by its other makes the approach to philosophy by its other a worthy task.

APPENDIX: LEVINAS' TEXTS FOR THE COLLOQUIUMS

#	Date	Topic	Levinas' text	Appears in
FOLLOWING PUBLISHED BY PRESSES UNIVERSITAIRE DE FRANCE (PUF)				
1	May 1957	—	—	—
2	Sept. 1959	Timidity/Audacity	On Rosenzweig	DL
3	Sept. 1960	Morality/Politics	Sanhedrin 99a	DL
4	Oct. 1961	Messianism/End of History	Sanhedrin 98b–99a	DL
Z	Feb. 1963	French & Algerian Jews	—	—
5	Oct. 1963	Pardon	Yoma 87a	QL
6	Oct. 1964	Temptations of Jews	Shabbat 88a–b	QL
7	Oct. 1965	Israel	Sota 34b–35a	QL
8	Oct. 1966	Does the World Need Jews?	Sanhedrin 36b–37a	QL
9	Jan. 1968	Israel	ABSENT	—
10	Mar. 1969	Judaism and Revolution	Baba Metsia 83a–b	SAS
11	Oct. 1970	Youth of Israel	Nazir 66a–b	SAS
12	Nov. 1971	Jews in Desacralized Society	Sanhedrin 67a–68a	SAS
13	Oct. 1972	Ish & Ishah, the Other	Berakhot 61a	SAS
14	Nov. 1973	Sabbath	ABSENT	—
15	Nov. 1974	Solitude of Israel	Makoth 23a–b	L'Herne
16	Nov. 1975	Facing the War	Baba Kama 60a–b	SAS
17	Nov. 1976	The Western Model	Menahot 99b–100a	ADV
18	Oct. 1977	The Muslim Community	ABSENT	—
19	Nov. 1978	Jerusalem	Makot 10a	ADV
FOLLOWING PUBLISHED BY GALLIMARD IDÉES				
20	Nov. 1979	Religion and Politics	Yoma 10a	ADV
21	1980	Community	Sota 37a–b	ADV
22	Nov. 1981	The Bible in the Present	Megillah 7a	HDN
23	Apr. 1983	Israel, Judaism, & Europe	Megillah 9a–b	HDN
FOLLOWING PUBLISHED BY DENOËL				
24	Jan. 1984	Idolatry	Sanhedrin 99a–b	HDN
25	Dec. 1984	Zeker: Memory and History	Berakhot 12b–13a	HDN
27	Dec. 1986	The Sixty-Nine Nations	Pesachim 118b	HDN
28	Dec. 1987	Money	"Socialité et Argent"	L'Herne
29	Dec. 1988	Question of the State	Tamid 31b–32b	
30	Dec. 1989	Reserve (*Quant-a–soi*)	Hullin 88b–89a	

CHAPTER 8

The Unique Other: Hermann Cohen
and Emmanuel Levinas

LEVINAS AND ROSENZWEIG intensify ethics by focusing on the interpersonal relationship between myself and an other. Their thought derives from the claim that this concrete situation of myself and another cannot be reduced to a relationship that could be grasped by pure reason. All the more striking, then, is the almost paradoxical parallels with one of the last great pure rationalists: Hermann Cohen. In this chapter I will explore the striking similarities between Cohen's and Levinas' accounts of my extreme responsibility. Those accounts focus on the uniqueness of the other person and on my unique, inalienable responsibility for that person. The arguments used are dissimilar, but both place each thinker at the outer margin of the philosophical school he espouses. Indeed, the struggle to intensify responsibility serves as an orientation for philosophy, which emerges as transcending the disagreement over the different schools of philosophy.

An added feature of this discussion, moreover, is that it allows us to sketch a map of four major figures in Jewish philosophy: Cohen, Buber, Rosenzweig, and Levinas. For Cohen's analysis of 'I' and 'you' is the seed both of the later developments and even of the disagreements between the other three figures. While both Rosenzweig and Buber drew directly on Cohen's work, it is not as clear how directly Levinas did. Levinas seems very close to Buber, until one looks more carefully. As the gulf between Buber and Rosenzweig widens, so does that between Buber and the Rosenzweigian Levinas. Indeed, there is a series of writings between Buber and Levinas that will display precisely the gaps between each man and Cohen and Rosenzweig. Thus in this chapter I will offer a simple prospect on the relations between these four thinkers through the various routes to the 'you' in each thinker.

We may begin by marking the distance between Cohen's rational idealism and Levinas' phenomenology. Levinas sets out from phenomenology, whose motto was "to the things themselves," but Cohen is the pure philosopher, the philosopher who refuses any contribution to knowledge or to ethics from experience, from empirical sources, from those 'things'. There is a sort of purity in phenomenological analysis, but it is a purification (reduction) of transcendent claims from experience. It is not the pure generation of experience from pure reason. Cohen's system is generated directly from reason, and it yields no place to empiricism or any other reflection based on experience. Husserl, on the other hand, devotes himself to meticulous exploration of the intentionality of experience, even though it is reflectively reduced to internal experience (the experience of consciousness). Although Cohen might have recognized in the new movement of phenomenology an ally against empiricism, and psychologism specifically, he remained wary of it.[1] His demand for critical epistemology left reason alone to generate its own categories and held even the reduced phenomena of phenomenology under suspicion. Levinas for his part, rarely mentions Cohen. He seems to regard him as a Platonic idealist of sorts and does not reject him but rarely examines him.[2] The problem seems to be that as idealist, Cohen must ignore the temporality of existence. Thus Cohen's idealism will not be able to give Levinas access to the nonformal existence of things in the world, much less access to others.

Yet before we dismiss the two philosophical visions as irreconcilable, we need to pause and consider the distance more carefully. Levinas' reading of Husserl is far removed from any sort of empiricism. Instead, Husserl appears most regularly in the guise of transcendental idealist. His analysis of consciousness is not a motion from the subjective ego to the objective 'real' world, but a motion within consciousness between the subjectivity of intentionality and the intended object of consciousness (TI 95–96/123). Levinas' reading of Husserl is debatable as a reading, but it makes phenomenology into an analysis of ideality and not a response to empirical data. Cohen's philosophical vocabulary could not serve Levinas as well, but the idealism at the expense of both empiricism and realism is shared by both schools. Cohen's and Levinas' analyses of the key concepts in this chapter are conducted in different vocabularies, but the orientation in both cases is toward a certain sort of idealism and away from a psychologism.

The tasks that Levinas and Cohen attempt in these two vocabularies strain each school. The two thinkers develop their central ethical concepts at the outer limit of their respective philosophical schools. They share an emphasis on the encounter with an other person, specifically with a stranger and with the poor. For both Levinas and Cohen the privileged experience is this encounter with the other, and through that I become myself in my responsibility and solidarity with the other. The priority of the poor and the stranger is unusual (even unheard of) in either school of philosophy. Idealism had never known such interest in the individuality of the responsible person, much less the route to my own selfhood through the other's poverty; and phenomenology was incapable of reaching to the radical otherness of the other person and so breaking with consciousness.

Cohen's Double Discovery of the 'You'

Cohen has two parallel discoveries of the other; one in his *Ethics of Pure Will*, and the other in *Religion of Reason out of the Sources of Judaism*. Once again we must note the consistency in these two works, as the 'you' of the *Religion* is not a bold departure or reversal from the discovery of the 'you' in the *Ethics*. In the *Ethics*, Cohen discovers the other as 'you' and not as merely an other thing. This discovery is prior to the emergence of an 'I', because the self does not come to self-consciousness except by standing in relation to an other. While Fichte might begin with an 'I' and then oppose it to a 'not-I', Cohen claims that ethics must begin with the other and then proceed to an 'I'. "The I cannot be defined, nor generated, except if it is determined through the pure generation of the other and then proceeds out of the other."[3] But if the now familiar detour through the other is clear, what is odd about Cohen's formulations is his insistence on purity and on generation. The discussion of the logic of origins in Chapter 2 of this book is again relevant, but now directly for ethics.[4] Purity means the independence from empirical sensation, but it also means the independence from affect, from feelings and desires. Ethics must be pure for Cohen if it is to manifest genuine freedom and not some naturalistic mechanism of forces. Cohen admits that feelings may be the motor of ethics, but that they may not be the motive. The problem becomes how my individuality (*Einzelheit*) can be generated purely, because even Cohen knows that my individuality is not a simple process of specifying a particular under a general class.

Even in the *Ethics*, Cohen marks out a division of pathways: religion with its love of the neighbor and philosophy with its generation of the other. I will follow the main route here (philosophy) largely because I will discuss the other route in the context of his *Religion*. The argument in the *Ethics* leads through lengthy reflection on the importance of jurisprudence and legal rights in understanding the pure ethics, as well as a justification of the state. Those reflections illuminate the constructive nature of legal persons (corporations, etc.) and the fact that the legal constructions are a rational way of constituting morally responsible persons. Not the perceptible person or group, but the 'legal fiction' (which Cohen prefers to view as a hypothetical person, or even a moral task), is the locus of ethics.

But beyond this emphasis on legality and the state under which the laws obtain their force, Cohen also offers an important challenge to social theory by contrasting the community (*Gemeinschaft*) with the cooperative (*Genossenschaft*). The cooperative as a social institution has roots in late-medieval Germany and could be either a consumer's or a manufacturing co-op. The idea was to form a voluntary corporation for mutual benefit. Its legal status was secured, even though a co-op need not be based on any natural, prior affiliation. Moreover, behind this economic practice is lurking the etymology—namely the companion, the one with whom one eats and shares enjoyment (*die Genosse*). Thus, while community would rest on something common to the members (common class, family, church, or fatherland), the cooperative was artificially based on the mutuality created in sharing or enjoying together[5]; it could therefore also be translated as companion (from the Latin *com* + *panis,* eating bread together), or even as *company* (!). Cohen makes this companionship so important that he then makes community depend on it to achieve self-consciousness as a form of society (*Gesellschaft*). He outlines the sequence of connections that determines the ideology of community, from land to people, to race, to marriage and family. This naturalistic interpretation of society falls vulnerable to the critique of capitalist society, which reveals the unethical and arbitrary nature of such society. The contractually formed cooperative allows the members to enter and to commit themselves freely, and in so doing to create a morally responsible entity.

Finally, that contract represents a demand for rights for the other members of the cooperative. That demand becomes an address to the others in the society, and so the other becomes a 'you':

> You is not he. He would be the other. He stands in danger of becoming treated as it. You and I simply belong together. I can not say you without relating myself to you, without uniting the you in this relation [*Beziehung*] to the I.[6]

This relation of I and you, which Cohen calls a correlation, is the result not of experience, but of the legal hypothesis of a contract. Through the contract that forms a cooperative, I can address the other as 'you'. And through that address to a 'you', I become me, a moral agent, free and responsible. The relation is mutual, but priority is given to the 'you'. The formation of a companionship is a task for the self, in order to become free and an 'I'. (This 'I-you' relation no doubt reminds many of us of Buber. Clearly the vocabulary, and even many of the concepts, are identical. In the fourth section I will discuss the importance of Cohen in interpreting Buber.)

This generation of the self, through a 'you', through a partner or companion, is balanced with the second mode of generation. The fullest exposition of the second mode is in the *Religion,* but it also appears in the *Ethics.* That other route in the *Ethics* focuses on the fellow (*Nebenmensch*) created by love of the neighbor.[7] Such love was viewed as sympathy (*Mitgefühl*), which broadened the self to include the fellow. The move was to make those who seemed further away, such as the stranger, into a relative (such as the widow or orphan). Cohen rejected this route to the fellow for ethics because the innate compassion, the love for the other, is not itself pure.

However, in the *Religion,* Cohen returns to this second route. Again, he is looking for the other in order to transform the self into an 'I'. At this point the focus is not only on the individuality (*Einzelheit*) of the person, but on their uniqueness (*Einzigheit,* or as *individuum*). Cohen's desire to achieve the most radical individuality in the 'I' brings him extremely close to the efforts of his existentialist students. The change in route is through the other, the 'I', but now the other is a co-person (*Mitmensch*) not the fellow (*Nebenmensch*). The fellow is one whom I might join with in a contract, but he is not someone whose wellbeing is my concern. His morality as the inner determination of his will, although invisible to me, is my concern, and so I encourage him to be moral. But whether he prospers or not is indifferent to me. Cohen notes, however, that my indifference leads to my subordination of the other, as the one who is near me becomes one who is my competitor and opponent, eventually becoming my underling (from *Nebenmensch* to *Gegenmensch* to *Untermensch*).[8] In contrast, the solidarity of the *mit,* of the co-person, allows me to say 'you' to the other. I learn that each of us is human and from my saying 'you', I first say 'I'.

But the way to the co-person is more complex. For this other is my neighbor whom I must love. That love must still be pure; it must not be an affect, but must originate in myself. What Cohen discovers here is that such love begins in compassion (*Mitleid*), which unlike sympathy can indeed be a pure feeling, one generated by reason itself. While in the *Ethics* Cohen had dismissed sympathy as too dependent on feelings, here he berates the Stoics, Spinoza, Schopenhauer, and others for not recognizing that compassion is not an affect but is purely generated from the self. Compassion becomes a task that I must perform, a reaching out to the fellow in order to feel with him.[9]

But the other, whom I must make my co-person, is my fellow turned underling. Here the distinctively human dimension of compassion appears, for Cohen argues that the suffering of humanity is poverty. The self is not independent from its fellows, but as social it is already an accomplice in the human suffering of the poor. To become myself, to become an 'I', I must recognize and suffer with the poor, with the other. The poor is not an empirical concept, nor is the poor man 'given' in experience. Rather, I must transform the fellow I meet, by use of pure will, by reason, into a co-person, a person with whom I suffer. I convert him by generating in myself the co-suffering of com-passion.

For Cohen, however, the 'I' and the 'you', even as co-persons, are not yet individuals. While the way to an 'I' is through a 'you', and only through social morality do we proceed toward uniqueness, the social ethics itself does not produce an 'I' who is more definite than the human discovered in the compassion with the co-person. The further step is through a discussion of sin and guilt. For there is a process of self-identification in the discovery of my own sin and in the struggle with my guilt. But the culmination of this discussion is that 'I' become 'I' not through my sin, but through my repentance. For in repenting I recreate my own self, exercising my pure freedom to become myself. Indeed, I sanctify myself before God in this act of self-creation. Self-sanctification requires a searching out of my ways, a confession of my failure, and a turning from evil ways. God in correlation forgives my sins, and a new community is formed: the congregation (*Gemeinde*).[10] That community forms to create a public space for confession, a space in which its members can collectively acknowledge their faults before God.

While these analyses are the climax of Cohen's *Religion* and, in addition, are the very analyses that most delighted Rosenzweig while he read the typescript at the front, we need not examine them closely here. What is striking for our discussion is that this second route leads through a different other (the co-person) to a different community and to a different realization of the self. For the self-sanctification that occurs in repentance is the taking on of suffering, the making myself suffer in order to release myself from my sin, from my unfreedom of following my desires. I learn not only to make the other's suffering my suffering through compassion, but also that I must take on my own suffering as repentance.[11]

In both routes, the 'I' is a task, for I must still become 'I' through the act of reason. And the distance between the two routes cannot be measured by a change in mind by Cohen. Even in the *Ethics*, Cohen refers to the prophetic discussion of redemption in introducing the issues of punishment, in order to emphasize the criminal's acknowledgment and confession as keys to a pure moral form of punishment.[12] But while in one way the other is a companion, in the other way she is my neighbor; in one we form a cooperative, in the other a congregation. And while the one is a constructive institution of socialism, the other discovers the suffering of poverty. The two ways to the 'I' both pass through the 'you' in Cohen.

LEVINAS' ACCOUNT OF THE OTHER

Levinas follows a not particularly different course. His method is phenomenological, until he must turn to the other person. Through phenomenological analyses Levinas portrays ipseity, the self prior to meeting the other. I am in my body in such a way that I am not merely a member of a species, but experience all of my life firsthand. My work with the world is one of assimilation, and my desire for something objective is constantly thwarted as I find that everything I touch I make mine. Thought itself seems destined to reduce the other things to a representation I make in my own consciousness. I am stuck with myself and my own intentionality, stuck like an insomniac who cannot find any way to escape the assimilating power of consciousness. This self as ipseity is isolated and secluded from God, from other people, even from the world.

And then some person meets me. This other commands me with her face. For the vulnerability of the other prohibits me from murder, and along with this command comes the astonishment that I cannot comprehend the other. I may not kill, and I cannot assimilate, the other. Instead, the duty not to kill now spirals, as the more I do for the other, the more I am obligated to do. An infinition of duty occurs, and my capacity for grasping reality is exceeded by the very duty that now grasps me. Levinas will say that I am thinking a thought (infinity) that is more than I can think. The very intentionality of consciousness is reversed: the other has intentions for me, and I find myself accused by the other. The isolated self has been interrupted by an other, by the intentionality of someone else, and so the self is extroverted.

The face of the other is not a perception of the other's physiognomy. In later work, Levinas shifts from the vision of the face to proximity to the other's skin. Again, the vulnerability of the other prohibits my violating the other. Like an aura, the other commands respect not by contact, but by an inviolable space that is not given to the scientific models of perception. Thus the aspect of the other that obligates me so distressingly does not itself appear. Levinas will say that the face is not a phenomenon. The infinity that happens in this experience is not an existent. The rules of sensible experience are broken and even reversed in this experience.

And so I find myself not the center, the ruler, of my life, but accused. Levinas puns that this is an indeclinable accusative, because the 'me' that is bound to this other cannot shake the responsibility. The possibility of refusing to be responsible occupies the next chapter, but here we see that the self, which had stored up treasures for its own use, now is the object of the other's intentions. I must now welcome the other, giving the other the very home, food, clothing, etc., that were for my own enjoyment. I suffer to relieve the other's suffering, and in so doing become myself in a way that is impossible through my own enjoyable life. I become myself—I become free in responsibility—only when I answer for the other. I am hostage for the other, says Levinas at his hyperbolic best. Thus I am not my own master, but am substitute for the other. I must take the other's place, and no one may relieve me of my burden to take that place. I am uniquely responsible. No one can take my place—the place before the other—the hostage for the other.

But all of Levinas' discussion goes on in a context of shadowy images. "The Other who dominates me in his transcendence is thus the stranger, the widow, and the orphan, to whom I am obligated" (TI 215/190). How many times does Levinas invoke this obviously Biblical series of 'others'? The other who commands me turns out to be the poor one, the one who suffers. Her moral height is coupled with her material humility, and the command is to lower myself in order to raise her material conditions. I come to be a responsible self, a person who responds to the other, in the context of the injustice done to the other, the injustice most of all of poverty. I must give the bread out of my own mouth to feed the other. I am accused, because I am an accomplice in the social injustice done to the other.

And yet, unlike Cohen, Levinas does not articulate a concept of poverty. The place of economics is increasingly marginal in Levinas' discussion, as will be examined in Chapter 10. In place of an analysis of who the poor are in contemporary or in biblical society, or even who the widow and orphan are, Levinas has recourse to more concrete but less economic concepts: alterity and nakedness. Indeed, this other is strangely undetermined, is almost *formal*, in its concreteness. The face is anyone we meet, is any other, but it is archetypically a poor person, one who is hungry. Ethics is an optics for thought, but its setting is being before the poor.

The logical issue of this approach of the other centers on uniqueness. Just as I, in this body at this place and time, do not fit under any class, so the other will also require a similar distinctiveness. Levinas develops uniqueness, however, not merely in the failure of genus and species classification, but rather in the working through of the other's interruption of my self-contained world. Levinas develops uniqueness in two directions. The main uniqueness is my own responsibility. Throughout his writings, the uniqueness that defies categories, that eludes rational classification, is my self: namely, the inverted agency of responsibility for others. No one can replace me as I stand accused before the other. The original isolated and almost solipsistic self of consciousness is not fully unique. Locked in his own consciousness, that self could easily enough be one of many such monads. But when the other interrupts me, I become responsible for that other; I and no one else. The true specificity of place and of time is found in relation to an other. Before that, the power of representation could suspend the temporal sequence and could always keep distance between the self and anything else. But I can neither suspend the urgency of the other's demand, nor hold myself back from proximity to her. Now, here, I, in my very corporeality, am responsible.

But in a few places, Levinas also grants a parallel uniqueness to the other. The very undefinability, the failure of any correlation between my knowing and the other, indicates that the other also is no individual in a genus. This is the insight for which he praised Rosenzweig (see Chapter 1). In a recent article, Levinas writes of love and ethical peace as he examines how one encounters the unique other beyond the individuality subordinate to a class. "The relation goes to the unassimilable, incomparable, other; to the irreducible other; to the unique other. Only the unique is absolutely other. But the uniqueness of the unique [*l'unicité de l'unique*], that is the uniqueness of the beloved" (EN 214). While Levinas had shied away from the term *love* for the relation with the other in earlier writings, here he uses it to find an experience that captures this uniqueness of the other. A beloved whom I love cannot be replaced by anyone else. A beloved is not just a member of a group, or a class, or a sex, etc., nor even simply a member of the human race; rather, we sense in our relationship that a beloved is unique. 'Only you, for no one else will do.' Love binds me together with an other who is absolutely other, in a relationship that exceeds the parameters of knowledge and creates a responsibility for the beloved that has no limits. Levinas thus replaces the notion of 'like loves like' with the keen awareness that I love a unique person, unique to such an extent that that person must be radically other from me. I then have a unique responsibility to love that beloved as only I can. 'Only you, and only I can love you as I can.' This is the type for responsibility, which makes me irreplaceably responsible for an other who also is unique.

THE OTHER'S FREEDOM / MY RE-SPONSIBILITY

Despite the difference in philosophical methods, both Cohen and Levinas are striving for the same goals. Both thinkers have two fundamental goals in portraying the self. First, both wish to wrest a genuine freedom for the other; second, both wish to emphasize emphatically, even redundantly and hyperbolically, that I am I because I am responsible for others. To do this, each exaggerates and stretches the concepts of their philosophical schools beyond their usual limits.

In Cohen's case we need to be alert to the often-voiced criticisms of the limitations of rationalism and idealism. Like Hegel or Kant, Cohen is often regarded as another example of someone who could not deal with the unique individual because reason does not grasp individuals. The very resistance to subordination under categories, the rejection of essentialism, the violence of the idealistic system—all stand as condemnations of Cohen as well. Indeed, Rosenzweig is largely responsible for that misreading of Cohen, as I discussed in Chapter 4. Cohen himself is convinced that the system must reach to the unique individual, both in the *Ethics* and in the *Religion*. Rosenzweig must not have read the *Ethics* seriously, else his own introduction to Cohen's thought would have noticed that correlation, the 'I' and the 'you', and the very concern with the individual person (Rosenzweig's 'first-and-last-name') were guiding concerns of the work.[13] Whether an ideal generation from reason alone can achieve the goals Cohen sets is another question. Clearly, Cohen goes further *in the systematic writings* than idealists have ever gone before.

But at this point Cohen's idealism itself requires some interpretation. In Chapter 2, we could see that idealism as an interpretation of divine freedom in creation. There the purity and idealism of cognition served as an image of the ex nihilo of God's creation. But here? What benefit is there in thinking ethics so purely, when the goal seems to be to recognize the existential freedom of the other? Why approach individuality through idealistic reason, if the goal is not a formalism? The introduction to the *Ethics* includes a thorough attack on the naturalistic attempt to found ethics on the empirical social sciences. Both psychology and sociology are criticized for making 'human being' simply 'natural being', and thus explaining ethics as derivative from causal laws of natural objects. (Here again we see a striking parallel to phenomenology, with its challenge to the primacy of naturalistic ontology.) The point is all too Kantian: If ethics is merely a branch of natural science, then it is not ethics at all. For ethics to be possible, ethics must arise from an unconditioned freedom. Thus any dependence on empirical sensation, any need for a given, (even of the other person as an existing reality) will entangle ethics in necessary causal relations and thus destroy ethics as such. In particular, if the freedom of the other person is the focus of the analysis—and Cohen derives my freedom and my consciousness from the other's freedom—then we need to be zealous in preventing her freedom from dissolving into a nexus of natural, objective forces. Were the other's freedom dependent on experience of her, she would turn back into an 'it', an object caught in the web of mechanical causes. An empirical source of the other refuses to permit that other her freedom for moral action. Even a thesis of underdeterminacy from experience limits the other. Why not accept the principle that my cognition of the other must start from reason in such a way that the other appears only as a source of freedom?

The parallel with Levinas and phenomenology is complex. At first glance, and that is looking from Cohen's perspective, phenomenology is a recourse to experience, or at least to an interpretation of intentionalities dependent on experience. Thus the attempt to discover the other through phenomenology is doomed, because the other will always be reduced to a mode of objectivity that dissolves ethical freedom. But that glance is only the appearance, because Levinas himself is forced to renounce the phenomenality of the face, of the other. If I insist on some phenomenological evidence of the face, I am frustrated. Levinas speaks of an immediacy, but it is more immediate than sight. Whatever else proximity is, it is not a phenomenon. Levinas introduced the concept of the trace for this nonphenomenal appearance of the other. The other leaves a trace, but the trace is fundamentally ambiguous. The 'appearance' of the other can be interpreted as either another correlate of my intentionality, or as the other in her freedom. Experience, in the normal sense of the word, cannot determine my responsibility.

Moreover, Levinas' own interpretation of phenomenology makes this excess, this break with phenomenology, all the more parallel to Cohen. For Levinas has made phenomenology into a transcendental idealism. The result has been that sensible experience is interpreted through consciousness and leaves no remainder from the assimilatory power of the self. Thus when the other confronts me, she is the first experience of an objectivity that refuses my intentionality. But as such, she may not be given in any normal, sense experience. Levinas, thus, must also stretch idealism to its breaking point—even when that idealism is of the phenomenological variety. What Levinas then proceeds to do is to reverse the flow: the face of the other is the primordial signification, from which all other signs take their meaning; the perception of the other is the true one, from which all other bodily perception ultimately derives. Here is 'the thing itself', at which phenomenology aimed, but its very excess—that I think what I am unable to think—reorients all of the previous categories of cognition. The desire for this unreachable other now becomes the passion of knowing—and the assimilatory desire of mastery of the object is made derivative.

The inversion of phenomenological categories like intentionality and signification serve a parallel function to Cohen's idealism. That is, phenomenology cannot do what Levinas requires of it, but by examining just what it can do, he can protect the freedom of the other. Only when the full range of mastery by consciousness in cognition and in perception is developed can the exceptionality and reversal of that mastery appear in its purity. Here, however, we seem to arrive not at Cohen's extension of idealism, but at Rosenzweig's inversion of it. Indeed, nothing echoes Rosenzweig's Cohenian constructions more clearly than Levinas' claims that the other *resists* thematization, *refuses* my concepts, etc. The logic from Chapter 2 appears again here. The other is not only someone who cannot be subordinated to a class, but is also someone who has the freedom to refuse my attempts to know the other—a freedom that would necessarily disappear were she to be given in sense perception. For then the assimilative power of consciousness could classify and appropriate her. Following Rosenzweig, Levinas opts for the preservation of the other's will by exploring the full limits of a totalizing self. The goal is shared, however: to preserve the other's freedom.

The second goal also involves a line from Cohen to Rosenzweig to Levinas, because the discovery of the 'I' through the self-sanctification before God is the recognition that I am the task of responsibility. In Cohen, the 'I' that emerges in the *Religion* is a guilty one who is forgiven and who is to make himself holy through suffering. This 'I' is not possible except through the love for the neighbor, but the further steps involve additional appropriation of the suffering of humanity. I become myself first by suffering with the other, and then by suffering for my own sin. But my self-realization—which is the process of making myself holy through my own freedom—transpires in correlation with God and happens before the other as an attempt to come near to the other.

Rosenzweig also has this self-sanctification before God as the key moment of becoming an 'I'. In the climax of the dialogue, I confess my sins before the other who has loved me first (see Chapter 3). In addition, the key moment in the Jewish community is the common kneeling before God in self-sanctification on the Day of Atonement—exactly as in Cohen (359f./324f.). I become myself through the other—the other who first individually and then communally provides the opportunity for my own repentance and self-sanctification.

For Levinas there is no gap between the encounter with the other and the self-sanctification before God: the two moments are entwined in the experience of the face of the other. While there clearly is a self before I meet the other, that self is hollowed out, obsessed, inverted, extroverted, denucleated, and so on by the encounter (the variety of metaphors point to various appropriations of Rosenzweig's logic of inversion/extroversion). Moreover, the 'I' becomes itself through its substitution for the other. This central concept will be the topic of the next chapter, but here I can note that I become this substitution, this de-centered self. My responsibility makes me me, and I cannot duck it. The 'I', as substitution, is a task of responding for the other—and as such becomes an infinite task through this inversion. Levinas calls this task ethics, but that is a translation of the 'Hebrew' term *sanctification*. The infinity of the task is the trace of God who has been here. Before the face of the other, near or in proximity to the other, Levinas finds the self-sanctification that Cohen and Rosenzweig found before the face and near to God. Levinas has thus brought the 'theological' dimension into the interhuman—but it is far from clear that this separates him from either Cohen or Rosenzweig.

Levinas now calls the other *him* and coins a new term, '*him-ness*' (*illeity*), to adjust the encounter with the other away from the 'you'. This adjustment reflects the intertwining of the human encounter and the divine dimensions (in the face of, near), and perhaps it is fitting that the two goals themselves—the radical freedom of the other and the ineluctable responsibility that makes me me—should be brought closer together. Only by freeing the other as completely as possible can my responsibilities be bound to myself so radically, making my identity depend on my responsibility.

COMPANION OR STRANGER?

Having come near to drawing some of the lines that connect Rosenzweig and Levinas, largely in order to bring Cohen and Levinas closer, I wish now to offer a sketch of the map of Cohen, Rosenzweig, Levinas, and Buber in relation to Cohen's two routes to the other. This map offers a certain clarity of distinctions, but more, it provides some important insight into the distance between Levinas and Buber. On the basis of that map we can have greater understanding of a published exchange between them.[14]

The basic tension to observe is between the constructions 1) of the fellow through the cooperative (*Genossenschaft*) and 2) of the co-person through love of the neighbor, leading to the congregation. Cohen observes that these two routes are in tension both in the *Ethics* and in the *Religion,* but especially in the latter he holds to the need for both. Much of Cohen's discussion could take us deep into his determination of the relation of ethics and religion, but perhaps the key note is that in the first construction I share through rational freedom itself in the formation of a legal companionship, but that in the second I share rational emotions in a community that replaces the state.

Rosenzweig adopts both routes, as both communities have a place in his work. First comes the love relationship, with its confession and self-sanctification before the lover, and second comes the companionship that forms the egalitarian community. He also emphasises that such companionship is not a political organization, but that the community of 'table fellowship' instead subverts authority. Rosenzweig avoids the term congregation, largely due to his allergy to religion as a category. But he also ignores the economics of companionship/cooperatives. He thus elevates companionship in his system, and he moves the self-sanctifying relationship forward in the sequence of relationships. Without interpreting the intricacies of relating the two routes in Cohen and Rosenzweig we can easily see that both sides of relating to the other occur in the works of both thinkers.

It is when we turn to Levinas and Buber that we get views that are truly more one-sided. Buber ignores the co-person and the economic suffering that leads toward self-sanctification; while Levinas ignores companionship and its more basic sharing. Buber's 'I-you' relationship is first of all a relation (*Beziehung*), drawing directly on Cohen's terminology. It is reciprocal, in that I cannot say 'you' to someone who does not also say 'you' to me.[15] Moreover, we can read the discussion of the genesis of the 'I' as emerging not from the 'I-it' but from the 'I-you': that is, that I come to be myself through the relation to a 'you'.[16]

Levinas has strong criticism on many levels for Buber's 'I-you'. In the concluding chapter, I will discuss Levinas' basic opposition to the privacy of the companionship of two people in a relation. But Levinas also criticizes Buber for hypostatizing the relation into 'the Between'. The result is that Buber does not break with philosophy as ontology and so leaves the ethical relation to fall under the sway of the assimilation of philosophy as the knowing of the totality. Levinas' own movement to an 'otherwise than being' is an attempt to escape the wiles of theoretical consciousness. A second criticism of Buber's philosophy of relation is that it is formal, for Buber held that 'I-you' relations could obtain not only with other people, but also with God, animals, vegetation, even rocks. While a more generous interpretation of Buber can allow that the human 'I-you' has a certain priority, and that the higher and lower relations are only intelligible because of the human ones, Levinas' interest in my relation to an other refuses the thought that ethics can appear as part of a species of relations. Buber's formalism makes his analysis again ontological and not ethical.

But Levinas makes a more basic critique of Buber: Buber's relationship is reciprocal. The result, according to Levinas, is that Buber provides for a relationship that does not recognize the height of the other and the fundamental inability to imagine the polarity reversed. To be addressed as 'you' by another is radically different from speaking to another. The very emphasis on the informal you (*du, tu, thou*) became the problem for Levinas—because I use that form of address precisely with those who also address me informally. Thus Levinas switched first to the formal *vous*, and then to that concept of 'him-ness', illeity, to accentuate the difference in speaking and being addressed. Buber, according to Levinas, was guilty of viewing the 'I-you' as a spiritual friendship (NP 40). In contrast to such a relation, which reflects Cohen's *Genossenschaft*, Levinas insists on the height and poverty of the other and on feeding the poor.

And thus Levinas prefers the absence of intimacy in the economic dimension of the second route, the requirement for love of the neighbor and compassion. There is no focus on the relation that obtains between the other and me for Levinas; the disrelation, the gap and separation, is the key. This approach of the other does not involve my responsibility only in order that we may enter into a rich relation. Levinas emphasises that I encounter a stranger who may never get to be my friend, who may always stand as one who commands me. Such asymmetry and absence of reciprocity of the 'I-you' characterize Levinas' interpretation of responsibility for the other. Buber's reply illuminates the gap:

> Levinas, in opposition to me, praises solicitude as the access to the otherness of
> the other. The truth of experience seems to me to be that he who has this access
> apart from solicitude will also find it in the solicitude practiced by him—but he
> who does not have it without this, though he clothe the naked and feed the
> hungry all day, it will remain difficult for him to say a true You.
>
> If all the world were well clothed and well nourished, then the real ethical
> problem would become wholly visible for the first time. (NP 45)

Buber invokes the first relationship to the other: that material needs are
not adequate to create an 'I-you', that we only achieve such a relationship
with a deeper level of openness and responsiveness to the other. Social
justice will not repair the gaps in the world. The fundamental turning of
repentance is not found through material transformation—thus, if
everyone's needs were met, we could then get on with "the real ethical
problem." While Levinas sees ethics as requiring concern without hope of
ongoing relation, Buber defines ethics as what happens in such ongoing
relations (which are not characterized by agreement, but by openness).
Which is ethics?

Levinas' responds to Buber's claims about ethics by returning to the
primacy of the ethics of feeding the hungry. He invokes Jochannan ben
Zakkai's "Great is hunger" and tells a Midrash of how the angels are
calmed in the protest against giving humanity the Torah by God's explanation that those laws are fit only for those who eat and sleep, work and
die, and so on (NP 46; HS 56–57). Are the angels calmed because they are
flattered, "Or did they, on the contrary, suddenly glimpse the superiority
of men on earth, capable of *giving* and of being-for-one-another and thus
making possible the 'human comedy', above and beyond that comprehen-
sion of being to which the pure spirits are devoted?"

Levinas, despite his more sympathetic reading of Buber in that responding essay, still does not budge from his emphasis on the asymmetric,
economic relationship; the relationship that need not produce any sort of
companionship. Not only do we not become friends, but we also do not
sit down together to eat. Instead, I must feed the other with bread from
my own mouth. The argument between these two relations is not easily
resolved.

Or perhaps it is simply a problem of one-sidedness. The companionship of friends, and even of enemies, who can say 'you' to one another is
highly valuable. But so, too, is the social, ethical responsibility that does
not aim for any 'relationship'. Cohen and Rosenzweig retain both routes
to the other, balancing them in terms of the different sorts of communities
and of the different theological resonances. Buber and Levinas seem to
split the two routes apart, and as a result both thinkers prove susceptible
to criticism for ignoring one aspect of responding to an other.

This sketchy map of the four thinkers is now complete, and the tension that exists between the two ways of responding to an other have been displayed in the tension between Levinas and Buber. But there still is one issue that remains for this essay: uniqueness. Uniqueness is a particularly difficult concept, difficult for rational idealism as well as for phenomenology. With it, questions of the unity of these four thinkers as modern Jewish philosophers, or as dialogical thinkers, or as . . . obtrudes precisely because of the unique qualities of each. Or again, uniqueness arises with the attempt to think what it means for Israel to be a unique people—a problem for all four thinkers. (Cohen, not surprisingly, finds Israel's uniqueness to be an external symbol of the need for the unique individual to take on suffering—Israel suffers for the world's redemption.)

The question of uniqueness is ultimately one of the Unique Other, of the One God. Cohen insists that God is unique, as opposed to merely a unified one. Cohen's method of correlation requires that we interpret that predicate as a moral goal for ourselves (and in this he is a Maimonidean). What is the meaning of God's uniqueness, if not the inalienable, irreplaceable, irrefusable duty to become a unique 'I', responsible for the others' sins, willing to suffer in order to make myself holy before that uniqueness? Levinas does not discuss this theological question, but the rigor and rhetoric of his ethics suggests that, for him as for Cohen, uniqueness as a logical or theological category can only be grasped as the unique responsibility that makes me me. The unique other person, as free and independent of me, is to transform me into a unique self, responsible for the other, the paradoxical correlate of the Unique God.

CHAPTER 9

Substitution: Marcel and Levinas

THE LOGIC of uniqueness displaces the focus of our thought from the self to the other. But responsibility requires a self who retains at least the capacity to respond. In the currents of postmodernism, the modern philosophical subject seems adrift, if not already drowned and vanished. Can any sense still be made of the concept of responsibility without such a subject? Can ethics survive the fracturing, de-centering, deconstructing of the self?

It is ironic that, long before the current hubbub called postmodernism, the de-centered self was already discovered—and in an explicitly ethical context. Dialogical philosophers found that interpersonal ethics was the foundation of the self, or rather, that the subject was not its own foundation, but depended upon others in order to be itself. And perhaps less ironic, the theme of that interpersonal self, that de-centered self, is directly correlate with traditional religious concepts. The antireligious agenda of postmodernism is not a necessary conclusion from the de-centered self.

Levinas' work continues that of the dialogical philosophers, and he is closely bound not only to the Jewish authors but particularly to Marcel. Levinas attended Marcel's soirées in the 1930s and there encountered Marcel's remarkable philosophical and religious approach to thought. Levinas has written on Marcel occasionally, and always with respect (HS 34f./EN 77f., 137–38). What I will discuss here is how Marcel's manner of writing grapples with the set of difficulties that concerned Levinas and also Rosenzweig. While a medieval Christian thinker might begin with a dogmatic claim that God created human beings and, therefore, that one must not hope to be one's own foundation, Marcel must struggle in a world that discredits the appeal either to authority (Rosenzweig's sense of dogmatism) or to merely idiosyncratic opinion (Rosenzweig's fanaticism). The task of de-centering the self in a world after Descartes must be performed through an engagement with the self, with the self's own conviction of its self-possession—and it must also be done in a way that is in principle communicable. Like Rosenzweig, Marcel must avoid dogmatics and also strive to overcome the threat from personal experience—of fanaticism. The solution, once again, is to look at the performance of speech.

The issue for this chapter is not merely a manner of thinking, but is, first of all, a question of how to display that my responsibility to an other constitutes the self. One of the most disturbing themes of Levinas' thought is that my spontaneous freedom is secondary, that I am responsible for another person before I can rationally choose to be so. In the first moment, I am not autonomous. The center of my agency is another person. Both Levinas and Marcel claim that there is a radical and ethical heteronomy. They explore the de-centered self, who is capable of substitution, as locus of responsibility—in opposition to an interpretation of the dispersion of the self, where there is no longer any responsibility. But if the self becomes responsible through the agency of the other, then with what freedom can I refuse or simply choose to ignore others? If responsibility precedes freedom, than how is it possible to be irresponsible or nonresponsible?

This chapter traces a motion from the freedom of the other, discovered in the last chapter, to the responsibility of myself. Marcel, even more than Levinas, focuses on the performance of speaking. The constraints of pronouns are explored to discover the nature of the relationship to the other. The practice of speaking displays how my freedom to resist the other itself rests on responsibility for the other. I do not first have a spontaneous freedom to choose whether to be for the other or to be for myself. A certain attention to the orientation of speech in its fundamental asymmetry will lead Marcel's reader to see that responsibility creates the possibility for the illusion of autonomy.

One more word of introduction, however. This chapter is a series of commentaries. I comment first on two texts by Marcel from the 1930s, and then on two texts by Levinas from the 1970s (all four texts are included in an appendix). Levinas' texts are from the final version of the central chapter of *Otherwise than Being*, a chapter titled "Substitution." I believe that you will find these passages extremely opaque if read on their own. More importantly, the structure of the passages itself performs the dislocation from a way of thinking about responsibility that begins with autonomy to one that displays how I am first of all substitute for the other. The Marcel texts are from his book of essays entitled *Du Refus à l'Invocation (Refusing the Call)*, or as it is translated, *Creative Fidelity*.[1] In contrast to Levinas' dense and obscure prose, Marcel's is colloquial. His texts reflect on utterances made to an other, although the written text clearly is not a transcript, but a philosophical reflection that discovers exigencies that govern the performance of speaking. Nonetheless, Marcel is also pushing the reader against the grain, leading the reader to recognize that the limitations on speech reflect a deeper insight into the de-centered nature of responsibility.

I have chosen to comment, moreover, not only because these texts are about the key question of this radical ethics; and not only because these texts themselves perform the de-centering by examining how speech itself de-centers (Marcel) and by examining thought (Levinas); but also because commentary itself reiterates or replays the actions of these various texts. The full justification of commentary can only come at the end of this chapter, after the place of substitution is clear; but as a preliminary thought, I suggest that first of all speech, then secondarily thought, and finally writing, are actions that put me at the service of the other—that my responsibility is not only for what I decide to say or to think or to write for myself, but always my responsibility begins with the other with whom I speak, for whom I think, to whom I write. Commentary, under this paradoxical view, is a privileged way to perform that responsibility.

Performing De-centering

Marcel began developing his thoughts on the other and intersubjectivity in the *Metaphysical Journal* and *Being and Having*. Many of the themes developed in these passages are continued in his later works, but the two passages I will examine in this chapter are both written in 1939 and republished in *Creative Fidelity*. The first is an excerpt from the essay "Belonging and Disposability."

In this text Marcel begins by examining the performative constraints on an assertion. Why does Marcel choose the assertion HE BELONGS TO ME? Because it epitomizes the aggression of self-interest. ME is the true subject in this utterance. I speak and make a claim to a listener about a third person. That third person, HE, is not a subject. I am trying to ASSERT that he is not a person with freedom. He becomes a peripheral object; I am the center, the self.

Marcel registers our shock, indeed our revolt. Notwithstanding the arguments of philosophers, the audience would be morally astonished by this degradation of a person into a possession. While a self may try to make itself the center, the addressee of such claims would regard them as worse than extravagant. Marcel also plays on the reader and listener with a reference to MY AUDIENCE. While he is not making this claim, nor even reporting a factual occurrence of what happened one day when he made it, he is casting the reader in the part of the addressee. He assumes the role of the speaker and indeed highlights the distinctiveness of the 'I' who speaks.

If I assert of a servant: *he belongs to me,* I would obviously provoke a genuine shock in my audience; assuming that I am not treated with the silent commiseration due an idiot, and am asked what right have I to assert that this servant belongs to me, I will answer that I treat him as a thing that I have acquired or that has been given to me, etc.

But the reader is encouraged not only to read, but to register his or her own shock and to take a part. Marcel identifies a quiescent reading (THE SILENT COMMISERATION DUE AN IDIOT) in order to jar the reader from a simply passive role. It says, as it were, "Don't just accept any claim advanced by a speaking 'I'." But the point is that we normally would not accept such claims, and we must attend to our resistance. More subtly, however, Marcel is also daring the reader to try to place oneself in the role of the 'I' who does say this unacceptable thing. The resistance from the audience is discernible in the difficulty in assuming the role of the speaker.

The speaker is asked WHAT RIGHT he has to make his assertion. This question challenges the degradation. Moreover, the response addresses the speaker directly. From the speaker's perspective the question comes directly to the 'I'. The question deals with the right to make assertions. Had the 'I' asserted "I feel sick," the audience would not be expected to question the right. But to assert possession of another person seems to presume a legitimation to say certain things that are not only illegitimate in this circumstance, but which in principle seem illegitimable.

Marcel answers for the first person, now taking the grammatical center that he deferred at the outset. In place of HE BELONGS TO ME, now the 'I' says: I TREAT HIM AS A THING THAT I HAVE ACQUIRED. Here the justification of the assertion focuses on the mode of taking possession of the third person. Such a justification is comparable to how one would justify an assertion such as "That book belongs to me." The 'I' mistakes the objection for a general question of how one comes to possess something.

Regardless of the reply, the audience would discount his claim. They object to the idea of possession and denigration of another person, not to the particular mode of taking possession. Despite the pretense of dialogue here, we cannot accept the claim of the 'I'. The resistance is on behalf of HIM, of the servant, the third person. I, as listener, cannot stand by while you enslave a third person. The injustice, the violation of right, is beyond the realm of the faked dialogue of question and answer. The protest against immorality toward a third brooks no reasons, no rationalizations. Indeed, the immorality of slavery is at least as much the communal tolerance of it as it is the aggression of the slaveholder. Injustice is not only a two-party relationship, as in Hegel's master-slave dialectic, but implicates the third party, the 'you' to whom the master speaks of his slaves.

Whatever the specified nature of the response, however, it is clear that it has every chance of not satisfying my questioner; on the contrary, it will seem to him an extravagant and unacceptable claim. Of course, it would have been otherwise when slavery still existed.

Marcel's challenge has been to accentuate what he takes to be our common refusal to allow someone to assert possession of a third person. He takes up the first-person speaker in order to locate us in the role of objectors, and from that position to make us aware of the structures of speech that make even the first-person role difficult to maintain. Moreover, we see Marcel's pragmatism: the difficulties he encounters are not eternal verities, but instead have to do with context (an era that has rejected slavery). The question of personal pronouns is not the sole linguistic resource for his analysis; rather, he moves from the constraints of those pronouns to an intimation of the contextually bound nature of those constraints. However, we now leave behind a third person and problems of justice.

The question is the relationship between the two terms of belonging. Marcel leaves the lecture hall, where I speak to a group of you about my relationship with him. In the new situation, I am face-to-face with an other, indeed with a 'you'. I no longer ASSERT, but now DECLARE something about me and you. Declaration is a different kind of performance, largely due not to the verb used but to the situation of address (from I to you) and the relation of the contents to that situation.

It is curious to note that the question is completely transformed if I happen to declare to another: *I belong to you.* Here we have completely shifted the ground.

Marcel reflects about the situational quality of this speech by inserting his authorial 'I' at this point: THAT I AM EVOKING. He calls attention to the distance that we interpose in reflecting on this speech from outside. We cannot really be audience or mere readers, because it CANNOT BE OBJECTIFIED WITHOUT ITS NATURE BEING RADICALLY CHANGED. Objectification has two related meanings here: First, that the first person cannot be replaced by a third person, not by an object or even by a 'him'. Why not? Because here we reflect upon the address to an other, the reality of saying to her, I BELONG TO YOU. Such reflection requires the 'I' be me, and not some objective 'one'; that I speak the speech, and not about the speech. The HE BELONGS TO ME is objectification because it is speech about a person as object, as third person. The second meaning of objectification has to do with the reflection about this situated speaking. Marcel may dare us to place ourselves in the midst of the situation, just as he turned the readers into the audience, in order to make us both acknowledge our objection and experience the failure to justify the assertion of another's slavery to me. The reflection looks like a move toward objectification, but in fact Marcel keeps reinserting us (his

First it must be observed—and this is essential—that I am evoking a situation that cannot really be objectified, strictly speaking; one, in any case, that cannot be objectified without its nature being radically changed.

readers) and himself in the situation where he (and we) must become the 'I' that speaks. When we read the sentence, he forces us to hear it coming out of our own mouths and so to discover what limitations and implications are performed in speaking.[2]

The RELATION, therefore, is ORIGINAL in the sense that our analysis must recur to the specific situated relation. The name, JACK, emphasizes that this is speech spoken to a unique person, a 'you' with a name. And then Marcel begins a sequence of explanations. Each involves a trust in 'you' no matter what you choose to do. Your will governs me; and what I am, I give to you.

Let us examine closely the original relation: Jack, I belong to you. This means: I am opening an unlimited credit account for you, you can do what you want with me, I give myself to you.

My self is now extroverted and exists outside my own center. My self is no longer mine, but yours. I GIVE MYSELF TO YOU is a 'translation' of the performative act of speaking the words I AM YOURS.

Notice that Marcel did not simply invert the HE BELONGS TO ME, into I BELONG TO HIM. In that case, we would have the slave's ideology. In

This does not mean, at least not in principle: I am your slave.

discussing HIM, I would objectify both the form of address and the situation of that address. I would now tell you about HIM, my master, and the addressee still would be guilty of complicity in or offended by the immoral possession of one by the other. But to belong is not simply to be a slave—at least not in this specific situation of an 'I' addressing a 'you'. While the objectified discourse of third persons does imply slavery, and the direct appropriation of the other (YOU BELONG TO ME) may also imply slavery, the address from 'I' to 'you' does not. The subtle play of pronouns makes apparent what could only be laboriously argued philosophically: that relations between two people surpass the alternatives of either master or slave. But this will be clearer later.

I am not enslaved, although I belong to you. I FREELY PUT MYSELF AT YOUR DISPOSAL. What is this freedom in the FREELY? The freedom of substitution (a term rarely used in Marcel's works). What would coercion be? YOU or HE BELONGS TO ME. In some sense, I can slavishly tell a third person that I belong to you—but always that is telling a 'you' whom I face that I BELONG TO HIM (a third), because the direct addressee becomes a 'you'. Only in an 'I-you' situation may I announce the substitution that is not slavery because of the performance of

On the contrary, I freely put myself at your disposal; the best use I can make of my freedom is to place it in your hands; it is as though I freely substituted your freedom for my own; or paradoxically, it is by that very substitution that I consummate my freedom.

speaking to the 'you'. The freedom in the act of speaking itself displays my capacity to bestow my own freedom and so, simultaneously, to act and to interpret my action. *I* perform the substitution, not *you*. The paradox, indeed, is that this freedom is truest, most perfected, CONSUMMATE. Autonomy itself is imperfect; the aggression of selfishness is immoral; only yielding freedom, the substitution of your will for mine, is fully free, because it is the freedom to not rule myself—which is not the slavery by which I am compelled by force to be ruled by another. But the original problem now returns, because the emphasis on FREELY suggests that I choose to belong to you, to substitute your will for my own. What choice do I make? If I don't have the choice, then we are back in slavery; if I do make the choice, then my own will precedes the substitution. At this point, the best solution seems to be that substitution completes my own will and that my own will is prior to that act of declaring that I belong to you.

Only by expressly considering the belonging to an Absolute You, to God, will the depth of Marcel's discussion become clear. Marcel explores the issue of self-possession in his essay, "Phenomenological Notes on Being in a Situation." Toward the end of that essay he returns to the issue of belonging to other people. He again observes the asymmetry of the 'I-you' relation: to say I BELONG TO YOU is to make a commitment; to say YOU BELONG TO ME is to make a claim. And he examines our offense at that claim in moves similar to the earlier discussion. But he does raise the possibility of certain contexts in which that claim would itself be tied to other counterclaims that might redeem the statement (such as lovers who affirm that they belong to each other or even to their love).

As a corollary to this discussion, Marcel raises the confusion that Christ's claim "YOU BELONG TO ME" provokes in him. At the outset, he explains the irritation and disavowal in himself this claim incites. As he proceeds, however, he attempts to justify the claim made *by* an 'I'. In fact, he can only justify the claim made *upon* an 'I', the claim that actually is the avowal of commitment (I BELONG TO YOU). Marcel never does justify the corresponding claim, from an 'I' to an other, to a 'you'.

The second part of my commentary begins with Marcel's resistance to the claim from Christ that he (Marcel) belongs to him, a claim Marcel encounters when "reading certain spiritual, or even properly mystical, works." This objection hinges on two points: 1) the resistance to anyone at all who claims that I must belong to him, and 2) the significance of a writer making that claim, even if in the voice of God. The first point claims that it is A TYRANNICAL INJUNCTION WHICH IS ADDRESSED TO ME BY SOMEONE SPECIFIC. If any particular person were to confront me with such a claim, I would not only question, but I WOULD REBEL. Here we

On the one hand, the fact that His word is transcribed, that it is addressed to me by means of a text, runs the risk of degrading it into a tyrannical injunction which is addressed to me by someone specific and against whom it is after all quite reasonable that I would rebel: What right has *some other* to claim that I belong to him?

find the 'I' trying to stand up for itself, for its rights, its self-possession, its autonomy. Marcel, in this objecting, senses the outrage of the confrontation—that if the claim were anonymous or general it might not rankle him so deeply, but how dare SOMEONE SPECIFIC make such a claim on me. This offense will slowly yield, as I will show in the following section.

The second point, of more subtle cast, is that the claim is not, in fact, made either in a face-to-face confrontation, nor even in some mystical or spiritual manner, but rather is made through a written text. The written text RUNS THE RISK OF DEGRADING IT INTO A TYRANNICAL INJUNCTION. Perhaps the objection to the specificity lies more in the ventriloquism of the written text. The problem is that HIS WORD IS TRANSCRIBED, that some later author, even the Apostle Paul, speaks for Christ, and then does not speak, but writes. In the face-to-face confrontation with a specific person, one might object or feel compelled to accept the claim that I BELONG TO YOU, but with a written text the issue is harder. I can neither challenge the author, who leaves me alone with the text, nor am I assured a confrontation with Christ. The text seems to offer yet another combination of pronouns: YOU BELONG TO HIM. Marcel registers the suspicion that such a claim, assigning me to a third—and not to the person in front of me—actually assigns me not to Christ, to Him, but rather to the author and the author's agenda. The author claims me for God in order, Marcel fears, to claim me for his or her own project. And by hiding behind God's claim, the author dons a protective cloak.

This problem is relevant for Marcel precisely because he will make this very claim and so must be alert to the same suspicion in his readers. What right has *some other* to claim that I belong to him? Perhaps the recourse to philosophical reflection will prevent his text from slipping into spiritualism or even mysticism, and so he can sidestep the suspicion that his readers no doubt hold: that when he (Marcel) claims that each of them belongs to God, he is only claiming it from his specific position. How can Marcel himself defuse this suspicion, this rebellion? (And, of course, this problem recurs in my commentary as well. Even as Marcel is commenting on a text that itself comments on an utterance, so this chapter comments upon that doubled commentary.) Only the most rigorous attention to the shifting pronouns will protect Marcel from provoking the rebellion he himself felt. That recourse to his own experience, to his vantage point with which he is uniquely familiar, is the key to a reflection about the claim of SOME OTHER upon a 'me'. But writing must carefully restore the integrity of the experience of each 'I' in order not to abstract utterly and leave every reader in the third-person role. The intrusion of Marcel's sensitivities in the voice of an 'I' induces the reader to replace Marcel with his or her own self. Marcel and the reader thus stay on the 'I' side of the claim being made and do not slip into the side of the claimant. Marcel does not become the ventriloquist of

God, but neither can the reader slide out of the position of being claimed by SOME OTHER.

Marcel's objection within himself is answered by the action of REFLECTION. The inner life of conflict and suspicion, desire and avoidance, itself has a dynamic that allows intervention from thinking. One of Marcel's great themes, the difference between thinking about something and thinking about my thinking about that something (which Marcel calls *secondary reflection*), lies in the discovery that in order to take up a thinking relation to some other thing, my own thinking must already be implicated in and inseparable from my perception of that thing. When I think about representing an object to myself, I discover a susceptibility in the subject that thinks, which provides a certain revision of my presupposition of a subject who thinks spontaneously and sovereignly. The 'I' becomes a permeable process, a being intrinsically open to the object. By exploring the recursive nature of subjectivity (thinking about thinking), Marcel eventually discovers that the subject who thinks can never become transparent to itself. The permeability and susceptibility, the passivities of the self, make the self opaque to a direct gaze of the subject upon itself. The deeper one bores into the self, the more one finds that the self is not the origin of the activity of thinking, nor is the self fully in control of the activity. And this otherness, this lack of closure and self-transparence of the self, is, indeed, exactly what confronts the 'I' in this claim by the other. INSOFAR AS HE IS MORE INTERIOR TO ME THAN I AM TO MYSELF, God makes this claim upon me. In other analyses, Marcel displays how the failure of the modern subject's project of autonomy discovers the presence of that subject's creator—a being more interior to the 'I' than is the self.

On the other hand, reflection quickly does justice to these false appearances: He claims that right over me precisely not insofar as He is truly some other one; but rather insofar as He is more interior to me than I am to myself.

What Marcel contrasts with this self unable to ground itself is an image of the self invaded from outside by something other. Marcel here is only explaining that there is a strange consolation in recognizing that the other who claims me is not simply anyone, but should instead be recognized as my very center, as closer to myself than the 'I' that thinks can be. That 'I' refuses the other the claim, but that 'I' itself will emerge as less central to myself than the other.

Marcel makes clear that the offense of refusing is STRICTLY REBELLIOUS. The prior commitment against which one rebels is yet to be discerned, but Marcel does wish us to see that what looks like autonomy, like rational assertion of myself, will have to be recast as a form of rebellion. The site of the rebellion was at my very

Hence I shall refrain from supporting the strictly rebellious claim that the *you belong to me* stirred up in my center. But it must be clearly noted that it is the value center. The issue is not the objective logic of who belongs to whom. Marcel's interest is not removed from this specific situation—for he must focus on what is specific to himself in this context. Thus the chief issue is what Marcel here calls THE VALUE. FORMAL POSSIBILITY refers to the possibility of anyone resisting any claim, of a generic refusal. But there is a question of value, of how his will achieves direction toward different ends.

rather than the formal possibility of the claim that is at issue.

To emphasize the speaking of the 'I', the 'I' for whom this is a question, Marcel inserts quotation marks. The written device notifies us that the following text is to be read as direct discourse; in this case, as an address from an 'I' to a 'you'. This quotable 'I' is less personal, less Marcel's own self engaged in self-reflection, than the 'I' who wanted to rebel. At the same time the quotable 'I' is more immediate to the reader, a voice observed not through an other's observation (even if the observer is the speaker), but a voice heard in its speaking. No move is more characteristic of the struggle to resist the temptation for writing to abstract from the situation than this breaking into quoted discourse.

"Indeed, who am I to pretend that I do not belong to You?"

What is even more noteworthy than the quotation marks is that the asymmetry of I and You asserts itself here. Once Marcel shifts from his reflections on speaking to speech itself, he cannot maintain himself in the second person. Marcel cannot explore YOU BELONG TO ME, but turns to the question of the I: whether I BELONG TO YOU. There is a complex aversion to examining the YOU BELONG TO ME: On the one hand, it involves setting words in the mouth of Christ. Here is the ventriloquism that seemed suspicious. But in addition, there is the more generic inability to speak the oppressive sentence. Even if inserted into a context in which the oppression itself is supposedly prohibited (when God says it), Marcel is bound by a humane reluctance or discomfort. The immediacy of quoting makes speaking this sentence (YOU BELONG TO ME) somehow wrong. The question of how much I can dissociate myself from the words I utter, even if uttered only to exemplify iterability, is raised by Marcel's subtle shift to the self-bestowing performance I BELONG TO YOU. And the interruption of the reflection about speaking by speaking, even in the written form of the text, brings with it the concreteness of the speaking situation. The written form can attempt to interrupt itself, re-placing the reader in the place of the 'I' once again. The reader notes this shift from YOU BELONG TO ME to I BELONG TO YOU and recognizes for his or her self the very resistance to speaking to a 'you' the aggressive claim.

Once we have made that shift, moreover, we resume the question of the last passage. Such belonging cannot be POSSESSION, cannot be the loss of my self. However, Marcel suspects that

"In effect, if I belong to You, it is not to say: I am Your possession; this mysterious relation does

finite wills (human or general wills) may reduce me to a thing. The insistence on infinity is key to preserving my self as self, even if I now am de-centered. An infinite power need not eradicate my self by claiming me; a finite one, Marcel fears, would.

"not occur on the level of having as would be the case if You were a finite power."

Marcel now takes substitution to its fullest extreme. Your will is mine; indeed, you are my freedom. But to belong to you is to receive my-self as a task. You originate my freedom, free-dom to belong to you and freedom to create myself—freedom to be a free person. If I could

"Not only are You free-dom, but You also will me. You instigate me too as freedom. You call me to create myself. You are this very call."

belong to a finite power only as a possession, as reduced to a thing, then to this infinite 'you' I belong in order to be free. Indeed, this 'you' is the exigency upon me to be free. This 'you' is the call to substitution. The other here is not another self for me, outside myself. This 'you' appears to me as a call to substitute your will for mine. The other is no object, no thing to be known. You are my call to freedom, to substitution.

Marcel develops, and will continue to develop, this thought within quotation marks in the speaking of direct discourse to a 'you'. That 'you' is capitalized in his text so that the reader may recognize that the 'you' is God; and more, that this speech is prayer. It is not a sentimental or pietis-tic prayer, but is instead a surprisingly vivid analysis of the reality of prayer. Speaking to God as a 'you' seems a form of 'I-you' dialogue, ex-cept that this 'you' never responds and, indeed, has no chance to do so. While the original discussion of speaking to an audience or to Jack led the reader to adopt each position in turn (the 'I' that spoke, and the other who listened and could speak), this prayer to a capitalized 'you' does not invite the reader to take up that position. The asymmetry of the 'I-you' space is parallel to the asymmetry of speaking to God: Marcel encourages the reader to understand that both the position of God and the position of the 'you' who claims that 'I' belong to him are not positions that the reader may easily assume.

What measure of free choice do I have? To what extent am I free to choose between alter-natives? The only alternative to the freedom of substitution, of belonging to the 'you', is to re-fuse the call, to maintain myself against your will. Can't I be autonomous? Marcel insists that autonomy is not the formal choice to be able to make a choice (what Levinas will call the temp-tation of temptation). A claim has been made upon me that makes my own freedom come

"And if I reject it, i. e., You, if I persist in main-taining that I belong only to myself, it is as though I walled myself up; as though I bound myself to strangling with my own hands that reality in whose name I believed I was resisting You."

from an other, from a 'you'. In that situation, to insist THAT I BELONG ONLY TO MYSELF is to persist in the image of autonomy. The ONLY allows that I have various connections, obligations, influences, etc., but claims that in the first instance I get to choose my own allegiances, that I have the capacity by my will to authorize, to validate, those complex connections. To belong only to myself is not to be a concrete island, but rather to have ultimate control of the coast and the harbors of myself. Then I can choose, in this specific situation, whether I shall belong to you. But such persistence is a refusal.

Marcel provides two images of that refusal: WALLING MYSELF UP, and STRANGLING myself. The first captures the solidity of the self, but it indicates that I can only make myself secure through an action of my own, that I am not first of all located within walls, but that I must build them. To make myself into a prison is to refuse the circulation with others that substitution requires. Such prison building is done in the name of self-possession, but as prison it denies me freedom. Strangulation pushes the image still further, because it implies that sealing oneself off will actually kill the self. What I lose by building those walls is not incidental to my self; it is the very air the self needs to breathe, to live. Better, the image of breathing indicates that respiration is the opposite of building: it is taking something deep within oneself and also letting something go. But STRANGLING MYSELF WITH MY OWN HANDS emphasizes how the action of the will is done 'autonomously'. The purpose appears to be the preservation of that REALITY IN WHOSE NAME I BELIEVED I WAS RESISTING YOU. My own will, which seems to require this strangling self-possession, in fact is the key victim of such will. I wish to believe that I am free before your call, and so I can stand up for my autonomy, but that use of my invested freedom is merely the act of sealing myself and refusing to let the one who calls me to freedom reach me.

Marcel restates these themes, still in direct quotation, and deepens the final point. Self-possession is dependent on responding to your call by substituting your will for mine. I become a breathing self, one who has the capacity to will, only when I accept the breath, only when I KNOW THAT I BELONG TO YOU. True selfhood is freedom from the prison of my own will. AUTHENTIC FREEDOM is responsive freedom, while the claim of originary autonomy, that there is first a freedom to choose whether to respond, is not a freedom I can truly claim. The substitution of your will for mine is my own freedom.

"If this is so, to know that I belong to You is to know that I belong to myself only on this condition—what is more, this belonging is identical to and united with the only complete and authentic freedom which I can claim."

I have no prior claim to this freedom you instigate because it is A GIFT. I do not earn it through moral struggle or deserve it inherently. My unique role is to ACCEPT IT. If I do not, it cannot be my freedom; it becomes mine only when I act in response. It is

"This freedom is a gift; even though I must accept it."

not coercion nor an intrusion of force. It is not the dissolution or the dispersion of the self, but rather the constitution of a self as originally de-centered, as responsive. The 'I' must accept it but cannot originate it. The other is the center of my freedom, and I still am free.

Here Marcel reaches his most challenging. Again we see the absence of a power prior to the call. I am not choosing the call, but the call itself gives THE POWER DISPENSED TO ME TO ACCEPT it. Even our power of refusing arises from the call. AND THERE IS A WAY FOR ME TO ASSERT THIS FREEDOM WHICH AMOUNTS TO A REFUSAL. The possibility of autonomy, or self-possession—TO ASSERT THIS FREEDOM—derives from the other's call. It is an inversion of the other's call. The ability to choose to accept is not rooted

"The power dispensed to me to accept *or to refuse it* is inseparable from this gift, and there is a way for me to assert this freedom which amounts to a refusal, and this refusal, addressed to the very thing that makes it possible, has the distinctive character of betrayal."

in a self-relation, but in the relation to the other. Here BETRAYAL appears as the use of a gift to deny the giver. The 'I' *asserts* its autonomy, ADDRESSED TO THE VERY THING WHICH MAKES IT POSSIBLE. ASSERTS here is parallel to the first use in this commentary—the usurpation of a person as a possession (IF I ASSERT OF A SERVANT . . .). The violence of asserting in response to this claim is what offends. Notice, moreover, that the gift is the freedom to be free of myself, to belong to you, to make your will my own. All autonomy, all denial of your claims to me, originates in this prior power to substitute. Prior to my acceptance or refusal, my substitution or my protests of autonomy, is a gift from you, from an other.

LEVINAS' SUBSTITUTION

Thirty years later, in 1967, Emmanuel Levinas developed similar themes in an essay which later became the centerpiece of his second great work *Otherwise than Being*. Here a markedly different rhetoric appears in passages which are among the most opaque in Levinas' works. Nonetheless, the repetition of themes from Marcel's texts is striking. While Marcel explored the speech between an 'I' and a 'you' and carefully led the reader to place oneself in the position of the 'I' upon whom a call to substitute was made, Levinas explores a rending of consciousness by an other without recourse to direct dialogue. Levinas' text stays in the realms of reflection, so he must disrupt the abstraction of reflection through means other than Marcel's. The reflection itself will have to turn back on itself, leaving the reader turning back against the presuppositions of the autonomy and spontaneity of thought.[3] Within certain limits, Levinas has argued that phenomenology is the most precise means of reflecting on the role of my own agency in my experience. The surpassing of phenomenology, which is not simply the rejection of it but the movement through and past it, happens in the reflection on substitution. That surpassing occurs through a shift in vocabulary.

PHENOMENOLOGY and THEMATIZATION forge the central link for Levinas, for phenomenology makes the manner of thought or sensation or experience appear to us. Phenomenology makes something implicit in our perception, for in-stance, into a theme, a topic for reflection. It brings it into the light of thought, in such a way that it can appear before our consciousness. As such, it presupposes, in fact requires, a correlation between the activity of the 'I' in thinking something and the thought the 'I' then has. The ade-quacy of describing both the intentionality of the 'I' and the thought that is thought is the measure of thematization. Language in particular plays a key role, as the phenomenologist uses words to effect the thema-tizing.

Phenomenology is able to follow the returning from thematization into anarchy in the descrip-tion of the approach.

The problem here is that THE DESCRIPTION OF THE APPROACH leads into a space without the transparency of phenomenological thematiza-tion. THE APPROACH refers to the approach of an other, it is the encounter that will soon appear as substitution. In *Totality and Infinity* this ap-proach was termed 'the face,' but in *Otherwise than Being*, Levinas refers to it as 'proximity'. He analyzes the moment of encounter when someone is near me, or perhaps better, draws near to me. That drawing near is a moment of vulnerability to the other's touching me. The approach is not the touch itself, but the proximity, the drawing near enough to be within reach of me. Levinas also plays on proximity as a neighbor, as the person who is nearest to me (see the discussion in Rosenzweig in Chapter 3). This approach of the other, this drawing near to me, this other becoming my neighbor, this approach of the face of the other is not thematizable. It is literally not a phenomenon and so cannot be described by the methods of phenomenology. Here, in this text, Levinas is reflecting on the very failure of phenomenology. But his interest is with the failing itself, not simply with what comes after it. The face is not a phenomenon for phenomenol-ogical description, nor is the approach an *arche*. An arche is a founding moment or principle linked by necessary bonds to subsequent moments, but those bonds also make the arche deducible in reverse from the later moments. The approach leads from what can be described and displayed phenomenologically, to the groundless, indescribable reality that is the other approaching me.

But where phenomenology FINDS ITSELF ABRUPTLY FLUNG in a PARADOX, ethical lan-guage interrupts and expresses the reality. PAR-ADOX because the other's freedom not only is ungraspable by my thought, even by the analy-

Ethical language comes to express the paradox where phenomenology finds itself abruptly flung. For ethics, beyond poli-

ses of phenomenology, but because the other at the same time now regards me and so sees me as the phenomenon. The other is no phenomenon for me, and at the same time I become a phenomenon for the other—and so phenomenology can only thematize the other as the one who thematizes me and cannot be thematized as such. But this is where the cognitive moves of phenomenology yield to some other sort of terms. Levinas pursues the question to the point of rupture with phenomenology, but when that fails, ETHICAL terms surprisingly serve to describe what is happening. The description, however, now must serve a different function, not allowing the reader a clear cognitive view, but somehow implicating the reader in the ethical relation of the approach.

> tics, is on the level of that returning.

The capacity for ethics to describe these events comes from its location ON THE LEVEL OF THAT RETURNING. THAT RETURNING is from thematization to anarchy, which means that in the approach of an other, the failure of thinking of the other that leaves me with no deducible relation to the other is an ethical moment. Ontology and epistemology here cross over into an ethics—an ethics BEYOND POLITICS, because Levinas will claim that the realm of politics is one of commensurable, thematizable relations between individuals and groups (this is a central theme for the final chapter of this book). Were ethics to be simply an introduction to politics when thematization breaks down, then even it would not occur at the level of anarchy. But because there is also an ethics that is part of politics, the reader is alerted that what Levinas will call ETHICAL LANGUAGE will not be the familiar vocabulary of ethical theories.

Here, a few lines later, Levinas takes up the question again, this time making still clearer the impossibility of thematizing THE APPROACH. Since the approach seems to be a sort of relation between the other and me, we might think that 'the approach' was a reflection, a name, or even

> The approach is not the thematization of any relation, but is that relation itself which resists thematization insofar as it is anarchic.

an existential category for the relation of the other and the 'I'. In short, doesn't Levinas prove that this relation can be thematized by his own thinking and writing when he calls that relation THE APPROACH? Levinas meets this objection by claiming that THE APPROACH IS NOT THE THEMATIZATION OF ANY RELATION: this name cannot represent or describe what is going on. Levinas finds himself in a familiar pickle for religious thought; indeed, for all thought of transcendence. How do you describe the indescribable, without disproving the claim that the indescribable is indescribable? Levinas makes recourse to one set of possible moves, beginning with the claim that the approach is not the *description* of an indescribable relation, BUT IS THAT RELATION ITSELF. Levinas is claiming that I can refer to the relation without thematizing it and that THE APPROACH is being used to signify what cannot be made to appear in consciousness. Here Levinas restores the basic capacity of words to refer, but he still must justify the possibility that a word could refer to something that is not itself describable; that the referent may transcend the capacity of my consciousness and its words.

Levinas' second move is to say that the referent of the approach RESISTS THEMATIZATION INSOFAR AS IT IS ANARCHIC. If the referent transcends the possibility of cognition, description, thematization, etc., then it must do so by refusing adherence to an arche. The strength of phenomenology is its a priori transcendental reflection: it displays the original rules and principles of possible experiences. If the referent of a word is accessible to an 'I', then we must be able to stipulate the possible conditions of the 'I''s access to it. When Levinas claims that the relation is anarchic, at least in part, he is excluding it from that sort of transcendental reflection. That relation RESISTS because, like the 'No' of Rosenzweig's elements, the other who approaches is free to have different intentions for me, and that approach of the other therefore cannot be thematized by me. The recourse to anarchy is a way to secure the approach, the referent of the word, from the logic of the 'I''s experience. An anarchic beginning is one that, again similar to the logic from Schelling and Rosenzweig, reason cannot deduce or produce, nor can phenomenology thematize.

Thematization, according to Levinas, must come after and only as a loss of the relation, the approach of the other. With the next appositive that loss becomes clear: THE ABSOLUTE PASSIV- | To thematize that relation is already to lose it, to leave the absolute passivity of the self.

ITY. Because thematizing requires the activity of the 'I', to thematize is to require the self to act. The approach of the other is the radical freedom of the other, before the self acts. Cognition, even of the transcendental phenomenological variety, requires activity of the self, the presence of the self in a way adequately described by philosophical analysis. But the claim that Levinas is expounding, by a similar sort of analysis, is that something—the approach of the other—cannot be adequately described and, indeed, requires an absolute passivity. But then what sort of agency defines the self (no longer the 'I') who is so approached? Is that self still a self?

Levinas now defines ABSOLUTE PASSIVITY. It must be an undergoing that precedes the split between passivity and activity. The key term here is ALTERNATIVE, because that implies that one must choose whether to act or to receive an action. Before the grammatical option between passive and active lies the sort of passivity of the approach of the other. MORE PASSIVE THAN ANY | The passivity this side of the passivity-activity alternative, more passive than any inertia, is described by the ethical terms: accusation, persecution, and responsibility for others.

INERTIA is not a grammatical image, but a physical one. Inertia carries not only the tendency to maintain itself in motion or rest, but also the sense of being at rest, inert. The passivity Levinas addresses is not merely the echo of matter, the inert stuff that maintains itself in rest, but rather a passivity in the face of the other that cannot be maintained or sustained, which is not the resistance in me to the other, which the other must set in motion, but is, rather, prior even to my capacity to stay at rest. A capacity that Marcel had called A GIFT, which arises utterly through the freedom of the other. A passivity that has no color at all.

Levinas develops the claim that such a passivity, such an encounter, can best be DESCRIBED BY ETHICAL TERMS. Phenomenological terms will not do, because they require some activity in the 'I', even if it is the activity of receiving sensations. Moreover, ontological terms require a universal subordination of everything to the category of Being. Substitution precedes that logic of particular and universal, preceding it by an excess (a description of which will appear in the following pages). Both for the freedom and the resistance to abstraction, the passivity of the self in relation to the other must move into another vocabulary. The ETHICAL TERMS, however, are the special vocabulary of Levinas: ACCUSATION, PERSECUTION, and RESPONSIBILITY FOR OTHERS. Each term seems odd to most writers on ethical theory, although each might have a place of sorts. ACCUSATION seems to be part of a juridical idiom and appears to require the division between justified and unjustified accusation. PERSECUTION seems a matter of extreme affliction and attack. It generally appears to deal with malicious prejudice against a class. Finally, RESPONSIBILITY FOR OTHERS appears almost paradoxical. One often is responsible *to* others, but responsibility seems to be largely for what one does or consents to having others do. To be responsible *for* others might mean to be bound to take care of them, a certain sort of paternalistic ethics; or, in certain legal contexts, it might refer to liability for what one's wards do. In short, these three terms do not seem the heart of any crisis in cognition and ontology. Levinas places them at the center of his ethical vocabulary, and the oddness is not due simply to the translation into English from French. The shift to ethics is, if not idiosyncratic, at least not a shift into a reasonable vocabulary of moral choice. Levinas suspects that such a vocabulary would thematize again, would objectify and restore the cognitive capacity and the authority of the 'I'. That the task is to define the passivity that proceeds moral choice is clear, but that these terms are actually ETHICAL and that they describe the passivity of the self is the task of the next few sentences of Levinas' text.

Levinas begins with PERSECUTION. The approach of the other persecutes me. But what is persecution? Persecution is displacement, a dis- The persecuted is expelled from his place and has only himself to him-

placement by force with no hope of return (expulsion). This loss of place is a fundamental loss of base or home for the self, without which one cannot enter into the world at large. The image self, has no place in the world to rest his head. He is pulled out of every game and every war.

of a prisoner in a concentration camp comes to mind, a person who does not even have his own place to sleep. Parallel to Marcel's description of your call and instigation of my freedom, Levinas' persecution is an unchosen initiative by the other. Persecuted, I lose my situation, my ability to establish myself. Even my thoughts run amok. I am de-situated and so cannot sit, cannot lie down. But this denial of my place, of my control over my space, means that I am PULLED OUT OF EVERY GAME. I have no space to play, there is no room. The initiative needed to play, to join the fray of the world, is impossible, as I am resourceless. But that also means that I am pulled out of EVERY WAR. From GAME to WAR, Levinas has moved the issue of leisure and reflection to that of life and death. The persecuted has no opportunity to relax and play at life, but he also has no place from which to fight to survive. Survival in a death camp was not part of the wars of the world. Persecution rips all weapons from one's hands and, by expelling one, leaves one no resources and no base for engaging with other wills through the use of one's own will. This seems the radical passive stance that Levinas is seeking.

Levinas now develops the other ETHICAL TERMS. The issue is still the attempt to discuss the approach of the other and the passivity of the self being approached. Levinas now contrasts two different concepts of the self's role in passivity. On the one hand is AUTO-AFFECTION, in which the 'I' is both agent and recipient of a feeling or of a law. Like a reflexive verb or the middle voice (which seem to be the way to avoid the split between passive and active) auto-affec- Beyond auto-affection—which is still an activity were it strictly contemporaneous with its passivity—the self is stripped in persecution, from which an accusation is inseparable, in the absolute passivity of the creature, of substitution.

tion makes the self its own cause. In ethics this produces autonomy, wherein the 'I' gives itself the command or the call to freedom. On the other hand is the persecuted self, where the other persecutes me prior to my self-consciousness, prior to my autonomy. This self is stripped of its interests and its games. The displacement in persecution requires more than a stoical (or Nietzschean) retreat to loving my fate. Even when the passivity is not consequent upon activity, even WERE IT STRICTLY CONTEMPORANEOUS, the self in autonomy is still active. Levinas seeks a passivity prior to activity, yet prior without being necessarily bound, and so consequent to activity, if only in an order of thinking. Contemporaneity makes the persecuted still in control, at least in thought, of his persecution. Levinas is seeking absolute passivity, freed of all initiative.

As the self loses its power not only over others in war but also over itself, loses its definition as self-constituting entity, it becomes accused. Persecution is bound with AN ACCUSATION. Even in the everyday sense of the terms, we recognize that a persecuted person is accused of some hideous viciousness or bestiality. The persecuted is accused in two ways: once as in a court, but also grammatically, as the direct object of an action and not as the subject. I find myself, as persecuted by the other, accused. But I also find myself in the position of the object of the approach, the one approached. Some other person approaches me. To be accused as a persecuted one is not to have done something, but rather to be accused in utter indifference to my own actions or traits. The persecuted does not cause the accusation. Similarly, the accusative case locates me in ABSOLUTE PASSIVITY. The face of the other draws near to me and I have done nothing to bring it about.

The self is stripped in persecution, from which an accusation is inseparable, in the absolute passivity of the creature, of substitution.

But Levinas now offers a third ETHICAL TERM, one which was not promised. For such ABSOLUTE PASSIVITY is that OF THE CREATURE. Here the creature, the object of creation, appears as that which has no say, neither as initiator nor as the one who accepts being created, nor even as one who assists by creating oneself. Here a term usually taken as theological is claimed for ethics. Levinas draws upon its meaning, even without requiring its implication of the creator, but he also seems to be correlating a theological claim with an ethical one; that is, anyone can identify the notion that a creature is radically dependent on its creator—if there is such creation. For those who are inclined to the theological claim, Levinas provides a correlate relation—in the precise sense of this book—from the passivity in the other person's approach to me.

But this is not without some retraction of the theological term, for a footnote to an earlier discussion of anarchy rejects theology as an attempt to thematize the transcendent. The defense of anarchy focuses on the failure of a correlation between the phenomena and the transcendence of the approach. That phenomenological correlation appears to be hopeless for theology, unless theology wants to be incredible (RINGS FALSE) or to become a language of myths. Levinas is well aware that much of the study of transcendence in religion has opted for the mythic, but he is wary of that route of a successful thematization. Indeed, the transcendence of a theological term will never be literal, will never be captured in a word. But if there is to be

Thus theological language pulls down the religious situation of transcendence. The infinite "presents" itself anarchically; thematization loses the anarchy which alone may accredit it. Language about God rings false or becomes mythic, which is to say, it may never be taken literally. (OB 155/197)

a correlation then of the sort I am examining, it will be between a theology that also displays the excess and the indescribability of its terms and its correlate in ethics, a relation that cannot be described fully. Correlation here is not making idols for worship, even out of rational morality, but seeing a parallel and reciprocal excess and unknowable dimension in both theology and ethics. Levinas can at least hope to display how the passivity in the relation to the other may give some meaning to the doctrine of creation, which itself remains beyond the range of consciousness. Levinas thus ties the sequence of what he calls ETHICAL TERMS to a correlational term, giving each a certain sort of weight, but also pushing the reader on toward the insight into the passivity of the relation to the other.

The momentum built from these terms concludes with the term that serves as the title of both Levinas' chapter and my own: SUBSTITUTION. This fourth term seems still less promising of ethics, because while the theological term may well borrow ethical vision to gain meaning, SUBSTITUTION seems merely the notion that things can be switched, one for another. Moreover, though creation may be suspect, it seems properly linked to passivity, even to absolute passivity. But does substitution also seem passive? Levinas will leave the term undeveloped in this passage, and my commentary will return to it in a few pages. Instead, Levinas now circles back to the motion through accusation to creation.

The Ego is the 'I' of the first sort of self, appropriating, authenticating, making its own, all experience and all affections, even those of passivity. The 'I' conquered every other source of experience and remained the subject of all of its passions. Levinas makes INDECLINABILITY function in a doubled way. First as a grammatical principle, of a noun or pronoun that cannot be declined through the cases—from a subject of action (nominative), to an addressee of speech (vocative), to a possession (genitive), to an indirect object (dative), to a direct object (accusative). Thus the 'I' of the self in control never undergoes a genuine grammatical declension: it is always the subject of any sentence in which it appears, even if it appears to be the direct object.[4] The 'I' that authenticates its own passivity is in this sense indeclinable—it refuses to become object, addressee, possession, or recipient. But the second sense of INDECLINABILITY indicates the question of agency more directly. The imperial 'I' refuses to decline agency. To remain in the nominative, to remain subject of my experience and my passions, is to retain agency.

In divesting the Ego of its imperialism, the hetero-affection establishes a new indeclinability: the self, subject to an absolute accusative, as though this accusation, which it does not even have to assume, came from it.

But now the 'I' is divested of that imperialism. HETERO-AFFECTION, the affect upon me by the other's drawing near to me, strips the 'I' of its role.

In place of such a self, the self is found now in A NEW INDECLINABILITY. NEW because the accusative indeclinability replaces the nominative one; INDECLINABILITY again in the doubled meaning 1) in a grammatical sense, it cannot go through a declension and 2) in the sense of agency, as a call that one cannot decline, refuse. Absolute passivity taken grammatically is being absolutely in the accusative case, to be the object.

To so be the object, in the accusative, is to be accused without even having TO ASSUME the accusation. Just as the persecuted does not precipitate her persecution, so the 'I' becomes accused without having to accept or to authenticate the accusation. The absolute passivity produces an accusation that sticks to me independent of any assumptions by me. But such an absolute accusative, in which I cannot hope to ever cooperate, much less authenticate, is AS THOUGH it came from me. The very incapacity to decline the accusation, my inability to escape it whatever I do, makes it seem as though the accusation must come from me, not freely but constitutively. Levinas' recourse to the subjunctive mood (AS THOUGH) preserves the origin of this accusation in the approach of an other, not in my own agency, but it also signals the path to substitution—that I must become my own accuser, my own persecutor. Not that I must accuse myself or persecute myself, that I will choose or act to initiate this passivity, but that I respond to the passivity by recognizing that I belong to that passivity. Marcel's echo is that I must accept—but that even refusal requires the prior reception of the gift. And Levinas twists this, so that one appears to accuse oneself. The other's accusation so defines me (INSTIGATE ME, TOO, AS FREEDOM), that I appear to be its source.

Levinas focuses on how persecution and accusation now become a reflexive verb: TO GNAW AWAY AT ONESELF. Responsibility is not an auto-affection, not something the self undertakes or even authenticates. But it is also not simply the dispersion of all agency. Its passivity produces a suffering that is reflexive, but without agency or control. Levinas alerts us to the danger of representing responsibility by the use of this ghoulish reflexive verb. The function of the self, of the reflexive pronoun *se*, is not to objectify itself. Such an objectification would be a way to think that the self reconstitutes itself in responding and so makes itself into an object (in the accusative case). If the self could become the author, could make itself objective, then passivity would again be eluded, and the other would again not be the cause of my passion. The 'me' is not capable of retrospectively making itself the subject and object of the approach of the other. Levinas chooses the gnawing away to indicate the drawn out, continuously painful quality of

The self of the *gnawing away at oneself* [le *se* du *se ronger*] in responsibility, which is also incarnation, is not an objectification of the self by me.

this passivity. It feels like I am chewing myself up as the accused and persecuted one, but in fact I not only do not originate that feeling, I also only think it at the risk of trying to make the accusation my own—which it is not.

And in the midst of this challenging sentence Levinas inserts an interruption, that that gnawing away IS ALSO INCARNATION. INCARNATION is this body that is mine, without being a possession, as Marcel often discusses. I do not produce this body. I am not in control of the self that devours me. The absence of a declension prevents incarnation from becoming either a possessive relation or one of a subject over its object. But Levinas has also inserted a new ETHICAL TERM that is also obviously *theological*. The fullest resonance of the gnawing away is that it is a bodily activity. To be incarnate is to be capable of gnawing away at oneself. The theological term is again correlate with the ETHICAL TERM (if GNAWING AWAY AT ONESELF can be so called). The two terms are bound together in their connection to a body and to an activity that seems to evade the self-control one assumes in a reflexive verb. Levinas is heading for a bolder theological statement as a correlate with this absolute accusative, but he moves through this difficult image.

Levinas now reiterates the sequence in order to move through the ETHICAL TERMS to the first term normally considered ethical. THE SELF (*LE SOI*) is the site of this approach of the other, the site of the relation of responsibility. THE SELF is apposite to THE PERSECUTED. Levinas makes frequent use of appositives, producing strings of replacements of parallel phrases. In the appositive, Levinas avoids joining the different terms with the copula, thus avoiding the statements of logical identity (A is B) and also avoiding the difficult relation to Being hidden in the copula. Each term interrupts the grammatical flow of the sentence in order to display another facet of the referent of the terms. Levinas also makes use of these interruptions to displace any illusion that the referent is actually given its proper name by a specific term. The nonthematizable quality of the approach is performed by this jumping about of appositives.

The self, the persecuted, is accused beyond its fault prior to freedom, and thus in unavowable innocence.

The accusation lodges itself without any freedom of mine. The PRIOR TO will take on clear relation to the deep past in Rosenzweig in the next passage for commentary. It is a nonarchaic kind of before. But the new twist here is the phrase BEYOND ITS FAULT. I cannot earn or deserve persecution. The BEYOND points to the irrelevance of the judgment of fault. Because the self is not yet free, it cannot be held to bear or not to bear fault for the persecution. The first normal ethical term, FAULT, is from a vocabulary of freedom that is too late for the ethics of this relation of the approach of the other. Fault is part of a discussion that thematizes and objectifies the relations with others.

But if fault is too late, then innocence is UNAVOWABLE. This is a further development of the indeclinability of the accusation. There the self could not refuse the accusation, but began to see itself as if it were the accuser. Here one cannot avow innocence. The persecuted is not able to affirm its own innocence. The self cannot even stand up and proclaim the truth about itself—such is the displacement in persecution. The self also is innocent, but with the sort of innocence that cannot be affirmed by an 'I', and, of course, the sort that cannot be claimed in a court. Here is an innocence that, like the BEYOND of the fault, lies outside the range of normal ethical terms. Levinas dares the reader to see that innocence emerges first in a situation without defenses, without thought and speeches, without will or initiative.

Levinas now most explicitly rejects a thought—a dogma of Christianity. Levinas' polemic against Christianity's dogmas is complex, but he requires an explicit rejection of this dogma because he seems to be dragging his own philosophy toward it. What else could ORIGINAL SIN be but the persecution of a person even before one acts, an accusation against one without requiring any will of the accused? But original sin requires a certain measure of fault and rejects the notion of original innocence (even be it unavowable innocence). However one chooses to interpret the Christian dogma, and Levinas is not exploring that theological issue, this persecution and accusation, even the gnawing away at oneself of incarnation, are not the deserved prosecution and punishments of sin.

> One must not think of it as the state of original sin; it is, on the contrary, the original goodness of creation.

The contrariness (ON THE CONTRARY) is an attempt to reverse the normal view of such persecution, of substitution. Not that a persecutor is good, but that the self as persecuted, as incarnate and so gnawing away at itself, as accused absolutely without any action of its own—that self is good. In place of seeing the corporeal passivity as a fault, as sin or the occasion of sin, Levinas proposes that the very goodness of creation is the absence of self-origination. Free adherence to the right is not the original goodness. To be a creature and not author of oneself is not a punishment or even a sinful moral state for which the solution is to become autonomous; rather, creatureliness in its vulnerability to persecution and its incapacity to refute the accusation and to affirm one's own innocence is good. Levinas claims that such vulnerability in one's body is THE ORIGINAL GOODNESS.

Here again Levinas is developing a correlation in the specific sense of this book. The theological term CREATION is made correlate to what Levinas will call ethical terms (PERSECUTION, ACCUSATION, UNAVOWABLE

INNOCENCE, SUBSTITUTION). Clearly, creation is changed in this correlation, as the passivity of the creature and its own vulnerability are made
the center of creation. The link back to Rosenzweig's interpretation of
death as the proper conclusion of creation, because death can open me up
to the power of love, is direct and interesting. Here one can clearly see a
whole tradition of Jewish reflection on creation surface, as human incarnation is seen as a positive moment. But Levinas has sharpened that flesh-
liness by linking it to the persecution and the innocence that cannot even
be asserted. The passivity of being a creature is made social because the
approach of the other alerts us to our vulnerability. Here, too, is an adaptation of Rosenzweig's claims that creation can only be re-cognized, and
then only because of the encounter with an other who calls me by name,
who places me in the accusative case. In a parallel motion, Levinas has
alerted the reader to the theological dimension of the approach of the
other—that the absolute passivity of persecution, of approach, and so on,
leads us to think of the condition of the self both as good and as that of
a creature. This ethical vocabulary is the logic of a creature. The passivity
of substitution is the accusative of being called to the Good by the other
and not by myself. I stand accused, in the accusative, because I cannot
originate my own freedom. And at the same time, creatureliness is ethical.
Creation is good not because I am rational, but, originally, because I can
suffer in the approach of another person. My creatureliness is my substitution for an other.

A second text from this essay, in its later revised form of 1974, takes us
from the passivity of the self in substitution to the fuller statement of what
substitution itself is.

I continue with a now familiar theme: the accusation that lodges itself against me without
my assuming it. The absolute passivity of the
last passage, however, is now linked not to corporeality in general, but to SENSIBILITY. The
passivity in sensation is not simply the positive

It [substitution] ac-
cuses without being as-
sumed, which is to say,
in the *undergoing of sensibility beyond the ca-
pacity to undergo.*

capacity for receiving. Such a capacity would be the paradigmatic case for
a thematizing description, for the adequacy of phenomenology. The correlation of that capacity, as something that is intentionally constituted by
my self, with the perception I hold of something, represents for Levinas
the auto-affection of an imperialist self. A capacity that is mine must be
able to yield to my own authority over that capacity. Therefore, sensation
is more than reception by my capacity. Instead, it is a passivity of receiving beyond my capacity to receive. The excess of undergoing (of passivity)
is the aspect of sensibility that involves the intrusion of the other.

DESCRIBES is a paradoxical term, tempting
and refusing the reader to imagine that the

This describes the suffering and vulnerability of

phrase UNDERGOING OF SENSIBILITY BEYOND   the sensible as *the other*
THE CAPACITY TO UNDERGO is a proper descrip-   *in me.*
tion. But Levinas breaks the italic phrase with a dash in the French text,
as though he is almost surprised that the rather odd phrase could serve as
a description. It serves because as a phrase it offers and then inverts:
offers a passivity that is comprehensible (UNDERGOING OF SENSIBILITY)
and then inverts by refusing to the self the capacity to undergo—but this
inversion plagues the reader, inverting the capacity to comprehend the
thought. What is it that I think I can undergo BEYOND THE CAPACITY TO
UNDERGO? To read this phrase is to disrupt my expectation of the concept
UNDERGO, but it also alerts me to another undergoing, an excessive undergoing. Hence it serves as a description of THE SENSIBLE. Levinas redevelops the vocabulary of accusation with the terms SUFFERING and
VULNERABILITY. Passivity now becomes a more direct reflection of suffering (a close analog of passion, or of undergoing). But SUFFERING also
carries with it the pain and the anguish that passivity or undergoing may
not. SUFFERING leads easily to VULNERABILITY. This vulnerability is that
of the sensible in Levinas' explanation that the excess of undergoing is not
only an interruption of the thought of undergoing and of the thought of
sensibility, it is also a violation, even an openness to violation.

But the passivity of accusation is now appearing as a description of
sensibility, a description that exceeds and inverts the very concepts of
receiving sensations. It breaks through into a new plane with the phrase
in italics in Levinas' text: THE OTHER IN ME. What is ultimately violated
is the 'I'. The integrity of the 'I' is broken in several ways, but first of all
in the way that Marcel would call permeability. The 'I' is not self-contained: some other got in here. Sensibility is the breaching of the walls of
the 'I'. To undergo beyond my capacity is for something which is not me
to get into me. Hence that phrase describes the vulnerability when sensibility is the other in me.

Marcel termed this "the mystery of incarna-   The other in me and in
tion": that in me there is something that is   the midst of my identifi-
other, that my relation to my body is not that of   cation itself. The ipseity
ownership nor of imprisonment, but of assign-   fractured in its return to
ment or of vulnerability. The paradox is that the   self.
other is found so deep within me that even MY IDENTIFICATION of my self
is not a reflexivity of me and my self. Levinas claims that such self-identification fails, and now in the context of sensibility, this commentary can
explore that failure. If sensibility is more than an auto-affection, if the
approach of the other requires a passivity more passive than any capacity
I may have, then in the midst of my self-identification the other has a
place.

IPSEITY is the self-actualizing of the self, parallel to Rosenzweig's introverted human. The self looks to be a process of self-determination,

whereby even the specificity of having my own body is appropriable by myself. The *this-ness* of being in a body is welcomed by a self that can make that bodiliness an extension of its own intentions. But now the return to self of IPSEITY is broken. Self-constitution is broken up as it tries to complete the circuit through others to itself. The self cannot recover itself through the other, but is fractured by its bodily vulnerability. The 'me' now includes the other. The invasion of the other into me makes the attempt for the 'me' to return to itself—with whatever that 'me' can grasp of the other—futile. But this ethical interpretation also controverts the phenomenological view of sensibility. If all sensation includes the other in me, then sensibility itself does not allow for the self-authenticating moves of the imperialistic 'I'. Levinas has brought the ETHICAL TERMS back to the home base of phenomenological description, challenging the ability of the self to return to itself even in the realm of sensation—a move that Marcel had also made earlier.

Accusation here is a SELF-ACCUSATION, but how that is so will become clearer at the end of the passage. But Levinas next introduces another ETHICAL TERM: REMORSE. *Remorse* is usually the activity of regret for a past failure. Levinas will require both a specific sort of past and a distinctive sort of activity for the self. Because remorse requires a past, Levinas can turn to it without fearing that it will become a spontaneous or autonomous agency. He plays with the word, moreover, because he lets it become a chewing over (*re-mordere*), which then gnaws away at the self-constituted self. Remorse then can become the gnawing at oneself of the last passage, a non-objectifying relation to the self. But remorse also carries a theological sense as part of the logic of repentance. That sense will become more prominent as Levinas moves through remorse to responsibility.

The self-accusation of remorse gnaws away even until opening the self, until fissioning it, gnaws at the closed nucleus and the firmness of consciousness—which always establishes equality and equilibrium between the trauma and the act—

What is gnawed away at is one's own attempt to enclose oneself. First it gnaws until OPENING THE SELF. This seems to be the breaking up of the capsule of the self. But next it is a FISSIONING of the self, in which the self breaks up at its very center. Levinas continues with the vocabulary of nuclear physics, referring to THE CLOSED NUCLEUS. Here is a sense of a center, a core of the self. Maybe the body cannot be simply assimilated to the self and retains a certain sort of passivity, but at least in my denser center, in the heart of my will, there I retain authority. The nucleus, indeed, repels the other—and yet there is a gnawing away at myself that splits that nucleus. Physics now leads to a language of CONSCIOUSNESS. The nucleus is the nucleus of consciousness, and consciousness struggles to assimilate the violation that occurs in sensation. The self wants to initiate itself, but if there must be some passivity, then the self wishes to make the passivity its own, to authorize it, if only after the fact, and so to make it appear to itself as coming from itself.

Consciousness is the struggle of the self to make its ACT balance THE TRAUMA of sensation, of suffering, of the approach of the other. But Levinas indicates that in this case the intent can stand in for the reality, as the consciousness can have AT LEAST SOUGHT the recovery from trauma even if it fails to establish equality. Levinas makes clearer that the method of the self is to reflect, to cast the trauma of violation in the SHAPES of thought; in short, to thematize. Suffering represented is not suffering, or at least is suffering that loses its sting. The trauma of accusation, of substitution, is made my own, my act through reflection, as though the other were not other but could be balanced by my thinking. The excess of undergoing, and with it the excess of duty, is reduced as reflection reestablishes a happy medium. The other is not protected from this imperialism, as only the 'I' remains, supervising the recovery of the 'I' by reflectively uniting the other and me and so failing to safeguard THE MULTIPLICITY OF SOULS. Indeed, the other's interruption is the fissioning, the accusation that the other in me cannot be rendered my self. The failure of equilibrium and even of my very effort to recover my self must be preceded by the interruption of the approach of the other.

Where this equilibrium is at least sought in reflection and its shapes, without having effectively ensured the possibility of total reflection and of the unity of Spirit beyond the multiplicity of souls.

Levinas has contrasted remorse, which disrupts the self-constitution of the self, with that effort to reflect on the suffering in order to remain myself, in power. Consciousness desires to keep conscious, to keep assimilating, even that which lies beyond its capacity to undergo. For consciousness, the question is always cognitive and the answers always originate in the intentionality of the 'I'. But remorse is a shift, not from one sort of theme to another, but from the self as thematizing to the self as bound and acting in response to the other.

Levinas then pushes from a metaphysical idiom to a political one, all in the guise of a question. He subtly shifts from the other in me to the OTHER IN THE SAME. That IN ME can be analogous to IN THE SAME depends upon the interpretation of the self as 'I', as assimilating and authorizing its own experience. That self makes everything and everyone into the same. The intrusion or violation of that self places the other in the same. But the question that confronts Levinas is whether the claim that the self is actually the substitution, the violation by the approach of the other, and that such an approach produces responsibilities—whether that claim does not in fact make THE EMANCIPATION

But isn't that the way, in itself, an other can be in the same without alienating it, and without the emancipation of the same from itself turning into a slavery to anyone?

OF THE SAME FROM ITSELF simply the SLAVERY TO ANYONE? *To anyone*, because whomever approaches can so violate me and displace my self-relation. The question arises from the assumption that either I am my own master and so inviolable, or the other is my master and I am a slave.

Levinas addresses this hidden question, this suspicion, much as Marcel had to address the suspicion of ventriloquism. He dislodges the assumption through the rhetorical question (BUT ISN'T THAT THE WAY . . . ?). Thus he alerts his suspicious reader that the discussion of passivity and remorse will, he hopes, lead beyond the assumption of self-mastery or slavery. The question does not provide the explanation, nor does it even make the claim as an assertion. Instead, it invites the reader to air the suspicions, and at the same time it lures the reader to explore the solution. One feels engaged directly, as the question reaches through the description, as strange as it has been, and finds oneself confused as to how this sequence of ideas can possibly be the answer to this suspicion.

But the answer follows: there is a relation in the deep past between the self and the other. The other interrupting the self does not enslave my self. The other frees the self from its own prisons of reflection, from its own will. To explain the possibility of this, Levinas refers to AN "IMMEMORIAL TIME," a past that was never present, a priority prior to all re-presentable priority (otherwise, consciousness will once again have restored equilibrium).

This way is possible because, since an "immemorial time," anarchically, in subjectivity the "by-the-other" ["*par l'autre*"] is also the "for-the-other" ["*pour l'autre*"].

The subject, in this deep past, endures the action of the other as its own action for the sake of the other. SUBJECTIVITY is not origination of action, but the connection between passivity and commitment. THE "BY-THE-OTHER" is the mark of the passivity that Levinas has described, but somehow that IS ALSO THE "FOR-THE-OTHER," the commitment to be substitute for the other. This connection, that what happens to me from the other can also be what I will for the sake of the other, is not a principle nor a deducible condition. Instead, the link is forged prior to all rational priority, in a past that is never present, that is not located on a time line, but that as deep past pervades any moment as the past that lies before and cannot be remembered. Being for-the-other appears to be the antithesis of the absolute passivity of the approach of the other, but Levinas explores how the odd modality of the other's approach turns into the similarly odd modality of this commitment, which is more radical than a rational commitment. Substitution is this connection, from undergoing an action by an other to undergoing for the sake of an other. I become substitute for the other. The way between self-mastery and slavery is still unclear.

But the next move is to rehearse the vocabulary of substitution. Levinas begins with SUFFERING, and he reintroduces fault. My innocence remains intact, but I substitute my self FOR THE OTHERS' FAULT. Levinas follows a subtle shift here. First there is the other, at fault, who causes me to suffer. This fault appears to be the first commonsense ethical judgment of the text, but substitution requires that I now bear that fault. The suffering is so passive that I appear as the one who can bear the fault. The subtlety is found in the shift from singular to plural, from THE OTHER'S FAULT to THE OTHERS' FAULT. The approach of the other is singular, as the suffering originates in one particular other. But the bearing of fault is plural, as I bear not only the fault of the one who makes me suffer, but, through suffering for that one, I also bear the fault of all others. In suffering there is an inversion of the self, from one who is made to suffer to one who exists as substitute for the others.

In suffering *by* the other's fault, suffering *for* the others' fault appears as *supporting* [*supporter*]. The *for*-the-other preserves all the patience of the undergoing imposed by the other.

Moreover, Levinas claims that this substitution for the others remains passive, never converting to an action I choose or initiate. Instead, the bearing of the others' fault is imposed upon me in the suffering caused by the other. The greater the passivity in my suffering, the more I can support or bear the fault for that suffering—because that bearing requires that I not be in control, that I not see it as meritorious or honorable. Levinas is challenging the reader to think what appear to be two opposed modes of agency: the absolute passivity of being made to suffer, and the superordinate virtue of bearing the fault of others. If one can glimpse the passivity that is not describable, can one similarly glimpse the bearing of others' fault? The shift to ethics seems most unsatisfying because Levinas dwells on a passivity that avoids a normal ethical context and now has overleaped all morality to arrive at an almost saintly goodness—which seems to be similarly bereft of ethical import. This dissatisfaction is linked back to the absence of thematizable content in the relation to an other. Levinas refuses to satisfy a reader's thirst for ethical theory, not out of mere French sophistication, but rather out of respect for the radical contingency of the other's freedom, which no theory can adequately protect. But the sequence of ETHICAL TERMS has one more term, which culminates the discussion here.

Levinas' final ethical term is EXPIATION. The resonance here is unmistakably theological. The task of correlation is similarly unavoidable here—Levinas is not hiding his ethics behind a theological authority, or even a spiritual experi-

Substitution for [*à*] an other; expiation for [*pour*] an other. Remorse is the trope of the "literal meaning" of sen-

ence. On the contrary, whatever use the theological terms may have is provided by their use
in what Levinas calls *ethics*. EXPIATION is SUB-
STITUTION—which, though excessive and in-
describable, happening in the deep past which cannot be remembered, is
still a purely interhuman, social event. The shift to expiation is accompanied by the insertion of the other person *(autrui)* for the other *(autre)*. To
be for the other is now clearly to be for the other person. I make his will,
his fault, his sin my own. With expiation, the discussion of fault points
now to one of sin. Again, I am not myself the faulty one; the other is. But
in a move of generosity not characterizable as willed or chosen but as
utterly passive, I now take on the punishment for the other's sin. To suffer
at the other's hand is to suffer for the sake of the other's sin.

In the last sentence of this passage, Levinas draws together the various
terms to bind them in the reader's mind. REMORSE recurs here. It is remorse that leads to expiation, but its meaning is not theological. Rather
sensibility itself is the trope for remorse—the chewing over of oneself
(re-mordere), the gnawing away at myself, is first an account of sensibility
and also an account of my relation with the other who draws near to me.
And to be remorseful is to accuse myself, or rather to need no longer to
distinguish BETWEEN BEING ACCUSED AND ACCUSING ONESELF. Remorse
does not produce the recognition of self-consciousness, by which I can
think of myself thinking. Rather, it produces a self-relation that is utterly
passive. To be accused in this passive way is to push out the bottom of
passivity to the point of not knowing whether the accusation comes from
an other or from me—because the accusation comes from the other in me.

The sequence PERSECUTION, ACCUSATION, INCARNATION, CREATION,
SENSIBILITY, REMORSE, EXPIATION constitutes a performance of the description of SUBSTITUTION. The sequence is clearly linked to Rosenzweig's account of the face-to-face encounter, with its motion through
remorse to atonement. Nonetheless, Levinas is adapting Rosenzweig,
making significant changes in the sequence. More significant, Levinas has
his eye set on the questions of agency and of the indescribability of the
passivity of being called to substitute. As similar as the sequence is, and as
profound as the new level of questions in Levinas is, what is even more
significant is that Levinas struggles to use theological terms as ETHICAL
TERMS. He requires the displacement of normal ethical terms in order to
preserve the indescribability of the relation to the other. Theological
terms already possess the desired absence of immanent reference, but
without a rigorous correlation to the ethical situation, those terms seem
to presume an access limited to believers. Whether or not Levinas is ultimately successful in correlating these terms to a human relation, the

motivation for this double displacement from cognition and ontology to ethics, and then from ethics as a theory of freedom to the disruptive performance of excess of responsibility in substitution, is now clear.

INTO MY OWN VOICE

One of the obscurities in Levinas' intellectual development is the respective relations to Marcel's and Buber's analyses. One of the tasks of this chapter has been to display some of the deep similarities to Marcel, particularly because Marcel recognized the asymmetry in my relation to an other. In addition, Marcel saw an isomorphism between the other and my freedom in the spheres of sensibility, of the relation with an other, and of the relation with God. Marcel holds to some sort of correlation between philosophy and Christianity, which makes him a cousin in the family resemblance scheme I propose for correlation. What is decisive for registering these accounts of substitution, in contrast to Buber's 'relations', is the attention to the performance of speaking. Marcel's method, drawn directly from close study of Royce, depends on the practices of speaking words, whereas Buber held that the 'I' and 'you' were not primarily the speaking of these words, but were primordial and hence prelinguistic words. Levinas' proximity to Marcel allowed him to find the responsibility of encountering another displayed in the situation of speech. In these commentaries I moved from Marcel's analysis of the performance of speech to the complexities of the passivity in responsibility. That my freedom depends on the other, and that even my refusal (my 'free' choice) originates in the other's freedom, is one of the most contentious and most important insights for Levinas (and Rosenzweig, for that matter). While autonomy, the cherished criterion of moral philosophy, disappears, the conclusion is not that everything is permitted. The rejection of the self-centered self is not identical to the dissolution of the self, nor the dispersion of agency into a fine mist of interwoven agencies, without any specific responsibility left for me. The self is de-centered by an other who then appears as the center of my agency, producing an other-centered self. This option is a valuable one for postmodernism. But autonomy, which ethics so often requires, whereby the self can found itself, appears in Levinas and Marcel as unethical. Autonomy is itself a mark of irresponsibility, of moral failing. Substitution, availability, responsibility itself are the source both of the agency for justice and of the illusion of agency that is the pretension to be autonomous.

Two gaps require further attention. The first is found between Marcel's speaking of substituting your freedom for my own, and Levinas' of substituting myself for the other. Marcel seems to prefer a vocabulary of freedom to one of responsibility, and so makes the substitution less complete (only freedom, not the whole self). But if the other's freedom is taken not only as his rational or moral will, but as his life, his sin, his faults, then Marcel's substitution is much closer to Levinas'. The deeper issue reveals the agreement, because each is trying to identify my dislocation, the penetration of my castle of consciousness by the other. Levinas moves away from the term *freedom* largely to accentuate the moves we found in Marcel. Marcel in the first passage can discuss freedom at length, but in the second, freedom becomes something that originates before my choice. Levinas clearly situates freedom after responsibility: I am first approached, called to respond, then able to respond, and, from that ability, freed to act. The moving back before freedom is a characteristic move of Levinas' as he tries to avoid the objectification of ethical theory. Moreover, freedom cannot be passive enough for the paradoxical responsibility that Levinas describes.

The second difference is more challenging, precisely because it verges into the theological distance between these two men, a converted Catholic and a Jew. Here the relationship of the cousins in the family of correlational thinkers is at stake. Marcel refers to the other in substitution as You with a capital Y, as God. He is meditating on the mystery of Christ in me, and while he sees an isomorphism with the relation to another person, he sets the relation to God distinctly apart. The separation focuses on the infinite vulnerability and the infinite power of Christ. Levinas criticizes both Marcel and Buber for that Absolute You, denying the possibility of such a relation with God (HS 50). Yet as he moves through incarnation to expiation for the other, when he extols the passivity, the suffering for the other's faults—well, aren't we in Christian thought? Are we?

Levinas develops a Jewish concept of our human obligation to be for-the-other, an obligation developed throughout the Jewish tradition before and after Jesus of Nazareth. Marcel in the earlier writings, before converting to Catholicism (his mother had been Jewish, but his stepmother/aunt was a converted Protestant), was aware of the priority of the other and the betrayal of the gift of freedom in autonomy. The themes of incarnation, creation, expiation, responsibility for others, etc., are as much Jewish themes as Christian ones.

Or maybe more. If a Christian thinker were to read Levinas, would she not have to recast Christology? Is not the other *in* me, the other person, and not the absolute You of God? Will not the correlation of ethics and theology require that the approach of a human other generate substitution? Is not the human other infinitely vulnerable (murderable) and so capable of requiring infinite responsibility from me? Am I substitute for the other only because of the intimate relationship of prayer, or rather because of meeting in a public space where anyone may find me? Must not any person, any other, be one for whom I substitute myself? Is the 'Christian' message anything else than that each of us is persecuted, accused by the other, and that that accusation makes us substitute for the accuser? Is not the truth of incarnation, that we are incarnate, vulnerable in our naked skin? That we are persecuted and so expiation for others, and not that some divinity is expiation for us? I make expiation and suffer for him, not *You make expiation for me* or even *He makes expiation for me*. Or less rhetorically, must not one read the Gospel as proclaiming that every person is the one for whom I must suffer, the one before whom I have infinite duties?—but then perhaps we would no longer need to worry whether substitution was Jewish or Christian.[5]

And perhaps the postmodernists need not be excluded by their disavowal of religion. The discovery that the self is not reigning in its own will can be, remarkably, the true discovery of others—the awareness that I am obligated toward others. If the egotism and solipsism of the subject is now readily dismissed, must we ignore this more ethical and more spiritual analysis of the human condition?

Finally, if there can be peace between the cousins on the matter of substitution, then there is still the issue of how to discuss substitution, and there is also the immediate problem of the justification of my commentaries. Were I speaking with you, then, according to both thinkers, I would be substitute for you, responsible for each of your faults, even your faults in understanding Levinas and Marcel. Levinas interprets speaking to the other as apology in the Greek sense, as an attempt to justify myself to you, you for whom I bear responsibility, for whom I am substitute. Substitution is thus prior to apology, ethics to reason, and so substitution bears speech itself. The transition from that relation with an other to a written text is complex.

One can follow the commentaries on Marcel provided here as a path from the performance of speaking to the reflection on the performance of speaking. The shift requires the use of direct quotation in order to induce the reader to step in, not into dialogue with the author—which is physically impossible—but rather into the roles of the speakers upon whom the text reflects. Marcel's use of first person quotation interrupts a reflection upon the performance of speech, provoking metalepsis by the reader into the voice and the perspective of a speaker. Marcel thereby asks the reader to confirm the author's reflections on what happens when the 'I' speaks to a 'you' by trying to imagine oneself as an 'I' speaking. The written reflection returns, in imagination, to the situation of speaking, and the reader may verify the interpretation of the author. But that appeal to the reader to verify that interpretation suggests how an author can be vulnerable to the reader; indeed, how the author invites the reader to substitute for the quoted speaker, without forcing the reader into the position of one who must substitute. It may in fact be easier to discuss I BELONG TO YOU in print, where the reader is only invited to see his or her role as the 'I', than to discuss it face-to-face, where the interlocutor may be more suspicious that the asymmetry the speaker promises is only a ruse, that the speaker is demanding that the interlocutor belong to the 'I' who speaks. The indirection of the written text seems remarkably suitable to the refusals to objectify and so demand the other's enslavement.

But when Marcel yields to Levinas, the question is how to write and to describe without thematizing. Levinas has recourse to various moves to displace his own descriptions, but what becomes clearer is that those moves themselves are the key to writing about the indescribable drawing near of the other. Substitution becomes something done, not something named. And the writing itself requires just that sort of slipping and moving in order to thwart the efforts of consciousness to assimilate and to claim its right to authorize the ethical relation with the other. As author, Levinas accepts responsibility for the reader's thoughts, and so he tries to steer the reader away from a thematic, disinterested view of ethics. He disrupts the reader's natural desire to know with the authority of spontaneous consciousness. If the reader fails, then Levinas in some sense holds himself substitute for the reader's fault.

Levinas does not return the reader to the scene of speaking by quotation, but conducts his challenge to the power of consciousness in the realm of reflection itself. The reader here is invited to take the place of the thinker thinking these thoughts and so to confront the excess to which the author bears witnesses (OB 190f./149f.). Levinas may fail in either of two ways: 1) He may offer a good thematic discussion of ethics, in which case the passivity and responsibility that is the goal will be refuted by his discussion, or 2) When he steps beyond the realm of description, he may write gibberish. The success is possible only if the performance of reading leads the reader to see the excess in responsibility, only if the text breaks down the sovereignty of the 'I' and drives the reader back to glimpse the origin of speech in responsibility.

But my task has been to examine the performance of reading these two thinkers. I invite my readers to place themselves in the position of readers of the pre-texts. As writer I substitute the authors for myself, allowing their texts to determine my text, to guide me and to abdicate my position as initiator. In place of reflection upon speaking, or reflection upon the failure of reflection upon speaking, I offer commentary on those two forms of reflection. Like Marcel, I use quotation to draw the reader back into the situation of speech. But like Levinas, that quotation does not necessarily lead all the way to speech, but may place the reader only in the arena of reflection itself, there to rehearse the excess of responsibility beyond reflection.

There is a certain sort of substitution under way here, an undertaking of your fault by me, but it is diffuse and risky. Writing, unlike speaking, is both an extreme invulnerability (I am not here when you read this) and an extreme vulnerability (but my work is now in your hands). Ultimately, a commentator must leave the reader with the other texts—and you can now substitute Levinas and Marcel for me, as I have withdrawn myself responsibly. And to be left with such texts is not to recognize their themes, but to perform a reflection that exceeds the capacity for reflection, to find oneself substitute for an other.

APPENDIX: PRE-TEXTS

Marcel: *Essai de philosophie concrète*, 64–65; *Creative Fidelity*, 39:

If I assert of a servant: *he belongs to me*, I would obviously provoke a genuine shock in my audience; assuming that I am not treated with the silent commiseration due an idiot, and am asked what right I have to assert that this servant belongs to me, I will answer that I treat him as a thing that I have acquired or that has been given to me, etc. Whatever the specified nature of the response, however, it is clear that it has every chance of not satisfying my questioner; on the contrary, it will seem to him an extravagant and unacceptable claim. Of course, it would have been otherwise when slavery still existed.

It is curious to note that the question is completely transformed if I happen to declare to another: *I belong to you*. Here we have completely shifted the ground.

First it must be observed—and this is essential—that I am evoking a situation that cannot really be objectified, strictly speaking; one, in any case, that cannot be objectified without its nature being radically changed.

Let us examine closely the original relation: Jack, I belong to you. This means: I am opening an unlimited credit account for you, you can do what you want with me, I give myself to you. This does not mean, at least not in principle: I am your slave; on the contrary, I freely put myself at your disposal; the best use I can make of my freedom is to place it in your hands; it is as though I freely substituted your freedom for my own; or paradoxically, it is by that very substitution that I consummate my freedom.

Essai, 154–55; *Creative Fidelity*, 100:

On the one hand, the fact that His word is transcribed, that it addresses itself to me by means of a text, runs the risk of degrading it into a tyrannical injunction which is addressed to me by someone specific and against which it is after all quite reasonable that I would rebel: What right has *some other one* to claim that I belong to him? . . .

On the other hand, reflection quickly does justice to these false appearances: He claims that right over me precisely not insofar as He is truly some other one; but rather insofar as He is more interior to me than I am to myself. . . .

Hence I shall refrain from supporting the strictly rebellious claim that the *you belong to me* stirred up in my center. But it must be clearly noted that it is the value rather than the formal possibility of the claim that is at issue. "Indeed, who am I to pretend that I do not belong to You? In effect, if I belong to You, it is not to say: I am Your possession; this mysterious relation does not occur on the level of having as would be the case if You were a finite power. Not only are You freedom, but You also will me. You instigate me too as freedom. You call me to create myself. You are this very call. And if I reject it, i.e., You, if I persist in maintaining that I belong only to myself, it is as though I walled myself up; as though I bound myself to strangling with my own hands that reality in whose name I believed I was resisting You.

"If this is so, to know that I belong to You is to know that I belong to myself only on this condition—what is more, this belonging is identical to and united with the only complete and authentic freedom which I can claim: this freedom is a gift; even though I must accept it; the power dispensed to me to accept *or to refuse it* is inseparable from this gift, and there is a way for me to assert this freedom which amounts to a refusal, and this refusal, addressed to the very thing that makes it possible, has the distinctive character of betrayal."

Levinas: *Autrement qu'être*, 155–56; *Otherwise than Being*, 121:

Phenomenology is able to follow the returning from thematization into anarchy in the description of the approach: Ethical language comes to express the paradox where phenomenology finds itself abruptly flung. For ethics, beyond politics, is on the level of that returning. . . . The approach is not the thematization of any relation, but is that relation itself which resists thematization insofar as it is anarchic. To thematize that relation is already to lose it, to leave the absolute passivity of the self. The passivity this side of the passivity-activity alternative, more passive than any inertia, is described by the ethical terms: accusation, persecution, and responsibility for others. The persecuted is expelled from his place and has only himself to himself, has no place in the world to rest his head. He is pulled out of every game and every war. Beyond auto-affection—which is still an activity were it strictly contemporaneous with its passivity—the self is stripped in persecution, from which an accusation is inseparable, in the absolute passivity of the creature, of substitution. In divesting the Ego of its imperialism, the hetero-affection establishes a new indeclinability: the self, subject to an absolute accusative, as though this accusation, which it does not even have to assume, came from it. The self of the *gnawing away at oneself* [le *se* du *se ronger*] in responsibility, which is also incarnation, is not an objectification of the self by me. The self, the persecuted, is accused beyond its fault prior to freedom, and thus in un-avowable innocence. One must not think of it as the state of original sin; it is, on the contrary, the original goodness of creation.

Autrement qu'être, 160–61; *Otherwise than Being*, 125:

It [substitution] accuses without being assumed, which is to say, in the *undergoing of sensibility beyond the capacity to undergo*—this describes the suffering and vulnerability of the sensible as *the other in me*. The other in me and in the midst of my identification itself. The ipseity fractured in its return to self. The self-accusation of remorse gnaws away even until opening the self, until fissioning it, gnaws at the closed nucleus and the firmness of consciousness—which always establishes equality and equilibrium between the trauma and the act—where this equilibrium is at least sought in reflection and its *shapes,* without having effectively en-sured the possibility of total reflection and of the unity of Spirit beyond the multiplicity of souls. But isn't that the *way,* in itself, an *other* can be in the *same* without alienating it, and without the emancipation of the same from itself turning into a slavery to anyone? This way is possible because, since an "immemorial time," anarchically, in subjectivity the "by-the-other" ["*par l'autre*"] is also the "for-the-other" ["*pour l'autre*"]. In suffering *by* the other's fault, suffering *for* the others' fault appears as *supporting* [*supporter*]. The *for*-the-other preserves all the pa-tience of the undergoing imposed by the other. Substitution for [*à*] an other; expiation for [*pour*] an other. Remorse is the trope of the "literal meaning" of sensibility. In its passivity it effaces the distinction between being accused and accusing oneself.

CHAPTER 10

Marx and Levinas:
Liberation in Society

LIBERATION is not a private affair. It is not consummated in an intimate relationship of two people. Even less is liberation a purely personal accomplishment. In opposition to a long tradition of ethics focusing on the perfection of the single individual, a philosophy of liberation is always social—looking at individuals in society, in communities. Liberation is not a flight from society, but a restructuring or a reorienting of human interrelationships and of society. But to invoke this social sphere need not be to dissolve the responsibilities of individuals, to absorb the individual person into a group. Totalizing over the community is not the distinctive move of liberation. It is an unfortunate heritage we have that mislocates ethics in individuality and sociality in totality.

There are many exceptions to this dialectic, two of which are Karl Marx and Emmanuel Levinas. Perhaps it seems odd to combine the father of communism with a phenomenological Jewish Thinker, but these two thinkers are combined with great creativity and skill in contemporary liberation thought, both theology and philosophy. The exploration of contemporary liberation thought, however, is not my task in this last chapter. Rather, I will try to take up social theory a second time, this time in relation to economics. In Chapter 5, I drew Rosenzweig into the context of Weber and Troeltsch; here, Marx and Levinas will complement that approach to social theory. My aim is to enhance our resources for considering the ethical dimension of sociality. The refusal of totalizing views needs to be joined to an insistence on economic justice; that is, joined to the materialist demand of ethics. This project is consonant with one central current of Jewish thought, a current not limited to the Bible, but actually most prominent in post-Biblical Judaism, in Talmudic Judaism. Levinas and Marx belong in that current.

I will draw out a mutual reading of these two thinkers, with the hope of illuminating their strengths in order to describe rigorous foundations for an account of the ethical in the social. I propose to read Levinas from a Marxian perspective, focusing on Levinas' economics, and similarly to read Marx from Levinas' perspective, drawing out a social ethical reading of Marx. At the limits of these readings lies a reflection about liberation as liberation in society, as breaking with totality, and so as a liberation from national politics.

IN THE FACE OF THE OTHER:
LEVINAS' ECONOMICS

The central issue in Levinas' thought is how we come into society. He argues not only that we are social beings, but even that our freedom to join society is the result of a previous interhuman relationship. Thus the freedom that founds social institutions itself rests upon a previous sociality—a face-to-face relationship with an other examined in the last chapter. The other invests me with my capacity to respond, and that responsibility makes me who I am. My identity and, as a consequence, my freedom and even my rationality, are social for Levinas.

But despite his focus on the face-to-face relation, Levinas claims that such responsibility involves a relationship with a third person. In this chapter, I will explore Levinas' social thought by coordinating my discussion around the theme of the third person. And while I do not wish to suggest a strong developmental theory of Levinas' writings, there are significant variations. I will note the change in the roles that justice and economics play in his thought. By emphasizing the eclipse of economics in Levinas' work, I hope to display the challenge in combining the rejection of totality and material duties. On the basis of the roles of justice and economics, I will raise the question about social institutions and the state.

From Two to Three

My point of departure for Levinas will be an essay published in 1954: "The Ego and the Totality"("*Le Moi et la Totalité*")(EN 25–52/CP 25–46). The purpose of this essay, and indeed of all of Levinas' mature work, is to describe the moral conditions for thought, to identify the moral experience prior to thinking that itself calls forth thinking and reason. Levinas inverts the question of much ethical theory, as he asks not, "Is it rational to be ethical?" but, "Is it ethical to be rational?" His answer involves tracing rationality back to a pre-rational moral experience of looking at another face-to-face (see also SAS 58/122). In this essay Levinas locates economic justice as the condition for thought; however, he contests two alternate claims: 1) that love, particularly in an 'I-you' relationship, is that condition, and 2) that reason provides its own condition for thought.

In more recent work Levinas has found more place for the concept of love, but in 1954 he criticized it. The problem is that love creates an intimate society of two and only two persons. It makes no space for unintended consequences of actions. In the context of love, I can always redress and repent any wrong to the beloved and so be forgiven, because the harmed person is a present 'you'. But if a third person comes into the scene, then by restoring your due to you, I may deprive the third of its due. In French grammar, there is no informal plural of the second person: two *tu*'s must be addressed as *vous*. Levinas calls the relationship between two, not justice, but either *beyond* or *before* justice (EN 32/CP 31).

Society, in opposition, involves the permanent risk of alienation of my freedom. Society is a relationship in which most of the others are not present, not known by me. What I do to them I will never know, nor can I remedy the harm I cause them. They do not have a personal relationship with me. Justice becomes an issue only with the possibility of a wound, or a tort, that cannot be repaired—in a situation wherein repair would cause other torts. Institutional injustices, such as structural inequalities and market distortions, are the primary forms of injustice, because I cannot find the others whom I oppressed through participation in institutions, and so I cannot redress the wrong. Levinas even goes so far as to speak of the harm to a third by the love of two—that their exclusivity can be this very sort of tort.

This theme recurs throughout Levinas' works, although purged of its strongly economic tone. In later works, he rejects a romantic, privatized interpretation of the face-to-face interaction. Levinas distances himself from the popular appropriation of Buber by insisting that the other is not to be a *tu* but a *vous*. Indeed, Levinas rejects the notion of an intimate relationship with God, an infinite *tu*, and prefers instead the emphasis on *il* (he), going so far as to coin a term for the thirdness of the face-to-face relationship: *illeity*. Thus, while Levinas concentrates on a face-to-face encounter, which appears to be an 'I-you' relationship, he retains this critique of the privacy of love as not just.

In this early essay Levinas also presents an argument that will move more and more to the center of his work, an argument that reason cannot found ethics nor, consequently, society. The basic argument is a reformulation of Rosenzweig's assertion that ethics 'appears' first in language, in speech. Spoken speech itself is an address from one person to another. But the performance of speech occurs not as an event seen from the outside, but as an existential occurrence: that is, when I speak, I experience my speaking as bound up with my existing, corporeal self. My words emerge from me, not from some individual human being, a member of the species. The process of reflecting upon myself and upon my speaking abstracts from my existing and allows my self to fall under a category of speaking animals, rational beings, etc. To know my self through reason, therefore, is to have lost my existing, pre-rational, speaking self. Moreover, reason itself emerges from this speaking, as the use of words produces an order in which abstract signs admit of universal significance (see the discussion of Cohen in Chapter 8 on the question of whether reason itself must be formal). The foundation of reason is the speaking 'I'. Levinas asks, "Can reason found the unique worth of each individual in his individuality?" If we allow this standard trope of existentialist critique of reason, we can follow the claim that reason will rest on linguistic praxis and that linguistic praxis itself will originate in a speech of an 'I' to an other. For Levinas, the primary encounter, which precedes and indeed demands speech, is of the 'I' with its other.

In the same essay, Levinas develops at length the concept of the face (*le visage*), later transformed in the concept of proximity. He claims that there is a moral condition for thought, that ethics precedes rationality. This moral condition is the one-on-one encounter, in which the other commands me by his face. The face is the nudity of the other in his vulnerability. The face of the other commands me, "You shall not murder." In later writings, Levinas backs away from a commitment to a visible presence of the other in the other's face and changes to an emphasis on proximity and touch, by which the other's vulnerability again nonviolently commands a prohibition of my possible violation of the other. The proximity to touch of a naked face becomes the central phenomenon, as Levinas tries to refuse claims that the other becomes a presence for my consciousness.

What remains constant from the earliest discussions of the face is that it is not simply an 'I-you'. Indeed, it does not depend on any intimacy and does not necessarily create intimacy. Thus one of the strongest tendencies of misinterpretation in Levinas must be checked: the approach of the other, the moment when my responsibility arises, despite its constitution as a relation between one other and me, is not exclusive, is not a withdrawal from others. This is critical because of the exorbitance of Levinas' rhetoric concerning this responsibility. He began his rhetorical descriptions with a reciprocal responsibility in "The Ego and the Totality." Soon, however, in *Totality and Infinity,* he made responsibility asymmetric: I alone am responsible to the other. Then, in ever heightened rhetoric, he moved to the idea that I am responsible for the other, responsible for the other's persecution of me, and ultimately hostage for the other, even in his persecution of me (*Otherwise than Being*).

The intensification of responsibility in this ethical 'experience' prior to reason, prior to intentionality and even to consciousness, produces an infinity of obligation. It is, moreover, an infinitizing spiral in which the more I do, the more I am responsible for, the more I find myself accused and so called upon to accept more. It is not long before one raises the question of how I can be infinitely responsible to two people at once, particularly insofar as each responsibility is independent of universal norms or principles. Since reason is derived from ethics, how can ethics be based on infinite obligations?—unless we return to the tempting misinterpretation that Levinas is discussing love and only cares about *private* ethics.

Levinas insists repeatedly that negotiation, measuring, even calculation of responsibilities begin with the entrance of a third person into my relationship with the other. In *Otherwise than Being* he refers back to *Totality and Infinity* (AE 201/158), where he all but quotes from his discussion in the earlier essay, "The Ego and the Totality" (TI 188/213). In that essay he discusses how the other is a third, that he institutes not an intimate love affair, but a society of freedom and of respect. Levinas had not yet discovered the asymmetry of responsibility, the fundamental non-reciprocal quality that he develops so persuasively in the major works. Thus the other is capable of being both face and third, and so requiring of me that I become a third by respecting the other and so myself.

> To respect is not to bow down before the law, but before a being who commands a work of me. But for this command not to allow any humiliation—which would take from me the very possibility of respecting—the command that I receive must also be a command to command him who commands me. It consists of commanding a being to command me. This reference from a command to a command is the fact of saying We, of forming a party. Because of this reference from a commandment to the other [*à l'autre*], We is not the plural of I. (EN 49/CP 43)

This command to command is what makes me also into a third, a person capable of giving commands. Whereas the intimacy of 'I-you' would seem to consist of two independent selves in relationship to each other, the possibility of a 'we' requires that we mutually invest each other with the freedom to command each other, for the sake of a third. In this essay Levinas articulates his strongest concept of mutuality and of community in his longest treatment of the 'we'. He insists that we give each other commands, we do works, all for the sake of social justice (EN 49/CP 44). Justice requires an equality of the persons. Mutual relation accomplishes this equality.

In Levinas' major works, when he develops the concept of the face and then proximity, when the ethical relationship is focused more exclusively on the one-to-one relationship, he avoids this 'we' more and more and distinguishes the asymmetric nature of ethicality from mutuality. But Levinas retains the importance of the third in order to avoid the honeymoon ethics he dismissed here. Despite the radical asymmetry of responsibility, that the other is higher than me, is my master, teacher, and commander, Levinas still insists on an equality.

> The poor one, the stranger presents himself as equal. His equality in this essential poverty consists in referring to the *third*, thus present at the encounter and whom, in the midst of its destitution, the Other [*Autrui*] already serves. He joins himself to me. But he joins me to him in order to serve. He commands me as a master. This command can concern me only so far as I myself am a master. Thus, this commandment commands me to command. The *you* [*tu*] is posited before a *we*. (TI 188/213)

The equalization of the other with me occurs by reference to the third, for whose sake we must both serve. "The presence of the face—the infinity of the other—is destitution, a presence of the third (which is to say, of all humanity which looks at us) and a command which commands commanding" (ibid.). Thus the other as the face is not only a concrete individual, but also obligates me with the whole world watching, as it were. Not only with his eyes am I seen and accused, but his eyes imply the eyes of everyone. I am not free to serve him in such a way as to harm a third. Thus we are in public, in the strongest sense. In *Otherwise than Being*, Levinas writes, "In the proximity of the other, all the others than the other obsess me, and that obsession already cries out for justice" (AE 201/158). Here is the emphatic denial of a private affair, supplanted by a one-to-one relationship that, in its imperative of responsibility, is before the eyes of the world. While I am obligated beyond measure by the other, by the face or proximity, that responsibility is a public duty.

Levinas interprets this interposition of the third as the very speaking of language. Words, instead of being idiosyncratic tokens of love, are universals, referring to all humanity as their potential audience (TI 184/208, 196/221). I speak to the other in response to the nonverbal command "Thou shall not kill" in an attempt to justify myself, to apologize in the Socratic sense. I speak to the other in response, but I cannot make a private deal with the other. By speaking I establish a public relationship, a relationship which reveals its intrinsic sociality. Words signify for the purpose of this apology, but by means of their generality, a generality which allows them to signify in other contexts, to other listeners. Levinas here is examining a tension between the specificity of the performance of speaking and the generality of meaning in the sign. That tension prohibits a spoken word from being merely private, even if the immediate context is of two people alone, for the capacity of words to abstract from that context means that they always bear a wider public, a potential universality in their use. While Levinas usually writes of the approach of the other, who must be singular and require a specific apology, he also usually refers to this third person as the others, or even all the others. The third, as the alternate addressee of my speech, can be anyone and, indeed, must be everyone in some sense. To use a word is to speak into a social realm in which everyone can listen. In the other's command to me, only the other and I are present; in my speech, all the others now are listening.

Institutions of Responsibility

As the generality of speech represents a pole of the apology to the other, so money also appears as a general sign that moves beyond the specific context of the other and me. I justify myself to the other by speaking, by invoking the public audience. But once invoked, that audience represents other claimants on my responsibility. To balance duties to the thirds requires calculation, which itself is a further demand for reason. Reason is first of all the ethical responsibility to balance and measure the infinite responsibilities I have to each other. I coin general or even universal concepts in order to adjudicate and then to justify the resolution of various responsibilities. Justice requires that quantified duties replace infinite duties, and so produces an economics: "Justice can have no other object than economic equality" (EN 50/CP 44).

In "The Ego and the Totality," Levinas introduces the concepts of work and of money as the means of accomplishing justice. He claims that both economic works and money are intrinsically social. Money serves to measure the immeasurable—the other. The very calculation and balancing of duties instituted with the third requires an economic calculus, and money serves for that. Money is always abstract from the specific context and does not require a specific context for its value. Money allows for a social commerce to replace the vendetta for unintentional wrongs. Society creates money as a way to negotiate the constituent infinite responsibilities, just as I invoke the public realm by speaking. To use money is to trade what is in itself useless, but what we trust others to honor in the future. Money is intrinsically social and is the key tool for instituting social justice.[1]

While money and speech will remain largely parallel in Levinas' different treatments, economics itself undergoes a shift from an intrinsically ethical function to a location that is pre-ethical. In the earlier theory, Levinas insists that labor and will are not conditions for thought, but that they rest on thought. This depends on his interpretation of thought in its generality as itself resting on sociality—on the third and on the ethical. According to the essay, we work in order to establish the justice commanded in the face of the other. Working, as opposed to enjoying, is to risk alienating my self in the work produced. We consign the work to others and abandon our control over it. Work is the production of something that will have social consequences beyond my intentionality, and thus it depends on a previous trust in the society.

Seven years later, in *Totality and Infinity*, Levinas moves economics prior to the experience of the face, in a pre-ethical world. The place that works held in the essay is now occupied by the will and its freedom. By the time of *Otherwise than Being*, economics is eclipsed totally and has no place in the text. This eclipse of economics, of work, labor, and money, is in some ways only a measure of Levinas' developing focus on the confrontation that is the face, but it also is a move away from an analysis of the material world and its social reality. Levinas retains some rhetorical gestures toward material needs, but he no longer has the interest to explore them philosophically.

In *Totality and Infinity*, Levinas creates a moment of enjoyment prior to the ethical. We live for the sake of the Same, for assimilating what is other into ourselves. Independent of others, we stake a claim and make a home. We enter the world from our home, and we go home when the day is through. Labor is acquiring what is other and transforming it into property, which can be stored at home. Labor now occurs in this pre-ethical world as my triumph over the resistance of matter, furnishing me with good things to eat, a house to be home in, clothes to protect me from the elements, etc. The key moment is the making mine by labor, the bringing it home—economics, in an etymological sense.

Levinas now locates this economic theory of labor and enjoyment as pre-ethical, prior to the experience of the face, in order to have the other break into my self-centered world. At that moment I must feed him with my food and bring him into my home. Without an an-ethical economic life, I would not be capable of hospitality, of receiving the other, of giving from myself. The introversion of the self in the world is an economic self, storing up goods at home, and that self is an introverted foundation for the de-centered self who becomes responsible for the other. The key move of ethics for Levinas becomes an inversion of the self from the one who brings other things home, making them its own, into a self who is bound to the other and gives to the other those same things. The ethical demand, however, is not in a different realm, in a nonmaterial realm. The demand from the other is not for some spiritual good, but for my material possessions. Economics is the milieu not only of pre-ethical experience, but also of ethical experience. Again, the demand for justice is a demand for economic justice.

In parallel fashion, Levinas relocates justice. In the earlier essay justice was the very goal of his project, and ethics was identical to economic justice. In the major works, justice becomes a third moment. First there is economics as the pre-ethical manufacture of the same, then there is the face and its infinitizing responsibility, and finally, there is justice as a negotiation and a weighing of those infinite responsibilities due to the presence of the third. It is not that Levinas no longer cares about justice, but that he focuses on the second moment. In logical moves parallel to Rosenzweig's in setting apart the three parts of *The Star of Redemption*, Levinas spreads out economics and justice. In order to interpret the moment of responsibility, he requires an independent analysis of economics. And in order to separate off the futural visionary aspect of social justice, Levinas must allow the approach of the face only to demand and not to provide justice.

However, in *Otherwise than Being* Levinas focuses on the middle moment, that of the approach of the other, to the point of almost excluding the other two moments. Not only is the third moment of justice pushed to the boundary, but the first pre-ethical moment all but disappears. Levinas narrows his perspective to the complexities of that moment of obligation, the meeting with the other as proximity. Although Levinas insists on the sociality of ethics, his focus draws ever more narrowly on the asymmetry and nonreciprocity of the face or proximity. But that is not itself a moment of justice, but rather a moment that precedes justice. Economics becomes a prior moment, and in so doing creates a permanent context for ethics and politics and religion—while justice becomes the desired result for Levinas, but not the question that most concerns him.

If economics has itself become a medium for the creation of justice, then Levinas must find what distinguishes the justice of the various social institutions. All social institutions will involve labor; all will be economic. But justice will emerge from one of the two basic routes from the original encounter with the other. In *Totality and Infinity*, Levinas develops two contrary forms of social institutions. Starting from the face, he moves in two opposed directions: 1) through love to fecundity and paternity, which he calls *religion*, and 2) through reason and the will to freedom, culminating in the State, which he calls *politics*. The first direction preserves the ethical dimension of interpersonal relations by looking to the discontinuity of generations from parents to children. The second direction is at best an ambivalent transformation of ethics. Politics tries to overcome time and change, but it betrays the infinite dimension of ethics. This contrast shows Levinas' adaptation of Rosenzweig's discussion of politics and its sublation: the Jewish community (see Chapter 6). A brief contrast of these two directions will display Levinas' hope for instituting responsibility.

Levinas sets out upon the first direction (religion) by drawing upon love. After criticizing private love as nonsocial, this move seems inconsistent. Levinas even asserts again that love is antisocial (TI 242/264–5), but he then explores love's ambiguity. Love is at once post-ethical and pre-ethical. On the one hand it is a pre-ethical desire for assimilation in the realm of one's enjoyment, but on the other hand it is an ethical relationship with an other. As merely love, the relationship to an other is exactly that isolated, private relationship I began by criticizing. The culmination of Levinas' analyses of voluptuosity, however, is the moment of sexual reproduction, the fecundity creating a child of the lovers.

This discussion of fecundity is a distinctive feature of Levinas' work. Neither Heidegger nor Husserl had explored the structure of having children at all. The discussion first appears in *Time and the Other* (1947) and then more fully in *Totality and Infinity*, but it disappears in *Otherwise than Being* altogether. Levinas argues that the father-son relationship is a positive form of sociality based on the approach of the face. My child is me, although I am not him; that is, I am responsible for him, but not the converse. The very separation of the other from me here appears as unconquerable, but at the same time as constructive for responsibility. I cannot assimilate my child to myself; he remains always free and stands separate from me, but I am now de-centered, responsible for whatever my child may do. Ultimately, I hope that my child will also be capable of responsibility, not for me, but for others. Indeed, I am responsible not only for my child's actions, but for my child's responsibilities for others' actions (see ADV 105–6/LR 227). The separation is a temporal one, as the new generation begins fresh, without the experience of my contemporaries and me. That newness produces a true experience of the future as not merely an extension of the present. The ability to respond for others is then reproduced, not for my sake but for other others, and so Levinas claims that the discontinuity of the generations creates a true time, an infinite future.

These exorbitant claims for sexual reproduction emerge from what is a quite simple claim: the responsibility we have for the other as free and independent (like that for our children) can be the shape of the future in all ethical experience. Just as we would die to save our children, as we would pay their ransom—even if they were ungrateful, indifferent, or even hostile to us—so must we be responsible for others in a nonreciprocal and asymmetric way. And just as we hope our children will become responsible, so the future always opens out as a hope for others to become responsible for other others. The child teaches me, and child rearing is not so much instructing my child as it is learning how to respond to my child's growth and changes. The child is to be my survivor; its freedom overcomes my own mortality, and its freedom may also become the freedom of responsibility. I discover that I live for my child, even after my death—that my effort to have my child live beyond death is a way of living not toward my death, as in Heidegger, but beyond it. All responsibility is responsibility for the other beyond my own death, opening up to a future of further responsibilities.

Moreover, fraternity arises from fecundity. Just as infinitizing responsibility is found in paternity, equality that arises with the third is a correlate of fraternity. Levinas states that "fraternity is the very relation with the face where both my election and my equality are accomplished at the same time, which is to say, the mastery exercised by the other over me" (TI 256/279). Just as the one-to-another relation involves the third, so fecundity creates fraternity. Ethics is the inception of true equality.

Levinas devotes much of *Totality and Infinity* to discovering a sociality that will preserve responsibility. His discovery of the family as a positive institution is contrary to Hegel's analysis in the *Philosophy of Right*, in which the family is an immediate social structure overcome in civil society. For Levinas the family is a nonimmediate sociality. Moreover, in the family structure Levinas finds the possibility of the asymmetry and infinitizing of obligation that lies at the core of ethics, and of the equality of justice. He is not canonizing the nuclear family as much as finding it a model for all sociality. But a fuller appreciation of this positive institution depends on a contrast with the other form: the political.

Politics rests on freedom, on the will. The will, for Levinas, is the engine of the economic life. However, in *Totality and Infinity* Levinas discusses the will at greatest length after the face, because what I make, my works, the fruit of my labor, is given over to others. My will becomes contradictory in my works (not unlike the earlier account of works), because it shows both the alienability of my will to others and also my attempt to make something my own (TI 202/227). By cooking the bread, I appropriate it and prepare to assimilate it, but I also then exchange the second loaf for some cheese. Thus my loaf is now the other's loaf; my labor is now at the other's disposal; my will is lost. Commerce itself displays the interdependence of oneself and the others, not just as an exchange of complementary needs, but as entrusting one's work, and so one's will, to others.

Moreover, my will is not satisfied by hiding at home, within me. It has no choice but to make works, to externalize itself. My will to survive, to live, to enjoy life requires that I make works for others. In one of the few simple appropriations from Hegel, Levinas agrees that a good will requires means outside itself to become true freedom (TI 218/241). As I exercise my will, I encounter not only the face of the other, but also the third. The very equality that the third brought to the other and to me now becomes a foundation for exercising freedom. Freedom, like the third, demands a universality. This universality in action is the exigency for reason.

Thinking, because of its abstraction and formalization in representing, allows for the balancing of competing wills and even of infinite responsibilities. As represented, as known, those infinities are reduced. In order to institute justice we must reason, we must use universal principles and concepts. The face cannot appear within rational discourse, but the face is the originary cause of that discourse. When the will expresses itself in speaking, it preserves freedom. In this expression, the will stays with its product: its word. A person stands behind his word, while he sells or commits his works to others. As long as the speech remains within the original context of apology to an other, the tension between the purpose and the generality of speech is retained. But once the words circulate independent of that purpose in speaking, they lose the tension and become only general terms.

In the social sphere, words in their generality become currency. Justice requires the move to public society. Will becomes separate from the specific context of face-to-face responsibility, as words become molded into written texts. Written laws preserve freedom by universalizing it, and reason is the tool for this task. We put an end to violence through law, through words in their universality. The state appears as the visible power of reason and universality, the totality within which markets and persons function.

Levinas criticizes this realm of reciprocal freedom, of universal rational order, of language and currency abstracted from the face-to-face responsibility. The very objectivity of this order is based on the reduction of the infinite responsibility I have toward the other. The universal discourse of reason cannot hear the unique apology of the 'I', the excess of responsibility which rests on me. I become a person, one of a species, with the universal duties that rest on us all. But I have lost the origin of the desire for freedom: the unique and personal responsibilities that devolve on me and for which no one can replace me. The rationalizing of responsibility is necessary in society, but it also betrays the prior sociality of the face. The state, as an institution of reason and of universality, is always drawn toward totalitarianism. In Levinas' terms, *politics*, as opposed to *religion*, is intrinsically a mistranslation, a betrayal, of ethics.

The key point, at least in *Totality and Infinity*, is that the state is based on a universal reason that reduces the infinity of responsibility—or barters away its own foundation. The family, on the other hand, is a model for a positive sociality wherein not only is the infinity of responsibility preserved, but also in which eternity can arise. Levinas elevates the family over the state and, indeed, suggests that it is unlike the state, even when the state makes room for it (TI 283/306). Thus there is a social program of sorts, based on the discontinuity and separation of selves in the family, which can stand as an alternative institutionalization of the responsibility demanded by the face. And that social program clearly points in the direction of the sociality Rosenzweig analyzed as the Jewish *Aufhebung* of political society.

The last step, however, is to explore the disappearance of religion in Levinas' later works. That disappearance leaves Levinas bound to explore how politics can be criticized without recourse to a second form of social institutions. Levinas binds criticism to politics and explains that binding with the emergence of skepticism as a permanent partner of philosophy. Levinas does not abandon philosophy and its reason for skepticism, but he retains the two in a dialogue, in which skepticism always interrupts philosophy's assertions. Similarly, ethics and politics now remain in a dialogue, without recourse to a religion that will exist outside politics.

In *Otherwise than Being*, Levinas finds responsibility in the *proximity* of the other, through which I discover my inalienable responsibility for what the other does. This responsibility precedes consciousness and intentionality. I have been assigned or accused from a moment that is in principle immemorial. And yet, the third enters, or, rather, in proximity to the other I am called before all others.

The relation with the third is an incessant correction of the asymmetry of the proximity where the face is faced. There is weighing, thought, objectification and, by that, an order that betrays my anarchic relation to him-ness [*l'illéité*], but where my relation is translated before us. Betrayal of my anarchic relation with him-ness, but also a new relation with it: it is only *thanks* to God that I am a subject incomparable to the Other, that I am approached as other among the others, which is to say "for myself.". . . The "passing" of God, of whom I can speak only by reference to this help or to this grace, is precisely the reverting of the incomparable subject into a member of society. (AE 201–2/158)

From society's viewpoint, my obsession with the other and my infinitizing responsibility for the other are impossible. Absolute responsibility, however, cannot be divested. So God appears in a reflective judgment. Rejecting fanaticism, Levinas claims that God's agency cannot be specified. Instead, the emergence of rational society out of the "dead end" of infinite responsibility requires this role (yet another version of the sociological argument for the existence of God in moral society, linked to at least as far back as Kant's *Religion*). But once, God only knows how, we gain reason, we start to think in terms of a society of three equals. Justice emerges from the previous ethical relation. The judge, upon whom the universal rational law hangs, is still a person, a person who is not outside the society, but within it—face-to-face with the criminal or the plaintiff. "The law is in the midst of proximity. Justice, Society, the State and its institutions—labour and markets—are intelligible from proximity: which means that nothing escapes verification by the responsibility of one for the other" (ibid.). Ethics verifies politics, the infinite is the measure of the finite.

Clearly society in this quotation is the society of politics, not that of religion. Religion's role has now been limited to the absent God who passed by, who authorizes the society by not participating in it. In his later writings, Levinas seems ever more interested in the theological issues of an absent, infinite God. Throughout *Otherwise than Being*, Levinas abandons the discussions of family and its alternate sociality. In *Totality and Infinity*, Levinas writes of the violation of individuals in politics and claims that justice centers on the right to speak, to offer an apology. "Perhaps it is here that the perspective of a religion opens. It moves out of political life to which *philosophy does not necessarily lead*" (TI 274/298) (italics mine). But in *Otherwise than Being*, we find that philosophy now leads only down the path to the state. Politics remains as the sole form of sociality.

The disappearance of religion transforms the discussion of reason and the state. Prohibited appeal to the more ethical social structure represented by religion, the ethical critique of reason and of the state become focal. And at the same time, we make room for an irresistible critique of philosophy. Philosophy, with no possibility of the detour into religion and social justice, must now become the rationale of the reduced responsibility of the state and of written laws.

What saves philosophy, and the state itself, is that philosophy is not only what is thought. The act of philosophizing is speech to another, to someone else. The praxis of thought and of communication provides a trace of what escapes and even interrupts the philosopher's reasoning. The freedom of the interlocutor transforms philosophy into apology. Philosophy's other is skepticism, which disrupts the systems and the universal reasoning. What skepticism objects to is not important; what is important is the perennial need for philosophy to apologize, to justify its answers to another. The return to the specific context of responsibility is possible because the words bear a trace of that responsibility, of the performance of speaking. In dialogue proximity breaks up reason's abstract government, and reason is criticized by the ethical moment. Thus the very vulnerability of the political to the objection of ethics is the privilege of skepticism to demand an apology, a justification by philosophy.

At that moment in his thought, Levinas has focused all of his sociological concern on a doubled dialectic within the state. Due to the freedom of the other, the ethical encounter remains both the origin and the perpetual interruption and critique of politics and its discourse: philosophy. But any full sociality of responsibility has become impossible as the family and its positive sociality is gone. Social institutions are now limited to political ones. We are left with an inevitable emergence of the state and a demand that the state always be subjected to critique, but not to abandonment. There is no liberation from politics, nor can ethics create its own institutions or realm. As long as the family could be held out as an alternative, we could claim that Levinas rejects the state. Now that the ethicality of the family is gone, Levinas sees sociality producing an intrinsically unethical state whose fortunes are linked to philosophy. Liberation becomes solely a praxis, but one which can never be established or instituted. There no longer is a positive model for social institutions, and so Levinas chooses, reasonably enough, to focus on the moment before reason, the ethical moment that subtends the demand for justice.

I would add that these moves are paralleled in several of Levinas' essays on Jewish topics—the most important of which are his commentaries on *Sanhedrin 99a* (DL) and the essays on Zionism in *L'Au-delà du Verset* (LR). In an essay written in 1971, Levinas affirms the state, but after tracing the theology of the Davidic kingship, he limits its function to an almost Hobbesian one of protecting us from each other because men act like wolves. He then explores the messianic politics and the question of whether it takes us beyond the politics of war and of oppression (ADV

216f./LR 274). Levinas' affirmation of Zionism is both dovish and religious—in both cases because he sees it as an attempt to transform politics towards a messianic politics (more like what he had called religion), and he insists on distancing it from nineteenth-century nationalism and *Realpolitik*. He sees Israel's political arena as especially open to the critique of ethics. The question of Zionism, however, is not my concern here. Rather, the affirmation of a very limited politics, a state that establishes order, but which must be vulnerable to ethical critique, is the issue. Even in his writings about Israel, Levinas invokes what he calls religion (see "Means of Identification" [DL2 78f./LR 263f.]) against mere politics. But in his later philosophical thought, he insists on the inevitability of politics and refuses the earlier hope for a religious social form.

Marx's Social Ethics

While the focus on the third and on economics provided a somewhat unusual perspective on Levinas,[2] the parallel overlap in reading Marx's work is more common. Not only are there Levinasian readers of Marx today both in Latin America and in France, but a general emphasis on Marx's social thought and earlier writings is a well-established trend. Levinas himself, however, makes very few references to Marx (see Appendix). While my reading of Marx is not intended as definitive, it serves to highlight the social ethics at the heart of the body of his thought. A supposition of this reading is that the young Marx's relation to Hegel provides a significant vantage point for his thought. I would also suggest that the descriptive and scientistic side of Marx's later works cannot be detached from these earlier, more philosophic writings. Yet if the historical dialectic and the economic analyses receive short shrift here, it is only in order to identify an important and challenging common ground with Levinas. I do not, in any sense, claim to exhaust Marx's thought.

Social Economics

Marx argues that human beings are fundamentally social beings—that they exist as human beings only through their relationships with others. However, this profoundly social nature of our being is distorted and obscured in modern (civil) society. To the extent that modern society can create the illusion that society is formed by the free assent of autonomous individuals, it has obscured the deeper material connections we all have with each other. Later I will discuss the significance of this illusion, but Marx argues not only that we are to become more truly social—that our relations will openly express our social nature—but also that this change is accompanied by a transformation of our own consciousness of our social nature. These claims about the advent of a truly human sociality are linked to the advent of communism through a revolution of the proletariat. Here I do not need to resolve the tension between the descriptive and normative nature of Marx's claim; rather, I will explore the shape or the form of the difference between modern and communist societies.

At the outset, then, let me refer to one of the lengthiest accounts of that difference: the *Economic and Philosophical Manuscripts of 1844*. There we find the account of communist society, wherein human social nature finally emerges as itself:

> Activity and enjoyment in both content and *mode of existence* are *social: social* activity and *social* enjoyment. The *human* essence of nature is first that of the *social* human; because here for the first time nature is there for the person as a *bond* with *people*, as an existent for the others and the others for it, as the element of life of human reality. Here for the first time nature is there as *foundation* of its own *human* existence. Here for the first time its *human* existence become its *natural* existence and what is nature to it becomes human.[3]

Clearly one of the key parallels with Levinas' thought is that one exists for others. This deep solidarity, that one's very existence is for the sake of others, is the heart of social ethics. Our activities are primarily our work, for we spend so much of our lives in the effort to make things, and that activity is ultimately social. In addition, our enjoyment (linked etymologically to the companionship discussed by Cohen and Rosenzweig) is also social.[4] We enjoy life with others in their presence and through their enjoyment. We work with others and for others, that they may enjoy with us the fruit of our labors. Moreover, this relation with others in work and play, in effort and enjoyment, is our very nature, a nature we have not fully experienced in current society.

Instead, the self-understanding we have in modern society is that we are first of all free individuals with free wills. This ideology of individual freedom is a central opponent of Marx's thought, and it represents the philosophical tradition for him, as I will discuss below. Marx argues that, nonetheless, our current lives also reflect our social nature—in our relationship to private property, first of all. The very possibility of selling or trading our property is what defines it as property (hence, as long as we want to keep it, it is not property). The right to do what we want with our property is merely the right to ignore the social reality of our property and the social consequences of our choice.[5] In addition, the structures that govern our sale of property also reflect society's presence.

Even my consciousness itself is for the other, because consciousness is bound up with speech.

> We find that people also have 'consciousness'. But this also is not from the outset 'pure' consciousness. 'Spirit' in itself has the curse from the outset of

being 'burdened' with matter, which here appears in the form of moving layers of air, tones, in short—speech [*Sprache*]. Speech is as old as consciousness. Speech is practical consciousness, both for the existing consciousness of other people, and therefore also for myself for the first time as existing, actual consciousness. And speech arises, like consciousness, first of all from the need, the necessity for exchange with other people.[6]

Here is a sequence familiar to us, but now located in the heart of Marx's early thought. From our relations to others we learn to speak. But in speaking we achieve, for the first time, consciousness of ourselves. Pure consciousness, the realm of reason, thus arises through speech, which arises through others and their needs. I translate *Sprache* as *speech* and not as *language* here to highlight the materiality of language (tones and moving air) and so to show that Marx is focusing on the performance of speech and not on the system of signs available for use.

Marx thus can both hold that our nature is to become fully social, fully directed to others, and at the same time show how even now, before overcoming the problems of modern capitalist society, we can discover that our current life, despite the illusion of nonsocial existence, is fully social. Why and how that illusion is produced is the topic of a later section, but here we notice that even in a capitalist, individualistic society, we are still living for others and still finding what meaning we can through our relations through others. All the more so in a society that takes as its point of departure that sociality.

In contrast to the distortions of fundamental economic interrelations to others in modern society we can examine the mutuality which reflects a fulfillment of our social nature (as Marx himself does). In his earlier works he focuses more on alienation and less on quantitative economic analyses (although these are not necessarily independent, much less opposing, themes for Marx). A set of concepts, moreover, is linked, and these concepts provide for the contrast I require in this chapter. The concepts are the division of labor, alienated labor, and private property.

In *The German Ideology*, Marx distinguishes between a division of labor that is naturally derived or indigenous and one that is voluntary.[7] That naturalistic division is linked to families and produces the break between the individual and the community. The fixed roles force each to do his or her own job, but such service to the community is not a fulfillment of the individual's interest.

That coercive role itself creates the alienation of labor. Alienation for Marx is not simply an externalization of my will, but, specifically, the expropriation of my labor. The labor that I put into the object, transforming it and increasing its value, becomes something other and external to me; but, more importantly, it also becomes something alien to me and ultimately something that rules over me.[8] The production of the object becomes the definition of my worth (instead of my will defining the worth of the object). The problem with externalization is a result of the modes of production (the division of labor): because one's labor is assigned by social structures that are not democratically and freely chosen, but are determined in one of several oppressive manners, the externalization means the expropriation of labor.

In order to expropriate another's labor, I must have a right to retain something that is not in use. Thus property rights arise as the result of different ways of dividing labor; without the possibility of holding property, the division of labor could not occur. The modern notion of private property, in opposition to earlier versions of property, is the result of the capitalist division of labor. Capital is the highest form of property, because it has no intrinsic relation to any estate or natural group; thus, the capitalist can be anyone. The hoarding of the workers' effort by the capitalist is the modern form of alienated labor. The conservation of alienated labor by private property characterizes economics in the pre-revolutionary society.

Marx claims that the laborer becomes not only dissociated from his labor, but also from his fellow and ultimately from himself. In a necessary cruel twist, landowners also become alienated from themselves and their tenants: their land comes to own them. The capitalist, too, becomes enslaved to his capital. Ultimately, the competition for the appropriation of things, for the accumulation of property, makes all human effort into a struggle for survival. Capital owns workers, landowners, even capitalists. The expropriation of ourselves by our things, the replacement of labor's effort by capital's dominion, also results in worsening material conditions for the workers. For Marx, the injustice of capitalism is that people serve their commodities as human faculties are reduced to a crude sort of animal materialism. Marx is not opposed to the material needs of humanity, but competition and commodification reduce such needs to the barest needs of survival.

And it is just this attack on the crude materialism of civil society that illuminates the reappropriation of materialism in terms of economics after the revolution. The key steps are the abandonment of private property and the communist approach to division of labor. Marx repeatedly discusses the abandonment of private property, including in the *Communist Manifesto*,[9] and it clearly serves to prohibit the hoarding of others' labor. But, in addition, it is also necessary to change the modes of production, and so the division of labor must become a spontaneous and free choice of the individual. In a famous passage, Marx writes:

> In the communist society, where each does not have one exclusive circle of activity, one can cultivate oneself in each branch at one's pleasure. Society regulates the universal production and thereby makes it possible for me to do this

today and that tomorrow; hunting in the morning, fishing in the afternoon, rearing cattle in the evening, criticising after dinner—just as I simply desire to do, without becoming hunter, fisherman or shepherd, or critic. [10]

Whether the utter spontaneity will involve the almost anarchistic quality of this passage is another matter, but the key contrast is clear: the fixed roles under all previous divisions of labor must be replaced by a creative and spontaneous process of working. In that way my labor will not produce something that oppresses me, nor will anyone be in a position to use my own efforts to suppress me. The abolition of fixed roles and of private property makes possible a truly social economic relation with others.

Marx discusses how even perception will become humanized—by which I take him to mean that we will no longer look at a thing only as a commodity with a price, but we will see it in relation to the human race, as a social product for social use. Our relation to objects will be changed; objects will no longer be that in which we lose ourselves through our labor, but will become what Levinas would call "expressions of ourselves." The decisive difference in the two economies is an inversion, for in civil society people are free individuals, free to pursue their own interest, but thus enslaved to the pursuit of property; while in the society to come, in a fully human society, human needs will become fully social, and one will find freedom through responsibility for others' needs. Each person's hunger will be that of his fellow, and so the satisfaction of those needs will be a social action.

A History of Institutions

The fulfillment of our other-directed nature, however, cannot be met except through a universal community. Just as the indigenous division of labor produced an unjust division of labor, the private communities of precapitalistic society are inadequate for understanding the fully human society. Marx does not rest positive sociality on the community (*Gemeinschaft*), and indeed is somewhat reluctant about the very immediacy of the community. Rational thought, in which I have no immediate community, is a stronger principle for the universality of social life. By thinking in universal categories, I discover myself as fully social.

Like Levinas' critique of the privacy of love, Marx seems suspicious of any private, immediate community. True sociality requires the intervention of universality—what Levinas called the third. And civil society has made it its business to dissolve immediate communities—the family and other 'natural' associations.[11] In the *Communist Manifesto,* Marx describes how the bourgeoisie has destroyed feudalism, the guilds, the dignity of the professions, etc. In civil society all value is reduced to price. But Marx sees this as a positive move in history because the earlier, direct communities are arbitrary and exclusivist. The integrity of landed property, to take an example, bestows value on the gentry, but it is hardly a rational or fully social value. Like Hegel, Marx accepts that the emergence of the rationality of modernity and that the destructive universality of civil society serves to sweep away these arbitrary social structures. The transition is accomplished by the replacement of the limited 'estates' by the rational and universally defined classes. The modern state serves the interests of the ruling class, in place of the feudal state which served the interest of the ruling estate. But to replace the one state by the other required the dissolution of the communities upon which the feudal state rested.[12] Like Levinas' third, this dissolution was accomplished by a weighing and calculation of the value of each thing—a commodification of all values, in which price determines worth.

Marx claims civil society will culminate in a capitalism so rampant that it will engender a universal class of laborers, a class that will hold no capital. The universality of civil society thus prepares humanity for the emergence of a fully social universality. While Hegel affirmed the state serving civil society, Marx claims that even that state cannot stabilize the universalization of competition and the destruction of communities. Even the artificial community of capitalists will fall prey to the competition of the market. Marx follows classical economics, but predicts greater and greater intensification of capital, coupled with ever worsening conditions for laborers. Ultimately, the ruling classes of the state and the cartels of capitalists will fall to a revolution of a universal class.[13]

The proletariat is that class. It will be the universal class opposed to class. In earlier society with immediate communities, class struggle resulted only in the realignment of classes, but since the dissolution of intermediary social structures, any class struggle now will result in the end of class structure. The very universality and totality of oppression of proletariats qualifies them not only to overthrow the capitalists and their state, but to stand against oppression itself, to be the last revolutionaries. The radicality of their oppression means that they can be expected to put an end to history and its social struggle. With the revolution, full sociality—social humanity—will appear.

The economic injustice of modern civil society is also coupled with a misperception of economic freedom. Earlier I commented that consciousness emerges from our material exchange with others through speech. But Marx analyzes the creation of ideas as reflective rationalizations of economic conditions. Thus, life determines ideas and not vice versa. The motion from premodern society to the modern civil society, therefore, saw not only the rationalization and universalization of capitalistic economic conditions, it also produced a more universalistic philosophy. Yet, insofar as the society is not fully social, human, etc., its universalism is still distorted and in fact justifies the very oppression that comes with the universalism of capitalism.

Marx, therefore, is one of the great critics of philosophy, displaying how its notions of freedom, of the will, of pure reason, and so on, all serve to hide the material reality of the injustice of the society. The more thought withdraws from the concrete, material conditions, the more absolute it can make the current conditions look. The recourse to eternal truth serves to obscure the reality of historical change and the worsening conditions for most workers. Thus more reflection, more abstraction, more universalization means the betrayal of the original demand for speech and thought: the other person's material needs.

The one exception, however, is the true universalism that will emerge in the communist society. The worldwide market of modern capitalism is an inverted condition of the genuine universal community of the communist society—and only in that universality, a universality of economic conditions, can individual freedom finally appear. While in civil society one can only be free by abstaining from society, by exercising an almost antisocial control over property, in this universal community individuals will achieve their freedom through their voluntary associations.[14] Clearly philosophy might become possible in this new society, but it will be utterly changed from the current discipline, precisely because it will reflect new material conditions in which the tension between individual and universal will be resolved in everyday life.

Without committing myself to outlining the altogether distressing and difficult issue of Marx's account of life after the revolution, I wish to take note of two important parallels with Levinas. I will not explore the dictatorship of the proletariat, or the withering away of the state, or the later reflections on the decentralized communes in Paris. The radical nature of the revolution, as a revolution against classes and against the state, makes all speculation impossible. All current social forms that partake of the oppression and alienation will be universally overthrown by the new, fully human society.[15]

On the other hand, what is interesting is that, like Levinas, Marx first finds that sexuality and the family form a positive image of sociality in place of the state, but in his later thought he finds that the rejection of the state becomes, to some extent, complicated and attenuated by recognizing the inescapability of the state. In the *1844 Manuscripts,* Marx discusses how the relations of men and women can be used as a measure for the development of society. In the positive relation of fully social humanity, sexuality reveals the positive sense of our natural needs, for the other person becomes, as human, my need.[16] The other is not a means to my satisfaction, but I have a social need, a need that can only be met by another human in her praxis as human. This is not the bourgeois family, which Marx interprets as prostitution, but is a natural structure that can be embraced only in a universal society in which we are a fully social human race.

On the other hand, Marx does not discuss this positive sexuality in his later works (so far as I know). And whatever the relationship of Lenin and later political developments may be to Marx's thought, still there is a temporary patience with a new state—the universal state which he calls the dictatorship of the proletariat. While Levinas must criticize the state and its politics precisely because it is universal and totalizing, and as such abstracts from the originary infinite demand of the other, Marx rejects the state because it should become superfluous. The state is always a tool of the oppressing class. The modern state emerges as a separate power structure to serve the middle class against the classes of nobles and churchmen. The state will have no such function in communist society because it is to be a classless society. Nonetheless, history has grasped hold of the intermediary state, the dictatorship of the proletariat. Even in later writings, Marx saw the state as losing its place, as yielding its powers back to the now fully human society.

Marx does not develop the sort of dialectic of politics and ethics that Levinas does. Instead, we have a much more Hegelian total-state becoming a non-state. And in parallel fashion, the dialectics of philosophy and skepticism are replaced by a critique of philosophy and the advent of a new communist science, again lacking the continuing tension that Levinas found ineluctable. The Marxists for their part make different choices in interpreting these claims. For this chapter the interesting issue is how the full sociality, communist society, has not only no need for the state, but similarly little or no need for social structures. While Marx avoids anarchism by his insistence on the changes in material conditions, the importance of spontaneity and creative associations within the new society leaves little room for the state.

REVOLUTION AND THE FACE

The task of this chapter, to draw together these two resources for social ethics, must also include notice of the strain in the mutual readings. While it is possible to discover similar sets of concepts in the two thinkers, their disagreement on the dividing point between the unjust economics and the just economics, between self-interest and responsibility, is significant. For Marx the practical action of revolution, of radical and even violent transformation of society, is the key to distinguishing two forms of society. For Levinas the dividing point is a personal one-to-another experience. Levinas would object that revolution does not put an end to totalizing social immorality and violence, while Marx would object that by focusing on the face, Levinas has overlooked the need for radical transformation of society and its economic structures. Even bearing in mind that Levinas is not proposing a private relationship, we miss the call for refounding society. Similarly, we regret that Marx insists on a new totality and seems oblivious to the violent reduction of responsibility in any totality. Revolution or the face?

If I have now led us to a chasm between the two perspectives, so that what we have found by this crossed reading only leaves us calling across, perhaps I can describe what sort of bridge might preserve the best each thinker has to offer. We stand in need of nontotalizing social structures for economic justice—liberation in society. The Hegelian dialectic, which both thinkers oppose and also presuppose, forces them to abandon any stopping point in society short of the state. Social practices and institutions must become subordinated to the total state. But we need to inquire whether there are possible models for radical but not totalizing social reform.

The central element, I propose, must be the vulnerability to critique—but taken in the most radical, Levinasian way. A society must be open to critique from outside, which means that it cannot conquer the outside, cannot be universalizing by inclusion, in the manner of the imperialism of church or market. In addition, it must not exclude the outside, silence it, for example, through the monopolies of race, gender, or capital. Such a view of nontotalizing sociality precludes the modern concept of nation-state, for the right of citizenship could not be withheld from anyone, nor could the military serve its functions. Liberation becomes, in this sense, liberation from the political—from nationalism and its state.

The space that is opened is one of sociality in various guises, without a hegemonic rationalizing power—no king of the castle. Liberation would mean the praxis of restructuring society to develop the originary responsibility. Ironically, Jewish 'normative' thought focused intensively on these in-between structures, precisely because political sovereignty was lacking. Without the power to conquer others, nor the threat of large influx—precisely because of their oppressed condition—Jewish thinkers framed institutions in a manner that is instructive for these thinkers and for us. The current in which Levinas and Marx float is one that flows through Rabbinic thought, thought which explored a society which need not engender totality. Without advocating a philosophy that is handmaiden to *Halakhah,* the traditional Jewish reflection on law and custom, I would suggest that a philosophical exploration of Halakhah would illumine the task of liberation. The development of institutions that could replace the sacral practices of the Temple in Jerusalem and priestly authority required a mode of reflection that holds particular interest for an attempt to develop social institutions that could replace the totalizing proclivities of modern states. If Marx and Levinas had drawn more deeply on the traditions of Jewish social thought about institutions, they might have produced more constructive insights into the partial remedies for our situtation.

With the deeper awareness that ethicality is social, we need not conclude that liberation is impossible, nor that it must dissolve all social institutions. We may resist the thought of the state totalizing over all sociality. Marx need not be totalizing, or at least we may learn from Marx the primacy of praxis and see that first of all in the economic dimension. Again, we may hear familiar strains from Liberation Thought, but the space for liberation must be freed from Hegelian totalizing dialectic even more radically than it was by both Marx and Levinas, and precisely by a less radical analysis of the social realm.

The possibility of drawing not only upon these two thinkers, but of broadening the correlation with Jewish thought, points back in the direction of the work of Rosenzweig and of Cohen. They began a struggle to interpret Jewish society in terms of the radical social ethics that both Marx and Levinas espouse. What Marx and, even more, Levinas contribute is a deeper awareness of fundamental and philosophical issues in liberation, but the correlation with Jewish thought could produce still more help in developing the society that liberates. The rejection of totality in the name of social ethics is liberation from the absolute claim of the state, and the work of liberation itself must take place in society.

Appendix: Levinas on Marx

It may seem paradoxical to write a chapter on two thinkers and relegate one's discussions of the other to an appendix. And so it would be, if only Levinas had not himself relegated Marx to a secondary, or rather tertiary, status. The references to Marx in Levinas' philosophical works can be counted on one hand. My task in this appendix is to indicate the variety of not only those comments, but also of other comments scattered in interviews and Jewish writings. I am afraid that it is hardly a rewarding investigation.

There are several comments by Levinas about the failure of Marxism, particularly in terms of Stalinism. The strongest identify the failure of communism as the ultimate refutation of the attempt to found a society on love or charity.[17] Levinas also criticizes the Sino-Soviet debate as displaying the re-emergence of nationalism—as an evil—in the midst of supposedly internationalist communism (DL1 227). This leads him in another location to suggest that the nationalistic divisions represent further needs that threaten the totalizing, rational, universal society that communism is supposed to be (HAH 36/87). This critique recurs in an essay about Kruschev, in which Marx is linked with Hegel (DL1 223). Even though the socialist society is opposed to fascism, Levinas still sees the universality of Marx as totalizing and incapable of maintaining individuals' freedom. What unifies these critiques is not merely the malaise of disappointment in 1968 with what Marxism could not deliver. Rather, the failure is traced back to the totalizing, rational society Marxism proposed. Such a society, for Levinas, will always violate the responsibility of its members. Moreover, the confidence, even naiveté, of wanting a society to be based on charity, and not on justice, produces the temptation of totality.

But if these various comments seems more like a critique of current events, the few substantial references to Marx in Levinas' philosophical works focus on the positive materialism discussed in this chapter. Not only is there a long praise of Marx for recognizing the sincerity of desire, that economics can be a realm without ulterior motives, and that hunger and thirst have good will (EE 69/45), but also that happiness is in meeting needs, in fulfilling our desires (TI 120/146). Levinas also admits that materialism has a part that is eternally true: that the human will is expropriable in its works (TI 204–5/229). With the preceding three citations, we exhaust the references to Marx in the main works. What they point out is a respect for the analysis of desire and also for the alienation of will in works. What is lacking, however, is a serious discussion of the sociality that Marx proposed. Levinas seems content to regard it as merely universalized material desire for assimilation/consumption. I tried to show that such a reading is not the best that Levinas' perspective can produce, although the question of rational totalization is serious in Marx.

There are also two concluding passages and a footnote in Levinas' works that I wish to mention. The footnote occurs in the midst of a discussion of whether the messianic age will bring the end of social injustice, in which Levinas cites the saying of Jochanan: "All of the prophets prophets prophesied only for the messianic age. But for the world to come: 'Eye has not seen, except for you, Lord, what you will do for those who await.'" (Sanhedrin, 99a). Levinas has his own interest in this passage, but he does say that this "singularly recalls the strange passages where Marx expects the socialist society with its modifications of the human condition, baffling all anticipation in fact of their very revolutionary essence" (ADV 218/LR 277). Levinas locates Marx within a Rabbinic argument, an argument about the need for politics and the persistence of suffering. Such a locating is in large measure one of praise.

The first passage is a still warmer affirmation of Marx's project, as the primacy of praxis. In an interview with Richard Kearney, Levinas states:

When I spoke of the overcoming of Western ontology as an "ethical and prophetic cry" in "God and Philosophy," I was in fact thinking of Marx's critique of Western idealism as a project to understand the world rather than to transform it. In Marx's critique we find an ethical conscience cutting through the ontological identification of truth with an ideal intelligibility and demanding that the theory be converted into a concrete praxis of concern for the other. It is this revelatory and prophetic cry that explains the extraordinary attraction that the Marxist utopia exerted over numerous generations. Marxism was, of course, utterly compromised by Stalinism. The 1968 Revolt in Paris was a revolt of sadness.[18]

Here is the appreciation of the primacy of praxis as social praxis—"concern for the other." Moreover, we find here the messianic echoes and prophetic critique identified in this chapter. That Levinas could see this in Marx and yet ignore him throughout his work raises questions that I cannot begin to answer about Levinas' own reflections.

There is a second text to consider, truly the only prolonged discussion of anything Marxian in Levinas' work: an essay, "On Death in the Thought of Ernst Bloch" (DVI 62f.). It represents for us exactly the point that Levinas is hardly unaware of or uninterested in Marxian thought, but that he feels little compulsion to go back and study Marx as he studies Heidegger, or Buber, or even Montaigne and Pascal. His position is relative to Marx and his contemporary followers, but he has no philosophical interest in either the Marx of the sociality I have discussed, nor a more economic Marx. The task falls on others who wish to consider how the two thinkers balance and counteract each other. And, not surprisingly, the liberation thinkers, the solidarity thinkers, and even the French Marxian thinkers, find social thought in need of a positive combination of the two.

Seven Rubrics for Jewish Philosophy

To conclude this book I would like to list an agenda of seven rubrics for contemporary Jewish philosophy. This list both presents a sketch of a family portrait, calling attention to certain key family resemblances, and in addition offers a regulative ideal for what Jewish philosophy should struggle to approach. Coming as a conclusion, this list can hardly be considered established or proven by the discussion in these pages, but, on the other hand, I believe that a reading of this book should produce at least the plausibility of this agenda.

This ideal agenda is not simply a summary of the two thinkers who caused this book, but neither is it a priori. It is a certain sort of ideal type which may never have empirically existed. Moreover, as an agenda for Jewish philosophy, it connects back to the traditions of the Sages and of the Bible. I do not suggest that this agenda is the plain sense of either the Bible or the Talmud, but neither is it merely the fabrication of modern and postmodern thinkers. The interpretative tasks with respect to the Sages and the Bible are completely beyond this work, but what I am suggesting is that when Jewish philosophers pursue this agenda they pursue it in part because it is consonant with Jewish sources, particularly Midrash and Talmud. It would be a great mistake to discount a view of the Jewish tradition that emphasizes a radical ethics as a mere rehash of nineteenth-century claims about the Jewish genius for ethics. The reflection on imperatives in the performance of speech and on the social dynamics of redemption are in no way foreign to biblical and Rabbinic sources. It is not happenstance that these same thinkers are directly engaged with those sources and also struggle to lead others back to them. Jewish philosophy does and ought to emerge out of the sources of Judaism, and it will have recourse not only to concepts from those sources, but also to architectonic principles and methodological styles. But the move of Jewish philosophy is from those sources to a philosophy and, hence, the first rubric on the list is

1. *Universality of Accessibility*
    Despite its postmodern locale, contemporary Jewish philosophy aims at a certain sort of universality. This is not the universality of universal assent of rational beings, much less the universality that subordinates individuals into a totality. Rather it is the messianic universalism: that someday we all will agree and worship the true God. That sort of particu-

lar universalism prevents the exclusion of anyone in principle. Hence, it is what I have called, following Rosenzweig, nonfanatic. It does not require a religious experience of grace, conversion, upbringing, etc., but attempts to address others through universally accessible experience, such as the experience of speaking or eating with another person.

I will not claim for these rubrics that they are uniquely Jewish, that only Jews have thought these ideas, nor that non-Jews only think them by becoming Jewish. What is Jewish may well also be accessible to poets, artists, writers, philosophers, theologians, scientists, social critics, etc., who are not Jewish. Quite the opposite, what truth there is in these philosophical analyses is accessible doubly: once through Judaism, but again through 'neutral' thought. But while a Jewish thinker might take as his starting point this set of concepts due to upbringing or experience, the conviction of universal accessibility governs the efforts in thinking.

2. The Primacy of Ethics

The primary concern is the transformation of praxis, not the cognition of truth. By this I do not mean that truth is not also a goal, but it is a practical goal—even theory requires a practical justification. For Rosenzweig and Levinas, the intensification of ethics is the focus, and indeed the fulcrum, for their work. In traditional sources the emphasis on law, on commandments, and on a pure heart all form a baseline upon which the intellectual life constructs its schemata. It is pointedly true that Kant and Plato also emphasized what the former calls the primacy of practical reason, but that does not make such an emphasis less Jewish.

3. Sociality not Individuality

The practice in question is social. This is not an ethics which only cultivates the virtue of the isolated individual; instead, it claims that ethics concerns what happens in relations between people. The social context is the origination of the self, even of reason and speech. Thus the concerns about the other and solidarity with others are the focus of this ethics. Society is not constructed out of individual moral agents who exist prior to it, but rather, society is something in which we always are already and so for which we always already bear some responsibilities. Through this social responsibility we discover a richer view of society, because we are bound to one another ethically and not merely for personal benefit. This sociality, moveover, is not simply a private club or honeymoon, but is the plural relations of public society. The task of ethics is to explore the range of responsibility in public society.

4. Prophecy and Messianic Politics

Society as we find it, however, is not just. The emphasis on society leads to a vision of a perfect society, one in which armed conflict ceases and economic suffering disappears, in which individuality persists in the midst of harmony. That sort of society is no longer political in the contemporary modes of politics, but is one in which responsibility is met in peace. This messianic vision serves the function of criticism of contemporary society. Prophecy as social criticism is linked to this messianism. Because a just society is possible, our present society requires criticism, but in addition, the prophet challenges the individuals in our society to change that society. The justification for speaking *to* others about their ethical responsibilities *for* others requires the category of prophecy. In Levinas the very capacity for speech becomes prophecy. Every word I utter is also an apology, the availability of myself to the other. All speech is prophecy—and so all speech is a challenge in the name of God.

5. *Resurrection and the Material World*

The messianic age is also the preface to the resurrection of the body. Leaving aside the embarrassment found in some medieval and modern Jewish thought, we may find in the resurrection of the body the promise of a new materialism, one bound to a refusal to denigrate human physicality. This ethics takes place in the world of material needs and is not a flight from or repression of those needs in the name of some higher needs. Levinas quotes Israel Salanter: "My neighbour's material needs are my spiritual needs." The very corporeality of Jewish observance is an affirmation of the reality of others' material needs.

The materialism of resurrection is not an inversion of otherworldliness in general; it is not pure hedonism, but is precisely the materialism of sociality, the material needs of the others. Social ethics is not a renunciation of materiality for some higher form of reality, but is a social and human relation to each other's material needs.

6. *The Suspension of the State*

The adoption of a messianic vision also causes a severe shadow to fall on the importance of the state. Insofar as the state is constituted by violence and operates through principles of strict subordination of individuals (as in Hegel's rational state), Jewish philosophy must reject the state as opposed to the very social ethics that concerns it. The national state, with its boundaries and its military, does not contribute directly to that social ethics based on mutual responsibility and peace. However, there remains the question of whether the state can be indirectly justified as conducive to that social vision. Were such justification to be possible (and Levinas adopts one later in his work, while Rosenzweig seems less flexible), it would refuse to the state the priority that the modern state seems determined to make its own. The traditions of the Ancient Empires and of the modern Absolute State, shifting into the Total State, seem to leave no possibility for the state not to be the ultimate source of power and legitimacy in society. Such a view of the state would have to yield to one in which the state was granted authority only in order to facilitate social responsibility and as such the state would have to remain perpetually vulnerable to ethical criticism. Clearly patriotism and militarism would be rendered much weaker under such a view. Primary allegiance could not be to the state or to the land, but would be to the radical responsibility for each other.

This accommodation of the state in many ways parallels the Sages' response to the world empires of late antiquity. Once they realistically accepted that national sovereignty was not possible, they discovered that Judaism could survive without an army, in diaspora. They created a society that suspended the state, accepting the authority of ruling powers, but locating primary value in social institutions that were not statist. The medieval culture with competing estates and nonabsolute authority allowed a certain flourishing of Talmudic culture. I realize that to invoke armiless and nonnationalistic Judaism is controversial today, but the agenda I propose requires that social responsibility come first—and so it threatens the modern reality of national states. Moreover, whether we have "outgrown" this *galuth* (exile) mentality, we need to account for the creativity and insight of a tradition that fashioned a durable communal existence without a national state for almost two thousand years. The key, I believe, is the last rubric:

7. *Halakhah and Social Institutions*

What is necessary for this social ethics is not the coercive state, nor the virtuous isolated individuals, but rather social forms that bind people together without totalizing over those individuals. Cohen saw this need and so formed two different concepts of such community: the cooperative and the congregation. Rosenzweig devotes much of *The Star of Redemption* to exploring how communities can form in nonpolitical ways. Levinas, too, adapts Rosenzweig's view of Judaism to propose the new use of the term *religion*. And all three are adapting, more and less, the insight that guides the halakhic structures the Sages developed; the communal structures they produced were neither totalizing nor atomizing, but managed to guide and to preserve the community in the absence of state force. I am not advocating philosophy as commentary on the *Shulkan Aruch,* the legal guide of orthodox Jewry, but rather that the sphere of society in which we can pursue radical ethics is in that middle range which now is sometimes called the new Gesellschaft. The Sages' reasoning and creativity can help us discover contemporary means of developing better social institutions for ethical sociality. Thus the suspension of the state serves to elevate the social (noncoercive) realm.

That elevation of the community, or congregation, or companionship, or socialist cooperative, etc., is the last in the sequence of rubrics. Their meaning is clarified by the analyses of this work. In addition, they fit together and so form an agenda. Contemporary Jewish philosophy includes other people doing other projects, but I hold that this agenda is the guiding one for the field. Moreover, I hold that this agenda is in fact the agenda for contemporary philosophy, that philosophy itself needs to pursue this agenda in order both to understand and to justify itself. For the activity of thinking is ultimately an interpersonal act for which we must acount to some other person. And that act rests on the freedom and solidarity of our relations with others and not on the fields of force that permeate our society. This reorientation of philosophy by Judaism serves to accentuate the deepest responsibility of philosophers and so displays the responsibility we have to bring Judaism and Philosophy into correlation.

Notes

INTRODUCTION
PHILOSOPHY AND ITS OTHERS

1. Elie Wiesel studied with Shushani at the same time and has described him, if ever so romantically, in *Legends of Our Time*, 87–109, and *One Generation After*, 120–25.

2. *Les Cahiers*, vol. 3, ed. Rolland.

3. Handelman, *Fragments of Redemption*.

4. *Les Cahiers*, vol. 1, ed. Olivier Mongin, Jacques Rolland, and Alexandre Derczanski.

5. *Der Philosoph Franz Rosenzweig (1886–1929)*, ed. Wolfdietrich Schmied-Kowarzik.

6. *The Philosophy of Franz Rosenzweig*, ed. Paul Mendes-Flohr.

7. Mosès, *Système et Révélation*.

CHAPTER 1
CORRELATIONS, ADAPTATION

1. Cohen, *Religion der Vernunft aus den Quellen des Judentums*, trans. Simon Kaplan as *Religion of Reason Out Of the Sources Of Judaism*.

2. See Tillich, *Systematic Theology*, vol. 1, esp. 62f.

3. See Husserl, *Ideas, I*, §90–91, in *Ideen zu einer reinen Phänomenologie*.

4. Cohen, *Logik der reinen Erkenntnis*.

5. See Steven S. Schwarzschild's discussion of reason and correlation in "The Title of Hermann Cohen's 'Religion,'" in *The Life of Covenant*.

6. There are only five references to such sources in *Totality and Infinity*: three to Scripture and two to Rabbinic texts. At the same time, there are at least ten philosophers who are cited five times or more. In *Otherwise than Being*, the Jewish sources become only slightly more prominent, totaling twenty references (fewer than to Plato), but there Ezekiel and Rashi are the clarion call of the frontispiece.

7. "Between Two Worlds: A Spiritual Biography of Franz Rosenzweig" (DL3 253–82/181–201), and "Franz Rosenzweig: A Modern Jewish Thinker," (HS 71–95).

8. In the preface to Stephen Mosès' *Système et Révélation* (reprinted in HDN 175–85) and in a discussion with Hans Henrix and Evêque Hemmerle in *Zeitgewinn: Messianisches Denken nach Franz Rosenzweig*, ed. Gotthard Fuchs and Hans Henrix (part of which is published in HDN as "Judaisme 'et' Christianisme," 189–95).

9. *Zeitgewinn*, 173. See also EN 213–17.

10. For a survey of the Jewish mystical background to the concept of the face, see Richard Cohen, "The Face of Truth in Rosenzweig, Levinas, and Jewish Mys-

ticism," in *Phenomenology of the Truth Proper to Religion,* ed. Daniel Guerrière, 175–201.

CHAPTER 2
THE LOGIC OF LIMITATION

1. Hegel, *Wissenschaft der Logik,* trans. A. V. Miller as *Hegel's Science of Logic,* 145/134.

2. Ibid., 155/142.

3. It is a recurring weakness in Rosenzweig that he underestimates the appeal of the uglier side of Nietzsche (and in Rosenzweig's later years, of Heidegger). This is most graphic in his comment that Nietzsche was both poet and philosopher and that his personal style was the most important aspect of his philosophy: "Even now what he philosophized is all but a matter of indifference. The Dionysian, and the Superman, the blond beast, the eternal Recurrence—where are they now?" (10/9). Rosenzweig's lack of foresight is not the central point; rather, the appeal to the irrational, as Nietzsche so well illustrates, is fraught with deeper political significance than Rosenzweig acknowledges—a weakness shared by some current reinterpreters of Nietzsche who again focus on his aesthetic style by ignoring his politics.

4. See Schwarcz, *From Myth to Revelation* (in Hebrew).

5. Schelling, *Weltalter,* trans. Frederick de Wolfe Bolman Jr. as *Ages of the World,* (citations to German only, as English includes German pagination) 212f. and 343f.

6. Schelling, *Weltalter,* 212.

7. "Das Neue Denken" (III, 148). "Schelling foretold a narrative philosophy in the preface to his ingenious fragments, the *Weltalter.*" See the opening sentences of Schelling for an obvious example of Rosenzweig's wit: "The past is known, the present is recognized, the future is anticipated. The known is narrated, the recognized is exhibited, the anticipated is foretold" (*Weltalter,* 199).

8. Schelling, *Weltalter,* 223, cf. also 235, 253, and 309.

9. Ibid., 255.

10. Ibid.

11. Ibid., 309.

12. See Gershom Scholem's discussion of the primordial contraction in Lurianic Kabbalah, *On the Kabbalah and Its Symbolism,* 110ff. Also of interest is Jürgen Habermas' discussion of Schelling and the Kabbalah in "Dialektischer Idealismus im Übergang zum Materializmus," in *Theorie und Praxis,* 172–228 (not included in the English translation).

13. Schelling, *Weltalter,* 261.

14. Ibid., 302.

15. Ibid., 209. Cf. *The Star of Redemption* (33/30).

16. Ibid., 334.

17. Ibid., 209, 211, passim.

18. Ibid., 225.

19. Ibid., 319, 335.

20. Cohen laid the foundation for his own system with a short work called *Das Prinzip der Infinitesimalmethode und seine Geschichte* (*The Principle of the Infinitesimal Method and its History*), which presaged his complete system. He used that method in the *Logic*, but it is not clear where Rosenzweig first encountered it. For a discussion of Rosenzweig's appropriation of the infinitesimal method, see Norbert Samuelson, "The Concept of 'Nichts'," in *Der Philosoph Franz Rosenzweig*, 643–56.

21. Cohen, *Logic*, 599.

22. Cohen, *Infinitesimal*, §88, 189.

23. Cohen, *Logic*, 459.

24. The contrast with Hegel is illuminating. While Cohen uses the infinitesimal to move from quality to quantity, Hegel uses it to recoup the qualitative within quantity (cf. *Wissenschaft der Logik*, 260/225). Though their interpretations of infinitesimal calculus have many similarities, the functions in the systems illuminate the difference between Hegel's dialectic and Cohen's *pure* idealism: Hegel cannot generate quantity out of pure thought, and he uses the infinitesimal to display how quantity *also* can be thought in terms of quality. Cohen, on the other hand, requires nothing but pure reason to think quantity and so can first generate quantity from quality itself. For Cohen the infinitesimal method is a bridge forward, for Hegel a way of bringing something external and alien back into the system.

25. Cohen, *Logic*, 134–36.

26. Cohen, *Infinitesimal*, §32.

27. Cohen, *Logic*, 93.

28. Ibid., 97.

29. Ibid., 106.

CHAPTER 3
SPEECH AS PERFORMANCE (I)

1. This in opposition to Fackenheim's discussion in *To Mend the World*, where Fackenheim interprets Rosensweig's disavowal of fanaticism as meaning only the rejection of the neo-orthodox axiom of revelation to Moses at Sinai (65ff.). Fackenheim, I believe, has been misled by Rosenzweig's own student, Leo Strauss, into assuming the problem was neo-orthodoxy. Rosenzweig's concern, as will be clear in this chapter, is to discipline experience, to constrict the argument from what people experience, so that it may become public. What both Strauss and Fackenheim mistake for fanaticism is dogmatism. In discussing the 600,000 witnesses at Mt. Sinai, Rosenzweig refers to dogmatism. For a fuller discussion, see Chapter 5.

2. Kant, *Religion innerhalb der Grenzen*, 266.

3. In "The New Thinking," Rosenzweig claims emphatically that *The Star of Redemption* is not a religious work and that the word *religion* never occurs in it (see Chapter 1).

4. See Searle, *Speech Acts*.

5. Austin, *How To Do Things With Words*.

6. Ibid., Lecture 11.

7. Evans, *The Logic of Self-Involvement.*

8. See his *Faith, Authenticity, and Morality,* 251.

9. Rosenstock-Huessy, *Angewandte Seelenkunde,* in *Die Sprache Des Menschengeschlects,* vol. 2.

10. Ibid., 786.

11. *How To Do Things With Words,* 1–3, 58–9. But for the record, look also at Austin's *Philosophical Papers,* in which mood can be "an intimation that we are employing language in some special way" (103) and, even more important, look at the programmatic statements about a future grammar (*not* a speech-act theory) that will be able to deal with the issues that Austin raises (231–32).

12. Rosenstock-Huessy, *Angewandte Seelenkunde,* 752, 754.

13. Ibid., 756.

14. It is worth noting that Austin, for all his adherence to actual ordinary speech, also cautions against making it simply the norm for our reflection. See *Philosophical Papers,* 69.

15. Rosenstock-Huessy, *Angewandte Seelenkunde,* 754.

16. Ibid., 758. See also p. 787, where Rosenstock-Huessy raises the problems in naming this mood subjunctive, optative, voluntative (and, as we will see in Rosenzweig, cohortative). The justification for counting only three moods comes from Latin grammar and not from Greek. Moreover, I will contest the exclusion of a fourth mood in the next chapter.

17. See Wilhelm von Humboldt, *Über den Dualis,* in *Schriften Zur Sprachphilosophie, Werke in Fünf Bänded* 3:113–43, esp. 128.

18. Rosenstock-Huessy, *Angewandte Seelenkunde,* 766.

19. Ibid., 774, 778.

20. See Bernhard Casper's discussion in *Das Dialogische Denken,* 117–55.

21. Rosenzweig is not a feminist. Not only is his God always male, represented occasionally as "ER" (HE), but he views the sexes as fundamentally different in their spiritualities; that difference is marked by the gender types familiar in sexist traditions. Rosenzweig on the issue of lovers and beloveds sees both a parity of the sexes and the preservation of the gendered view: "Between man and wife the roles of giver of love and receiver of love go back and forth. The higher the plants of love between them thrive, the more they reach above themselves and distance themselves from their subterranean roots like a true palm-tree; although the roots of gender ever restore the univocal relationship to nature" (189/169). I certainly do not wish to explore whether women have a different relationship to love then do men, but were there a difference I doubt that it would be so closely linked to our socially constructed genders. Rosenzweig as a thinker is not comfortable with the question of gender. Indeed, he comments in a notebook that gender difference is a hard problem for ethics (III, 86). All of which is to say that we may wish to reapply grammatical thinking to this problem, but that would also entail exploring the complex relation between grammatical genders and social genders in general.

To take the example of pronouns: Rosenzweig focuses on German grammar, but the 'you' of Hebrew grammar is gendered. It is not hard to imagine a language in which even 'I' was gendered. Clearly the third person is gendered in many languages, but there also is the possibility of neuters. Both the empirical base for grammatical thinking (which languages?) and also the question of gender require further examination.

22. The status of the biblical text in this interpretation of speech is a subject for the next chapter.

23. The contrast with speech-act theory is marked, for Searle devotes a section to the problem of reference with proper names, but never discusses the vocative and the use of names in reference to the addressee. (See his *Speech Acts,* 162ff.)

24. This process of self-purification is the central spiritual theme in the section of Cohen's *Religion* that Rosenzweig read at the front and recommended so highly to others. The way that speech accomplishes such self-purification will be a subject for the next section, but see also Chapter 8 for the relation to Levinas.

CHAPTER 4
SPEECH AS PERFORMANCE (II)

1. A very helpful discussion can be found in Paul Mendes-Flohr's essay, "Franz Rosenzweig's Concept of Philosophical Faith," in the *Leo Baeck Institute Yearbook,* 34:357–69.

2. This interpretation draws heavily on "The New Thinking," written in 1925. I believe that a greater emphasis on temporality emerges there, but that *The Star of Redemption* was not in any way falsified by Rosenzweig's own interpretation. If any emphasis was lost, it may have been a greater sense of spatial orientation in *The Star of Redemption.* The specific distance between the work and its interpretation (or as Rosenzweig calls it, his hennish cackling over his own eggs) is complex and cannot be resolved here. See Nahum Glatzer's essay, "The Concept of Language," in *The Philosophy of Franz Rosenzweig,* esp. 182–84.

3. Rosenzweig links not only Part II, Chapter 1, to Part II, Chapter 2, in this way, but he also links Part I to Part II; Part II to Part III; and even Part II, Chapters 1–2, to Part II, Chapter 3. See his discussion of the various relations of Creation, Revelation, Redemption and proto-world, world, and super-world (327/294).

4. Altmann, "Hermann Cohens Begriff der Korrelation," in *In Zwei Welten,* 377–99. I might mention as a companion piece Steven S. Schwarzschild's essay on Rosenzweig's anecdotes, which contests the personal side of Cohen's supposed return to Judaism in his old age. Schwarzschild debunks several of Rosenzweig's favorite anecdotes, showing how Cohen could not have said what Rosenzweig reported and why Rosenzweig would have mistaken Cohen through repeated pathetic fallacy. "Franz Rosenzweig's Anecdotes about Hermann Cohen," in *Gegenwart im Rückblick,* 209–18.

5. Cohen, *Logic,* 145.

6. Ibid., 378.

7. Cohen, *Ethik des reinen Willens,* vol. 7 of the *Werke,* 211–13.

8. Cohen, *Logic,* 14.

9. Ibid., 47, 143.

10. Cohen, *Ethics,* 248.

11. B. T. Yoma 85b, *Religion* 260/223 and frontispiece.

12. Cohen, *Religion*, 228/195. In this context, the extensive treatment of confession in the work of Joseph Soloveitchik is noteworthy. Soloveitchik wrote his dissertation on Cohen and reinterprets Maimonides on the topic of the function of confession in the work of repentance. See *Soloveitchik On Repentance*, by Pinchas Peli.

13. Cohen, *Ethics*, 377f.

14. Cohen, *Religion*, 228/196.

15. For (God, world, man), 'Yes' is (A, = A, B), while 'No' is (A = , B, B =). The three equations (A = A, B = A, B = B) and their six terms of 'Yes's and 'No's contain a code for the whole of *The Star of Redemption;* that explanation, however, is not the task of this book, nor do I expect that anyone could crack the code from the symbols without first having read the rest of the book.

16. Islam becomes a mere placeholder for theology without inversion (for a kind of idealism). Rosenzweig does not care if it is historically accurate for Islam to hold this place; we are free to interpret the place being held but obliged to qualify, even to abandon, Rosenzweig's historical claim. See the next chapter for a fuller discussion of placeholders in *The Star of Redemption*.

17. Jabès, *The Book of Questions*, 1:164.

CHAPTER 5
ETERNITY AND SOCIETY (I)

1. Two excellent articles on Rosenzweig's views of history are juxtaposed in one volume. See Altmann's "Franz Rosenzweig on History," 124–37, and Mendes-Flohr's "Frans Rosenzweig and the Crisis of Historicism," 138–61.

2. Rosenzweig, *Hegel und der Staat*, 1982 reprint of 1920 edition.

3. Meinecke, *Weltbürgertum und Nationalstaat,* trans. Robert B. Kimber as *Cosmopolitanism and the National State*.

4. Ibid., 18/22

5. Vol. III of Weber, *Gesammelte Aufsätze zur Religionssoziologie: Das antike Judentum,* trans. Hans H. Gerth and Don Martindale as *Ancient Judaism*.

6. See Weber, *Gesammelte Aufsätze zur Religionssoziologie,* first footnote (1–6/425–29).

7. See Gager, "Paul and Ancient Judaism. A Critique of Max Weber's Interpretation" in (German), in *Max Webers Sicht des antiken Christentums*. The volume as a whole analyzes the value of Weber's work in a modern context. Gager raises questions about both the historical adequacy and the theological blinders that Weber inherited. Of similar interest is Frank Crüsemann's essay in the same volume.

8. "Apologetisches Denken," translated in *The Jew: Essays from Martin Buber's Journal Der Jude, 1916–1928,* ed. Arthur A. Cohen, 262–72. Rosenzweig refers to this essay in "The New Thinking."

9. Cf. (III, 686) and Arthur Cohen's introduction to essay 264.

10. Schelling, *Philosophie der Offenbarung,* 689–726. (There is a different edition based on the Paulus manuscript, edited by Manfred Frank, but Rosenzweig did not have access to that manuscript.)

11. Ibid., 702–4.

12. Ibid., 712–13.
13. Published in 1911 and trans. Olive Wyon in two volumes.
14. See Dietrich, *Cohen and Troeltsch.*
15. Troeltsch, *The Social Teaching,* 1007.

CHAPTER 6
ETERNITY AND SOCIETY (II)

1. Some Israeli commentators are eager to overcome this difficulty in appropriating Rosenzweig and so point to a few letters in which he backs off his extreme *philosophical* opposition to the Zionist movement by praising some Zionists. We cannot resolve the question of what Rosenzweig might have said about the State of Israel; however, we might well observe that he would be troubled, for on the one hand he expresses a deep commitment to the Jewish community, but as thinker he stands against the 'normalization' that gaining a nation-state requires. In addition, his commitment to the people is tempered by a sense that theological concepts such as revelation and redemption must norm our valuing the empirical reality of today's Jews (see "Atheistic Theology" [III, 687ff.]). The question is a philosophical-theological-sociological one, and the championing of alienation and exile as social categories is not an exclusively Jewish question—Augustine's concept of the pilgrim (literally, *resident alien)* addresses the same problems.

2. Again we find that the revival of Hebrew in Israel, already begun in Rosenzweig's time, is not our problematic. The alienation from one's own life, which the reservation of Hebrew for holiness brought, is the point of his analysis. The loss of that alienation, if that is the Hebraist or Zionist agenda, would be, for Rosenzweig, truly to become a nation like the other nations: mortal.

3. *Daily Prayer Book,* ed. Joseph H. Hertz, 208–11.
4. Ibid.
5. See Chapter 1, the fifth explicit influence on Levinas.

CHAPTER 7
CORRELATIONS, TRANSLATION

1. See the bibliographical appendix to this chapter. The key secondary works for the Talmudic readings are the following: David Banon, "Une Hermeneutique de la sollicitation," in *Les Cahiers de* La nuit Surveillée: *Emmanuel Levinas,* 3:99–118; Fabio Ciaramelli, "Le Judiasm dans loeuvre de Levinas," *Revue Philosophie de Louvain* 81 (1983): 580–99; and Edith Wyschogrod, *Emmanuel Levinas: The Problem of Ethical Metaphysics,* 159–99.

2. Citations list colloquium number followed by a reference to the book in which the commentary appears. If the colloquium number is not followed by a book abbreviation, the reference (e.g., #5, p. 478) is to the page of the Proceedings, which record Levinas' and others' comments in debates. A complete list of the colloquiums, topics, and corresponding texts appear at the end of this chapter.

3. Poirié, *Emmanuel Levinas, Qui êtes-vous?* 117.
4. Ibid., 110.

5. Ibid., 129.

6. Joyce, *Ulysses*, Penguin, 1960, 471, and Jacques Derrida, "Violence et Métaphysique" in *L'écriture et la Différence*, trans. Alan Bass as "Violence and Metaphysics" in *Writing and Difference*, 228/153.

CHAPTER 8
THE UNIQUE OTHER

1. Cohen, *Logic*, 56–57.

2. A careful reading of the two explicit mentions of Cohen, as well as a generally constructive and insightful treatment of the two thinkers, is Edith Wyschogrod's "Moral Self: Emmanuel Levinas and Hermann Cohen."

3. Cohen, *Ethics*, 212.

4. The best recent exposition of Cohen's ethics is Steven S. Schwarzschild's essay, "The Tenability of Hermann Cohen's Construction of the Self."

5. Cohen, *Ethics*, 239

6. Ibid., 248. I offered a different discussion of this passage in Chapter 3, focusing on the performative force of speech.

7. Ibid., 216.

8. Cohen, *Religion*, 148/128, 158/136, 170/146.

9. Ibid., 164/141.

10. Ibid., 230/197.

11. Ibid., 267/228.

12. Cohen, *Ethics*, 299ff.

13. For the claim that the 'later' and 'Jewish' discovery of correlation was Cohen's only way of access to the being of the other, see Rosenzweig (III, 209). On the other hand, Cohen explicitly criticized those who thought that they must turn to experience to discover the individual (*Ethics*, 234).

14. Robert Bernasconi has explored this exchange in detail in "'Failure of Communication' as a Surplus."

15. Buber, *Ich und Du*, 19–20.

16. Ibid., 22–25.

CHAPTER 9
SUBSTITUTION

1. Marcel, *Essai de Philosophie Concrète*, trans. Robert Rosthal as *Creative Fidelity*.

2. The clearest discussion of this I know is Lyotard's account of metalepsis in Plato. See *Le Différend*, 47–48, trans. Georges Van Den Abbeele as *The Differend*, 26. See also Rosenzweig's *Star of Redemption*, 194/173, and Alan Udoff's interpretation of it in "Rosenzweig's Heidegger Reception and the re-Origination of Jewish Thinking," in *Der Philosoph Franz Rosenzweig (1886–1929)*, ed. Wolfdietrich Schmied-Kowarzik, 923ff.

3. The most rigorous exploration of the different pragmatic effects of Levinas' text is Jacques Derrida's essay, "En ce moment même dans cet ouvrage me voici," in *Textes pour Emmanuel Levinas*, 21–60, trans. Ruben Berezdivin as "At this

very moment in this work Here I am," in *Re-Reading Levinas*, ed. Robert Bernasconi and Simon Critchley.

4. See the discussion in Chapter 3, wherein Rosenzweig makes this claim. It is noteworthy that Rosenzweig was working with German which has full declensions, while Levinas is writing in French which generally lacks declensions, except for the personal pronouns.

5. Levinas has engaged repeatedly with Christian theologians on these points. He is particularly interested in the concept of *kenosis*. See, for instance, "Judaism and Kenosis" (HDN 133ff.) and the comments in conversation with Henrix (HDN 194–95).

CHAPTER 10
MARX AND LEVINAS

1. In a recent article, "Socialité et Argent," in *L'Herne* (134–41), Levinas does not return to this earlier view but instead reiterates his later views that the economic is encountered first of all prior to the encounter with the other.

2. The only serious study of Levinas' social theory is by Roger Burrgraeve: "The Ethical Basis for a Humane Society," in *Emannuel Levinas: Une Bibliographie primaire et secondaire*.

3. Marx, *Ökonomisch-philosophische Manuskripte aus dem Jahre 1844*, 537–38, trans. Dirk J. Struik as *Economic and Philosophic Manuscripts of 1844*, 136–37.

4. Here a contrast with Levinas occurs, because Levinas discusses enjoyment as nonsocial (prior to the face). The absence of companionship in his thought is a topic of Chapter 8.

5. Marx, *Deutsche Ideologie*, trans. C. J. Arthur as *German Ideology*, 63/ 81; and *Zur Judenfrage*, translated as *On the Jewish Question*, in *Selected Writings*, 365/53.

6. Marx, *Deutsche Ideologie*, 30/50–51.

7. Ibid., 53/33.

8. Marx, *Ökonomisch-philosophische Manuskripte*, 512/108.

9. In this sense, the theory of the communists may be summed up in the single phrase, "Abolition of private property." Marx and Engels, *Manifest der Kommunistische Partei*, translated as *Communist Manifesto*, 475/23.

10. Marx, *Deutsche Ideologie*, 33/53.

11. Marx, *Ökonomisch-philosophische Manuskripte*, 531/129.

12. Marx, *Zur Judenfrage*, 368/55.

13. See the famous passage in *Towards a Criticism of Hegelian Philosophy of Right*, in *Critique of Hegel's 'Philosophy of Right'*, 390/141–42.

14. Marx, *Deutsche Ideologie*, 74/83.

15. See Appendix and Levinas' reference to this topic in a footnote (ADV 218/ LR 277).

16. Marx, *Ökonomisch-philosophische Manuskripte*, 535/134.

17. Poirié, *Emmanuel Levinas, Qui êtes-vous?* 134

18. Interview with Richard Kearney in *Face to Face with Levinas*, ed. Richard Cohen, 33.

Select Bibliography

WORKS BY ROSENZWEIG AND LEVINAS

See Abbreviations and Citations, with the addition of the following:
Rosenzweig, Franz. *Hegel und der Staat.* 1920. Berlin: Scientia Verlag, 1982.
For a bibliography of Rosenzweig's publications, see Stéphane Mosès, *Système et Révélation.* Paris: Éditions de Seuil, 1982.
For a bibliography of Levinas' publications, see *The Provocation of Levinas,* ed. Robert Bernasconi and David Wood. New York: Routledge, 1988.
For English-language publications and for all publications on and references to Levinas, see *Emannuel Levinas: Une Bibliographie primaire et secondaire,* ed. Roger Burrgraeve. 3d ed. Leuven: Center for Metaphysics and Philosophy of God, 1991.

SECONDARY AND GENERAL WORKS

Altmann, Alexander. "Franz Rosenzweig on History." In *The Philosophy of Franz Rosenzweig,* ed. Paul Mendes-Flohr, 124–37. Hanover and London: University Press of New England for Brandeis University Press, 1988.
———. "Hermann Cohen's Begriff der Korrelation." In *In Zwei Welten,* 377–99. Tel-Aviv: Verlag Bitaon, Ltd., 1962.
Austin, J. L. *How To Do Things With Words.* Cambridge: Harvard University Press, 1975.
———. *Philosophical Papers.* 3d ed. Oxford: Oxford University Press, 1979.
Banon, David. "Une Hermeneutique de la sollicitation." In *Les Cahiers de* La nuit Surveillée: *Emmanuel Levinas.* See *Les Cahiers,* ed. Rolland.
Bernasconi, Robert. "'Failure of Communication' as a Surplus: Dialogue and Lack of Dialogue between Buber and Levinas." In *The Provocation of Levinas,* ed. Robert Bernasconi and David Wood, 100–135. New York: Routledge, 1988.
Buber, Martin. *Ich und Du.* In *Das Dialogische Prinzip.* Heidelberg: Verlag Lambert Schneider, 1979.
Burrgraeve, Roger. "The Ethical Basis for a Humane Society." In *Emannuel Levinas: Une Bibliographie primaire et secondaire.* 3d ed. Leuven: Center for Metaphysics and Philosophy of God, 1991.
Les Cahiers de La nuit surveillée: *Emmanuel Levinas,* Vol. 3. Ed. Jacques Rolland. Lagrasse: Editions Verdier, 1984.
Les Cahiers de La nuit surveillée: *Franz Rosenweig,* Vol. 1. Ed. Olivier Mongin, Jacques Rolland, and Alexandre Derczanski. Lagrasse: Editions Verdier, 1982.
Casper, Bernhard. *Das Dialogische Denken.* Freiburg: Herder, 1967.
Ciaramelli, Fabio. "Le Judiasm dans loeuvre de Levinas." *Revue Philosophie de Louvain* 81 (1983): 580–99.

Cohen, Hermann. *Das Prinzip der Infinitesimalmethode und seine Geschichte.* Ed. Werner Flach. Frankfurt am Main: Suhrkamp Verlag, 1968.

———. *Ethik des reinen Willens.* Vol. 7 of the *Werke*, reprint of 2d ed., 1907. Hildesheim: Georg Olms Verlag, 1977.

———. *Logik der reinen Erkenntnis.* Vol. 6 of the *Werke*, reprint of 2d ed., 1914. Hildesheim: Georg Olms Verlag, 1977.

———. *Religion der Vernunft aus den Quellen des Judentums.* Reprint of 2d ed., 1928. Wiesbaden: Fourier Verlag, 1988. Trans. Simon Kaplan as *Religion of Reason out of the Sources of Judaism.* New York: Frederick Ungar Publishing Co., 1971.

Cohen, Richard. "The Face of Truth in Rosenzweig, Levinas, and Jewish Mysticism." In *Phenomenology of the Truth Proper to Religion*, ed. Daniel Guerrière, 175–201. New York: SUNY Press, 1990.

———, ed. *Face to Face with Levinas.* Albany: SUNY Press, 1986.

Derrida, Jacques. "En ce moment même dans cet ouvrage me voici." In *Textes pour Emmanuel Levinas*, 21–60. Paris: Jean-Michel Place, 1980. Trans. Ruben Berezdivin as "At this very moment in this work Here I am," in *Re-Reading Levinas*, ed. Robert Bernasconi and Simon Critchley, 11–48. Bloomington: Indiana University Press, 1991.

———. "Violence et Métaphysique, *Essai sur la pensée d'Emmanuel Levinas.*" In *L'écriture et la Différence*, 117–228. Paris: Éditions du Seuil, 1967. Trans. Alan Bass as "Violence and Metaphysics: An Essay on the Thought of Emmanuel Levinas," in *Writing and Difference*, 79–153. Chicago: University of Chicago Press, 1978.

Dietrich, Wendell. *Cohen and Troeltsch.* Atlanta: Scholar's Press, 1986.

Evans, Donald D. *Faith, Authenticity, and Morality.* Toronto: University of Toronto Press, 1980.

———. *The Logic of Self-Involvement.* London: SCM Press Ltd., 1963.

Fackenheim, Emil. *To Mend the World.* New York: Schocken Books, 1982.

Gager, John G. "Paul and Ancient Judaism. A Critique of Max Weber's Interpretation." In *Max Webers Sicht des antiken Christentums* (German). Frankfurt am Main: Suhrkamp Verlag, 1985.

Glatzer, Nahum. "The Concept of Language in the Thought of Franz Rosenzweig." In *The Philosophy of Franz Rosenzweig*, ed. Paul Mendes-Flohr, 172–84. Hanover and London: University Press of New England for Brandeis University Press, 1988.

Habermas, Jürgen. "Dialektischer Idealismus im Übergang zum Materializmus— Geschichtsphilosophische Folgerungen aus Schellings Idee einer Contraction Gottes." In *Theorie und Praxis*, 172–228. Frankfurt am Main: Suhrkamp Verlag, 1971.

Handelman, Susan. *Fragments of Redemption: Jewish Thought and Literary Theory in Benjamin, Scholem, and Levinas.* Bloomington: Indiana University Press, 1991.

Hegel, G.W.F. *Wissenschaft der Logik.* Vol. 5 of the *Werke.* Frankfurt am Main: Suhrkamp Verlag, 1969. Trans. A. V. Miller as *Hegel's Science of Logic.* New York: Humanities Press, 1969.

Husserl, Edmund. *Ideen zu einer reinen Phänomenologie und Phänomenologis-chen Philosophie*. Husserliana Bd. III. Den Haag: Martinus Nijhoff, 1950.

Jabès, Edmond. *The Book of Questions*. Vol. 1, *The Book of Questions*. Trans. Rosmarie Waldrop. Middletown: Wesleyan University Press, 1972.

Kant, Immanuel. *Die Religion innerhalb der Grenzen der blossen Vernunft*. 8th ed. Ed. Karl Vorländer. Hamburg: Felix Meiner, 1978.

Lyotard, Jean-François. *Le Différend*. Paris: Les Éditions de Minuit, 1983. Trans. Georges Van Den Abbeele as *The Differend*. Minneapolis: University of Minnesota Press, 1988.

Malka, Salomon. *Lire Levinas*. Paris: Cerf, 1984.

Marcel, Gabriel. *Essai de Philosophie Concrète*. Paris: Gallimard, 1940. Trans. Robert Rosthal as *Creative Fidelity*. New York: Crossroads, 1982.

Marx, Karl. *Aus der Kritik der Hegelschen Rechtsphilosophie. Kritik des Hegelschen Staatsrecht*. In Marx and Engels *Werke*, Vol. 1, 261–313. Berlin: Dietz Verlag, 1957. Trans. Joseph O' Malley as *Critique of Hegel's 'Philosophy of Right.'* Cambridge: Cambridge University Press: 1972.

———. *Zur Judenfrage*. Vol. 1 of Marx and Engels *Werke*. Berlin: Dietz Verlag, 1957. Translated as *On the Jewish Question*. In *Selected Writings*, ed. and trans. David McLellan. Oxford: Oxford University Press, 1977.

———. *Ökonomisch-philosophische Manuskripte aus dem Jahre 1844*. In Marx and Engels *Werke*, Ergänzungsband, Erster Teil. Berlin: Dietz Verlag, 1968. Trans. Dirk J. Struik as *Economic and Philosophic Manuscripts of 1844*. New York: International Publishers, 1964.

Marx, Karl, and Friedrich Engels. *Deutsche Ideologie*. Vol. 3 of Marx and Engels *Werke*. Berlin: Dietz Verlag, 1968. Trans. C. J. Arthur as *German Ideology*. New York: International Publishers, 1970.

———. *Manifest der Kommunistische Partei*. Vol. 4 of Marx and Engels *Werke*. Berlin: Dietz Verlag, 1968. Translated as *Communist Manifesto*. New York: International Publishers, 1948.

Meinecke, Friedrich. *Weltbürgertum und Nationalstaat*. Munich and Berlin: 1908. Trans. Robert B. Kimber as *Cosmopolitanism and the National State*. Princeton: Princeton University Press, 1970.

Mendes-Flohr, Paul. "Franz Rosenzweig and the Crisis of Historicism." In *The Philosophy of Franz Rosenzweig*, ed. Paul Mendes-Flohr, 138–61. Hanover and London: University Press of New England for Brandeis University Press, 1988.

———. "Franz Rosenzweig's Concept of Philosophical Faith." In the *Leo Baeck Institute Yearbook* 34 (1989), 357–69. New York: Secker & Warburg, for the Leo Baeck Institute.

———, ed. *The Philosophy of Franz Rosenzweig*. Hanover and London: University Press of New England for Brandeis University Press, 1988.

Mosès, Stéphane. *Système et Révélation*. Paris: Éditions de Seuil, 1982. Translated as *System and Revelation: Philosophy of Franz Rosenzweig*. Detroit: Wayne State University Press, 1992.

Poirié, François. *Emmanuel Levinas, Qui êtes-vous?* Paris: La Manufacture, 1987.

Rosenstock-Huessy, Eugen. *Angewandte Seelenkunde*. In *Die Sprache Des Menschengeschlects*, Vol. 2, 739–810. Heidelberg: Verlag Lambert Schneider.

Samuelson, Norbert. "The Concept of 'Nichts' in Rosenzweig's *Star of Redemption.*" In *Der Philosoph Franz Rosenzweig (1886–1929)*, ed. Wolf-dietrich Schmied-Kowarzik, 643–56. Munich: Verlag Karl Alber, 1988.

Schelling, F.W.J. *Philosophie der Offenbarung*. Vol. 6 of *Schelling's Werke*, ed. and reorganized by Manfred Schröter. Munich, 1927.

———. *Weltalter*. Vol. 8 of *Sämmtliche Werke*, ed. K.F.A. Schelling, 195–344. Stuttgart and Augsburg: 1861. Trans. Frederick de Wolfe Bolman Jr. as *Ages of the World*. New York: AMS Press, Inc., 1967.

Schmied-Kowarzik, Wolfdietrich, ed. *Der Philosoph Franz Rosenzweig (1886–1929)*. Munich: Verlag Karl Alber, 1988.

Scholem, Gershom. *On the Kabbalah and Its Symbolism*. Trans. Ralph Manheim. New York: Schocken Books, 1969.

Schwarcz, Moshe. *From Myth to Revelation* (in Hebrew). Tel Aviv: N.p., 1978.

Schwarzschild, Steven S. "Franz Rosenzweig's Anecdotes about Hermann Cohen." In *Gegenwart im Rückblick: Festgabe für die Jüdische Gemeinde zu Berlin 25 Jahre nach dem Neubeginn*, 209–18. Heidelberg: Lothar Stiehm Verlag, 1970.

———. "The Tenability of Hermann Cohen's Construction of the Self." *Journal of the History of Philosophy* 13 (1973): 361–84.

———. "The Title of Hermann Cohen's 'Religion of Reason out of the Sources of Judaism.'" In *The Life of Covenant: The Challenge of Contemporary Judaism, Essays in Honor of Herman E. Schaalman*, ed. Joseph A. Edelheit, 207–22. Chicago: Spertus College of Judaica Press, 1986.

Searle, John. *Speech Acts*. Cambridge: Cambridge University Press, 1969.

Soloveitchik On Repentance. Ed. Pinchas Peli. New York: Paulist Press, 1984.

Tillich, Paul. *Systematic Theology*, Vol. 1. Chicago: University of Chicago Press, 1951.

Troeltsch, Ernst. *The Social Teaching of the Christian Churches*. N.p. 1911. Trans. Olive Wyon in two volumes, reprint of 1931 edition. Chicago: University of Chicago Press, 1981.

von Humboldt, Wilhelm. *Über den Dualis*. In *Schriften Zur Sprachphilosophie, Werke in Fünf Bänded*, Vol. 3, ed. A. Flitner and K. Giel, 113–43. Stuttgart: N.p., 1963.

Weber, Max. Vol. 3 of *Gesammelte Aufsätze zur Religionssoziologie: Das antike Judentum*. Tübingen: J.C.B. Mohr, 1923. Trans. Hans H. Gerth and Don Martindale as *Ancient Judaism*. New York: Free Press, 1952.

Wiesel, Elie. *Legends of Our Time*. New York: Holt, Rinehart, & Winston, 1968.

———. *One Generation After*. New York: Random House, 1970.

Wyschogrod, Edith. "The Moral Self: Emmanuel Levinas and Hermann Cohen." *Daat* 4 (Winter 1980): 35–58.

———. *Emmanuel Levinas: The Problem of Ethical Metaphysics*. The Hague: Martinus Nijhoff, 1974.

Zeitgewinn: Messianisches Denken nach Franz Rosenzweig. Ed. Gotthard Fuchs and Hans Henrix. Frankfurt am Main: Verlag Josef Knecht, 1987.

Name Index

Subject Index